China Fortunes

A Tale of Business in the New World

John D. Kuhns

WILEY

John Wiley & Sons, Inc.

Published by John Wiley & Sons, Inc., Hoboken, New Jersey.
Published simultaneously in Canada.

For general information on our other products and services or for technical support,
please contact our Customer Care Department within the United States at
(800) 762-2974, outside the United States at (317) 572-3993 or fax (317) 572-4002.

Wiley also publishes its books in a variety of electronic formats. Some content that
appears in print may not be available in electronic books. For more information about
Wiucts, visit our web site at www.wiley.com.

Library of Congress Cataloging-in-Publication Data:

Kuhns, John D.
  China fortunes: a tale of business in the new world / John D. Kuhns.
  p. cm.
  ISBN 978-0-470-92804-2 (cloth); ISBN 978-1-118-00562-0 (ebk);
  ISBN 978-1-118-00563-7 (ebk); ISBN 978-1-118-00564-4 (ebk)
  1. International business enterprises–China. 2. Investments, Foreign–
China. 3. Businesspeople–United States. 4. Businesspeople–China. 5. Business
ethics–China. 6. China–Commerce. I. Title.
  HD2910.K845 2011
  338.8′8851–dc22

                                          2010037954

For my sons—Jack, Joe, Casey and Dylan.
This is your story now.

Contents

Prologue   ix

Book 1: The High Life   1

Chapter 1   Chinatown on the Rio Bravo   3

Chapter 2   Born to Run   7

Chapter 3   Fortune Cookie   15

Chapter 4   Squeeze Play   41

Chapter 5   Mistakes Were Made   45

Chapter 6   The Right Man for the Job   55

Chapter 7   Token Poet   61

Chapter 8   Token Poet's IPO   75

Chapter 9   Chinese Walls   87

Chapter 10   The Year of Living Dangerously   103

Chapter 11   Easier Said Than Done   107

Book Two: The Crevice   **111**

Chapter 12   A Leopard and His Spots   113

Chapter 13   Talk the Talk, Walk the Walk   121

Chapter 14   The New World Power   131

Chapter 15   A Date with a Monkey   145

Chapter 16   Once Burned, Twice Stupid   157

Chapter 17   Tell Me Something I Don't Know   183

Chapter 18   False Starts   189

Chapter 19   The Worst of Times   193

Chapter 20   Seven-Year Itch   199

Book Three: Hainan Jack   **205**

Chapter 21   Rather Be Lucky than Good   207

Chapter 22   Monkey on His Back   209

Chapter 23   Hearts and Bones   215

Chapter 24   China Fortunes   223

Chapter 25   Killing Two Birds with One Stone   237

Chapter 26   The Man to See   245

Chapter 27   Original Sin   253

Chapter 28   Living Large   259

Chapter 29   Jack, It's Chinatown   267

Chapter 30   What Happens in China Stays in China   271

Chapter 31   Finders, Keepers   275

Chapter 32   The Future of China   285

Chapter 33   Chinese Coverage   305

Chapter 34   The Fish Will Die   317

Chapter 35   As Little as Possible   333

Book Four: Hydro King   **337**

Chapter 36   Sand Pebbles   339

Chapter 37   Chinese Water Torture   351

Chapter 38   Soldier of Fortune   367

Chapter 39   Hydro King   379

Chapter 40   Timing Is Everything   393

Chapter 41   Who Knows Where the Time Goes   401

Chapter 42   You Learn Something New Every Day   411

Chapter 43   The Place to Be   415

Chapter 44   Bulls in the China Shop   425

Chapter 45   Gum on Your Shoe   429

Chapter 46   There and Back Again   433

Chapter 47   Close but No Cigar   443

Chapter 48   Penny Wise, Pound Foolish   449

Book Five: China Hand   **455**

Chapter 49   Men and Women   457

Chapter 50   Catch and Release   463

Chapter 51   China Hand   467

Chapter 52   Chinese Handcuffs   471

Chapter 53   Midnight Train to Baoding   483

Chapter 54   Chinese Checkers   493

Chapter 55   Chinese Fire Drill   499

Chapter 56   A Walk on the Wild Side   507

Chapter 57   One Rainy Night in Lijiang   513

Chapter 58   Tea and Oranges from China   529

Chapter 59   Knock on Wood   533

Chapter 60   Fortune Fish   537

Chapter 61   It's Enough to Make a Man Religious   541

Chapter 62   A Chinaman's Chance   547

Chapter 63   Be Careful What You Wish For   549

Book Six: The Long Walk Home   **555**

Chapter 64   Trial and Error   557

Chapter 65   Third Time's the Charm   561

Chapter 66   Two Out of Three Ain't Bad   565

Chapter 67   Easy Come, Easy Go   569

Chapter 68   High-Water Mark   573

Chapter 69   The Long Walk Home   575

About the Author   579

Prologue

If the water is too clear, the fish will die.

Chinese Proverb

I never had a plan involving China. Swept repeatedly by life's vicissitudes onto the Middle Kingdom's beaches, it took me a while to realize that I owed it to myself to record the events.

In 1984 when I first set out for the Mainland, I was simply a businessman pursuing a commercial goal, an inexpensive alternative to costly Western hydroelectric turbine equipment. Looking out the window on the ride from the airport to the factory in Chengdu, I saw nothing to bind me to the place—the country was raw, uncouth, and otherworldly, in the midst of shaking off the detritus of a century of purgatory. A week later, a purchase contract in hand, the vigorously negotiated 25 percent cash deposit having gutted my bank account, I departed, wondering if I'd ever see my turbines and sure I would never return, the gravelly airstrip trailing off in the smog behind me.

Back stateside, China's remoteness overpowered any other sensibilities I had picked up during the trip. It was as if I had just completed a transaction on Mars. Yes, the Middle Kingdom was 9,000 miles away, but time and distance weren't the half of it. Part of the difficulty was the inadequate communication technology of the day: a telephone call to my Chinese counterparts at the turbine supplier to check on the status of my equipment was impossible—the company had a single telephone for local calls—and their telefax messages, fluttering in curlicue sheets covered with incomprehensible Chinese characters down in a pile on my floor, were as ephemeral and useless as snowflakes on a warm afternoon. In the short week that I had been there, there had been no way to tell if the Chinese were people like me. While we had signed papers saying we had a deal, there was as yet only a nascent concept of contract law in the PRC. Would they honor their commitments? I crossed my fingers and toes, and second-guessed myself for six months.

The turbines finally came, more or less on time. And they worked well, thank God. I began to get comfortable with my Chinese counterparts, and they with me. And China's business trajectory was just beginning. When the country needed foreign investment capital for electric power and other industries, I was an obvious candidate for *cooperation*, their ubiquitous term that can mean so many things. As a partner in a joint venture developing hydroelectric projects on the Minjiang river in Fujian, as well as an investment banker raising money for some of the earliest privatized companies tapping the American equity markets, I jumped back into the now roiling Chinese waters, gaining a much closer perspective on the country and its people, but my Chinese counterparts and I were still at opposite ends of the pool. I was getting to know them better, but the view was not always positive. My long flights to China were laden with anxiety and dread, and there was little opportunity for intimacy across 9,000 miles. But China was beginning to absorb the world's fascination, and back home, my stories were getting attention at cocktail parties—everyone wanted to hear more about the hope and dashed promises, the ecstasy and the tragedy, of the potentially golden, unpolished land. I started to think about putting some words down on paper.

Most people don't get a chance to raise the curtain on a third act, let alone one involving a third business opportunity in China, but when I needed to draw yet another winning hand, China was still calling. By this time hardened and cynical, I went back Chinaside desperate to make one last fortune in the crucible of the now self-congratulatory country, firmly convinced that as tough as China's business challenges would be, the sustenance of anything more than a commercial relationship was unattainable.

But this time there was a major difference. As an owner of businesses in China, the Chinese with whom I interacted were my partners and employees; they were on my side, working with me, some diligently, others clumsily, all of us pulling on our collective oars to build a business and enjoy the glittering potential awaiting entrepreneurs in the greatest business expansion in history. After a long train trip with some memorable events and characters, I spent the 12-hour return plane ride to JFK making notes on my computer. The next day, I woke early, went to my office and kept writing. And a curious thing happened: I couldn't wait to get back.

I had crossed the cultural chasm separating the Occident and the Orient, and was not only viewing firsthand the landmarks of my pilgrimage—the laziness, duplicity, and venality causing treachery and heartbreak, the tireless work ethic, loyalty, and selfless desire-to-serve giving rise to affection, admiration, and more—but recording them. And the dry pages of nonfiction couldn't do them justice—a story was required. Reality is disappointing—China is better.

While based on my own experiences, *China Fortunes* is fiction; the majority of the novel's characters are fictitious, and any resemblance in name, description, or action they may enjoy with real people is purely coincidental.

John D. Kuhns
Lime Rock, Connecticut
November 2010

Book One

THE HIGH LIFE

Chapter 1

Chinatown on the Rio Bravo

The big flatbed truck rolled up shortly before noon. Its driver tried to downshift and apply the brakes at the same time. The truck almost stopped, lurched forward, crawled the last few yards to where the two men stood waiting, and wheezed to a halt, the Rio Bravo River running blue green and silent just beyond.

The air was dry and still. Dust thrown up by the truck billowed and shimmered in the sun and began to settle. Under a blue California sky, the Sierra Nevada lay low on the eastern horizon, a pine-and-snow-topped backdrop for the foothills above the river, their high grass already brown and parched even though it was only April.

Jack Davis stood upstream about 20 yards. He had been looking at the river, running clear and high, trying to see the trout swimming in the shallows, but turned and watched as the truck pulled in.

Up closer, the two men walked toward the truck, eying its cargo. The near side door of the cab creaked opened slowly and a small, trim Asian man climbed down. "Excuse me, do you know where I can find Whitey Davis?" the man asked. He looked to be about 60 years old, was dressed in good casual clothes, and wore heavy black glasses.

"That's me," said one of the men, stepping forward and removing his sunglasses. "Professor Cheng?"

"Hello," Professor Cheng said, extending his hand. "I'm glad we found you. The road's a little confusing once you come off the highway down at Bakersfield."

"Welcome to the Rio Bravo hydroelectric project," said Whitey. He was Jack's brother and the project manager for Catapult Energy, Jack's power company and the owner of the project.

The second man with him walked slowly alongside the rig, looking up at the big pieces of hydroelectric equipment lashed to the flatbed. "This gear have a manual in English?" he said, standing in his Oakleys facing the rear of the truck, his back toward Professor Cheng.

"Professor Cheng, this is Pete Bright, Catapult Energy's chief engineer," said Whitey.

"Very nice to meet you, Mr. Bright," said the professor.

Pete Bright didn't respond, but kept studying the flatbed's cargo.

On the flatbed, a collection of raggedy men began to crawl out from the spaces between the equipment where they had been riding on makeshift mattresses and bedding. The men were small, brown, and wiry, their pants tied with rope or twine at the waist. Some of them wore flip flops, others what looked like the disposable slippers they hand out at the hospital.

Professor Cheng spoke to the workers. One of them answered, standing on the truck bed and speaking nonstop for about three minutes in Chinese. Soon all the men on the truck were talking among themselves in Chinese.

Jack Davis stood and watched, the sun moving up in the sky, burning down on his wavy brown hair and tanned, roughhewn face.

"He says they can install the turbines quickly," said Professor Cheng.

"That's not what I asked you," said Pete Bright. "Where's the manual?"

Professor Cheng spoke once more to the Chinese man on the truck who appeared to be the foreman. He replied in Chinese for several minutes, while the others kept speaking back and forth to one another.

"He says the men are very tired. They've been up since we unloaded the units from the ship in Long Beach yesterday," said Professor Cheng.

"Jesus Christ! Can you just answer my question? Where's the manual for this stuff?"

The Chinese men all stopped talking and turned and stared at Pete Bright.

The professor looked at Pete, then turned and asked the foreman a question. The foreman spoke more slowly but kept talking. The professor started to raise his voice, and the foreman raised his. "*Meiyou.*"

The professor spoke in what sounded like reproachful language to the foreman, who spit back, "*Meiyou!*"

"What does 'mayo' mean, Professor?"

The professor and the foreman stopped talking and together looked back at Pete Bright.

"Is anyone going to answer me?"

"There is no manual, Mr. Bright," said Professor Cheng.

"No manual at all? Christ Almighty! How the hell are we going to install this iron? Jack, you're out of your goddamned mind buying this junk," Pete Bright yelled upriver toward where Jack Davis was standing.

"Pete, we all inspected this stuff in Wuhan," Whitey said. "We know it works. Besides, they install it, not us. Quit being such a control freak. We don't have to get involved. Let them sort it out."

"Yeah, that'll work out just fine," said Pete. "Look at these guys. You expect me to believe they're going to be able to assemble two turbine gensets and install them in our project without screwing everything up? It doesn't even look like they brought winches and cranes."

"Mr. Bright, I assure you these men know what they are doing."

"Yeah, but when it comes to my machines, Professor, I want to know what they're doing, too."

"I'll personally see to it we get a manual delivered to you from Wuhan immediately," the professor said.

"Yeah, and it'll probably come in Chinese, right?"

"Pete, lay off him, for God's sake," said Whitey. "He's just Wuhan Turbine's agent. What do you expect from the guy?"

The men stood in their respective groups, looking at each other.

"Professor Cheng, I've made some reservations at the local Holiday Inn for the crew," said Whitey. "If you want, they can get their gear and I'll drive them over there to get cleaned up. It sounds like they've had a long night."

"Holiday Inn? Oh no, that's very kind of you but I don't think they'll be interested in staying there," said Professor Cheng.

"Well, where are they going to bunk? That's the only hotel around here."

Professor Cheng turned and looked upstream at a flat stretch of grass running along the river where Jack Davis was standing, seeing him for the first time. "If it's all the same to you, they can pitch their tents right over there."

Chapter 2

Born to Run

Jack Davis turned away from the men and went back to looking at the Rio Bravo, refocusing on the trout swimming lazily right below the power plant construction site where the water had formed a deep pool and ran still on the surface. Standing between the ascendant sun in the eastern sky and the edge of the river, his shadow— much larger than his six-foot, 200-pound frame— spilled onto the surface of the water and spooked the fish whenever he moved.

He liked watching the fish; he had always liked it. It relaxed him. Whitey and Pete would sort things out with the professor. Starting out in business, when he thought he had to do everything himself, Jack used to get all exercised over the little things too, before he learned to talk less in order to think more.

Whitey walked over. "Watching those fish?"

"Yeah. It takes your mind off things, you know?"

"Things like Pete's nonsense, for example."

"You know Pete—he's not happy unless he's got something to gripe about," Jack said. Pete liked to complain and play his badass role around strangers. He thought he fooled them into thinking he was in charge, which was important to him. "Let's worry about something worthwhile."

Whitey was usually the one giving Jack advice about people. Like their mother, Whitey had studied psychology in college and had gone on to get a graduate degree in counseling before becoming dissatisfied with his practice and chucking it all to join Jack at Catapult Energy.

"Yeah, you're right," Whitey sighed. "One last thing."

"What's that?"

"You ever wonder if there's a connection between you and the fish and owning a water power company?"

They laughed together easily and talked for a while about the progress of the job and then Whitey went back to organizing arrangements for the new arrivals.

Jack turned his attention to the equipment on the truck. The Chinese turbine generators, coated in bright blue paint, lay disassembled in pieces lashed down to the flatbed. The last time he had seen the equipment had been four months ago when it was sitting on Wuhan Turbine's loading dock. It had been his first visit to China.

㊗ ㊗ ㊗

China had been Yu Cheng's idea. Before Jack started his power company, back in 1983 when he was still an investment banker, he had backed Yu, a brilliant Chinese inventor, before anyone else in Silicon Valley believed in him.

A year later, sitting with Yu in his Palo Alto laboratory in the technology park on the ridge above the city, Bruce Springsteen's *Born in the U.S.A.* playing on the radio, Jack hadn't paid any attention to the music or the tech geeks running experiments across the room, talking among themselves and trying to sound cool in front of the stranger in a jacket and tie who looked to them like a Republican. He was trying to absorb everything Yu had been telling him about the technical aspects of hydroelectric equipment.

The company Jack had just started, Catapult Energy, developed hydroelectric power projects. It had invested in a group of hydroelectric sites around the country, filed permits, obtained power sales contracts and done all the obvious things any developer was supposed to do to be successful. But the American hydroelectric equipment manufacturers had closed their doors, forcing him to deal with European vendors: Swiss, Germans, and Austrians. And while their equipment was jewel-like, it was over-engineered and ridiculously expensive. If forced to pay their prices, Catapult Energy's projects wouldn't be financeable, let alone profitable. And Jack's carrying costs were adding up fast. Unless he found an alternative soon, Catapult Energy would be broke.

Yu had a solution. He sat across from Jack, telling him in a matter-of-fact tone that Chinese equipment cost a fraction of Western gear, and was reliable. It was difficult for Jack to accept—Chinese hydro-electric turbines and generators?—but Yu knew his hardware, and was conservative when it came to mechanical things.

Yu's cousin in Beijing, a professor and head of the physics department at Tsinghua University, moonlighted on the side as a sales agent for Wuhan Turbine, a manufacturer of hydroelectric turbine generator sets located in Wuhan, a large city in China. Cousin Yu was tasked with finding American customers.

Describing the technical qualities of the Wuhan Turbine products and charting their power curves for Jack, Yu had sounded convincing. "All right, how many American hydroelectric power companies have bought equipment from Wuhan Turbine?" Jack asked.

Yu hesitated, and then turned his head and looked Jack in the eye. "No one."

"No one? Maybe I'm asking the wrong question. How many American hydroelectric power companies have bought hydroelectric equipment from *any* Chinese manufacturer?"

Yu sighed. "No American party has bought any hydroelectric equipment from any Chinese manufacturer. You would be the first." Yu looked with resignation at Jack, as if suspecting his honesty would end the conversation.

Jack stood for a moment digesting what he had just heard. "And you're telling me this stuff performs the way you've demonstrated and costs what you've quoted me?"

"That is correct."

Neither man said anything for a long time.

"Yu, you might just have yourself a customer. How long does it take to fly to Wuhan?"

Both men smiled at each other, Yu slowly moving his head up and down, his face displaying only a hint of his underlying relief, Jack trying to get comfortable with the notion of betting millions on Chinese hydroelectric equipment when no one else stateside was inclined to do so.

水 水 水

Coasting down into their first stop in Mainland China, Jack had worried some more when he looked out his window and couldn't see any lights.

It was a winter day in 1984 and Jack, Whitey, Pete, and Kalin Gao, the licensed Chinese agent Jack had hired to represent Catapult Energy in China, were on their way to Wuhan in central China. Their ride was a beat up DC-3, the kind of old propeller-driven plane whose tail when parked on the ground was much lower than its forward cabin, forcing passengers to walk downhill to get to their seats.

Taking the ferry to the Mainland from Hong Kong, clearing customs at the border, and flying north from Guangzhou in the darkness of early morning, they were passengers on a milk run hopping up the east coast of the country before turning inland to Wuhan. Their first stop was Xiamen, a seacoast city on the Straits of Formosa.

"Can you see anything, Whitey?" Jack asked his brother.

"Nothing," Whitey said from his seat across the aisle, his face pressed to the window.

Descending rapidly, the plane dipped its wings and made what felt like an approach turn. Jack stared out the window into the soupy brown air. Maybe they were still over water. Hopefully, the airport was right off the beach. The plane kept descending. Jack's eyes strained to find a landmark or a light in the murk below—what the hell was the pilot doing? At this rate, they would soon land in the drink.

Finally, the outlying reaches of Xiamen loomed up out of the smoggy mist a thousand yards below. Reportedly a city of three million people, whoever was down there was making do in the predawn darkness without the benefit of electricity—Jack couldn't see any lights on in the buildings beneath them or along the road outside the airport.

"Jesus, does anyone live down there?"

"Yeah, I can see lots of people over here, just no lights or cars," Whitey said.

They landed a few minutes later. Following the crew's instructions to wait inside the terminal while they took on fuel and cargo, they walked down the metal stairway and set foot in the interior of the People's Republic of China for the first time.

"Just remember, this was your idea," Whitey said, half kidding.

The small group of passengers headed toward the terminal. Red-brown dust and grit swirled on the tarmac and blew into their eyes. The air smelled musty and acrid, a combination of expended fuel and combusting refuse. Men wheeled baggage carts and fuel wagons by hand toward the plane, staring at Jack and Whitey and Pete as they passed by. Most of the workers wore shorts consisting of pajama-like bottoms rolled up to the knees, tee shirts, and crummy slippers. Even though it was December, the South China air was humid and clammy.

Whitey was right. China *was* his idea. It had been easy to rational-ize. They needed to come here. Catapult Energy was desperate; the company had borrowed money from the banks, but wasn't close to turning a profit.

But few others assessing Catapult Energy's difficult circumstances would have identified a plane trip to China as the solution. And Jack had to admit his justification of the trip wasn't flawless. Pete Bright, his chief engineer, had pointed out that other foreign manufacturers in less exotic places around the world made inexpensive hydroelectric equip-ment. But Wuhan Turbine was not just the cheapest by a long stretch—it was located in China: the self-proclaimed center of the universe, a mysterious destination that had beguiled explorers and thrill seekers since Marco Polo.

Who wouldn't want to try their hand in the Middle Kingdom? Any sane person seeking to avoid uncertainty and hardship, Jack sup-posed. But those things had never bothered him. Especially now. China had recently thrown open its doors to foreign investment, attracting everyone from multinational corporations to pioneering entrepreneurs. For anyone with the temerity to believe they could surmount the country's cultural and business challenges, a chance to build an empire waited on the ground floor of the wide open, teeming land.

Still, when it came to taking such a questionable step, he knew himself well enough to stop and examine his motives. Jack could persuade others to do a lot of things, but the most dangerous thing he could do was fool himself.

He stood in the Xiamen terminal, watching the sun try to poke through the haze. His judgment wasn't perfect, not by a long stretch. He'd made a lot of mistakes in the name of misguided adventure; that was for sure.

When was the first time? Probably when he had stolen the car.

He remembered the end the most—driving slowly up the hill in downtown Silver Spring at two o'clock in the morning, bringing the car back to the dealer lot where they had taken it a week earlier, trying to stay calm, the radio on, and *Wouldn't it be Nice* by the Beach Boys playing. The streets were empty. A light fog covered his tracks as he coaxed the Volkswagen along—he had worn the clutch to the bone, and the little car couldn't get up the traction to go more than 15 miles per hour. He looked up in the rearview mirror and saw the cop car come around the corner behind him, moving up silently, only its running lights on, looking like a sinister white shark. Jack pissed in his pants, the warm urine making a puddle in his seat.

Jack stopped the car as the cop's red and blue flasher lights blinked on and circulated. He just sat in his seat. He didn't know what else to do. He watched in the rearview mirror as the cop emerged from his vehicle, his uniform splashed red and blue by the lights, and came up alongside the VW.

"License and registration."

"There isn't any."

"What's that supposed to mean?"

"There isn't any license and registration, sir."

"You mean you left them at home?"

"Not exactly."

"Well—exactly then—what are you talking about?"

Jack sat in the car, the urine dripping down his pant leg. He knew what he had to say; he just didn't know how to say it.

"I took this car from the VW dealership up the street a week ago, sir. I was returning it. I don't have a driver's license yet and I think the dealer must have the registration. Sir."

"So you're telling me you stole this car a week ago and now you're returning it?"

"Yes, sir."

"Why would you do a fool thing like that, boy?"

"I felt bad for the owner. Sir."

"Forget the sob story. Why'd you steal the car?"

Jack didn't answer.

"So what'd you do with it for a week?"

"Drove my friends to school."

The cop sighed. "Get out of the car, kid. I've got to take you down to the station."

Jack got into the back seat of the squad car and looked at the hand-cuff rack. He was out of chances. He'd have to give the thrill-seeking stuff up, go straight.

He was 13 years old.

The Xiamen airport workers finished fueling and loading the plane and wheeled their empty carts back across the tarmac. As they passed the window of the terminal, they all stared through it at Jack, Whitey, and Pete. One of the workers pointed at them and laughed.

"What are they looking at?" Pete said.

"Us, I guess," Jack said, looking over at Kalin Gao as he spoke.

"You're *laowai*," their agent said simply, averting her eyes and gazing out the window.

"What's that?" Jack asked her.

"Foreigners."

"They act like they've never seen one of us before," Whitey said.

Kalin turned and looked at Whitey. "They haven't."

Chapter 3

Fortune Cookie

Five hours later, they landed in the Wuhan airport and coasted up to the weathered terminal. Their plane was the only one on the tarmac. A big, dusty bus full of people chugged out to meet them from the terminal building.

"Are those connecting passengers?" Jack asked Kalin.

"I don't think so, Mr. Davis," his agent said.

"What are they doing in that bus, then?" Pete Bright persisted, staring out his window as the bus stopped at the foot of the metal stairway being rolled up to the door of their plane.

Saving Kalin from having to answer, the attendant opened the door and the passengers began filing off the plane down the stairway to the tarmac. The bus's passengers lined up and waited for them, all wearing identical white shirts and logoed baseball caps, standing stiffly and staring straight ahead. Two men, boys really, wearing a different type of military-like uniform and helmets stood at attention at either end of the line, holding salutes. They seemed a little ridiculous.

Kalin hurried down the stairway ahead of the others to the man in an ill-fitting jacket and stringy tie standing in front of the receiving line.

She and the man shook hands and spoke in Chinese as they waited for Jack to catch up.

"Mr. Davis, I'd like to present Deputy Manager Wen, the Deputy General Manager of Wuhan Turbine," Kalin said. "The line of people behind him are his top engineers."

Deputy Manager Wen and the engineers all smiled and bowed at Jack.

"Hello," Jack said, sticking out his hand. "I'm very pleased to meet you." He hadn't asked Kalin whether he should bow, but decided not to. As he shook Mr. Wen's hand, the engineers all applauded.

Pete Bright came down the ramp behind Jack. "Kalin, what's going on? How far's the factory? I've got an agenda to adhere to."

Kalin checked with Deputy Manager Wen. "About three hours."

Jack watched as Kalin spoke to Pete, wondering if her hard, business-like edge with others was ever going to rub smooth. In the few weeks Kalin had worked for Catapult Energy, she had catered only to Jack, paying little attention to the other members of his management team. Probably a Chinese thing—serve one master, or something like that. And while she was polite to everyone, she went out of her way to let her charges know she was a professional, not their servant.

Two days into the trip, her patience with Pete already seemed to be wearing thin. While Jack and Whitey were happy to interact as Kalin instructed with Chinese people who didn't speak English, Pete demanded Kalin translate every word, as if he might miss something important hidden in gratuitous conversation. It was becoming obvious Kalin avoided Pete. She didn't address him directly, but only answered his questions, which she tended to treat as interruptions.

"Okay then, let's get going," Pete said. "Who are all these people standing in line and why are they clapping?" he asked as he noticed the Wuhan people in front of him for the first time.

"I'd like to present Deputy Manager Wen and Wuhan Turbine's hydroelectric engineering team," Kalin said. "They are clapping to show our team their respect."

"Is Deputy Manager Wen the head of Wuhan Turbine?"

"No, that would be General Manager Wang."

"So why isn't he here?" Pete demanded.

"That would be beneath General Manager Wang. We won't meet him until later."

"Why not now? We here to give him biggest order of year; he no come greet us?"

"Hey Pete, there you go again talking funny," Whitey said to Pete, winking at Jack. For some reason, Pete's speech devolved into pidgin English whenever he attempted to converse with Chinese people, even Kalin.

Kalin ignored Pete's silly speech and tried to explain. "General Manager Wang knows this trip is preliminary for our evaluation of his company's products. He would lose face if he extended himself and we declined to purchase his equipment."

"Do they know my position with Catapult Energy?"

"Yes," she sighed, "they know you are the chief engineer."

"Well, why are all these people here at the airport?"

"They came here to greet Mr. Jack Davis and the Catapult Energy team."

"Yes, you told me. That's very nice, but what are they going to do now?"

"Nothing; they will return to the factory with us."

"But you said the factory's three hours away. Thirty guys drove three hours one way just to say hello?"

㊖ ㊖ ㊖

Kalin Gao was Yu Cheng's idea, too. Born in Taiwan before moving stateside, she was fluent in English and in both of China's major dialects, Mandarin and Cantonese, and licensed by the PRC government to represent foreigners seeking business deals in China. She did most of her work out of New York in conjunction with the United Nations and lived on the Upper East Side.

Jack had called her and explained his plans to visit the Mainland to buy Chinese hydroelectric equipment. She listened to his story, and agreed to come by the next day for an interview.

He had expected someone different from the woman waiting in his reception area. The Chinese girls he had hired to help him research his China business plans had been mousy, their faces wan and thin and framed with glasses that looked like the kind they hand out to watch a 3-D movie. Instead, the woman in front of him was striking—close to six feet tall, with deep, almost sad eyes and long black hair falling down her silk blouse to her waist.

"Mr. Davis? I'm Kalin Gao," she said, standing up from her seat and holding out her hand, smiling slightly as she gave him time to recover.

Jack couldn't help staring at her. "Hello. Call me Jack."

"Here's my resume," she said, both of them just standing there eying each other in the reception area. "I spoke to Yu Cheng about your requirements. I can do a great job for you. I'm licensed by the PRC and am an excellent interpreter. More importantly, I'm honest. You're going to need that where you're going."

Jack just kept looking at her. "Is that all?" he said finally, starting to laugh and ignoring the receptionist rolling her eyes and shuffling things on her desk to remind them she was in the room.

"I'll bring you good luck," Kalin added. "I'll be your good fortune cookie."

Even though she had been twice as expensive as he could afford, he hired her on the spot.

㊍　㊍　㊍

Deputy Manager Wen had organized two ancient British Leyland Land Rovers to ferry the visitors from the airport to the Wuhan Turbine factory. Jack and the others climbed in and the drivers wheeled their charges out of the terminal, following the engineers' bus. Leaving the airport's two-lane access road, Jack didn't realize the quarter-mile stretch of unfettered roadway represented the only quiet interlude he would encounter until they reached their destination hours later.

Around the corner, life changed. Entering the first village, a scene of chaos smacked Jack like something thrown at him. The drivers began leaning on their horns every five seconds. People, animals, and wheeled assemblages of all kinds wandered everywhere with no sense of direction or logic. Oblivious of motorized traffic, men pedaling bicycles piled eight feet high with nets of coconut shells hogged the roadway, moving at a snail's pace. Odd contraptions assembled from tractor parts and fan belts pulled carts laden with commodities, stopping every few blocks to sell shovelfuls to customers.

A fetid haze of incinerated garbage wafted over the road like a slimy mist, smoke from charcoal cooking fires and the aroma of ammonia-laced animal excrement cutting through the stench. As men pulled lines of water buffaloes roped nose to tail against the traffic, mud rolled off the beasts' hairy thighs and joined their droppings in piles along the road. Flocks of dirty white ducks waddled by, depositing bean-like turds in their wake. As the Land Rovers plowed through, dozens of ducks quacked and flapped their wings at once, their human handlers screaming and whacking them with long bamboo poles.

The drivers were more hazardous than the obstacle course. Jack was convinced the driver of his Land Rover had obtained his license just the previous day. When Kalin said something to the man in Chinese, he turned and looked at her to answer, stopping the car dead in the middle of the road.

Coming into Wuhan from the north, the Land Rovers crossed a steel bridge taking them hundreds of feet above the Yangtze River. No trout in there, Jack thought as he looked down; it was hard to believe anything could live in the yellowish brown sludge. Along the stone bund lining the shore, he saw scores of boats—sampans and paddle wheelers and ocean-going barges—moving in and out of the docks like a vast flock of waterfowl paddling on the river's turgid surface.

In the car, Deputy Manager Wen explained that Wuhan, containing eight million people, was formed from three old cities—Wuchang, Hankow, and Hanyang—at the intersection of the Yangtze and Han Shui rivers. Wuhan Turbine's works, one of the city's three biggest industrial complexes, were in Wuchang, on the south side of the Yangtze, along with Wuhan's steel and cement companies—all state-owned enterprises, Wen said. Kalin called them *SOEs*.

Moving haphazardly down the main drag of Wuchang, their driver pulled into the main entrance of Wuhan Turbine's factory, passing underneath an iron gate topped by an orange fiberglass statue portraying a curious creature. At least 10 feet high, the statue was half man, half monkey, resembling a mutant orange cousin of the monsters defending the Wicked Witch of the East in *The Wizard of Oz*. Posed in a battle-ready, mid-stride stance, the creature wore a uniform and cap, and brandished a spear.

Jack got out of the van and looked back up at the gargoyle-like figure.

"I assume someone's going to tell me about the monkey," Jack said to Kalin.

"I'll leave that to General Manager Wang," Kalin said. "I'm told its story is very important to him."

"When will we meet the Great Wang?" Pete asked.

"My guess is that depends," answered Kalin.

"On what?"

"Whether you give him an order, of course."

A boy appeared with hard hats for the visitors, and guided by Deputy Manager Wen, the Catapult Energy group set out on a tour of the Wuhan Turbine factory.

Viewing the complex for the first time, Jack was chagrined. It was difficult to imagine how anything of value could possibly be manufactured there. Covering several square acres, the factory was immense but ancient. Most of the structures appeared to have been built around the turn of the century, and much of the workplace was outdoors, where men and machines were exposed to the weather. While the shop floors teemed with both male and female workers, most worked without the benefit of tools, pushing and pulling things with their bare hands.

Jack and the others paused in the main work yard to watch a team of men hoisting a turbine up into the air to place it in a test stand. The hoist was nothing more than a collection of wooden poles arrayed in a crude, teepee-like structure, the turbine hanging by ropes in the center. Dozens of men fanned out in all directions, pulling at the ropes and slowly winching the turbine upward.

"Jesus, Pete. Look at that. Those guys are pulling that turbine up to its test stand by hand," Jack said.

"I'm watching them."

"How much do you think that goddamned thing weighs? At least a ton, right?"

"Jackie, that's one of the turbines we're thinking of buying—more like two tons."

No one but Pete ever called him Jackie. "Well, at least it's a manufactured product—hard to believe they actually make turbines here."

"I'm more worried about the generators," Pete answered.

"Kalin, where's the foundry?" Jack said after a half hour of wandering around the yard. "Please thank Deputy Manager Wen for showing us the general layout of the place, but I'd like to see some stuff actually being made."

Kalin pulled on Deputy Manager Wen's sleeve and spoke to him. He nodded to her, and took them down a back alleyway to a worn brick building belching black smoke.

Looking inside, Jack could see men with long metal poles pushing charcoal into the blue-orange flame of a blast furnace smelting chunks of ore, while others drained orange molten metal from a crucible. As the molten metal was poured in to a cooling mold, two hefty women with grimy faces and babushkas gushed water from fire hoses into the sand around the mold to quench the hissing, steaming heat of the metal.

Jack, Whitey, and Pete just looked at one another. Kalin stood off to one side, a quiet smile held in the corners of her mouth.

"Jesus, this looks like something out of the Industrial Revolution," Whitey said.

"I don't think it's history here," Jack said.

"Take a look at the finished product," Pete called from where he stood across the room. Jack and Whitey joined Pete to look into the entrance of the adjoining workspace where a cacophony of metal-on-metal sounds clattered and whined as men with hand tools ground and sanded dull-edged metal shapes into the shiny, bladed curves of a water turbine.

"Will that work?" Jack asked Pete.

"You know, Jackie, for what it's worth, we're looking at a hydro-electric rotor being fabricated by hand," Pete said. "As far as its efficiency, I'll still need to review the test stand results, but a turbine built this way ought to last a lifetime."

"Why don't they make them by hand in the West?" Kalin asked.

"Forty dollars an hour plus benefits prevents you from making a lot of things," Jack said, as he and the other *laowai* continued to watch the half-naked men in bare feet shuffle around on the sand floor. "When you think about it, it's counterintuitive for us, but I guess in China anything labor-intensive is a good thing."

"What about the generators, Kalin?" Pete asked.

She turned to Deputy Manager Wen and spoke to him in Chinese. "They're wound on site," she said to Pete.

"On site? You're kidding me," Pete said.

"Is that bad?" Whitey asked.

"I guess not," said Pete, shaking his head. "Just more of the same—it's very labor intensive to wind a generator on site. Like the turbine, the generator is essentially handmade. The cost would be prohibitive for a foreign manufacturer."

"But Pete, this stuff's still commercial, right?" Jack asked.

"It should be fine, but we won't really know what we've bought until it's assembled and operational," Pete said. "Should deserve a preliminary price discount; I'll bet the installation manual will make for interesting reading."

"I don't think price should be an issue," Jack said. He didn't care about shaving the price of the machines—they were already dirt cheap; he just wanted to know they worked.

"You know, it isn't supposed to be this way," Pete said to Jack as the Catapult Energy group walked away from the foundry and headed toward the loading dock to inspect the finished goods awaiting shipment.

"What way?" Jack asked.

"Why did America spend all its resources building up a mammoth industrial complex if a bunch of guys in pajamas can make a similar product for a fraction of the price?"

"You can worry about that if you want to," Jack said, walking around the corner and coming face to face with a phalanx of finished hydroelectric machines on Wuhan Turbine's loading dock, "but I'm happy they're doing it."

He had seen enough. A photograph of the finished equipment would probably have done it for him, but seeing the big, fungible turbines six feet away was even better. Only a fool wouldn't grab the opportunity sitting in front of him, he thought as he asked Kalin to tell Deputy Manager Wen he was a customer subject to normal conditions. His squeamishness over Wuhan Turbine's antique surroundings a distant memory, Jack's remaining concern was who was taking delivery of the turbines on the loading dock. Hoping they weren't going stateside, he prayed Yu Cheng had been correct when he said no American competitors had yet discovered Chinese hydroelectric equipment.

Deputy Manager Wen guided Jack, Kalin, Whitey, and Pete up the steps of the company's headquarters building and down the first-floor hallway. The air hung heavy in the corridor, full of the acrid incineration omnipresent in China's air, garlic-intense cooking odors, and ammonia-laden bathroom stench. Jack breathed through his mouth.

They passed a bathroom area where women were rinsing mops and rags in industrial sinks, toilets consisting of slit holes lined up beyond the sinks. A man stood in an open stall urinating, the cleaning ladies oblivious. Along the hallway, girls with dirty gray rags wiped the dusty floors, walls, and doorframes of the corridor in long circular strokes.

At an open doorway marked by a red sign with gold stars and Chinese lettering, an older woman waited for them as they walked down the last length of the dark hallway. Deputy Manager Wen spoke to the woman as Kalin whispered they were entering General Manager Wang's family apartment.

Kalin had told Jack most factories in China provided dormitories to house managers and workers, but the dwelling they were entering was not part of a dormitory—it was right in the middle of the company's administration building. Jack looked up and down the hallway and saw no other signs of habitation. As they nodded their heads and said hello to the woman, she offered them a dull greeting with no change of expression, and ushered them into the rooms, disappearing to the right into a space functioning as a kitchen.

Composed of a row of dank, interconnected compartments, the apartment was a collection of old offices converted into a bleak living space. Some of the doorways were nothing but holes chopped through the walls to allow access. There were windows, but no light came through the ratty blankets arrayed as crude drapes to keep the sun out.

Straight ahead, a naked light bulb hung from the ceiling, providing the room's only illumination.

Just below the light, sitting at a steel case desk as large as an aircraft carrier, was a man who Jack figured must be General Manager Wang. Dressed in what appeared to be an army uniform, the man's face was swarthy but unlined, his head practically bald. He didn't get up initially, instead pushing papers around on his desktop, trying to give the visitors the impression he was a very busy man with a lot on his mind.

Another man sat off to the side in the dark, a plume of bluish cigarette smoke curling up behind his head.

Jack stood in the middle of the room, not knowing what to do next, while Deputy Manager Wen spoke in Chinese to Kalin. Absorbing the impression of being in some sort of bomb shelter, Jack's attention was drawn to the drab greenish walls. All four sides of the room were covered with hundreds of picture frames, plaques, photographs, and framed articles.

Jack moved closer to the wall nearest him and began scrutinizing the items he could discern in the dim light. When General Manager Wang saw Jack studying the memorabilia, he dropped his pretense of being otherwise engaged and emerged from behind the desk. Slight and bent, he straightened up as best he could, gave an acknowledgment to Kalin, and began speaking in Chinese to her.

"Mr. Davis, this is General Manager Wang," said Kalin. "He is honored you have visited him and his family in his private quarters."

Not waiting for Jack to say anything and paying no attention to Whitey and Pete, Wang took Jack's elbow and motioned him along the wall, talking excitedly and pointing to a framed article from the *New York Times.* The article contained a photograph of a younger General Manager Wang standing on a street corner in New York City, and described his attendance at the International Rotary Club's annual convention. Probably not a lot of hydroelectric turbine customers there.

As General Manager Wang moved down the wall, chattering about this plaque or that certificate, Kalin followed behind and described their significance, but Jack could read them for himself: *Greater Sacramento Chinese American Club's International Guest of the Year,* one of them proclaimed; *Who's Who in the Chinese Community in Everett, Washington,* said another; a third was a letter from the *Greater Tuscaloosa Chamber of Commerce,* thanking General Manager Wang for passing through.

Jack did his best to appear interested as General Manager Wang continued in Chinese to describe the items, happy to talk about himself and paying no attention to anyone else in the room. Consumed by his importance, the man would have been pleased to yammer on all night if they had let him.

Getting to the corner of the room, Jack tried to bring the show to an end by giving General Manager Wang his business card. Using both hands, he presented the card to General Manager Wang, who was careful to show respect to his guest by studying the card. He appeared to have genuine interest in Jack's card, quizzing Kalin on the particulars of Jack's title and responsibilities.

"He says you look very young to be in such a responsible position," Kalin said, turning and smiling at her boss.

"Tell him that's because unlike him, I'm not an old mossback who's survived 50 years of political infighting," Jack said.

Kalin was concentrating on her translation, sorting through the words, and Jack's inept attempt at humor caught her by surprise. Her smile disappeared; she stammered, and turned to look at him, her eyes wide open and confusion on her face.

Jack realized his joke had backfired badly. "No, no, I didn't mean for you to translate that," he said, rubbing his face so the others wouldn't see him laughing. "I'm sorry. It was just a stupid attempt at a joke," he said to Kalin. "Please thank General Manager Wang for his compliment."

"Why do you American guys always have to try to be funny?" Kalin said, leveling a reproachful glance back at Jack before recovering her professional mien.

The Chinese in the room watched the interaction between Kalin and Jack with blank expressions, shuffled around, and waited for the introductions to continue. General Manager Wang motioned to the man behind him, who came forward. "This is Jensen Chen," Kalin continued. "General Manager Wang says Mr. Chen is his Hong Kong investment banker," she said to Jack, raising her eyebrows in what Jack took to be a cautionary expression.

Jensen Chen spoke a clipped, barely recognizable form of English that extended only as far as introductions. He offered Jack his card. It was embossed with cheap, crinkly gold ink, and listed numerous titles and professional affiliations no one stateside would ever put on a business card. He wore a crumpled double-breasted navy blazer with gaudy plastic buttons and some type of insignia limply sewn on to the breast pocket, a pair of dirty yellow linen pants, white socks, and shiny black patent leather shoes with big buckles.

General Manager Wang went to a box on his desk, got a card, came back around where Jack stood and presented it. It was in Chinese, and featured a logo of the orange man-monkey guarding Wuhan Turbine's entrance gate.

Thankfully, the picture show ended as the old woman reappeared with tea, and they sat down around a table on the other side of the room. As the woman placed the tea service and a dish of sunflower seeds in the middle of the table, Kalin spoke to her in Chinese and confirmed to Jack she was indeed General Manager Wang's wife. Knowing it might be counter to protocol but wanting to show her some small indication of respect for what he imagined life had been like for her, Jack intentionally introduced himself to her anyway, giving her his business card. Flabbergasted, she didn't know what to do. Kalin helped her make the tea to calm her down.

General Manager Wang picked at a sunflower seed and made a motion to Jack to join him. To be polite, Jack cracked a few seeds open. It was an impossible process; there wasn't much inside and what was there tasted like salted cardboard. Who would do this? he thought to himself, before answering his own stupid question: starving Chinese.

As the others talked, Jack watched General Manager Wang's wife and Kalin bend over the table, laboring through the tea service. Dropping twiggy loose tea into a bowl of hot water, they squashed the leaves into the steaming liquid with porcelain spoons and strained off the water into a pot, then repeated the process until they had collected a full pot of amber tea. Rising from the table, the old woman crept around behind her husband and his guests, pouring the tea into tiny cups, and then returned to her perch and repeated the process.

Jesus, Jack thought. The tea was good, but not *that* good, the ritual as unproductive as picking at the sunflower seeds. Thinking about what would have been offered at a table of guests stateside, he felt spoiled and wasteful. The Chinese had no idea what was coming their way—disposable income was going to change a lot of habits around China. There would probably be more seeds and tea leaves left lying around, too.

As the discussion gravitated to the subject of Wuhan Turbine's business, General Manager Wang grew less animated, and was content to let Deputy Manager Wen handle things. When Wen got to the company's revenues, General Manager Wang interrupted with the number, but when Jack asked about profits, Wang was noncommittal. Jack got the impression he didn't know his own company's profit line, and cared less.

Wang's wife had just poured her third round of tea when Jack asked Kalin if General Manager Wang would mind telling them the story of the man-monkey.

Kalin repeated Jack's request to General Manager Wang, and the man's face lit up. Reenergized, he talked and talked. As Jack was learning, dialogue with Wang wasn't like other conversations Jack had experienced in China in which one person speaks, followed by translation, and then the other person responds. General Manager Wang had his own style. He did all the talking; everyone else just listened.

Across the table, the glazed expression on Deputy Manager Wen's face indicated he had heard the speech many times. Jack pretended to be consumed with Wang's diatribe. Finally, when it seemed Wang might continue forever, Jack interrupted out of desperation. "Kalin, what on earth is he talking about?"

General Manager Wang looked over at Jack, faltered for a moment, and Kalin was able to explain to Jack what he was saying. "He says he was a businessman until the Cultural Revolution. Then he was identified by the Red Brigades as a Capitalist Roader, thrown into a pit with no food or water and left to die. Many times he was thought to be dead, but whenever someone checked on him, he surprised them. Some of the cadres started a rumor Wang had magical powers, like an extinct breed of orange-colored monkey that according to local legend once lived in the nearby forest. More and more people in Wuhan learned about Wang's survival skills, he became a semi-mythical figure, and soon afterward they let him out of the pit."

Jack put on his best expression of admiration as he turned and looked at Wang, who was looking at him as if to extract his due.

"That's just the beginning, I'm afraid," Kalin continued. "The City of Wuhan had problems at Wuhan Turbine, and General Manager Wang was asked to fix things. According to him, he turned the place around and made it profitable. Now he's one of the most respected men in China," she said, making sure to add, "according to him," "and the city erected the statue of the man-monkey to honor him."

The session in the sepulchral apartment mercifully ended—it was time for dinner. Kalin told Jack and the others the meal would be an important event: along with General Manager Wang, Wuhan's mayor, and more importantly, the head of Wuhan's Chinese Communist Party, would attend.

Jack, Kalin, and the Catapult Energy group left the factory and were driven to their hotel, Wuhan's official guest house, owned and maintained by the city for important visitors, to freshen up. The guest house's rooms contained essentials—beds, toilets, and most importantly, Mah Jong tables—but no telephones or elevators. Its halls and public areas smelled no better than the corridors at the factory.

After changing and putting on a jacket and tie, Jack sat on his bed and looked at the cigarette holes in the grungy carpets, watched the faucet drip in the bath tub, and felt the prickly mattress filled with cotton and straw.

The surroundings couldn't dampen his spirits. He was feeling good, and after a few drinks at dinner, he would feel even better. Visiting Wuhan Turbine had not been a mistake, but a piece of extraordinary good fortune. China would not only give his company life—with a pipeline of inexpensive Chinese equipment in place, his hydroelectric projects would surely be profitable—but also allow it to become a thriving enterprise. He allowed himself to speculate about an IPO–an initial public offering, the universally accepted indicator of success on Wall Street, would assure the financial viability of both the company and his bank account.

He was going to be spending a lot more time in places like the one he was in, but it was going to take more than one visit to get accustomed to some of China's oddities.

Like the English language being unexpectedly omnipresent. "Please fasten your seatbelts; the airplane is about to depart." Flying from Guangzhou to Xiamen, when the flight attendant issued the standard takeoff precautions in English, it escaped his attention. Until she did it again on the way from Xiamen to Wuhan. A flight attendant had just told a packed plane of Chinese passengers to fasten their seatbelts *in English,* and Jack, Whitey, and Pete were the only *laowai* on the plane.

Like one time zone. The United States, with the same land mass as China, had four time zones in the lower 48 states. China got by with one, and didn't even use Daylight Savings Time. Wuhan's winter mornings were pitch black. He couldn't imagine how they could function in the far western reaches of the country—it had to be dark there until noon. Kalin said Chairman Mao said the country's stability was enhanced by everyone having the same time on their watch.

Or like uneven floors. Most of the public spaces he had entered in China were booby trapped. Crossing the lobby of the guest house, he had been walking over to the breakfast cafe when he had stumbled and gone down hard. The floor of the cafe was three inches higher. Maybe the cafe had been a later addition; perhaps the ground underneath had been a little higher. Whatever the reason, no additional excavation was required—the cafe floor was just installed three inches higher than the main lobby floor. Sitting and having tea, he watched several customers knock themselves silly in the course of an hour.

He heard a knock at his door. It was Kalin. "Mr. Davis, are you ready for dinner?"

"Sure," he said, shutting the door of his room behind him and following Kalin to the end of hall where the stairs led down to the lobby.

"How's your jet lag, Mr. Davis?" Kalin asked.

"What's with the Mr. Davis stuff?" Jack said to her as they wound down the dusty stairs poorly lit by a single blue-white fluorescent bulb at each landing. "Call me Jack," he said, reminding himself to breathe through his mouth as the odor of urine wafted up the staircase shaft.

"Oh no, that wouldn't be professional. Addressing you by your first name here in China is not respectful of you and your position."

"Come on now. It's just me and you here."

"I might call you Jack in private if you gave me permission," Kalin said.

"Permission granted," he said. "Perpetually."

"But not in public. You're an important *laowai* businessman. I wouldn't be doing my job in China if I addressed you by your first name in a business setting."

"Look, I'm not important, and I'm an easygoing American, remember?"

"You're important to me. And we're in China."

"Fair enough. I've got another question. I heard Wen and Wang address you as 'Gao Lin.'"

"Gao Lin is my Chinese name."

"Last name first?"

"Yes, like all Chinese names."

"And one uses both names like that?"

"Yes."

"So you're telling me all your friends call you Gao Lin."

"Well, in China they do. At least in front of others in a business setting. Sometimes friends use nicknames."

"What's your nickname?"

"Little Lin."

"You're not little," Jack said.

"It's a common nickname in China. It means young."

"Where'd Kalin come from?"

"I made it up."

"You made it up."

"I had to chose an English name and I wanted one that sounded like my real name, but different."

"So you just picked an English name?"

"Everybody does that when they study English in school.".

"What if you changed your mind?"

"Then I would change my name. Don't you like my name, Mr. Davis?"

"It's Jack, remember? Of course I like your name. I was just curious. But you could change it if you wanted to? It's not official?"

"No, it's not official; I have girlfriends who have changed their English names several times."

"Just like clothes or boyfriends."

"What? I don't understand."

She could be so serious, and she was so beautiful. He liked it that Kalin seemed to want to do a good job for him, and he liked her. It would be nice if he could make her laugh—he wished he was funny or witty—but he wasn't. He knew it, and he knew she knew it.

"Never mind. So why do you call me Mister Davis? Why don't you address me as Jack Davis—or Davis Jack, I guess—using both my names the way Chinese people address you?"

"Because you are my boss. You are Mister Davis in English, or in Chinese, Director Davis—*Daviszhong*. It's disrespectful for a subordinate to address a superior using their regular name."

"You're not a subordinate to me."

"In China I am," Kalin replied.

"All right, I'm not going to fight you about it."

They kept walking down the musty, spiraling staircase.

"I guess I should have asked you this before, but I didn't realize names were so important here. So what should I call you?"

"You can call me Kalin."

"Not Kalin Gao or Gao Lin."

She shook her head as she led him down the last of the stairs.

"And not Lin."

"Only my husband calls me that," she said.

The dining hall did not feature a large, open dining area, but rather a warren of private rooms. Jack and Kalin were ushered into one end of a large room where Whitey and Pete and the Wuhan Turbine engineers were already seated around a conversation area filled with overstuffed fake leather chairs and couches; a kitchen and dining room adjoined. The room contained two console televisions, one showing a soccer match in French; the other, BBC news. They were the first televisions Jack had seen in Wuhan. "What's with the TVs?" Jack said across the room to Kalin over the din of the conversation and the television and kitchen noise. "The announcers are speaking in foreign languages— these guys can't possibly understand them."

"Status symbols," Kalin said across the room, giving Jack a non-plussed shrug and turning back to her conversation with Deputy Manager Wen. Jack looked around; none of the Chinese were watching either one of the televisions.

The restaurant staff, a half dozen young Chinese girls attired in long, sheath-like dresses, moved around silently taking drink orders. One asked Jack in English what he wanted to drink. Kalin looked over to help, but Jack said, "*Shue,*" and congratulated himself when the waitress recognized his request for water. When the girl returned, she set down a glass, poured some water from a bottle, swept her hand over his drink as if to announce its presence, and said "*Pleasssse.*" She did that every time she served him anything for the rest of the night.

Even though the table was set for 20 people, it didn't appear the restaurant would be serving a set meal. While the others talked, General Manager Wang sat in the corner poring over a large, plastic-covered menu, replete with descriptions of each dish, including color photographs. Deputy Manager Wen left his conversation with Kalin to help his boss. The two of them flipped through the menu for 30 minutes before they were satisfied. If they were stateside, the meal would have been practically over.

The government officials arrived, first an entourage including the mayor, and then another one led by Wuhan's Communist Party head. As he was introduced to the officials, Jack exchanged cards. All of the officials had cards in Chinese, with the Chinese state symbol in a red circular background and the five stars in gold. The party head's card had a hammer and sickle with embossed gold lettering, and the mayor's card had an English version on the back.

People milled around until Wang and Wen finished ordering, and then it was time for dinner. Jack looked at his watch: it was barely six o'clock in the evening.

As they moved from the sitting area to the large banquet table, Jack went for the seat nearest him but Kalin directed him to the rear of the room where the seat for the guest of honor, designated by a ringed napkin folded stalk-like into the air, faced out toward the door.

"There?" Jack asked Kalin.

"Yes. You are the guest of honor, and that seat has the best *feng shui,*" she said. Jack had tried to discuss *feng shui* with Kalin once before, but her description made it sound too much like religion, and he had dropped the subject.

"Sit down," Kalin said, motioning for Jack to take his chair. She stood behind her chair two seats to his right.

He went to help her with her seat.

"No, no, that's Western style—here the big boss sits down first," she said, pushing him away and telling him again to take his seat so everyone else could sit.

Jack sat down and watched as an unusually gregarious General Manager Wang fawned over the Wuhan officials. Wang held the party head by the hand and was trying to drag him over to the seat on Jack's right. "*La, la, la,*" Wang said in Chinese, Jack figuring he was saying "sit here, sit here," while the man protested but allowed himself to gravitate over to the seat on Jack's right and sat down. Deputy Manager Wen was doing the same thing with the mayor on Jack's left.

Jack raised his eyebrows over at Kalin.

"Seating is a big deal here," she said loudly to be heard over the din, as several debates around the table were going on as to where people would be placed. "You are the honored guest, but the most important people in the room other than you are the party head and the mayor, so they should sit on either side of you. They are saying to General Manager Wang that he is the important one, and he should be sitting next to you, but he knows better. These men are his bosses."

Now they were making a fuss about where Whitey and Pete would go. Deputy Manager Wen said something in Chinese to Kalin, who responded, after which Whitey was placed to the left of General Manager Wang while Pete took his seat next to Deputy Manager Wen.

"They asked me who was more important at Catapult Energy," Kalin explained to Jack, "and I said they were equally important but reminded them Whitey was your brother. That's all they needed to hear," she said, laughing. "Blood is much thicker than water in China."

As the seating carousel sorted itself out, Jack studied the table and the array of hardware in front of him. Each guest received three glasses: a tumbler, a wine glass, and a tiny shot glass filled with a clear liquid. When he asked Kalin what it was, she smiled and said, "Mossback liquor."

"Very funny," Jack said, laughing. "Seriously."

"*Baiju*," she said. "White liquor. All the government officials drink *baiju*." Jack's waitress noticed him looking at his glasses and asked Kalin something in Chinese. "She wants to know if you want wine, beer, or juice. Chinese white wine is terrible; the red wine is all right."

"I guess red wine then," Jack said. "I love Chinese beer, but only after a workout."

Kalin told the waitress, who poured a thimble full of red wine into Jack's wine glass—one sip, and it would be empty again. He watched as the waitress poured an orange-yellow concoction into Kalin's tumbler.

"What is that?"

"Corn juice," she said.

He tried not to think too much about that.

"Would you like some?"

"I don't think so."

"You might like *baiju*," she said.

"I have a feeling I'm going to find out before the night's over."

In the center of the table was a glass Lazy Susan arrayed with dishes of appetizers—he recognized black mushrooms and *bok choi* and what looked like peanuts—with the waitresses loading more dishes onto the glass wheel every minute.

In front of him lay a large dinner plate, chopsticks, and a serving spoon. He went to take his napkin and a waitress snatched it out of his hands and arranged it so it was secured under his plate and flapped over his lap. Then she made a big deal out of presenting him with a knife and fork—"Pleasssse"—but he didn't need them. He had been eating Chinese food with chopsticks stateside for years.

But not Chinese food like this. Not that he hadn't prepared himself. He had assumed he would be consuming strange animals and unspeakable body parts, and figured on staying away from things he didn't recognize and eating food he could identify: cold sesame noodles, spring rolls, General Chung's chicken with cashews, stuff he had eaten a hundred times in the Chinese restaurant around the corner from his house in New York.

But as he surveyed the table, he didn't see anything that looked remotely like General Chung's chicken. Still, the food the waitresses were bringing out of the kitchen smelled great. The food kept coming—

dishes containing celery, spinach, tofu, some kind of cut-up birds that looked like chicken or quail but turned out to be pigeons, beef, pork, two kinds of whole fish, small lobster and crabs, noodles, rice, and dumplings.

If people didn't start eating soon, there was going to be no place to put everything.

"You're the guest of honor; they're waiting for you," Kalin said.

Jack picked up his chopsticks and speared a clump of broccoli. It was very fresh—probably harvested earlier in the day—with a light peanut sauce.

All the Chinese men smiled and started speaking excitedly to Kalin.

"They're very impressed that you can use your chopsticks," she said, looking at him with approval.

During the dinner, Kalin ate little, helping Jack and the other *laowai*. When there was something Jack didn't recognize, all he needed to do was glance over at her.

"Duck tongue," she said as Jack's chopsticks hovered hesitantly over a small dish of browned strips resembling crispy bacon. He ate one. Delicious, he grabbed another before the Lazy Suzan took them away from him toward his neighbors. "Sea cucumber," she said when the waitress put a small plate with a brownish, tube-like thing in front of him. He took a bite, resolved never to eat sea cucumber again, and moved the plate off to one side.

When everyone had consumed a comfortable amount of food, General Manager Wang stood up, picked up his shot glass of *baiju,* hurled a bunch of Chinese words across the table that Kalin fielded as the other men began to clap, and looked over at Jack.

"He's welcoming you to Wuhan," Kalin said. "You must stand up and toast him back," she said.

As Jack stood up and grabbed his shot glass, everyone pushed back their chairs and stood up around the table, raising their shot glasses.

"They're going to say, '*Gambei,*'" Kalin said. "It means 'bottoms up,' but you don't have to drink the whole thing if you don't want to."

"*Gambei,*" cried General Manager Wang, downing his *baiju* in one swallow and turning his glass upside down to Jack to indicate it was empty—a sign of respect.

"*Gambei*," said Jack, throwing the firewater down his throat and feeling the kick of the hard liquor as he turned his glass over, following General Manager Wang's lead. General Manager Wang and the others cheered, and then they all sat down as quickly as they had stood up and went back to their food and their conversations.

"That's only round one," Kalin warned Jack across the table. "You don't have to drink the whole thing every time. All the officials drink a lot—it's part of their job—but they all fantasize about being able to outdrink a big American like you, so you need to watch out. They'll be trying to get you drunk."

"Look, don't worry about me. The *baiju* has a kick all right, but it's just a thimbleful of booze," Jack said to Kalin over the noise at the table. "If these guys think a few shots of this stuff is all it takes to get me drunk, they're in for a disappointment."

"Just be careful, and don't let them know how you feel."

After General Manager Wang's toast, the party head and the mayor followed suit. Just as before, everyone at the table got up from their seats, hoisted their glasses, echoed "*Gambei*," threw down the firewater, sat down, and went back to eating as the waitresses rushed around replenishing their glasses. Kalin whispered to Jack that it was his turn and he and Kalin stood up and Jack gave a toast to Wuhan Turbine and the city of Wuhan as Kalin translated.

Four down and feeling fine, Jack said to himself as he sat down. No one had touched their wine.

"Kalin, I'd like to make a toast," Pete said, starting to stand up.

"No, no, you can't do it that way," Kalin said to him quickly, motioning for him to keep his seat as Pete hesitated, a confused look on his face. "Watch what happens next," she said as Pete kept looking at her for directions.

A moment later, Deputy Manager Wen got up from his seat, came around the table, and stood behind Jack, shot glass in hand.

"He doesn't have standing to offer a toast to the table, so he's showing you his respect by offering you a toast personally," Kalin said to Jack, making sure to speak loudly so Pete could hear. Jack stood up and turned to Wen, clinked glasses with him, drained another round, and sat back down.

"Like that," Kalin directed across the table to Pete as Deputy
Manager Wen went back to his seat.

"Why?" Pete asked. "I want to toast the table, too."

Kalin didn't answer him, picked up her chopsticks, and grabbed a
green bean.

Pete sat considering his options, and after a minute, got up with
his glass and looked to Kalin for further instructions. "Start with the
party head," Kalin said, not letting him out of her sight.

Pete teetered over to the party head's chair. Pete couldn't hold his
liquor and was only good for a drink or two before showing it, but
with Kalin translating he reeled off some flowery nonsense wasted on
the party head, who stood tentatively beside his chair, a plastic smile
on his face, until they finally clinked glasses and Pete wobbled back to
his seat.

Soon the table was surrounded by Chinese jumping beans as the
secondary government and company officials began hopping up and
making their rounds, each starting with Jack and then hitting the party
head, the mayor, General Manager Wang, and on down. The waitresses
worked hard to keep the *baiju* flowing, and everyone was watching
Jack out of the corner of their eye to see when he was going to topple
over.

Pete sampled one dish that looked like squiggly french fries. "Hey
Jack, what do you think these are?" Pete asked, holding one up in the
air with his fork. "They're the only thing I've found that I like."

Jack looked at the squiggles and turned to Kalin, who, trying to
suppress a laugh, told him. "You don't want to know," Jack said as he
turned back to Pete, who stopped chewing.

"You're going to tell me worms," Pete said, his mouth full as he
mouthed the words.

"Deep-fried caterpillars," Jack said.

Pete stopped chewing, then started again. "Too late now," he said,
shrugging his shoulders. "Besides, they're good. Kalin, when do we get
our fortune cookies?"

"We don't have fortune cookies in China," she said. "They're just
another China thing invented in America, like the notion that Chinese
women are all compliant China dolls."

"You mean they're not?" Jack asked.

Kalin had turned away; he couldn't tell if he had made her smile or not.

㊛ ㊛ ㊛

Two hours after they sat down, the meal was over. The televisions squawked away and the Chinese guys were gathered in groups, leaving the *laowai* to fend for themselves. Whitey and Pete were each three chairs away, and it wasn't worth it to Jack to yell over a government official's head to engage in small talk.

He looked over at Kalin, deep in conversation with a few of the Chinese guys. Jack hoped she would loosen up and enjoy herself a little. Jack wanted to like Kalin, but she was hard to get to know. She was good at her job and worked hard at it, but he couldn't see into the rest of her, at least so far. It didn't hurt that she was good to look at.

As opposed to the art on the walls. Jack looked around the room at the cheap copies of traditional Chinese paintings. Having been an artist before he had gotten into business, he knew he should be more appreciative of the technique and serenity of the work, but he couldn't help it: the stuff was hideous. How many geishas, gazebos, and fat Buddha-like characters could someone take?

Reminding himself he was in no position to criticize anyone else's artistic efforts, he thought back to his conversation with Virginio in Italy six years earlier.

"I think it's time for me to do something else," he had said to Virginio, the Italian sculptor and professor he worked for.

It had been noontime on a summer day in 1978 in Carrara, the quarry town in Italy where the finest marble in the world lay buried under the Tuscan hills. They were eating lunch in a grassy meadow above the cavernous quarry pits. Virginio Ferrari, a professor of fine arts and the sculptor in residence at the University of Chicago, had received a commission from the City of Chicago for a marble piece that would stand on Dearborn a block south of the Picasso bull, and he and Jack, his student and apprentice, were in Carrara to pick out the stone. Below them, the men worked the mules pulling the cutting wires back and forth across the mountain, slicing the big blocks of stone the same way it had been done for centuries.

"What happen?" Virginio said, turning to look at him.

Jack had been avoiding the topic, but it couldn't wait any longer. He knew Virginio was going to be disappointed. "I've just got to face it, Virginio. I don't think I'll ever be that good at this," Jack said.

"You can be good. You have a good feel for the stone. I like the buttons very much," Virginio had said. Jack was carving a series of large round shapes of stone with holes in the middle, and Virginio had seen them and christened them "button stones."

"Well, thank you, but they're not important. You do important work; your friends Manzu and Marini in Milano do, too. I don't think I'll ever get there."

"You must be patient."

"You know, Virginio, I think that's part of the problem. I want it too much. I think it colors my work, makes it seem ambitious. There's nothing worse than ambitious art. I think I'm going to do something else."

"So, you will go back to football?" Virginio laughed. Jack knew he wasn't being mean, just teasing. Playing football hadn't been the answer for Jack, either. Before he had showed up at Virginio's studio, he had worked out for a couple of NFL teams, but while he had been a good player and the captain of his college team, he wasn't good enough to play professionally.

"No," he said. "That's over."

"What, then?"

"You wouldn't believe it if I told you."

"What?"

"I think I might go to the Harvard Business School."

"What? You want to be good at something; what you think you can do in business? They eat you alive, those guys."

"I won't taste too good."

Chapter 4

Squeeze Play

"So I just want to know. How much do those turbines really cost?" Jack asked.

The trip to Wuhan concluded, he was back in Palo Alto with Yu Cheng in his laboratory office. Late on a December afternoon, shade washed the lawn with a bluish hue. A gap in the top of the Coast Range allowed the last of the sun's rays to sneak through and cover the buildings still in direct light with a coppery sheen.

Yu took off his glasses and began polishing them using the handkerchief he kept in the left rear pocket of his trousers. He didn't look at Jack, but kept polishing his glasses.

"Ten million?" Jack asked.

"Ten million what?"

"Samoleans. Dollars, for God's sake."

"I thought maybe you meant renminbi."

"Dollars. Why would you think I meant RMB when we've been speaking in dollars the whole time?"

"I wasn't sure, that's all."

"I get the feeling you just don't want to discuss this subject, Yu. But I really need to know."

"You've got the invoice from Wuhan Turbine. What more do you want?"

"The invoice just tells me the price I pay them; that's not what I'm after. I want to know what it costs the company to make these machines and sell them to me. Then I'll know how much money they're making."

Yu sighed. "You mean after all costs?"

"Yes, of course—all costs."

"What types of costs are you including—just hard costs, right?"

Jack stopped pacing idly, turned and walked to where Yu sat and faced him. "Look, I get nervous when people don't answer questions about dollars and cents. I'm not fooling around; I want to know how much you think those turbines cost, including all costs—hard costs, soft costs, whatever. You must have a good idea, and I need an answer."

"Jack, I'm just their sales agent. They don't tell me everything."

"But you've got to have a realistic idea."

"Including fees?"

"Yes, for God's sake; including fees."

"Whose fees?"

"Yours, for Chrissakes."

Yu looked at Jack. "My fees from you, my fees from them, or both?"

Jack stopped pacing once more and stared at Yu. "Are you telling me Wuhan Turbine's paying you a fee as well?"

Yu tried to look Jack in the eye, failed, and stared down at his feet. "Jack, that's the Chinese way. Everyone makes the squeeze."

"The squeeze? What's the squeeze?"

"Getting paid from both sides."

Jack just stood there.

"We've got to make something on this deal ourselves, Jack," Yu offered lamely.

Jack still didn't say anything, still trying to assess how he felt about what he was hearing.

"Besides, what difference does it make?" Yu asked, anxious to change the subject. "You're still getting these turbines for 30 percent of the world market price."

"Yeah, but what if they really cost just 10 percent? It makes a big difference to me. That's just the way I am. I want to know what the other side's profit is. I can't stand it when I pay more than I should. And not knowing who's paying who is even worse."

"Well, now you know—the total cost of this equipment includes fees from both you and Wuhan Turbine."

Jack shook his head slowly, scratching the back of his neck. "Any other surprises?"

Yu sat polishing his glasses. "In your calculations, have you included Wuhan Turbine's fee to Kalin?"

Chapter 5

Mistakes Were Made

Five months later, Jack stood on the banks of the Rio Bravo River watching the Chinese workers unload their gear from the truck bed.

He looked at the fish in the river one last time. The trout were running up and down the Rio Bravo, hiding in the shadows, drifting down into the deep holes as the sun continued to rise and the temperature warmed up and they became comfortable with their surroundings, floating slowly upward to sample the nymphs escaping from the depths toward the surface, and then darting up or downstream when they felt Jack move on the river bank.

Watching them didn't really take his mind off anything—just the opposite. Focusing on the trout, he could lock out everything else in the world. If he was lucky, all of his remaining consciousness would be filtered by the white noise of the ripples, riffles, and gurgles of the stream.

"Jack, you're out of your goddamned mind buying this junk."

Pete's lament found its way through Jack's concentration, and he laughed to himself. Pete knew the equipment wasn't junk. In Wuhan, they had checked it out thoroughly. Pete probably just hadn't slept well. But his quirky behavior didn't bother Jack; he loved the guy most of the time. Sure, Pete could be insufferable and arrogant, but he was loyal to Jack and totally dedicated to Catapult Energy. And as soon as the people he offended showed him respect, Pete reciprocated and became their best friend—especially if they were engineers.

And after working with him for over a year, Jack knew Pete worked hard to protect him from himself. Jack took chances, but he was smart enough to have people like Pete around, people who were good at what they did and could keep him from making mistakes. People like Kalin. He wanted her to like him, and to laugh at his jokes. But nothing more than that. Jack loved his wife.

Anyone else would be a big mistake, and he wasn't going to do that. That would be taking too big a chance, and it would be a big mistake all right, and he didn't want to make a mistake where his wife was concerned.

Because there was nothing anyone could do to help him if he made a mistake like that. Stealing the car had been one thing, but if he was to make a list of chances he had taken, the subject of women would come up pretty quick. No doubt about it. Not that he was blaming the women. It wasn't them, but the mistakes he made where they were concerned.

He thought about Patricia. She was the first.

Waiting for his brothers to drift off to sleep and the house to go quiet for the night, Jack had lain in bed thinking about Patricia, her hair and her face and her *Je Reviens,* her mother's perfume that gave her the smell he loved.

He lay there thinking about her, fighting to stay awake, waiting for the moon to come up. He finally decided it was time, got up, listened one last time to make sure he could hear his brothers breathing in their sleep, and put on his clothes and shoes. He moved across the room to the second floor window looking out over the lawn below, opened it, and stepped up and out as quickly as he could, shinnied down the slate-covered corner eave and dangled his toes down to where they found the gutter. He sidled along the gutter for 10 feet until he came to the scratchy branches of the cedar tree, climbed down, looked through the dining room window to make sure no one was still awake downstairs, and then slipped through the azaleas to the street.

The warm air of the Washington summer night bathed him in a light mist of humidity as he walked up Takoma Avenue until it ended, turned right on Ritchie Avenue and headed for the Piney Branch Parkway.

He saw the headlights of the first car about the same time he heard it behind him. He ran off the street and hid behind a tree, standing there upright until the car had passed and gone on up the hill. Jack watched the car carefully. It wasn't a cop, just someone driving slowly up the road.

He could do this all the way across America if he had to, lying low behind bushes and trees, just in case he had to hide from someone. No one could ever catch him. He didn't understand why fugitives always seemed to get nabbed down at the train station in the light of day. Why couldn't they just do what he did, walk the streets on foot at night, jump behind trees when the cars came, and cross the country that way?

Jack forgot all about the intrigue of getting there and began focusing on Patricia. She would be up waiting for him. He came around the corner of her street and looked up at her house. She stayed in the basement in the summer, telling her parents it was cooler down there.

Jack mounted the lawn and went around the back of the house to the basement entrance where Patricia had left the door ajar, opened it slowly and walked down the dark hallway toward her bedroom. He came in to her room in the darkness, seeing her lying under the covers. As he leaned over, she reached up and pulled him down to her and kissed him, then wouldn't let go, pulling him into her bed. He kept kissing her as he kicked off his shoes and climbed in. Whatever he did, he had to somehow wake up and get out of there before it got light.

Jack was a year older than when he had stolen the car. Patricia was much younger.

Jack went back to watching the trout. There were a lot of them. It was after midday. The air was warming up, and the temperature of the water in the Rio Bravo was rising. Looking at the languid surface of the pool below the tail race of the powerhouse, he was surprised. It was early in the season, but he could see hatch coming up off the water, and ripples where trout had started to feed; it looked like some of them were taking food off the surface.

He went into a room on the back side of the powerhouse and fetched the fly rod and vest he stored there. Rigging up the rod and threading the floating line through the ferrules, he thought about using a wooly bugger. He didn't have a lot of time; it was going to be a busy afternoon.

He knew the fish were down below, so he could go ahead and use a wooly bugger or another big nymph. The wooly buggers were surefire—they looked just like worms. But every time he used one he felt bad, like he was cheating, not giving the fish a chance or himself a challenge. A dry fly made for better fishing, and might work—it looked like they were taking flies off the surface—so he tied on an elk wing caddis, using the fisherman's knot his father had taught him a lifetime ago. He wouldn't have any time to change flies later.

He came out of the darkness of the powerhouse back into the bright sun. Ducking down low so his shadow wouldn't spill over the surface of the water and spook the fish, he crawled up to the edge of the river, kneeled, pulled 20 yards of line out of the reel of his rod and let it lie on the ground, held the fly off the ground in his left hand, and prepared to sling it down into the pool.

He looked upstream to where the Chinese workers had started to set up camp. They had all stopped what they were doing and were standing there watching him.

He pumped the rod tip back and forth off his right shoulder and shot the line out into the pool. The floating line landed with a quiet slosh, the tippet running on out toward the opposite bank and the fly landing at the end, pinging a tiny circular ripple on the quiet pool of dark water running in a circle below the dam.

A surge fractured the glassy surface of the pool. Jack stood up and lifted his rod into the air to set the hook and started reeling the line back out of the river as the surface of the pool quivered, the lucky fish who weren't hooked bolting to the shoreline and shooting lines of rippled motion out in all directions from the center of the pool, the water looking like something was shaking the ground beneath it.

He heard excited Chinese exclamations behind him.

Keeping the rod above his head and the line taut, Jack kept reeling line as he headed down the bank from the powerhouse to where the ground met the river, keeping the line tight on the fish as he walked, and when it had grown tired, hauled the trout over to the bank. It was a big German Brown, easily two feet long and probably weighing over four pounds. He put his rod on the bank, wet both of his hands, took the trout firmly in one hand as it thrashed and wiggled in the reeds, and using a pair of tiny pliers attached to his vest, detached the fly from its mouth and released the big fish back in to the Rio Bravo.

The commotion behind him reached a crescendo, and he turned around. The Chinese workers were all issuing various sounds indicating their profound dismay; it was probably the first time they had ever seen a fish released.

He thought about trying to catch another one. But that would be a mistake. It was always a mistake to keep fishing a hole after he'd caught one there. The other fish had been warned and they wouldn't behave the same way in their world for a while.

Going after another fish in the same hole in a river was a bad idea, but not as bad as some other mistakes he had made, truly bad choices about the really important things—not so much the choices themselves, but not knowing how important they were at the time.

He hoped his marriage would never turn out to be a mistake. He didn't like even thinking about that. That was the one thing that couldn't be a mistake. They would be married forever. He had loved Alicia the day he met her, even though he didn't know her, and he still loved her, he knew he did, even though she was different now and they were different now.

He remembered the first night, when everything was so good. It always started out that way, with everything so good.

Jack had to work that night. He slung on his leather jacket as he left his townhouse and climbed on to his motorcycle, a metallic purple 750cc Norton Commando, the fastest thing on two wheels at the time. He kicked the Norton over, stomped it into first gear, let out the clutch and sped up Prospect Street on his way to his night shift tending bar at the Tombs. Taking the bike through its gears, approaching 50 miles an hour, the wind blowing in his wavy brown hair, he was a junior at Georgetown without a care in the world.

The professional baseball player and his date came into the Tombs about eight o'clock.

The player was Rick Richards, the new outfielder for the Senators, the guy the sportswriters were calling the "Bonus Baby," and the presumptive savior of Washington D.C.'s perpetually dismal baseball team.

Richards was standing in the entrance in the middle of a group of fans, and at first Jack didn't see the girl with him. Obscured by the crowd, she finally stepped forward to keep from getting crushed. Jack couldn't take his eyes off her. She was a knockout. Looking around for a place to sit, she gave Jack the impression she didn't want to be there as she found her way to the bar, Richards breaking away from his public to follow her.

"Beer okay, Alicia?" Richards asked her as she chose a bar stool and sat down in front of Jack.

"I think I'd rather try a daiquiri," she said to her date.

"I was going to order a pitcher; it's cheaper," the baseball player said.

"Oh, of course, that's fine, Rick; whatever you think," she said.

Jack served them a pitcher of beer. The guy was an oaf. Jack felt bad for the girl. They got up to leave a little while later. Richards asked for the tab, looked at the total, raised his eyebrows, and threw some bills on the bar; he didn't leave enough for a tip. As the girl looked back at him while leaving, Jack thought it would be a long time before he saw someone as beautiful as her again.

Later that night, an hour before last call, two stragglers came in: Alicia and a friend. Alicia looked excited, her eyes sparkling, her friend giggling like they were in on a secret. They didn't acknowledge Jack, but took a table in the dining area.

A few minutes later, Phil Tucci, the waiter handling the back room, came up to the order rail.

"Two daiquiris."

Tucci picked up the drinks and headed back to the dining room to deliver them. Phil Tucci was on the football team with Jack and was staying temporarily in Jack's townhouse during August as the team went through summer practice. Tucci wasn't a very good football player. Jack liked him well enough to let him stay at the townhouse and hang around, but as far as football, Tucci got injured too much.

Tucci came back out of the dining room.

"Jack, I think I've got a live one. These two girls in my section are hungry and the kitchen's closed. Are you okay with me inviting them over to the house after work so I can make spaghetti?"

Jack sighed. He couldn't believe she would reduce herself to going home with Tucci, but he had misread women before.

"Sure, Phil. I didn't realize you were such a gourmet."

The girls left and Tucci hustled out after them. Jack stayed behind to check the night's liquor inventory, balance the evening's accounts, and lock up. Stopping around the corner at his art studio, he stuck his head in to tell the guys he wouldn't be working late after all, and headed home.

He arrived back at the townhouse five minutes later. The lights were on; it was about two o'clock in the morning. Inside, a small crowd congregated in the kitchen. His brother Whitey and his roommate Dave Goranski were seated on bar stools drinking beer, winding down from their bartending shifts. Tucci was wrestling with some pots and pans on the stove. The two girls sat quietly in the corner.

Jack ignored the girls. "Dave, I'm going to take a spin. You want me to lock your bike to mine when I come back?"

"Sure, JD," Dave said. "I'd do it myself except I don't want to miss any part of Chef Tucci's performance. Phil, seriously, when do you boil the water—after you add the sauce or before?"

Jack looked over at the girls. Alicia looked back at him and smiled, looking uncertain. He turned and walked back out the door.

He was unchaining the Norton when he saw her come down the steps of the townhouse and across the street toward him. She got as far as a few feet from him and stopped.

Jack straightened up and looked at Alicia. Her face made up by the moonlight, she gazed back at him, beautiful but nervous.

"What happened to the Bonus Baby?"

"I asked him to take me home."

"Before you had dinner?"

"It wasn't going well. I thought I may just as well go home."

"What got you out again so late at night?"

She stood looking at him and didn't say anything.

"Well, in any event, Phil's going to take care of you guys—I'm sure you'll get enough to eat."

"Phil told me he lived with you. That's the only reason I agreed to come."

"Not wild for spaghetti?"

"I don't like spaghetti that much, but I was actually quite hungry."

"Are you still?"

"Yes."

"Well, I suggest you go back in there then. No way Tucci can harm spaghetti that much; you'll be fine."

"Where are you going?"

"I was going to go up to the All Night Bakery Café. The bartending crowd will all be there."

"Can I please come with you?"

"What about your friend?"

"Trish came for Tucci—I came for you."

Jack stood holding the bike chain and looked at her. "Go get your things then."

He watched Alicia as she recrossed the street and headed back into the townhouse. The heat of the day dissipated slowly in the black August night. A taxi lumbered up Prospect Street toward Key Bridge, momentarily drowning out the hum of the cicadas.

Football practice was about to begin. Jack had worked out on his own all summer, pushing himself hard, up to 500 pounds on the squat machine and 10 reps of 225 on the bench press, his thighs too big for his jeans and his neck a size 19, getting ready for the free agent tryout with the Redskins that the coach had promised him if he had a standout season.

And he had tended bar every night for three months straight to pay for next term's tuition and books. Now that he had made enough money, before practice started, he planned to take a weekend off, go down to Ocean City, and do some surfing.

Work hadn't been all bad; he'd picked up girls every night he was in the mood all summer. It was easy; everyone wants to know the bartender, and by the time he told them he played football at Georgetown, the girls were giving him their phone numbers unrequested. Some of them were college coeds staying over for summer school, some were women working on Capitol Hill, and a few were high school chicks.

They meant well but didn't have anything much to say, not that conversation was really the subject on anyone's mind, but things would begin and end quickly and then there was nothing else.

Alicia was different. He could tell. She seemed so nice. And she was so beautiful. Jack didn't care if he was with anyone else ever again.

She reemerged from the townhouse with her pocketbook. Jack kicked the Norton into gear, reached back and pulled down the passenger foot pedals, and motioned Alicia to get on behind him. She sat on the seat and wrapped her arms around his waist. As he dropped the bike into first gear and gunned it up Wisconsin Avenue, he felt her pull her arms tightly around him and put her head against his back.

They pulled up to the All Night Bakery Café a few minutes later. Motorcycles lined the curb out front. Inside, the place was jammed. Jack and Alicia waited their turn in line, exchanging small talk about what they were studying in school, until a small table opened up in the corner.

Alicia sat down, Jack spent a moment saying hello to a bartender from Clyde's, and Whitey and Dave came in and sat down at the table next to them, being careful not to act like they were surprised to see Jack and Alicia together.

"Doughnuts better than Phil's spaghetti?" Jack asked.

"For everyone except Trish."

Jack went up to the counter to order some things to eat and coffee.

"Oh, no thank you," Alicia said when he returned and offered her a glazed doughnut.

"You're turning down the world's best doughnut."

"They're not good for you," she said to him. "And they can make you fat."

"We could eat a hundred of these tonight, and after practice tomorrow we wouldn't have gained an ounce," Jack said, looking over at Dave and the others in the process of proving him right.

"But you shouldn't form bad habits; one day football will be over."

"Don't tell me that. What else is there?" Jack asked, only half joking.

"What about your art?"

"Well, other than that, I meant," Jack said as he saw she was serious. He didn't want to think about the rest of his life. But at least she cared enough to ask. He really liked that. He started mixing some warm milk into his coffee, making a café au lait.

"No, no, Jack; not that way. Let me show you," Alicia said, taking his cup and the milk. "You always put the sugar in first. That way the coffee stays hotter and the sugar dissolves quicker."

Jack did what he was told, slowly stirring the sugar into his coffee, looking at her. It was very noisy in the café; better to just eat than try to talk.

"What do you want to do after this?"

He could tell she heard him. She stared at him but didn't say anything. Whitey and Dave concentrated on their doughnuts.

"How about we take the Norton and drive down to Rehoboth Beach, sleep out on the sand?"

She moved into the townhouse a short time later. Jack never asked her what her favorite color was, how she liked to spend her day, how she wanted him to spend his, how she was about money or other women in his life or whether she would love him as much as their sons, and he never considered the sorrow they would feel when their lives together were over.

He just knew he loved her.

His rod and vest returned to storage, Jack came out of the powerhouse and looked at the Rio Bravo one more time. A lot of trout were taking flies off the surface of the river, but it would be a mistake to try to catch another one. He didn't have time. He wished he could just watch the fish forever.

Chapter 6

The Right Man for the Job

In the trailer that functioned as Catapult Energy's office at the Rio Bravo job site, Jack finished his phone call with Kalin, said goodbye, and rang off. She would call Wuhan Turbine to make sure an installation manual in Chinese was shipped to her in New York, translate it, and Pete would have an English version in two weeks. Not a perfect solution, but workable, just like most of the things involving Wuhan Turbine. Not perfect, but workable.

As opposed to Kalin. As far as doing her job, she was close to perfect. Take the manual. With difficult technical language translation, the other Chinese students Jack had hired just shrugged their shoulders. Too complicated—it just couldn't be done. But Kalin did it.

And while she was an excellent translator, she was an even better agent. Jack had watched the other translators who accompanied the Wuhan government officials when he had been in Wuhan. They were mainly interpreters, lost when it came to business issues. When presented with a hard question or a difficult issue—like in Wuhan when Pete tried to tell the mayor he needed traffic lights—they folded. Getting a confused, almost frightened look on their faces, they became speechless, their client allowed to take off on another verbose soliloquy, the troublesome issue ignored.

Not Kalin. She had substance, too; she evaluated people, passed on her thoughts to Jack, and was usually right. Asking her to telefax a document stateside, she gave him the original and a receipt the next day, time stamped two o'clock in the morning—she had waited up to make sure delivery was confirmed. After dinner, she stayed up nights reading anything Jack made available to learn more about his business. He liked to look at her when something they were speaking about excited her, when she got emphatic and breathed hard, her face flushed and her breasts moving up and down as she talked.

He wanted to believe Kalin was good, that he was right to like her. But believing good things about people could be a problem for him—it had to be based on reality, not hope. Believing in them didn't make them good; they had to do the rest themselves. Most people weren't all good and didn't change, and he couldn't change them, either.

It was hard for him to determine whether people were good or not, and from what he had seen, it was going to be harder in China. He wanted to believe Chinese people were good, especially Kalin. He didn't want to know the bad things about her.

And she was sure good to look at. He had thought about her that way. Looking at her, who wouldn't? Kalin was bright and shiny, but hard. Very hard. He only knew a few other Chinese women, and had never taken things any further in his mind as far as they were concerned. They were probably all like Kalin. He heard a lot of them ate garlic.

Kalin was good at her job and good to look at, all right. It was the rest he found puzzling. Like the part about the squeeze.

He confronted Kalin when they were back at his office in New York, bringing up the subject as soon as they had sat down. No use avoiding things. At first, she just stared back at him without saying anything. Her jaw started to quiver and the muscles under her lower lip slumped. He found himself looking at the top of her head as she looked down at the floor.

"I'm really sorry, Jack," she said, still looking down, almost as if she was bowing.

"Kalin, look at me, for God's sake. Yu Cheng told me—everyone in China plays the squeeze. We know each other better now, so forget about it."

"We're not all like that."

"I'm sorry. You know what I mean."

"I didn't really know you in the beginning."

"Don't worry about it."

He was about to change the subject when she started to cry.

"Hey, come on now," he said, sitting up in his chair. "Jesus, don't do that." He got up and closed the door to his office, leaving it open only a crack. He hadn't thought she'd cry.

She stopped crying, pulled a Kleenex out of her purse, and dabbed her eyes. "I don't want you to think I'm like everyone else. I wanted to be good for you; especially for you."

"Look, don't be so hard on yourself. We all make mistakes."

"What else am I doing wrong?"

"Kalin, come on. Nothing. Really. You're great at what you do. I mean it. I'd tell anyone that."

"Well, I don't want you to think I'm just good at my job. That I'm not a good person."

"I know you are," he said. "I mean it," he emphasized when she sat there not saying anything.

"I wanted to be a good person for you. That's what I want now. To be good for you."

"You are, Kalin."

They both sat there in the quiet of his office as she tried to recompose herself and he puzzled over what being good *now* meant, and why she wanted to be good for *him*. What about her husband?

Turned toward the window, she finished fixing her makeup, stared out the window and then looked back at him. "So what do you want to be good at?"

"What do I want to be good at?" He looked at her, relieved she was dropping the subject of the squeeze, but surprised at her question. He didn't know if he wanted to answer. That would mean being serious with her, and he didn't know if he wanted to do that. He could give her a sarcastic answer, but that probably wouldn't go over too well. Besides, she didn't think he was funny.

"Why?" he finally asked.

"I'm just curious."

"You're just curious."

"I really don't know you very well, Jack. You don't have to answer me if you don't want to."

"I used to think I wanted to be well-rounded."

"Well-rounded?"

"You know, good at a lot of things."

"But not anymore?"

"Well, that was before I realized life wasn't going to allow me an infinite amount of time."

"What do you mean?"

"It's difficult to be good at a lot of things if you're not gifted or smart. You run out of time trying; know what I mean?"

"I hadn't really thought about it."

"Anyway, being well rounded is really kind of meaningless. It's probably better to be excellent at one thing. So hopefully next time I can pick the right thing."

"So what do you want to be now? I hope you're not going to tell me a comedian." She croaked a laugh.

"Not likely," he said, grinning. "Something that doesn't take much more time, I think."

"Now you have China," she said, reopening her mirror and checking her face once more.

"You think? I'm not sure what China means for me. It's a long way to go to find something to be good at."

"China is the best thing for you, Jack," Kalin said as she breathed hard, still recovering from her cry.

"I don't know. I don't know what to think of the place."

"You should take advantage of what you mean to Chinese people."

"What do you mean?"

"They accept you because they expect you." When Jack looked at her with a quizzical look on his face, she continued. "Chinese people need money, but they're not going to take it from just anybody. Where they get their money is very important. Receiving money from a *laowai* means status, especially a *laowai* like you."

"Why me?"

"You're not young."

"So I'm old to you."

She wasn't going to talk about that. Jack didn't say anything. He hadn't thought of himself as old before—he wasn't even 30, for God's sake.

"You look like you have a lot of money. And they know you went to Harvard."

"But people in China like brand names. My business doesn't have a brand name like Morgan Stanley or Goldman Sachs."

She shook her head back and forth. "Wuhan Turbine isn't going to do business with those big American firms, no matter what General Manager Wang tells you. And even if the Americans from the big companies were interested, the people don't sound right."

"Don't sound right?"

"They speak too fast, in buzz words and sound bites. Chinese people like someone who talks like you—slowly, in complete sentences, looking at them when you speak to them."

"Someone else told me that once, a long time ago."

"And your voice is deep," she continued, "and you're taller than them—like from central casting," she said, laughing, her face getting red as she looked away. She was breathing hard again.

Jack watched her chest go up and down as she composed herself, said something about how nice she was to say that, and then asked, "Why does a deep voice and being tall matter?"

"They want to look up to you."

"But I thought they didn't like foreign devils telling them what to do."

"They don't."

He just looked at her.

"They're Chinese." She smiled.

Chapter 7

Token Poet

Jack hadn't started out in the electric power business. Three years earlier, when he was about to graduate from business school, he had hoped he was going to be an investment banker. On the day of his first job interview, at Salomon Brothers in New York, Jack had sat stiffly in his seat trying to adjust to his surroundings. He was nervous. Thinking he could become a good investment banker was probably as crazy as some of his other bad ideas.

It was a sunny spring day in 1979, the kind of day when Jack looked outside in the morning and told himself nothing could go wrong. He sat opposite Jimmy Laurel, who sat at his desk smoking a cigar as he read Jack's resume, his knee bouncing up and down. Jimmy wore a suit of lightweight blue serge, together with a pink shirt, royal blue suspenders, a striped tie, and penny loafers. His face was tan, and he was sweating slightly down his temples and cheeks. To Jack, the temperature in the office felt like 60 degrees.

"Mr. Laurel, Ronnie over at Lehman's on the line," a woman said on the intercom. Laurel picked up his telephone. "Helen, call down to Pine Valley and get my tee time tomorrow," he said, "and tell that moron from Lehman I'll call him back."

Waiting for Laurel to finish reading, Jack looked out through the floor-to-ceiling glass wall at a secretary. At least he thought she was a secretary. He really didn't know, because he wasn't sure what any of the people out there were doing. All he knew was the woman was very attractive, wore expensive clothes and jewelry, and had an outstanding figure. As Jack watched her, she dropped off some documents with a clerk in the middle of the floor and returned to her desk, a tiny outpost jammed in a row of trading stations, swivel chairs, computer equipment, and telephones.

Jimmy was a bond trader at Salomon Brothers, the greatest bond trading firm in the history of Wall Street. He was one of the top partners in the firm, a fabled partnership that doubled as a shark tank where once a year survivors divided up huge profits and started thinking about next year's ritual the same day. Trim and athletic, many would have called Jimmy handsome, but to Jack his brown, furtive eyes and nervous tics gave him a ferret-like quality and an air of unapproachability.

Jack was surprised Laurel took so long reading the resume—he had heard that traders were gruff and crass, with extremely short attention spans. Jimmy paused, removed his glasses, breathed on the thick, Coke bottle–like lenses, polished them with his silk striped tie, looked sideways for a moment at Jack, and then turned back to the one page document and kept reading.

As he turned back to look out at the trading floor, Jack saw a reflection of his face in the glass and felt sheepish about his glasses. He didn't need glasses—he had perfect vision—but had purchased a pair of tortoise shell frames with clear, nonprescription lenses in anticipation of his interview. They would make him appear more studious.

For the interview, he had spent most of the balance of his checking account purchasing, in addition to the artificial glasses, a new suit and dress shirt, an Hermès tie, a pair of suspenders and, at Alicia's insistence, a pair of garters to hold up his socks. The glasses were his idea; the suit, shirt, and tie, obvious; and the suspenders were something he had learned about from his classmates at business school. They said every man working in an investment bank on Wall Street—at least the traders, salesmen, and deal people—wore suspenders. The more flamboyant, the better.

Dressing before the interview, Jack had hesitated before donning the suspenders. Some of his classmates had told him suspenders were something to be earned, and wearing them prematurely would brand him as a parvenu. However, the people who provided this information seemed like they knew less about investment bankers than he did, but just acted like they knew more. In the end, he wore the suspenders, and kept his jacket buttoned just in case.

It was early morning, but the activity outside the glass-walled office, located right off the trading floor, was palpable. The throb and din of the big room washed in as a clerk opened Jimmy's office door to deliver some reports, then receded again as he left. Across the big room and up and down its aisles, men stood or plopped down in swivel chairs at their trading turrets surrounded by screens filled with oscillating green numbers. Sure enough, most of them wore suspenders. He looked carefully down toward their feet—he didn't spy any garters, and made a mental note to throw his out as soon as he got home.

Whatever they were doing out there, he got the clear feeling it was important, and told himself he could be really good at it if they just gave him a chance.

"Did I ask if you wanted a cigar, kiddo?"

"Yes. No, thank you, Mr. Laurel."

"That a no?"

"Yes, sir."

"You don't have to be so polite around here."

"Yes, sir."

Laurel put his cigar down and began filing his nails, balancing Jack's resume on his knees.

"You know how to write letters?" Laurel asked, for the first time looking directly at Jack through the thick lenses of his glasses.

"Yes, sir. I'm good at writing letters, sir."

"How about adding columns of numbers?"

"Yes, sir."

"That a yes?"

"Yes, sir, I can add columns of numbers."

"'Cause you got to be able to add columns of numbers here. See that guy over there—Bobby McDermott?"—Jimmy said, pointing through the glass window to where a guy Jack's age sat at a nearby turret. "We'll be bidding on fuckind $100 million of New York State Power Authority

Nines, the bid's due in 20 seconds, it's our ass if he's wrong—and McDermott types in the bid without flinching. And's never wrong."

"Truthfully, sir, I have never done anything like that. I think I could learn but I'm not sure. Sir."

"What's your name again, kiddo?"

"Jack Davis, sir."

"Well, Jack Davis, I'm going to hire you. I need a person to write letters. Someone who graduated from Harvard ought to know how to do that."

㊌   ㊌   ㊌

No one would ever believe him. First, after earning undergraduate and graduate degrees in fine arts, he was admitted to Harvard Business School as a "token poet," the admissions people wanting to add some diversity to the student body. And now he had just been hired by Salomon Brothers, the most powerful bond house on Wall Street, because he could write letters.

He took Alicia out to celebrate that night. She was ecstatic about his job offer.

"What will you do there?"

"I wish I knew," he answered.

"Jack, don't tell me that," she said, half teasing but replacing her smile with a serious expression.

"Look, I told you—the man said he's hiring me to write letters."

"What kind of a guy would do that?"

Jack didn't have it wrong. He worked long days and nights generating language and paperwork for the senior members of the department and then, as new business began to pour in, went out on the road carrying their bags to make the presentations.

In six months, he was pitching new clients on his own, and he and Alicia felt secure enough to start a family. In an 18-month period, Alicia delivered two sons—Irish twins.

One day two years after he had joined Salomon Brothers, Jimmy invited Jack to go to lunch, a first.

"Hey kiddo, you feel like a piece of pizza?"

Jack had learned Jimmy called people kiddo when he couldn't remember their names, which was often.

"Sure, Jimmy."

"You know what's going on around the firm, kiddo?" Laurel asked as they walked in their shirtsleeves down the block to the pizza joint on the corner.

"No idea, sir."

"A bunch of us are getting screwed on our payouts and we're not going to take it any more—we're leaving. I'm going to start my own investment firm—J.J. Laurel and Company."

"I haven't heard anything about that, sir."

"I want you to come with me—be my junior partner."

"Me?" Jack stopped and looked at Jimmy, who kept walking to get his pizza.

"Yeah, you," Jimmy said when Jack caught up with him. "I need someone to do all the proposals and letters we're going to need to get out to the clients. Besides, you talk like a farmer and people like that."

"I talk like a farmer?" Jack wasn't sure he wanted people to view him that way, but he suspected it was true.

"Yeah, you talk slow, not like most guys on Wall Street. People out there across America understand you. When you talk slow like you do and then use a big word, you sound even smarter. So what do you say?"

"I guess I don't get to go home and talk to my wife about this."

"Not if you want the job."

"Okay, count me in, Jimmy."

❀   ❀   ❀

"I don't know if you're going to like this," he had said that night to Alicia, and then proceeded to tell her about Jimmy and J.J. Laurel and Company.

"He asked you to be his partner? Why Jack, you should be so proud," she had said, putting on her best smile but delivering it along with the hesitant catch in her voice and quizzical look in her eye he had expected. "But do you really think going with Jimmy is better than staying at Salomon Brothers? You could be a partner there, too.

I know you could." That's why he loved her, he said to himself: she supported him.

"Maybe, Alicia, but how long will that take? I don't have a lot of time. Besides, I think Jimmy's right; I could be really good at this. Better than football; better than sculpture. This could be the best thing I've done."

"You could be good at Salomon Brothers, too, Jack. I don't know why you can't wait. But it doesn't matter. I won't stand in your way. Do what you have to do," she had said, a woman still in love. She kissed him, and that was that, just like when they took his motorcycle to the beach.

Jimmy called later that evening and announced he needed to go out west on a three-month sabbatical to get himself mentally and physically ready for the stress of running the new firm. In the meantime, he needed Jack to get everything organized. The following afternoon he'd be leaving for Vail, so he needed Jack to drive out to his horse farm in western New Jersey in the morning to review the office budget, Jimmy's general instructions, and Jack's compensation before he left.

Saturday morning, Jack kissed Alicia goodbye and took a rental car to Jimmy's house, making it through the tunnel before seven o'clock. Heading west on the new stretch of Interstate 78, Jack watched the trees losing their last leaves to a stiff November breeze and slowed down as a family of wayward deer wandered across the highway. Oncoming winter didn't put a dent in his mood—he was too young.

Jimmy's place was plain compared to some of his neighbors, but he had already explained to Jack he didn't believe in grand, trophy houses.

"The main thing is to avoid corners. You don't want too many corners."

"Corners?"

"Right," Jimmy had said. When you built a house—and every house Jimmy had ever lived in had been newly constructed—you didn't want any more corners than absolutely necessary, he had explained. Weather would kill you. That's why those modern houses they build out in the Hamptons are white elephants, he had said. Too many corners—the weather will jack the utility bills through the roof.

"But that means the best house is just a square box."

"Exactly."

Coming up Jimmy's driveway, he could see Jimmy had not exaggerated his aversion to architectural nuance, but it didn't bother him.

Nothing could today. Jimmy was standing at the kitchen door, directing Jack to park his car in a space beside the house. He went inside the kitchen to the smell of wood smoke from a fire burning on the hearth and coffee Jimmy's wife had waiting.

"All right. We don't have a lot of time." Jimmy pulled out a dog-eared piece of paper. "First thing, kiddo, we need space. I can't see how we can have an address that's not on Wall Street, can you? People see my business card for the first time, they will have never heard of me or J.J. Laurel and Company, but if we're on Wall Street, we've got to be good, right?"

"I think that's right, Jimmy."

"'Course it is. Next thing, we've got to have a car that looks like a limousine, so when we get a client coming in from the Midwest, they get picked up at the airport and they're impressed. Right?"

"Most of my clients just grab a taxi, Jimmy."

"Yeah, but your clients are farmers building power plants out in Wyoming somewhere. I'm talking about real clients from real companies. Like Shell Oil; that type of thing. I know the chief financial officer from Shell Oil—North American operations, that is—he's going to hire us for sure. Kiddo, did I tell you we're going to be the next Salomon Brothers?"

"That would be great, Jimmy."

"You can take it to the bank. Okay, where were we? Right, the limousine. I'd get a Cadillac, but a lot of people across the country are more conservative, and don't like investment bankers spending all their money, so I'm thinking about going with an Oldsmobile. Not as fancy, but with the driver wearing a uniform and a hat and all, we'll still get the right image across. What do you say?"

"I don't know if this matters, Jimmy, but Oldsmobile is a brand I've always associated with old people."

"Exactly. I knew I was right to hire you. How old are you, kiddo?"

"Twenty-seven."

"Yeah, twenty-seven going on forty. You're right. Those board members will get the right sense of us when they see the Oldsmobile; conservative, stable, that type of thing. I'll have my stable girl, Nancy, wear one of those morning suits, the ones with the black coat and gray pinstripe pants, that type of thing."

"Your stable girl?"

"That's right, kiddo. Can't have you do it. You're going to be too busy writing proposals," Jimmy said as he paced back and forth in the kitchen. "I've got to get out of here soon. Take a look at this punch list. I want all this done by the time I get back so I can just walk into the office and everything I need has been taken care of: receptionist, secretary, analyst, copy machine, telephones, faxes, supplies; it's all there. Here's your budget—I figure we should be able to get all this done for $100,000, right?"

Jack eyeballed the budget and didn't answer at first. "The $100,000 doesn't include salaries?"

"'Course it does. Includes everything. $100,000's a lot of money, kiddo."

Jack acted like he was studying the budget some more, but he just didn't want to say what he knew he had to.

"It'll be more like $200,000, Jimmy."

"What? For Chrissakes. We're spending it faster than we're making it now, for sure."

"Not including me."

"For Chrissakes. God almighty, how much are you?"

"You were going to tell me this morning, remember?"

While Jimmy had fun skiing out west, Jack got to work. He located space at 100 Wall Street and signed a three-year lease. He arranged for the building to paint and carpet the space, and to replace the standard door with a double door, walnut entrance, including a brass sign with the firm's name and logo. He ordered furniture, including nice things for Jimmy—a mahogany desk, red leather drawing room chairs, and a couch and stuffed chairs in a navy brocade fabric for Jimmy's sitting area—and serviceable furniture for the other offices.

Once Jimmy returned from vacation and came to the office every day, Jack was certain the clients would start to pour in. When he got back and nothing happened at first, Jack wasn't overly concerned—Jimmy just had to get warmed up.

After a few weeks, though, Jack knew something was wrong. He sat in his office, listening to the flies buzzing in his window, praying for the phone to ring. What was Jimmy doing? Jack tried to listen for Jimmy's outgoing calls, but the only sound was the air-conditioning system humming in the background. He peeked in when Jimmy's door opened; his desk was piled high with old newspapers Jimmy saved to take with him when he went to the bathroom.

Finally one weekend, after confessing his concerns to Alicia and being more alarmed by the look on her face than his own previous perception of the predicament, Jack resolved to take matters into his own hands. Monday morning, arriving at the office before seven o'clock, he opened up his big Standard & Poor's Utility Manual and started going through the entries for the hundreds of electric, gas, and water utilities listed. The data included financials, bond indentures, names, and telephone numbers—anything a reader wanted to know about the enterprise.

Jack opened the manual to the As. *Anaheim Electric, Light and Water* was the first utility he saw; it was located in Anaheim, California. Disneyland. A muni, Jack thought—a municipally owned utility. Good. They probably didn't have a lot of financial sophistication, and might not hang up on him when he called. Jack studied the information available. To find something to talk about with utility managers, the best idea was to become knowledgeable about the most difficult part of their business, the things they avoided. Then, any help would be genuinely appreciated.

He waded into Anaheim's bond indentures. No utility manager wanted to deal with bond indentures. Anaheim's indenture, the contract governing the deal between the utility and its bondholders, was old-fashioned. The utility's bonds had been issued ages ago and had only a few years outstanding.

Then Jack saw his opportunity. It lay in the specifications of the reserve fund required by the indenture. The reserve was specified at a minimum of $5 million, and had been pegged to equal 10 percent of the original size of the $50 million bond issue. But the bonds were almost all paid off—there were only $8 million outstanding. A $5 million reserve fund to secure $8 million of bonds was a waste of money. If J.J. Laurel and Company could underwrite a $10 million issue of refunding bonds, they could pay off the old bonds, hand the Anaheim utility a $5 million check, plus $2 million of working capital.

Jack waited until it was ten o'clock, or seven in the morning Pacific Time. Like many people on the West Coast, the Anaheim management might start the day early. He dialed up Neil Hoyt, the general manager.

Not only was Neil Hoyt in his office, but he answered his own phone. Jack introduced himself, and paused, politely giving Mr. Hoyt an opportunity to make some excuse to end the call. But Hoyt didn't, instead asking Jack what was on his mind. Jack launched into his analysis. Hoyt didn't say anything when Jack was done, then asked Jack to repeat the name of his firm. Hoyt thanked him, said he'd get back to him, and rang off.

Jack kept going through the S&P manual until Jimmy arrived, took a break, got his checklist of tasks from Jimmy for the day, and returned to his manual and his phone. Shortly before noon, the telephone rang. The receptionist told Jack a Mr. Neil Hoyt from Anaheim was calling.

J.J. Laurel and Company was hired, Mr. Hoyt said. The firm had its first client. Now Jack knew what to do, and just kept at it. Plowing through the entire S&P utility manual, he spent every day analyzing electric companies, gas utilities, water companies, even sewer authorities, looking for angles that he might use in a telephone pitch to get retained. Within months, J.J. Laurel and Company had 10 clients.

㊛　㊛　㊛

At the end of the J.J. Laurel and Company's initial fiscal year, Jack told Alicia the firm had turned profitable. She told him every dollar would help, since she was pregnant again. This time she delivered real twins, two more boys, and they were now a large family. They would have to move soon.

But even though the six of them were jammed into a small Upper West Side apartment, they were happy. The only issue was Jimmy.

Jimmy had been a trader at Salomon Brothers, and he had been very good at it. But Salomon Brothers, with its huge capital base and extensive intelligence and infrastructure, could make a trader better than his natural limitations. And while Jimmy might have been a good trader, he was lousy at most other things.

His foibles were all right with Jack, who tried to get Jimmy to leave more and more of the overall business to him, suggesting that Jimmy just focus on being chairman-like. But they were not lost on Alicia.

A little under a year after they opened the firm's doors, Jimmy invited Jack and Alicia out to his horse farm for dinner. As Jack pulled the rental car up to the front door, Jimmy and his wife Marianne came out to greet them, Marianne taking Alicia by the hand into the drawing room and Jimmy bringing Jack into the bar.

"Vodka martini okay, kiddo?" After all this time, Jimmy still couldn't remember Jack's name, let alone that he didn't drink vodka martinis. Without waiting for an answer, Jimmy grabbed a tumbler large enough to serve lemonade, stuffed it half full of ice, and poured Stolichnaya over the cubes until the liquid filled the glass. "Come on, let me show you my new horse," Jimmy said, pushing open a double door to the terrace and walking across the lawn down the hill to the horse barn, with Jack trailing behind.

Jimmy had inexplicably decided that Jack, like Jimmy, should join the Essex Hunt, and was completely absorbed by the subject. By the time Jimmy had shown Jack his new jumper, asked Jack how much he weighed, how tall he was, and whether he wanted to start off with a Western saddle or take his chances with an English one, Jack was loaded, having drained his martini as he struggled to keep up with Jimmy's staccato delivery on the merits of fox hunting. Finished in the barn, they returned to the house, cutting through the bar again where Jimmy refilled their drinks on their way to dinner.

Dinner was a blur. The only thing he remembered of the latter part of the evening was seeing Marianne looking at him out of the corner of her eye as he realized he was eating with the serving fork for the green beans.

Jack was slowly navigating back east on Interstate 78 toward the city when Alicia said, "Look, I've got to tell you, I think you were right to leave Salomon Brothers because I know you like being your own boss, and I know at J.J. Laurel and Company you're really the boss because Jimmy is incapable of doing anything. But Jack, his name is still on the door."

"And?"

"To quote your father, the man doesn't know his ass from third base. He could do something stupid and blow the firm's capital, and the results of all your hard work—our hard work—at any time."

Exhausted and still wobbly from the martinis, Jack was just concentrating on getting them home, and did his best to appear like he was listening.

"I don't like the look in his eye," Alicia continued. "Back that man into a corner, and he's capable of anything. And when that happens—not if, but when—he's going to take advantage of you; of us."

He kept driving, reminding himself sporadically to stay no more than 10 miles over the speed limit.

"Do you have everything in writing?" Alicia asked as they descended into the gloom of the Lincoln Tunnel.

㊌ ㊌ ㊌

After the new year, Bobby McDermott came over from Salomon Brothers, and Jack finally had a capable partner. They shouldered the load of managing the firm together, built a growing business, and closed some noteworthy transactions.

But as well as the firm was performing, Jimmy was increasingly frustrated. They were not making serious money, big money, Jimmy said. While not bothersome to Jack, for Jimmy, merely making a living was equivalent to contracting a loathsome Asiatic disease. He began trading larger positions. Sometimes his bets paid off, but most of the time the firm lost money. He started to complain about mysterious medical ailments.

And then it happened, just as Alicia had predicted.

Jack and Bobby arrived at the office early one Monday morning in December. Surprisingly, Jimmy was already there. He looked awful. He invited them into his office, shut the door, and told them he had lost most of the firm's capital by investing in some wildcat oil and gas wells in Louisiana that had come up dry.

Jack and Bobby were stunned. They couldn't look at each other, let alone Jimmy, and for a long time sat in their chairs just starring at their shoe tops. Bobby wasn't saying anything, but Jack couldn't help himself. All he could think of was Alicia saying, "I told you so" when he got home that night. "We don't know a damn thing about oil and gas, Jimmy."

"Well, you win some and you lose some, Jack. To make a big score, you've got to take risks. It's not like you've got any better ideas."

Easy for him to say. Jimmy could afford to go home to his horse farm and forget about the day's events; Jack couldn't.

"Well, Jimmy, at least I know enough not to invest in something I know nothing about. Next time you're going to throw away all our capital without telling us, at least put it into something we know something about."

"Like what?"

"Well, like hydroelectric projects. We've been helping all these utilities raise money to build hydroelectric projects and now Congress has changed the law so that non–utilities can own them. I'd rather own a hydro project than a dry oil well."

"I don't know what the fuck you're talking about—you got something for me to read, I'll take a look at it."

Sitting in Jimmy's office that morning, Jack made up his mind to form Catapult Energy. The company would be a new, non–utility, independent power producer. He had been thinking about the possibility of the company for a while, but now it took on a separate urgency. Catapult Energy would allow him to get loose from Jimmy.

Jimmy couldn't teach him anything more. Jack had thought about finding another mentor, and had looked around. There wasn't anyone out there. He had gone as far as he could as a follower. Now, he was going to have to find his own way.

Jack wrote the plan for Catapult Energy by year end, and in early 1984 incorporated the company. With Jimmy and Bobby, he went down the street to the private equity unit of Bankers Trust and borrowed $2.5 million to start things up. Jack was the CEO, Bobby would continue running J.J. Laurel and Company so they had something to live on, and Jimmy would stay the hell out of the way if they were lucky. They had two years to do an IPO of Catapult Energy before the money ran out and the loan had to be repaid—two years to go public or go broke.

Chapter 8

Token Poet's IPO

The first thing Jack needed to do was find some good hydroelectric sites. The most hydro-rich region of the United States was California, so he spent the first months of his new career on the Golden State's back roads and highways, prospecting for hydro locations. Running into scores of competing developers who had staked out claims on project sites, he soon learned most of the good sites were already taken, the remainder marginal.

"This is going to be harder than I thought," he said to Alicia.

"You'll think of something."

Searching for an angle, Jack spoke to his friend Yu Cheng about the merits of Chinese equipment, but he still needed a site. On a hunch, when Jack learned that a rancher named George Penny had a marginal site near Bakersfield for lease, he faxed him a proposal and arranged to see him.

Mr. Penny set down two frosty lemonades for himself and Jack as they settled into wicker chairs on the terrace of the ranch house of the Rio Bravo Ranch, Mr. Penny's spread lining both banks of the Rio Bravo River. The ranch, one of the largest in California, ran from the foothills of the Sierra Nevada all the way to the bottomland of the

Central Valley. From their spot on the terrace Jack could see south past the intersection of the Rio Bravo and the Kern River to the outskirts of Bakersfield and the shimmering smog hanging over what passed for civilization 10 miles away.

"Mr. Davis, I'm an old rancher and I believe what goes around comes around so I've got to tell you straight—this site's a money loser. I never wanted to develop it but my wife kept pushing me, saying it would be a good thing to do in the long run. I shouldn't have listened to her. I'm not sure what you think you're doing here—I heard you're planning on using some newfangled kind of equipment—but things are different here in the Central Valley. I've got enough money; I don't need to steal yours. I won't be angry if you want to rethink this deal."

"Call me Jack, Mr. Penny. Thanks for your concern, but I guess I'll be all right."

"Jack, I just don't want you coming back later and suing me, saying I swindled you."

"Yeah, I see what you mean, Mr. Penny. No, I'll be all right. Really," Jack said as he reviewed the site's economics in his mind, thinking maybe what he should worry about was Mr. Penny coming back and suing *him* over the excess profits he was due to earn if everything Yu Cheng had told him about the Chinese hydroelectric equipment was true. On the other hand, if he was wrong, Catapult Energy would have a short life.

With the Rio Bravo site in hand, the next critical element of his plan was a smart hydroelectric engineer. He scanned the advertisements in *HydroWire,* the industry trade journal, and made some phone calls.

Pete Bright stopped by Jack's New York office a few days later. "I understand from the message you left on my telephone you're interested in purchasing my hydroelectric modeling software," he said as he stuck his head into Jack's doorway.

"Well, not exactly, although I'm sure it will come in handy," Jack said.

Bright stared at Jack. "Oh, okay, let me get this straight. You answer the advertisement for my software, and leave a message inviting me down here. I come all the way downtown on my own nickel; and now you tell me you're not really interested. I must be imagining this, right? Very nice to meet you, too."

"Mr. Bright. Pete. Relax. I've got something in mind I hope you'll agree is much better."

"What could that be?" Pete asked.

"I'd like to speak with you about joining Catapult Energy as its executive vice president and chief engineer. We're going public in another year or so. You'll be in on the ground floor."

"Catapult Energy is going public?"

"That's the plan."

"How? Are you an engineer?"

"If I were an engineer, I wouldn't be talking to you. I'm in the investment business; a deal guy. We'll make a perfect team. I've been taking other companies public as their investment banker, and you're a mechanical engineer building other companies' hydroelectric projects. Now we can finance and build our own projects, and do an IPO ourselves."

"And I'm in charge of engineering?"

"Completely in charge."

"Do I get a piece of the action?"

"Of course."

"What kind of staff do I have?"

"You're the first guy on board, so it's up to you. However, one thing I can tell you, this is not just any engineering assignment. Catapult Energy will be, by necessity, dealing with unconventional hydroelectric sites and equipment."

"Look, I'm not stupid. What kind of a hydro company has no employees?"

"I've always thought a company should only bring on employees who can truly add value. You're the first one I've been able to speak with who fits that description."

"You've just told me you're not an engineer, so what do you know about hydroelectric equipment?" Pete asked.

"Nothing specific, but I know most of the equipment manufactured by the European vendors is too expensive for the remaining marginal hydroelectric sites in this country, so for any developer to make it here, they're going to have to use new technology, or old technology manufactured in a new way—like standard equipment made in emerging growth countries—or both."

Pete just looked at Jack.

"So what do you say?" Jack asked.

"Where did you come up with that stuff?"

"I didn't get it from anyone else, if that's what you mean."

"Those are your ideas?"

"Sure. It's pretty obvious, right?"

"Not to everyone," Pete Bright sighed. "Count me in."

(水)　(水)　(水)

After he validated the Wuhan Turbine equipment, Jack scrambled to obtain rights to a dozen hydroelectric sites around the United States—some medium-size sites like Rio Bravo, and a huge one, the Vidalia project on the Mississippi—and ordered a corresponding number of additional turbines from Wuhan Turbine.

As the projects were developed and constructed, Catapult Energy started to show the promise of earnings. When Rio Bravo was commissioned, the company became profitable for good, and its cash flow began to take off.

Wall Street took notice. Investment bankers began to drop by the office, armed with proposals and pitch books. The IPO Jack needed to pay back Bankers Trust was no longer just a dream.

(水)　(水)　(水)

After a round of presentations, lunches, dinners, and pricing discussions, Catapult Energy gave Donaldson, Lufkin and Jenrette the mandate to manage the company's IPO. The road show was to be launched in the fourth quarter of 1985, only a few months before the Bankers Trust loan was due. The offering was hardly a foregone conclusion—there had been few successful IPOs recently.

Bill Martinette was the DLJ investment banker in charge of their deal. Martinette stood five feet four inches, and wore the same clothes every day: a dark blue serge suit, double breasted with extra silver buttons lined in two rows up and down both sides of his chest, the jacket always buttoned up tight; black English-cut tie shoes; and a dark red tie with a stickpin. Martinette worked in his office at a stand-up desk he supposed had been favored by bankers in the City of London in the heyday of the British Empire, claiming he needed the desk because of a bad back.

In November, Martinette came over to the Catapult Energy office to meet with Jimmy and Jack and rehearse for the IPO road show, two days away.

"Gentlemen, let's huddle up here. I'll take you through the presentation I want to use during the road show."

"Who the fuck you talking to?" Jimmy said. "We don't need you to tell us what to say. We'll make the presentation. You just sell the fuckind stock."

After the meeting, Jack told the rarely reticent Martinette that Jimmy wasn't as bad as he seemed, but DLJ should figure out how to muzzle him. Martinette seemed intimidated, though. For a guy who liked to give everyone the idea he was in charge, Martinette faded fast.

The road show began the following Wednesday at eight o'clock in the morning at the offices of Royce Morgan and Associates. Jack, Jimmy, Bill Martinette, and Paul Foster, DLJ's head of institutional sales, arrived on time and jammed themselves into a small conference room with Royce Morgan, the head of the investment management firm.

One of America's best small cap portfolio managers, Morgan was physically almost as diminutive as Martinette. He wore a bow tie and socks the same color as his tie. Once he started talking, however, Morgan's physical size and quirky dress were forgotten. His questions were sharp and efficient; Jack had never seen anyone dissect a pitch better.

Jimmy was all gunned up, listening to himself and liking every word he heard. "What Harriman was to the American railroad industry, I'm going to be to the American power industry," he said to begin.

Eight minutes later, Royce looked at his watch. "I think I've got it. Sorry, but I have another appointment. Thanks for coming."

Jimmy, Jack, and the DLJ guys shambled out the door, Jimmy in a daze, Martinette and Foster depressed. Jack just shook his head. What had just taken place in Morgan's office was bound to continue.

Things got worse at lunch. Instead of a one-on-one setting, the standard forum for IPO road show presentations, DLJ had opted for a luncheon format at the New York Analysts Society. There would be about 50 people in attendance. The larger forum was promising but risky. If the presentation went well, they would have 50 buyers; if it went poorly, they would disappoint a lot of people.

Jack looked around at the audience. Many of the attendees appeared to be most interested in the free lunch. However, not even free food could force them to stay for Jimmy's diatribe. He served up the Harriman line again, and by the time the salad course was cleared, the audience was thinning noticeably.

After lunch, Martinette waved a caution flag. "Let's cancel the rest of the day and regroup before the meetings tomorrow. Jack, we should speak later."

Martinette and Foster called Jack at four in the afternoon. Martinette did the talking. "Jack, this deal is going to crater unless you get Jimmy the hell out of the way."

"I tried to warn you guys. Give me until tomorrow morning. Believe it or not, this is going to come as a big surprise to him."

"What a moron. I've never met a guy on a bigger ego trip."

"Look at it this way, it could've been worse," Jack said. "If he had been mildly obnoxious instead of a complete asshole, we would have gone three weeks before bringing him up short, and lost three weeks' worth of buyers in the process."

Martinette was not assuaged. "Yeah, but the Street talks. That fiasco at lunch is already fodder for jokes being hatched on every trading desk in the industry. 'The Harriman of the power business.' Christ Almighty."

"So where do you think we stand?" Jack asked.

Martinette sighed; he sounded ready to throw in the towel. "We need two minor miracles. We need you to replace Jimmy and flat out mesmerize people, and we need a bell cow order—an order for at least 10 percent of the deal from a lead investor—or we're fucked. So we're probably fucked."

"Bill, listen to me. Just worry about the second part."

"Jack, this isn't child's play. I've been doing it for years. It takes a natural aptitude and a lot of presence—I just wish I could do it for you."

"Can you get me a lead investor or not?"

Martinette put his hand over the receiver and conferred a moment with Foster. "Too early to tell. I'll speak to you as soon as I know something."

"Just get me a lead investor. Or tell me who to call and I'll do it myself."

"Fat chance," Martinette said, and hung up. Catapult Energy's IPO was probably going to be over before it could begin.

❀   ❀   ❀

About five o'clock, one of the girls at the reception desk poked her head through the door of Jack's office. "Jack, there's a Mr. Morgan on the phone."

Jack reached for the phone.

"Hi, Mister Morgan."

"Call me Royce. Can you get up here before six tonight?"

Jack was uptown sitting in Royce Morgan's office 30 minutes later. "It says here you're the chief executive officer of Catapult Energy," said Royce, reading from the prospectus he had received that morning. Jack could see Royce's copy of the prospectus was lined and annotated.

"That's right."

"So why did Laurel make the presentation, not you?"

Jack took a deep breath. "You've got to know Jimmy."

"You have to put up with him, is that it?"

"Something like that."

"But you really run the business, correct?"

"Yes, sir."

"So take five minutes and tell me about Catapult Energy." Royce leaned back in his chair, put both of his feet up on his desk and focused his eyes on Jack.

Jack knew Royce meant what he said. Guys like Royce wanted to see if Jack thought about his business so much—like every waking hour and even when he was asleep—he could distill the essence of the company down to a five-minute description without a rehearsal.

"So you really think these Chinese turbine generators work?" Royce asked when Jack had finished.

"I know they do."

"And all these marginal hydro sites around the United States can be profitably harnessed using this equipment?"

"Right."

"And you've got an iron-clad relationship with a good hydroelectric equipment supplier in China?"

"Wuhan Turbine, one of the best in China. We've already ordered and installed their equipment in the Rio Bravo project, our first. So far, there have been no problems, and I don't expect any."

Royce sat there for a minute.

"I like your business model," he said, looking out his window up the Avenue of the Americas to where the road entered Central Park. He sat thinking a little while longer.

"I'll tell you what I'm going to do. On one condition, I'm going to give DLJ an order for 10 percent of your IPO. Don't take my word for this—you should speak to DLJ—but my order should ice your deal. You'll get the IPO done before Christmas now."

"Yes, sir; I know. Thank you, sir."

"Call me Royce. Here's the condition. You've got to personally assure me you're going to run Catapult Energy. I never want to see that idiot Laurel again."

With Royce Morgan's 10 percent order in hand and Jimmy relegated to his office, the Catapult Energy IPO was oversubscribed at $10 a share, and closed in mid-December. The company listed its shares under the symbol CE on the New York Stock Exchange.

Six years out of Harvard and barely 30, Jack Davis was rich—
between his ownership stakes in Catapult Energy and J.J. Laurel and
Company, his net worth topped $30 million—and famous.

Lionized in the financial press, articles trumpeted Jack's intrepid
venture into China, his ability to find value where others had failed,
and rapid financial success. Courted by the investment banks as a featured speaker for their investor conferences, some called him a genius;
others, a "Renaissance Man."

But he knew better—he was no genius, and what he had done
wasn't really that extraordinary. He was just the embodiment of the
Wall Street maxim—"Better to be lucky than good."

And while he had helped make some of his luck, that still didn't
mean he was smart enough to know that when things seem good, they
almost always turn bad soon afterward.

㊌ ㊌ ㊌

He had promised himself and Alicia a few things when he made serious
money.

With their four sons, they lived in a cramped apartment on one
floor of a five-story brownstone townhouse on the Upper West Side.
Jack wanted to live in a real house. Not just one floor of a house, but
a house like the one he grew up in, with an upstairs, downstairs, and
a backyard. Shortly after the IPO closed, he bought out the other
tenants in the townhouse, gutted it, and converted it into a single family
home, and hired a Filipino couple, Romeo and Lydia, to help Alicia
manage the household.

The townhouse was expensive. Jack didn't care; it would make
his wife happy. And that was more important than ever. Since the
boys had arrived, things had changed in the Davis household. With
the advent of the boys in Alicia's life, Jack was no longer the undis-
puted king of the household; respected as the breadwinner, his
position was nonetheless very different from the one he had occupied
before.

Which was not necessarily fair compensation for his labors. Working
seven days a week, Jack hadn't been fishing or bird shooting in years,
and if the trend continued, was growing concerned he would become

just another guy with a Rolex and suburban aspirations. With his obligations to his family satisfied, Jack looked for a retreat in the country. Alicia was dead set against it—it was far away, she liked sleeping in on Saturdays, transporting the children was a schlep—but he was adamant, even if it meant he would be going there by himself.

He contacted a real estate agent in Connecticut who proposed showing him a place in Lime Rock, a small New England village a two-hour drive from midtown. As they drove up to the property, looked up and saw the pagoda commanding the hill above the house, Alicia asked, "What is that?" The agent told them it had once been the water tower for the estate.

"A pagoda in New England? Next to a trout stream? It can't be a coincidence," Jack said as Alicia rolled her eyes. He bought the property a month later.

㊍   ㊍   ㊍

Jack Davis developed a daily routine for the first time in his life. Rising at five o'clock in the morning, he would run around Central Park for the next hour. He liked being out in the morning in the quiet, running around the reservoir looking at the flocks of seagulls on the water and listening to the low roar of the traffic as it rolled across Central Park like the sound of beach break at the shore.

Showered and shaved by seven, he had Romeo drive him to the office where his secretary had coffee and the newspapers waiting— the *New York Times,* the *Wall Street Journal, USA Today,* and the *Bond Buyer.* He didn't read magazines or watch television; if he read the papers every day, he figured he would know everything worthwhile.

One day after lunch at the Harvard Club, as they finished their cigars, Jack looked over at Bobby McDermott and asked, "What are you going to do now?"

Bobby looked back at Jack. "What do you mean, 'What am I going to do now?' Nothing different, I hope. I'm perfectly happy."

"Me too."

"So why'd you ask?"

Jack relit his cigar. They were never as good once they had to be relit. "I don't know. Everything seems too easy. I'm not sure we deserve all this. We pulled off the IPO and got rich overnight, we're both married to beautiful girls and have great kids. I'm not complaining, Bobby, but this can't be real, can it?"

"Jesus, Jack, don't talk like that. You go looking for trouble, it'll come and find you. Come on, let's get back to the office."

They walked east from the Harvard Club back toward Park Avenue. The morning's heat, already furnace-like, wiggled the white paint of the warning stripes at the crosswalk and melted the tar on the street. Ahead of them, their platform waited, a broad, stable craft that no longer rocked or pitched, a vehicle that could pay for Park Avenue rents, junior employees to do most of the work, managers to do the rest, drivers to take them home at night, and hours of long-distance telefax charges and airplane tickets to China, the mysterious, brooding source of their fortune.

Chapter 9

Chinese Walls

"I'll be happy to meet with Chu-Yi, but I know what she wants—inside information—and we can't give her that," Jack said to Kalin.

Kalin had telephoned Jack to describe her conversation with Chu-Yi Chen, Donaldson Lufkin and Jenrette's research analyst. Technically, Kalin didn't work for Catapult Energy, but Chu-Yi always contacted Jack through Kalin. It was okay by him; he figured they liked to chat and Chu-Yi wanted to stay up on her Mandarin.

"She says we can. She claims there's an approved barrier at DLJ, a 'Chinese wall' that effectively restricts information flow between research and the other departments at their firm," Kalin explained to Jack. "She says whatever we tell her is confidential, and won't be leaked."

"Yeah, right, and I'm the tooth fairy. By the way—this isn't a trick question; I really don't know the answer—why do you suppose they call it a Chinese wall? Why not a Japanese wall?"

"A Chinese wall is an artificial confidentiality barrier in a Wall Street firm."

"Kalin, I know what it is. I'm just curious what makes it Chinese."

"Don't ask me; I'm Chinese and I never heard of a Chinese wall before working for you. It's probably just like fortune cookies, something stupid you foreigners choose to call Chinese that we never had anything to do with. In the meantime, our appointment with Chu-Yi is set for breakfast tomorrow morning. Seven o'clock at the Waldorf Astoria. See you there."

Early the next morning, Romeo picked Jack up in front of the town house in Jack's BMW 750 and headed the big sedan down Riverside Drive to the 72nd Street exit. Romeo wheeled around the circle to the east off the Drive and took the streets toward the East Side. It was a clear, cold morning in December. Columns of steam rose straight up to the sky from the manholes dotting 64th Street, like so many fumaroles in a geothermal field.

Chu-Yi wasn't Jack's idea of a great way to start the day. She was pushy. Not only would she try to extract inside information from Jack, but if after a few questions in English she couldn't get him to open up, she would turn to Kalin, start speaking in Mandarin, and try to trick her instead.

He knew what Chu-Yi wanted: advance confidential information about the Vidalia hydroelectric project. Vidalia was the company's biggest deal so far, a 200-megawatt, $600-million project located on a channel of the Mississippi River. Operational and being tested before final acceptance, Vidalia was already printing money every day. But the company wouldn't be ready to release financial information about Vidalia to the investor public before the issuance of the company's annual report at the end of March, several months away.

Chu-Yi thought she was smart, but she was focused on the wrong subject. She and the other analysts covering Catapult Energy didn't know half of the truth about China; they were naive about the place. Even though Chu-Yi was Chinese, she had little real experience in-country, having been born there and then departed. For purposes of writing her reports and persuading investors to buy Catapult Energy shares, it was convenient for her to write as if Jack had a virtual patent on the Middle Kingdom. But that was not only lazy, it was wholly inaccurate.

All right, he was inside China, doing business in the mysterious, far-off place, and he had relationships. But things were tangential at best. As far as his business, sure, he was buying inexpensive hydroelectric turbines. But it was a one-way street. The turbines were valuable to Catapult Energy, but the cash he was paying Wuhan Turbine was doing much more for them—Wuhan Turbine was becoming a very valuable company, and it was mainly from Jack's purchase orders. For his trouble, Catapult Energy owned no equity in Wuhan Turbine, and didn't even have an exclusive on its machines. Wuhan Turbine could raise their prices tomorrow, or even sell their turbines to one of Jack's competitors. And as far as relationships in China, he hadn't gone anywhere else in the country beyond Wuhan.

As he entered the hotel lobby with its big clock in the center, Jack saw Kalin and Chu-Yi already seated at a table in Peacock Alley, the restaurant off to the north side of the lobby. Chu-Yi wore expensive clothes and black heels so long and pointy they looked like they could hurt someone.

Jack said hello to them both, sat down, and ordered some coffee while the women went on speaking in Chinese for several minutes.

The conversation turned to the subject of the Vidalia project. Chu-Yi asked Kalin a question in Chinese. Turning to Jack, Kalin said "Jack, Chu-Yi is asking how much the Vidalia project will contribute to this year's earnings per share." Kalin knew better than to touch that one.

"Chu-Yi, you know we don't make projections to investment bankers," Jack said.

"Jack, I'm not an investment banker; I'm a research analyst. As you know, there's a Chinese wall between research and the other departments at DLJ, and our two firms have mutually agreed I'm 'over the wall.'"

To be polite, Jack acted like Chu-Yi was telling him something he didn't know, and waited for her to finish. "Thanks, Chu-Yi. Now I get to ask you a question. You're Chinese. So tell me, why does everyone on Wall Street call this confidential barrier you've described a 'Chinese' wall? What is it about the wall that makes it Chinese?"

Chu-Yi looked at him with a blank expression on her face.

"I think I know," Kalin laughed, having had some time to think about Jack's question. "What's Chinese about the wall is exactly what you're worried about, Jack. A wall is not supposed to have any holes, but in China, somehow information still gets through."

"The China I've come to know," Jack said. "Totally secretive, but everyone knows everything."

There was more than one kind of Chinese wall, but he was not going to elaborate with Chu-Yi.

The one he was concerned about at the moment was inside Wuhan Turbine. It appeared as if the Wuhan Turbine people calculated the minimum level of data required to snare Jack's money, and that was all he was ever going to learn about the internal financial workings of their organization.

When he spoke to Kalin about it, she told him to get used to it. Wuhan Turbine, like every other company in the PRC, was a state-owned enterprise, she said. Not just any SOE, but one of the largest in Wuhan. No one there was going to say a word to Jack except for the party line espoused by General Manager Wang.

But he couldn't help himself; he knew enough about the company to want to know more. He had figured out how the company priced its machines. It wasn't sophisticated. They simply assessed worldwide prices for hydroelectric turbines, and quoted a number they thought customers like Jack would accept. But their quote had little to do with actual cost. Once he had seen their factories, Jack knew Wuhan Turbine could probably make good money at much lower prices—slave labor doesn't cost much.

If someone with some cash and business sense—mostly just cash—could get control of the company, the opportunity was truly global. The more he thought about it, he didn't just want access to their machines—he wanted to own the company. Wuhan Turbine for starters; maybe others later.

His friends on Wall Street would think he was out of his mind.

Preparing for their next trip to China, Jack asked Kalin to arrange a personal meeting with General Manager Wang to discuss larger issues.

She reported back in a few days: General Manager Wang agreed to the meeting; he had his own strategic agenda to discuss with Jack; and was looking forward to receiving Jack in two weeks. Their meeting would be private—no engineering or procurement personnel.

Maybe now he could get somewhere.

They left 10 days later, traveling by way of Hong Kong. But this time, they wouldn't just change planes in Hong Kong and continue, but stay overnight in Hong Kong at the Mandarin Oriental, the grand dame of the city's hotels.

They checked into the hotel in the early evening as the breezes crossing Victoria Harbor were beginning to dissipate the city's subtropical heat. Sending their luggage up to their rooms, they headed to the Captain's Bar, Hong Kong's most important watering hole.

Off the hotel's lobby down a short flight of stairs, the bar's single room was windowless and darkly lit. Seating to the right and along the rear wall was arranged around red leather banquettes and low, circular red leather stools.

It was barely five o'clock in the afternoon, but the place was already jammed. Together with scores of British expats, there was an equally large crowd of big, beefy Americans. Utility types, Jack thought after a quick look, no doubt in town trying to grab China's big power and telecommunications deals. The *laowai* held down all the tables, barstools, pretzel bowls, and available females in the smoky room, occupying themselves puffing on cigars and ordering drinks the proper Hong Kong bartenders could only vaguely identify.

Jack ordered a Tom Collins and a Cohiba cigar. Kalin hesitated, and then ordered chrysanthemum tea.

"Mr. Davis?"

"I thought we were past the Mr. Davis stuff."

"We're not alone; look at all these people."

"Trust me, we're alone. No one in here can hear a word we say, and cares less."

"Jack."

"That's better."

"I actually was thinking of having a drink."

"You mean a drink drink?"

"Yes."

"A splendid idea."

"But I don't know what to order. We Chinese don't drink much, but I'm suspicious of any drink they list in a menu. They never list drinks in menus stateside."

"You should be. How about one of these?"

"What, a Tom Collins? It sounds like a man's drink."

"Well, it's not really for a man or a woman; it's gin, that's all. Or how about a daiquiri? They're made with rum; you'd like rum."

"I like the sound of that. All right, I'll try a daiquiri."

Jack signaled the waiter, a Chinese man in a white dinner jacket and black bow tie, and ordered a daiquiri for Kalin and a refill for himself.

They sat quietly in the midst of the hubbub and commotion of the room.

"Do you think those women are business people?" Jack asked Kalin as he surveyed the crowd.

She looked up and eyed the groups of women gathered at the bar. "Not the Chinese ones."

"Prostitutes?"

"Maybe. Some of them for sure," Kalin answered.

The waiter returned with their drinks. "Call me Billy," he said to Jack, putting down the drinks and some pretzels.

Kalin took a tiny sip of her drink. "It's good," she said.

"Are there a lot of prostitutes in Hong Kong?"

"You should see Shenzhen," Kalin said.

"Are they here because of the *laowai*?"

"Of course."

"You say 'of course,' but what do you mean? Are those Chinese women talking to the *laowai* because of the money, or are they attracted to them?"

"It's the money," Kalin said after hesitating a moment. "It's not attraction. You shouldn't flatter yourself, Jack. A lot of *laowai* men do. You know, many Chinese women are not attracted to *laowai* men."

"You mean culturally," Jack said.

"Yes, that too, but actually I meant physically."

"Physically? I thought Chinese women thought *laowai* men were handsome. Someone told me Chinese people liked long noses."

"It depends. Most of you guys are big and fat—I'm not talking about you," she said, laughing darkly as Jack's expression registered, "but take a look around if you don't believe me. These guys all drink and sweat too much, and they have hair all over their bodies."

"Chinese people sweat; everyone sweats."

"Not like *laowai*."

"And everyone has hair on their bodies," Jack said.

"Not like *laowai*."

Jack didn't say anything. He had hair on his body, that was for sure. He watched the women at the bar, trying to see some indicator that they were in it for the money. None of them looked like they were holding their noses.

"If it makes you feel any better, the common assumption is that *laowai* are better lovers," Kalin offered.

"Really? Why?"

Kalin shrugged. "Search me. Maybe the long noses." She laughed, but he got the feeling she wasn't kidding.

Kalin had never spoken to him like this before. It must be the liquor. He liked her more when she was this way.

"My husband's a *laowai,* you know."

Jack swung around from watching the crowd at the bar and looked at Kalin. "You've told me. So you're in it for the money," he joked, watching her face.

"No. I'm Chinese," she said.

"What does that mean?"

"You'll never know," she said, looking back at him through her Mona Lisa smile.

They left the hotel early the next morning, drove across the border to Guangzhou, and clambered on the same rickety, propeller-driven DC 3 they had taken two years earlier for their first flight to Wuhan.

The plane fanned up a storm of dust as it taxied into the terminal at the Wuhan airport three hours later. Deputy Manager Wen and a driver were waiting for them when they exited baggage claim.

Their first stop was the factory. Two hours later, as they crossed the bridge over the Yangtze from the airport, ocean-going steamers and tankers plied their way down the eastern end of the river toward

Shanghai, while upstream smaller craft headed west toward the Three Gorges.

After an additional hour, their car cruised under the orange man-monkey and into the courtyard of the headquarters building of Wuhan Turbine. An assistant led Jack and Kalin to a meeting room on the second floor. As they entered and sat down in front of the obligatory bowls of fruit and cups of green tea, it felt to Jack like they were walking into a frozen meat locker. He hadn't brought a coat. The last time he had been there, it had been December as well, but the weather had been comfortable. Now it was frigid.

General Manager Wang and some of his assistants came in, all wearing standard issue floor-length olive green army coats, sat down, and started talking about the arrangements for the following days as if nothing was up. It was difficult to concentrate; the room couldn't have been more than 40 degrees Fahrenheit. After 10 minutes, Kalin was shivering noticeably and Jack was about to lose his temper over the petty negotiating tactic.

"Jesus, Kalin, it's freezing in here. Tell him to turn up the heat."

"We're on the south side of the Yangtze, Jack. Get used to it."

"What's the Yangtze got to do with anything?" Jack said, looking at the fog made by his breath as he spoke.

"When China emerged from the Civil War, Chairman Mao decided everyone north of the Yangtze got heated buildings, while everyone south of the river didn't. But it can still get cold here," she said, shrugging her shoulders.

"I'll say."

General Manager Wang was watching them speak, and said something to Kalin. When she responded, his face erupted in a toothy grin. He barked loudly in Chinese to one of his aides, who ran out of the room and reemerged a minute later with army coats and fur hats for Jack and Kalin. Both sides had a good laugh.

General Manager Wang had a surprise for them; on the weekend, the weather was expected to warm up, and they would go to the company's getaway meeting place, a company-owned resort hotel on a lake south of the city. Jack had a hard time juxtaposing his notion of a resort with what he had seen so far of rural China, but he wasn't going to object. He just needed to talk to General Manager Wang.

After spending the night at the Wuhan guest house, they left by car for the country the following morning. After two hours, they pulled into a gas station. Their driver said some words to Kalin in Chinese.

"He says you should use the washroom here if you need to," she said to Jack, getting out of the car on her side and heading around the back of the building.

Jack let her go, stretched, and took a look around. Gasoline was selling for less than $1 per gallon, much cheaper than stateside. He had heard it was subsidized. To the left of the gas pumps, a small kitchen-like restaurant adjoined the service station. Off to the right, several families of Chinese squatted along a wall, selling apples, pears, and plums arrayed on the hard dirt ground in front of them. As flies swarmed over the fruit, children fanned crude brooms back and forth over the offerings to scatter the insects, the men and women calling out to would-be customers walking by. Everyone stared at the *laowai*.

Kalin came back around the front of the gas station, went inside the kitchen for a minute, emerged with two small packages, and handed one to Jack.

"What's this?" he asked, examining a soft orb the size of a tennis ball wrapped in a long green banana leaf with a rubber band.

"Sticky rice," Kalin said. She had already shucked the leaf wrapper and was eating hers.

Jack unwrapped his and took a bite. It was surprisingly good, the unrefined rice hulls tender and plump and flavored with a meat sauce that bound the rice ball together.

Finished, he needed to wash his hands and use the men's room, so he walked around to the rear of the building where Kalin had gone. Circling a pile of garbage running down the hill behind the kitchen that looked like it had accumulated over a hundred years, he looked for the men's room but could only find a dark doorless entrance, filled with hoards of flies buzzing in and out and a stench that would make a weaker man vomit.

As he stepped through the doorway and his eyes grew accustomed to the light, he saw a row of slit trenches along the ground and realized a woman was standing inside in a half squat at the end of the row, urinating over a hole. As she turned her head away from him and acted like he wasn't there, he stumbled backward and retraced his steps to the front of the gas station. He could hold it until the hotel.

Turning off the main highway, they took a two-lane, asphalt road that remained hard-topped for an hour, then became one lane, and then a gravel path. Dust billowed up behind them as the drivers sped along, blowing their horns as they whisked by bicycles, people, and animals. Both sides of the byway were lined with trees every 20 feet or so, each with the base of its trunk painted with white paint. Jack's first instinct was to wonder how expensive it must have been to get people to paint the thousands of trees, before he reminded himself there were millions of people in every pocket of rural China desperate to work for a dollar a day.

They swung around a corner and crossed a bridge over the inlet of a reservoir, its pea-green water severely depleted. At the edge of a 30-foot ring of exposed rocky soil surrounding the perimeter of the half-filled reservoir stood General Manager Wang's resort.

The exterior of the building was nice enough. With a motif vaguely reminiscent of French Rococo, the edifice was constructed completely of stone. The Chinese could do amazing things with stone and concrete, Jack thought to himself as their cars pulled into the hotel's circular entryway; he tried to recall having seen a single wooden structure in China, and couldn't.

A red plastic banner with yellow Chinese characters hung across the front portico of the hotel. In the middle of the banner, he could read in English the words "Catapult Energy" and "Jack Davis." A team of young, smiling men and women waited for them. As they got out of their car, one of them presented Kalin with some flowers and gave Jack a basket of fruit. Other than their reception party, there were no other people and no cars.

They clattered behind General Manager Wang up the stairs of the front entrance and across the lobby's wide marble floor under a gaudy chandelier to the reception area. General Manager Wang and a man who looked like the hotel manager greeted each other in boisterous voices, laughing and slapping each other on the back; after a while, Wang grabbed Kalin's arm and harangued her as well.

She nodded her head and turned to Jack. "General Manager Wang insists you stay in the president's suite, the rooms he usually takes."

Despite Jack's protests, the manager led him and Kalin out of the lobby along a terra cotta breezeway bridging a goldfish pond to a small separate stone building with tall, double-hung wooden doors. As the manager unlocked the room and Jack stood in the entrance examining the wood of the doors—fiberboard with a streaky walnut stain—he smelled the overpowering, musky scent of airspace uninhabited for months. He could see his breath.

He didn't care; it would be better than a sleeping bag on a rainy night. He just needed to use the bathroom. Kalin told him where she would be down the hall. She would come by in 15 minutes to pick him up for dinner.

He shut the door and walked through the suite's large living room furnished with French reproductions and overstuffed neoprene couches and a sideboard with glass doors housing the obligatory collection of fake porcelain vases and antique seals. A calligraphy set, intended to be a clear indicator the room belonged to a man of high stature, sat unused on a desk along the wall. Looking for a toilet, he passed a study, a walk-in closet, and two bedrooms.

Off the larger of the two bedrooms, he found a bathroom and lifted the toilet seat. The water in the bowl was a deep, almost viscous slime of green. Jack breathed through his mouth as he tried to flush it. Nothing happened. He walked through the bedroom and tried the toilet off the other bedroom. Same thing. No problem; he'd just prime the toilet by filling it with water from the sink. He turned on the water faucet. No water.

He checked all the other faucets, including the one in the wet bar in the living room. The president's suite was grand enough, but it wasn't plumbed.

He went out to find Kalin. As he walked down the hallway, he passed the door of a room with several mattresses on the floor where a group of Chinese maids in hotel uniforms sat on overturned wooden cartons. They were living there. When he passed and looked in, they all jumped up, stood up straight, and smiled. "*Ni hao.*"

He smiled at them, said, "*Ni hao,*" kept walking down the hallway to Kalin's room, and knocked on her door.

"Hey Kalin, sorry to bother you," he said through her door. "The president's suite doesn't have any water. I just need a regular room."

Kalin opened her door.

"I just need a regular room," he repeated to her, "so I can go to the bathroom."

Kalin was about to respond when one of the Chinese maids came up behind Jack and started speaking in Chinese to Kalin. She listened to the maid, asked her a few questions, nodded her head to the maid, and turned to Jack.

"How bad do you need to go?"

"I haven't since we left Wuhan."

"You went at the gas station. I saw you."

"I didn't." He wasn't going to say anything more to Kalin about the gas station. "What's the problem?"

"There's no water in this wing," she said, putting on a tired smile for Jack.

"What do you mean, in this wing?"

"There's water in the wing where General Manager Wang is staying."

"Well, let's stay there, then."

"We can't," Kalin said with a sigh. "They'll lose face. The maid said the other rooms are crummy. General Manager Wang doesn't want us to know. We're in the only fancy rooms. There's just no water. They ran out of money."

Jack stood there for a moment. "Nice of them to tell us."

"She said General Manager Wang doesn't know. The hotel manager has been hiding it from him."

"All right," Jack said. "No matter. Two things. First, please ask this woman if there's a back door I can use. Next, they're living right down the hall themselves—what do they do for water?"

Kalin spoke to the maid. "She says she'll take you to the back door; that's what they do, too. And they use buckets and washcloths for showers."

"That ought to work fine. What are we going to be here for, two days? Now I've only got one problem left."

"What's that?"

"There's no toilet paper in my room."

"It's China, Jack," Kalin said, trying not to laugh. "You're supposed to bring your own."

Dinner was winding down. The others were having a long conversation in Chinese. Jack watched everyone try to deal with the Lazy Susan. For General Manager Wang, only the latest in modern conveniences would do, so the Lazy Susan at the center of the dining table was mechanized, spinning round and round automatically. Unfortunately, it didn't stop, so if someone wasn't quick about it, he would help himself to the soup and be forced to hold the ladle until the bowl came all the way around the table again.

General Manager Wang seemed like he was playing right into Jack's hands.

For most of dinner, he had ranted about money—or more specifically, his lack of it. First griping about his company's situation, he then got personal. He didn't have any money, Kalin told Jack, nodding her head at Wang as she listened, trying to appear sympathetic. Wuhan Turbine, the city of Wuhan—it didn't matter—they couldn't pay him. Wouldn't pay him. He had turned the company around and put Wuhan on the map, and he was doing business and rubbing elbows with world leaders and moguls who were all filthy rich—but he was penniless. His counterparts all had beautiful houses and fancy cars and bank accounts, and what did he have? Nothing.

"Can't the company give him a raise and get him out of his apartment into a decent house?" Jack asked Kalin. "I've seen some houses around Wuhan that look reasonable."

"Are you kidding?" Kalin said. "They've got very strict rules about those things."

"Wait a minute, Kalin. You've told me all about other guys in China who have figured out how to play that game."

"I know, but it's not just the state rules that are a problem for him. He's put himself in a box. He imagines himself a 'man of the people.'"

Jack shrugged. "So should I forget about my idea?"

"We're here. You might as well try."

Jack launched his pitch, describing to General Manager Wang the worldwide opportunity available for Wuhan Turbine; commiserated regarding his shortage of equity capital; and as a solution proposed an investment in the company. They could begin with a small equity stake, and more money could change hands later.

When Kalin had finished translating, the room went silent, the Lazy Susan whirring around and around. When General Manager Wang finally spoke, he didn't respond, but just repeated how important Wuhan Turbine was becoming in China, and then rambled on.

Kalin leaned over and whispered, "I don't think you're going to like this. It seems like if you are proposing a solution that benefits only the company, he's not interested. He's saying he has been thinking about a good way for you to get what you want—a strategic relationship with Wuhan Turbine—and he proposes you prepay for a large order of equipment. He would give it to you at a significant discount."

Jack sighed. "That's a nonstarter—the blank check approach. He'll probably just want a big enough payment so he can skim some cash off for himself. What kind of an idiot does he think I am?"

"Don't let General Manager Wang see your anger," Kalin advised him. "That won't do you any good."

He looked across the table at General Manager Wang, a residue of bitterness covering his ruddy, nut-brown face. Jack's offer had fallen on deaf ears. Wang didn't care whether the company was successful or not. Unless a deal offered an opportunity for personal gain, he wasn't interested. In the long run, it was going to be impossible to do business with the guy. He was no partner; that was for sure. The current arrangement was mutually beneficial, but things could change. Betting Catapult Energy's future on Wang was not just risky, it was stupid.

"Fair enough," Jack responded to Kalin, forcing himself to be calm and not dwell on how he had come around the world to a rock pile in the middle of nowhere to hear what he had just heard, "but seriously, I don't think that man has any sense of his problem. And I know he has no understanding of mine."

It just wasn't time yet. The time would come, though—he didn't care what the government regulations said. He would take their approach, just wait them out. At the rate they were going, he would be around longer than they would.

For some reason, Kalin was wearing perfume; she smelled good, like summer lilies. He looked around, wondering what he was going to do until they left. "I thought Chinese women didn't wear perfume," he said to her.

"You'll never understand Chinese women, Jack," Kalin warned him, wearing the mysterious version of her smile.

"I don't think I'll ever understand Chinese people, period."

Chapter 10

The Year of Living Dangerously

When the secretaries in his office began asking him for stock tips, it was clear the end was near. Living in a golden age of debt, a gilded era of easy money fueling record levels of Wall Street financings, who could blame any of them for being dazzled?

Catapult Energy's share price approached $30. As Jack's net worth rose, he came up with more things to spend money on. He plowed cash into the townhouse. When the farm down the road from his country house came on the market, he bought it and converted its farm house into a weekend office. And when Jimmy's heart condition worsened and he called Jack to tell him he was retiring and closing J.J. Laurel and Company, Jack bought out Jimmy's interest and changed the investment firm's name to Davis Brothers.

Accessing funds was simple; he just sold some stock, or better yet, took out margin loans against his shares, careful to not tell Alicia, who kept warning him things couldn't stay good forever. Catapult Energy's stock price kept rising, and it hadn't seemed like a lot of debt at the time.

㊛ ㊛ ㊛

Sensing things had been too easy didn't make it better when the crash finally came.

At nine o'clock one Monday morning in October, Jack was sitting in Royce Morgan's office giving him Catapult's quarterly update when the opening bell sounded and the market roared downhill to close off 23 percent, the biggest one-day loss in Wall Street history. Royce was cool under fire, giving his traders orders to buy as the market slid out of sight while Jack sat there helplessly, watching the price of Catapult's stock collapse and feeling like he was about to go down the big hill on a roller coaster.

That afternoon, everyone at the company offices left their televisions on, monitoring the financial destruction. Jack refused to watch, and left early. Rather than having Romeo drive him home, he decided to walk. It would help clear his head, and something told him he should probably get used to walking again. Going up Broadway late in the afternoon, the shadows creeping across the garden medians and the last of autumn's leaves swirling along the curbstones, he stopped in the Ginger Man to have a drink.

As he glanced up at the television screen over the bar and saw the bright red graph describing the day's market carnage, Catapult Energy's symbol ticked across the closing tape at $6. He would have to get used to walking, all right—he wouldn't even be able to afford the subway. Before arriving at Royce's office that morning, he had been worth over $60 million; sitting at the Ginger Man bar, he was worth next to nothing and owed $3 million more in uncollateralized margin loans to the bank.

What was he supposed to do? The words to *That's Life,* the Frank Sinatra song, materialized in his head and hung there. But bad luck wasn't the whole story, and he knew it. He had overextended himself when he did not need to, spending money like a big shot, and now he was going to pay.

He should have panicked, but he didn't. Maybe he was in shock, or maybe it was just that he was still young. The ache that should have accompanied losing his fortune sailed over his oblivious forehead, the numb chaos that accompanies financial meltdowns a new experience still to come for him. Sitting at the Ginger Man bar, he didn't feel any different. He had had a good run. He could do it again. Sure he could.

He ordered another drink, downed it, and took one more look at the television. They were interviewing people who had lost everything, some forlorn, others wild-eyed. With no thought that he resembled anyone on the screen, he paid his tab, walked back out to Broadway and headed north toward home. Along the way, he noticed for the first time the faces coming at him the other way, tried to see if they were all right, and realized that that was why they were looking at him.

His wakeup call was standing at the front door. Alicia was waiting for him, a pained, hollow expression on her face. The day that could never happen had been the one she had predicted for over a year. She was sure he hadn't margined his Catapult shares, she said as she let him in. Surely he hadn't been that foolish with money they had worked so hard for.

Reviewing the grim financial situation with his furious wife that night, they confronted the inevitable, Jack calm, Alicia livid: with his stock under water, the townhouse was now their largest, most liquid asset. In order to pay bills, they would have to sell and move out of the city to the house in Lime Rock.

They were still young, but he had lost her. It wasn't what she said; it was what she didn't say. She offered no encouragement, not even resignation, just something much worse, coming from the only woman he had ever loved: disgust.

Turning from each other, neither of them realized what they were throwing away. It came along every day, didn't it?

The morning after the crash, Jack didn't hesitate, calling an emergency meeting of Catapult Energy's shell-shocked board of directors. With the stock at $6, they feared the worst. The world as they knew it had ended; with no access to capital, companies like Catapult Energy would die. It was unanimous; they would put the company up for sale.

"What about China?" people said to him in the aftermath of the crash. What about it? She seemed like part of another galaxy. Sure, last week she had sat beckoning, an alluring temptress for an ambitious traveler. But this week and for the foreseeable future, China couldn't help him—without financing, cheap Chinese hydroelectric equipment was meaningless—and he was in no position to help her.

Not that the Chinese didn't ask. Despite the absence of Western press in Wuhan, General Manager Wang and the others must have learned of the crash, but he received no acknowledgment of it or expression of sympathy, only continued requests to buy more turbines and send more money. It had been a one-way relationship, all right.

And Kalin, the medium through which he existed in the Middle Kingdom, was no different from the rest of them. After the crash, she had called and told him how sorry she was, saying she was confident he would get back on his feet. He thanked her, she paused a moment, and then reminded him to make sure he mailed her her monthly check.

He didn't blame her. Like the squeeze, it was just part of her world, a place in which relationships were important as long as they were one way—the right way. She called him weekly for a while, then once a month, and then less often than that, each time telling him she believed in him and would wait for him, as China and Jack floated apart at opposite ends across the expanding mist of the Pacific.

Chapter 11

Easier Said than Done

It had been about five months since the stock market crash. The first thing Jack had done was organize an auction for Catapult Energy, hiring Drexel Burnham to canvass buyers. Next, he entered into a workout agreement with the banks holding his margin loans and put his townhouse up for sale, planning to move his family and what remained of Davis Brothers to Lime Rock as soon as the transactions closed. In the meantime, Alicia barely spoke to him; he concentrated on work and tried to avoid her.

Initially, Catapult Energy's prospects remained moribund. The equity markets were closed, and the company's stock price hovered around its low.

When Boone Daniels, a well-known takeover artist, and his son Tim, backed by a Canadian hydroelectric conglomerate, bid $22 per share to buy Catapult Energy, they surprised everyone. Catapult Energy was undervalued, they argued to business journalists and anyone else willing to listen. The China connection was the key, they said. When the media called Jack for his opinion, he offered no comment.

The Catapult Energy shareholders were ecstatic; most of their other investments had yet to recover from the crash. Jack was a genius once more.

Privately, while distressed over having to part with Catapult Energy, he was prepared to move on. If Daniels wanted to pay three times the current market bid per share, and twice the IPO price, Jack would take it—his proceeds would be about $15 million. Not nearly what it would have been if he had sold at the peak, but still enough money to settle his margin loans and give him a cushion so he could start over.

The Chinese would never deal with Daniels, but for some reason no one ever asked.

On April 1, the day of the closing, Jack rose early, ran around Central Park, returned, changed, and left before Alicia awoke and had a chance to ask him what he was going to do next.

Genesis's *Invisible Touches* blared from a construction worker's boom box as Jack crossed Park Avenue at the corner of 54th on the way to his attorney's offices. In the flower boxes lining the medians, the daffodils were giving way to tulips.

Looking at the ambitious eyes of people walking toward him, the morning's agenda sunk in. For close to $1 billion, Jack was selling Catapult Energy, the company he had started from a concept three years earlier. Up until that moment, he had spent little time reflecting on the once-in-a-lifetime nature of Catapult Energy, let alone whether he could repeat its success.

Alicia had been right to worry. The Catapult Energy formula—cheap Chinese equipment—had fallen into his lap. He had no idea what to do for an encore, and less conviction as to whom to do it with.

The sale of Catapult Energy closed at 11 o'clock in the morning. Anticlimactic, the event was mercifully brief. Tim Daniels told Jack he would come by to take over after lunch. Jack and Bobby left as quickly as they could without being rude, and returned to the company's offices. When Daniels arrived, Jack would introduce him to the company staff, say goodbye to his employees, and get out of there.

Back at the office, Jack peered through the stacks of packing boxes, taking a last look around. He had thought he would be there forever. The company had occupied the space, the entire 18th floor of 245 Park Avenue, for the two years since the IPO. Jack's office was on the northeast corner of the building looking out over the East River. On clear mornings he would cut short his morning run and go to the office early to watch the big orange sun come up over the river, sitting there looking east through the Long Island mist, trying to convince himself that he was entitled to be the CEO of a New York Stock Exchange–listed company with a corner office at 46th and Park.

Sitting at his conference table, he was just lighting a cigar when Bobby came in and sat down, taking a cigar himself while not saying anything.

"So what are you going to do?" Jack asked Bobby when he felt like talking.

"Go to California," Bobby said.

"What's out there?"

"A paycheck. Cynthia isn't going to stop using her American Express card just because we sold the company."

Jack kept smoking his cigar, not saying anything. Bobby had to get on with his life.

"How about you?" Bobby asked.

"Jack, Mr. Daniels is here," Grace, one of Jack's secretaries, announced. Jack and Bobby got up from the table and headed for the door.

Grace led them toward the reception area, Jack following her, watching her trying to balance on her high heels. Most Wall Street executives, including Jack, still had secretaries. Jack used two, Grace for his Catapult Energy work, and Mary for his investment banking work. He didn't use a computer; nor did he answer his own phone or make his own travel reservations. He was an inefficient dinosaur; he just didn't know it yet.

Tim Daniels came down the hallway, not waiting for them to come out to the reception area and collect him, showing the Catapult Energy people he was taking charge. The expression on his face indicated he thought he was going to have an opportunity to make some kind of statement or do whatever an amateur whose father had bought him a business thinks he is supposed to do in similar situations. As Daniels was preparing to serve up his opening words, Jack handed him his keys and corporate American Express Card, wished him luck, turned, and started for the elevator, Daniels stammering in his wake.

"Jack, what will you do now?" Grace asked, her stockings hissing as she walked fast to keep up as he strode down the hallway.

"I wish I knew."

The elevator swallowed him up.

Book Two

THE CREVICE

Chapter 12

A Leopard and His Spots

Out of the hole. And by God, he was never going back.

As soon as Jack received the proceeds from the sale of his Catapult Energy shares, he paid off his margin loans and put the balance in his bank account. The same month, he sold the townhouse for $3 million. Back from the brink, the view of his net figures was nonetheless painful—after taxes and margin loans, less than $9 million left. A lot of money to most people, but a fraction of what he had been worth a year earlier.

He was just beginning to learn about crash aftershocks. Catapult Energy was gone, and with it the hefty salary and expense allowance he had taken for granted. Davis Brothers hemorrhaged cash. Optimism had been sucked out of people; with no buyers, there were no deals. Jack sold down the firm's trading positions, disposed of its branches, and let everyone go except his compliance director Robert Gander and other key staff who agreed to relocate to Lime Rock once he got the farm house renovated into an office.

Jack needed to get some cash coming in the door fast, and recoup the fortune he had lost. The temporary ambivalence about his career path was gone, replaced by resolve. Catapult Energy hadn't been a fluke—he would prove it by starting a new power company.

At least he wouldn't have to begin from scratch, working out of a telephone booth the way he had started his first company. He had cash; it just wasn't a lot, and would need to carry him a long way, all the way back to where he had come from. And he hadn't lost his confidence—he just didn't have any margin for error.

Acquiring Grizzly Power Corporation, a small hydroelectric power company near Bay City, Michigan, felt like second nature. Owned and managed by Carl Underwood, a retired accountant, Grizzly was being offered cheap—it was losing money—but could be turned around. Jack flew up to Michigan to inspect the facilities and review the company's papers.

"Anything else I should know?" Jack asked Carl, closing up the financial files and legal books after three hours.

"Nossir, nothing comes to mind," Carl answered. Way past retirement, Carl looked tired. He wore a flannel shirt and baggy pants held up by suspenders, not nice fabric ones but the crummy elastic ones with metal clips to snap on to your pants, the kind people wore in places like Bay City.

"I should probably speak to your company counsel," Jack said.

"Don't have one," Carl answered.

"How can a power company not have a lawyer?" Jack said.

"Hell, anything a lawyer can do, I can do better, and for half the cost."

Jack had never heard of such a thing. Out of compliance regarding its operating licenses, it was no wonder Grizzly couldn't find a buyer. "I expect you'll be happy to get this place sold," he said as he packed the due diligence materials back into their file box.

Carl just looked at Jack.

"So what do you want for this outfit?" Jack asked.

"Ten million."

"Three, and you ought to buy me lunch."

"You going to get a general manager?" Carl asked.

"Does that mean we have a deal?"

"I guess it does."

"Are you buying me lunch?"

"I've got a better idea," Carl said.

"What's that?"

"I'll take you out back, give you a rod, and you can fish for yours."
"Sold."

Jack searched across the nation to buy some more hydroelectric projects, but other than damaged goods like Grizzly, there was nothing for sale.

America's power market had changed. Utility conglomerates had taken over the independent power industry Jack had helped create, and there was no room left for small entrepreneurial players. He had wanted to keep things simple, not take any risks, but if he wanted to get back on Wall Street's main stage, he would have to swim outside of the mainstream.

Hydroelectric power in the United States was conventional, but emerging markets were different. No competition there. And with the crash dampening domestic prospects, his buy-side friends told him investments overseas looked more appealing. Other renewables, like wind and solar, were definitely not mainstream. No competition there, either. He liked renewables—what wasn't to like about no fuel and no emissions?

After Grizzly, Jack spent another $3 million acquiring Bayview Power Corporation, a wind farm in California's Altamont Pass, and $2 million more for North Vermont Solar, a solar company with installations around the world, added Bobby McDermott to his board of directors, and started looking at renewable opportunities overseas. Catapult Energy had been the nation's first independent power company; his new organization—the New Land Power Corporation—would be the world's first renewable power company.

But while admirers said Jack was being consistent, doubters said his consistency merely marked a leopard that couldn't change its spots. Once again, he was adventuring down the road less traveled, miles ahead of everyone else—sometimes that made a guy a genius, other times just a dreamer, or worse.

Spending time on his new business was better than going home to their transplanted household and confronting Alicia.

Alicia hated Lime Rock. Far away from her friends and New York activities, she found nothing redeeming in the country. She didn't care about the woods or the streams or anything Jack loved about the place, while in town there were no stores, no schools, and no nannies. The house was old. When it had been the family's weekend retreat, she and the rest of the family rarely used it; Jack went up by himself most weekends. Now strained by the pressure of eight inhabitants, every major system in the 200-year old building—heating, plumbing, electrical, sewage—malfunctioned and required replacement.

Lydia and Romeo, the Filipino help Alicia depended on, lasted until the first snowfall. Jack found Alex and Helena, a local Polish couple, and installed them as caretakers in the woodcutter's cottage at the end of the property, but Alicia was dismissive; they were rural peasants, she said, possessing no sense of the type of household she required.

Jack's long hours at work grew harder for Alicia to accept. In the old days when he had come home late, she had understood. Now she couldn't. Alicia was steadily being reduced to something neither of them could stomach, an angry woman biting her nails, worrying about money, and thinking her husband ignored her.

Arriving on a chilly June morning in 1988 to his office in the farm house, still under renovation, Jack brought in some logs from the wood pile, dodged the workmen lugging the remains of the root cellar up the basement stairs, and lit a fire in the fireplace. He got the mail, shut his office door, and sat at his desk, looking out the windows over the cornfield to the Lime Rock ridge behind his house a mile away. On the banks of the bass pond in the middle of the cornfield, one of Virginio Ferrari's sculptures presided silently over a flock of Canadian geese.

Jack lit a cigar. The workmen were taking a long coffee break, and the phone was silent. It felt good just to sit there. He never got to do this. Jack sifted through the mail, throwing out the catalogues, stacking the letters, telling himself not to sift through them, but open the one on top. He wasn't going to rush through things. The first letter was a bill. He forced himself to review the itemized information.

He couldn't comprehend what the figures meant, and cared less. He studied the data anyway, determined to go through the mail as he imagined other people did. But he wasn't any good at this, really. After a few minutes, Jack got up, went down the hall and made himself some coffee, returned, put the bills aside and started reviewing a description of a hydroelectric site in Costa Rica.

As the geese took off from the pond and headed upriver beyond the grove of sycamores, Whitey opened his door and told Jack he had a phone call from Kalin Gao.

Jack forced himself not to grab for the phone.

"Hello, Jack. I've missed you."

"Same here. What's up?"

"Good news. You might have a chance to own a hydroelectric project in China, after all. The central government in Beijing has just announced they're deregulating the electric power industry. Beijing is encouraging local companies to find foreign partners to build new power projects in China."

"China seems pretty far away, Kalin."

"Please don't be shortsighted, Jack. This could be a home run for you. The central government is pushing General Manager Wang to act. He likes the limelight, but now he needs to deliver."

"The problem is, in General Manager Wang's mind, all that means is someone's supposed to deliver something to him."

He tried to talk himself down, but still, it was indeed a tantalizing opportunity, representing what he had wanted before—an ownership stake in China—but not problem free. Maybe a hydroelectric project in Costa Rica wouldn't offer the same panache to investors, but it would probably be a whole lot easier.

"He told me he doesn't want anyone else for his partner," Kalin said. "You're his number one. He's got a whole list of projects waiting for you."

"I don't know, Kalin. I was hoping my next power company could do business in a country where they supply toilet paper in the restrooms."

"Very funny, Jack, but that's not fair. China was very good for you."

"In spite of General Manager Wang. He didn't feel like a partner to me, more like someone looking me over to find an opening. A country's a pretty lonely place when you feel that way."

"I was there for you, Jack."

"Yes, you were."

"Please?"

"What would I have to do?"

"General Manager Wang needs a joint venture proposal from a foreign partner with money. If you can put one together and send it to him, he'll meet us late in the year and we can start the business."

Neither of them said anything for a moment.

"And he'll open up about things this time?" Jack finally asked.

"Come on, Jack. He's Mainland Chinese. But he's going to need a lot of money to build his projects. He'll have to meet you halfway if he wants the cash. Right?"

"Halfway? I don't think so. Do you? He'll just make the Chinese wall a little lower, is all."

"Don't be so pessimistic," Kalin said. "The pressure from the central government is already intense—he's got to show results, and for that, he needs money—and soon. You've got leverage. I think he's prepared to give you some really big deals."

"You're overlooking the most important thing—the cash. I sold Catapult Energy last year. I don't have a public company anymore."

"Jack, who're you kidding? That never stopped you. Do an IPO for your new company—China's the perfect hook for new investors, and you know it better than anyone. This is a really big opportunity—you've got to do it."

"I don't know." Who knew what it would take for him to do a second IPO?

She let him think. "How long will an IPO take?" Kalin asked.

"If I could get everything lined up? Probably six months."

Kalin exhaled. "That should work. The legislation doesn't get passed until January. We can meet him December in Hong Kong, iron things out, and be ready to go in the new year."

Hong Kong was nice in December. "I had wondered if I'd ever be back there."

"So should I set it up?"

"Let me think about it." He didn't say anything for a long time. "I guess so."

"What is it?"

"I'm just thinking about Alicia."

"What about her?"

"Think about it, Kalin. Alicia hates it enough in Lime Rock already, and I'm going to walk into the house and tell her I'll be away in China two weeks out of every month and she's got the four boys by herself."

"What does she expect you to do? Work for the Post Office?"

Jack was surprised. In four years, Kalin hadn't ever mentioned Alicia, let alone with invective.

It didn't matter. He knew he had to go back. Staying in the United States would be like using a wooly bugger. The small fish were there, and he could stay home and catch one, but it wouldn't be enough. If he really wanted to fish well and catch a trophy, he had to use a dry fly and try to take the trout as it leaped in the air. But he couldn't make any mistakes, and he didn't have a lot of time.

"See you in Hong Kong in December," he said to Kalin, and hung up.

Chapter 13

Talk the Talk, Walk the Walk

"New Land sounds great, Jack, but where'd you get the money?" Bobby asked when they met for lunch the day Bobby left for California. "You sent your scratch from the sale of Catapult to Switzerland, right?"

"If I did that, how was I going to start a business?" Jack retorted, trying not to second-guess himself as he looked over the menu. The truth was, Jack had burned through most of his net worth acquiring and funding his company, something no self-respecting Wall Street guy did.

"Look, what about taking care of Jack Davis? You've got to have a margin for error, some cash offshore where your wife and the IRS can't find it. Everybody knows that."

"Great, so I'll have some cash in the bank, but no way to earn a living."

"If running a business is so important to you Jack, fund it with other people's money," Bobby said, waiting for a response from Jack, who instead was looking around for their waiter.

The next day Jack drew up a list of investment bankers, private equity investors, and venture capitalists, and starting at the top, invited

Richard Abderman, his investment banker at Drexel Burnham, to lunch at the Harvard Club.

In the stone-floored dining hall, the waiter's voice echoed as he read them the specials and took their drink orders. Jack filled out the order card for their lunch. "Richard, give me your club number so they don't mark up your lunch. Now that I don't have a big company paying the tab, I've got to conserve every nickel."

"A1312. I'll start with the vichyssoise and follow with the cold poached salmon," Richard said, putting down his menu and looking at Jack for the first time. "Look, Jack, you know we love you. But an IPO for a renewable power company? Hydroelectric projects in China? Why get so crazy? Look right under your nose. We're being inundated by all these guys looking for capital to develop gas-fired cogeneration projects. You could run circles around them. Keep it simple. Put a plan together to do what everyone else is doing, and we'll back you—simple as that."

"Richard, you just said, 'Everyone else.' And you're right—there are a million guys in independent power now and they're all doing—sorry—predictable things like gas plants. In a few years, that market will be a disaster."

"But Jack, look at the size of the deals. They're billion-dollar projects. Close one deal and you're set for life."

"Richard, you're talking about hydrocarbons. In the long run, coal and gas projects are going to have big problems. Renewables won't."

"Jack, in the long run, IBG and YBG."

"I beg your pardon?"

"I'll be gone and you'll be gone. Let someone else worry about the long run."

Jack laughed and shook his head. "Richard, I can't base a business on a quick buck. And don't forget about China—there's lots of upside there. It's going to be New Land's linchpin."

"But that's the most worrisome part," Richard said, ordering some fruit for dessert before he continued. "Hydroelectric projects in China? Look, it's one thing to buy some Chinese equipment to use in America, but I can't imagine how you're going to get money to actually put up projects on PRC soil. There's no law there, Jack."

Richard was no different from the rest of Wall Street—every investor has 99 reasons to say no and only one reason to say yes. "Look, I don't want to push my business plan down your throat," Jack said. "It doesn't sound like you're overly enthused. How was your lunch?"

"Fine, thank you. You're right; China and renewables scare the hell out of me. Just the same, don't go hiring any other investment bankers until you come back and give us the last word."

"Sure, Richard."

He wouldn't say so, but Richard's response meant no, so Jack dropped his plans involving Drexel and focused on getting Dennis Galileo interested. Employed at Morgan Joseph, a smaller Wall Street firm, Dennis couldn't afford to be picky, and with the market down, he was hungry for a deal.

Dennis invited Jack to dinner at the Water Club a few days later, and asked him to bring Lee Fu, the Chinese guy hired to be New Land's chief financial officer. Jack readily agreed, since they would have Dennis's full attention, and he was picking up the tab, too.

After desert, Lee excused himself, leaving Jack and Dennis to talk over cigars and cognac in the grille room.

Dennis waited until Lee was safely out the door. "Jack, I don't like the way he talks."

"What, no marbles in his mouth?"

"I'm not kidding. He sounds like a Chinese cab driver from Brooklyn. And where'd he get those clothes?"

"Sorry to disappoint you, but he's from Flushing. Trust me; Lee's the right guy for the job. What do you think about New Land's business plan?"

"It's not just where he's from, Jack. It's the whole package. The way he mumbles when he speaks, his clothes. He doesn't look me in the eye. I can't sell him."

"Dennis, you're entitled to your opinion, but you're wrong. You're overlooking his fundamentals: he has an MBA from an Ivy League school; a CPA; even a CFA. Best of all, he's Chinese, and speaks the language fluently. I need someone to keep Wuhan Turbine honest. Don't forget, I'm not just buying equipment from them this time around."

The waiter returned with the bill, and Dennis concentrated on filling in the gratuity, not saying anything.

"So what about the business plan?" Jack asked. "What about China?"

"China?" Dennis asked, looking up. "China's 9,000 miles away, Jack. I'm still worried about a guy from Flushing."

Jack admitted to himself he should have given Lee his basic rule as far as haberdashery was concerned—when pitching a deal, sitting for a job interview, or any time there's money on the line—overdress.

Speaking to Lee the next day, Jack spelled things out. "Look, Lee, I should have warned you. Dennis is a stickler on the cosmetics. But he's not the only one—most investment bankers will judge you the same way. So when you talk to these guys, look them in the eye and speak loudly. And any time you're having dinner with someone who's going to raise you millions, you've got to wear a suit. And I mean a real suit. From Bergdorf's, Tripler's, or Paul Stuart's—nowhere else. Shoes? Tie shoes—no loafers, especially the ones with tassels. No police shoes. Know what I mean? Those fake Florsheims with the two inch soles? Forget it. And please—no square toes. So get yourself some clothes; we've got several presentations coming up."

"Jack, I'm sorry. I'll improve, I swear."

That's what Jack loved about Lee. He was the smartest financial person Jack knew—Chinese or otherwise—and epitomized the American dream. Maybe someone had to show him the way the first time, but after that, Lee figured things out in a hurry.

"You don't need to improve. You're terrific just the way you are. But you've got to see these guys coming. Get some clothes, speak confidently, and look them in the eye, that's all."

"I'll take care of it. As long as we're on the subject of tomorrow, what do you want me to say?"

"Just don't forget, whether we're meeting with investment bankers or investors, they get nervous when the CEO answers financial questions. You've got to—I can't do it for you. And another thing—these guys assume since you're the CFO, you're thinking about New Land's numbers 24 hours a day. So memorize every New Land financial fact: unit sales, revenues, costs, earnings, margins, and share prices, for the last two years and the next three at least. And no notes."

Jack couldn't stand the private equity guys, an antipathy developed through years of experience across the table from them as an investment banker. "We love this deal, Jack," they would say; "We'll put up all the money—don't call anyone else." Smelling a closing and a payday, Jack and his staff would work hard to finish up. Then, the day of the closing, he would get hit with the same punch every time: "Jack, we're still prepared to close, but we've learned some things in our due diligence requiring us to price the deal differently. You'll have to reduce your fee 50 percent."

Greed was one thing. But their other mantra—control—would be a deal-breaker for New Land. How many times had Jack heard them say to one of his clients, "Congratulations on building a great business—we'll take it from here." What the hell did these guys know about running a hydroelectric project in China?

Despite showing up in the correct wardrobe, Jack and Lee struck out with the private equity types. China and renewables were not hot topics, and predictably, the few interested in New Land's business plan wanted control from the start.

Jack didn't even try to discuss the deal with the venture capitalists. As bad as private equity investors were, venture capitalists were worse.

Instead, he called Paul Foster, his friend who at the time of the Catapult Energy IPO had headed up institutional sales at DLJ. Jack had always liked Paul, but he lost his judgment when he drank too much, which had been often. After one particularly long lunch, Foster had quit DLJ in a rage over some trivial matter and had subsequently descended down a spiral of firms, finally hitting bottom at Iowa Capital, a tiny boutique run by Mason Swartzwald, a former Marine Corp drill sergeant. Floundering even there, Paul had called Jack one day sounding incoherent. A day later, Jack helped Paul check in to a rehab clinic.

After months of the usual denial and recrimination, followed by the acceptance and abstinence experienced by the lucky ones, Foster was back on the outside, sitting over at Iowa Capital with time on his hands.

"Paul, I've got a proposition for you," Jack said after asking Foster how he was doing and Paul going on like all recently converted AA guys about how he never felt better and was taking it one day at a time. "I need to raise $10 million. How'd you like to take New Land public?"

"Jack, that's not even funny," Paul replied.

"Who's joking?"

"How's Iowa Capital going to take New Land public? This crummy place has no salesmen, no capital, and no research. They can't get arrested, let alone underwrite an IPO."

"Not even if I handed it to them?"

Paul didn't say anything for a moment. "Davis, what are you cooking up? Don't fool around with me, goddammit. If there's a way to catch a break and make some money, you know I'd jump at it. So just tell me. What's your idea?"

Jack explained. "I can't raise money through the private equity guys or the venture capitalists. I need to do an IPO. And for that, I need an investment bank. The institutions will love this deal, Paul. I've already talked to a lot of them. Guys like Royce Morgan have said they'll buy shares in New Land as long as it's publicly traded."

"So you just need an investment bank for its broker dealer license. You'll do all the rest—prepare the book on the company, write the offering documents and sell the deal. Right?"

"Exactly," Jack said. "Mason lets me use you for however long it takes to sell the deal, Iowa Capital underwrites the IPO, and makes a big fee for doing nothing."

"Listen, if you think he'll buy this, I'm game."

Jack and Paul sat down with Mason Swartzwald, who agreed to Jack's proposal but drove a hard bargain. Refusing to take any risk, he demanded a 10 percent underwriting fee, a prepaid retainer of $200,000, firm orders of 200 percent to close the offering, and a prepaid cash deposit to amortize Foster's expenses.

Jack didn't have any choice. He wrote out two checks to Mason, one for the retainer and one for the expenses. It was the middle of the year. They planned to issue the red herring version of the prospectus as soon as the SEC allowed, embark on the road show after that, and close in the winter.

Jack and Paul drew up a list of every institutional investor with whom they had even a remote acquaintance in the money centers of the world, including more than 200 mutual funds, insurance companies, banks, and pension funds, and then shut themselves in Paul's office.

Jack wrote up the pitch, the short sales script they would use over the telephone, consisting of a one-liner describing New Land and a reference to Jack's track record. If they got that far, the best thing was to shut up and get prepared for when the person started asking questions. Paul started dialing accounts. His first calls were people they knew best, like Morgan Royce and others who had been happy shareholders of Catapult Energy. Those guys, representing approximately 20 institutions, would meet with them for sure.

But the balance of the institutions, some they knew only vaguely, needed to be sold. They were being asked to give up the most valuable thing a portfolio manager possessed—time—and they were universally parsimonious. None of them answered their own phones, and their assistants were trained to protect them from unsolicited calls.

And there were protocols to deal with as well. No self-respecting financial institution in the City of London would take a meeting with anything less than several weeks' notice. The rest of the United Kingdom and Europe were much the same.

After a month, Jack and Paul had lined up 20 institutions in Europe. In late September, leaving Lee to address the SEC's comments on the initial draft of the New Land registration statement, they arrived at the British Airways terminal at JFK for the overnight flight to London.

㊉ ㊉ ㊉

Jack made his first mistake outside of Heathrow Airport in London. After the eight-hour red-eye flight, he was still groggy as they passed through customs. Out of habit, Jack flagged a taxi. Ten minutes later, mired in rush hour traffic, watching the meter spin and wasting pounds, not dollars, Jack kicked himself—they could have taken the underground for half the price. If he didn't close the New Land IPO, he'd be broke for sure.

Their first appointment was at Foreign and Colonial, one of the oldest trust companies in the world. Geoffrey Roakes, the F&C portfolio manager handling micro cap equities for North America, had been a shareholder in Catapult Energy. If Geoffrey liked the deal, he would refer them to a dozen other institutions in the City. Assuming Geoffrey bought in, they would too.

Entering a glass-clad building near the Tower of London, Jack and Paul rode the lift to the twentieth floor where they were greeted by a group of three prim but sleek girls hidden behind a reception desk. One of the receptionists checked them off her roster and escorted them down a long hallway punctuated by thick fruitwood doors leading to pitch rooms. As Jack and Paul walked by, the startled occupants paused and looked up distractedly, then turned back to the grind of extolling their companies.

The receptionist deposited them in a conference room appointed with antique sideboards and crystal wall sconces, a boardroom table complete with multiple electronic features, and the obligatory plate of cookies placed in the meeting rooms of all U.K. financial institutions.

Before she was out the door with their coffee orders, Paul snatched the Saran Wrap off the cookies and downed three of them. Like most recovering alcoholics, he needed a sugar fix; they'd been in the taxi for over an hour and he was making up for lost time.

A minute later, Geoffrey and his assistant Christine knocked and entered, Geoffrey attired in a suit with wide chalky pin stripes and Christine in a designer dress and heels. Armed with the New Land packages Paul had sent them, Geoffrey and Christine were all business. Their materials were lined and dog eared, indicating they had prepared for the meeting—a very good sign.

"Right," Geoffrey started. The meeting was handed over to Paul, who as Jack's investment banker made brief introductions.

Afterwards, Jack began with the pitch one-liner: "The New Land Power Corporation is a renewable-based power generating company building several new hydroelectric projects in the People's Republic of China," then dropped in a summary of the company's financial performance to maintain Geoffrey's interest, segued to a description of the company's basic business, summarized the provenance and credentials of the management, addressed competition and valuation issues, thanked Geoffrey and Christine for their attention, and asked if they had any questions.

His presentation had lasted 30 minutes. They were right on schedule.

Being British and experienced, Geoffrey and Christine had politely sat through Jack's presentation with only a modicum of interruption.

Now, they consulted their notes and began their questions. Once done with the fundamentals, they turned to the important items.

"How much money do you have in the company?" Geoffrey asked.

"About $8 million," Jack answered.

That seemed good enough.

"How about family relationships? Any wives or girlfriends on the payroll?"

"No," Jack said, "but my brother Whitey is a senior manager." When there was a silent pause, Jack added, "As he was at Catapult Energy, you'll recall."

"How about salaries, stock options, and so forth?" Geoffrey said.

Jack listed the salaries of the senior management, and indicated that bonuses and the stock option plan were controlled by the compensation committee of the company's board of directors, a group of independent members of the board.

"How many members of management are on the board?" Christine asked.

"Only me."

The one-on-one lasted almost 90 minutes, an ideal length. Geoffrey appeared to be nearing the bottom of his list. "What are your other business interests? Do we get 100 percent of your time?"

"Absolutely, other than the small amount of attention I must give Davis Brothers."

"What haven't we asked that we should have?"

This was the time Jack could show Geoffrey he was honest without it costing him anything. "Most renewables need subsidies," Jack said. "Eliminate the subsidies and, whether it's a wind farm or a solar panel, the economics don't work."

"Are there any renewable power projects that don't require subsidies?" Geoffrey asked.

"Hydroelectric projects in China," Jack answered.

"So you're saying on a worldwide basis, as far as you know, renewable power projects need subsidies, with the exception of hydroelectric power projects in China?" Christine asked.

"Yes."

"And why are hydroelectric projects in China so blessed?" Geoffrey asked.

"Hydroelectric projects are 75 percent civil works—concrete and men—and there's no other country in the world where those ingredients are so inexpensive."

Geoffrey scribbled a few more notes, and then looked up at Jack as Christine kept writing. "So while Catapult Energy bought Chinese equipment and used it in the United States, now that they're changing the law in the PRC, you're switching gears, going to China to build and own hydroelectric projects there," he said.

Jack nodded his head.

"Very promising. I guess there's only one last thing. If I were going to invest, I'd want the issuance to be in preferred stock. That way, outside investors receive a liquidation preference vis à vis your founder's common," Geoffrey said, watching Jack as he spoke.

"Well, that's a little draconian," Jack said before he could catch himself. If the company were sold or liquidated, the other shareholders would have the right to receive all their money back plus a preferred return before Jack got a dime. But it really didn't matter, did it? As long as the company was a success and was sold at a high enough premium, everyone would be happy, including Jack. And sitting in the comfort of Foreign and Colonial's drawing room, that was the only outcome Jack could envisage.

"Do we have an issue, then?" Geoffrey said, looking like it indeed would be if Jack answered in the affirmative.

"No; all right by me," Jack said.

"Right," Geoffrey said. He turned to Paul and gave him an order to buy 20 percent of the offering, and promised a list of other potential City buyers. The New Land IPO closed two months later.

The day the closing was announced in the papers, Richard Abderman called. "All right, all right, I was wrong. I guess there really are investors interested in China and renewables. But you made it look easy, Jack."

"Who said this stuff is supposed to be hard?"

Chapter 14

The New World Power

Leaving the New Land closing dinner, the first thing Jack did was fill his Suburban with gas; he hadn't purchased more than a quarter tank at a time for a year. After a miserable Christmas the year before, he looked forward to the holidays; surely, the company's IPO would smooth things over with Alicia.

On the Taconic Parkway going north, deer stood under bare trees in the moonlight as he guided the Suburban along the road. An hour outside of the city, the first snow cover appeared. By the time he got to Lime Rock, there was a foot on the ground, and more coming down.

He pulled the car up the long driveway to the big white main house, waded through the snow to the porch, unlocked the side entrance and went into the kitchen for the first time since the IPO road show began six weeks earlier. Inside, it was very cold. Alex, the Polish woodcutter who lived in the cottage with his wife, Helena, had fires going in the kitchen, the parlors, and the bedrooms to save fuel.

His four sons and his bird dog Ritchie were waiting for him, asleep in the parlor. He woke them, they put their arms around him, and all hugged in a big pile on the cold chestnut floor while Ritchie tried to lick their faces. After they talked about the boys' school and the football games he didn't get a chance to see, Jack took them up to the third floor, tucked them in, and read them two chapters from *Kidnapped*. A half hour later, they said their prayers and went to bed. Before turning in, he sat in their room another 20 minutes, watching the fire's orange light flicker across their faces.

Alicia was in bed, and didn't stir. She hated the cold. Jack got in on his side. His feet were ice cold. Tomorrow, he would tell her about the closing, and that everything was going to be all right again, just like before. They would decorate the main house and put up a Christmas tree, hang wreaths on the doors of the main house and the outbuildings, and big ones on the pagoda and Virginio's sculpture at the farm. The next day he would go with Ritchie and the older boys shooting birds in the snow in the early morning, and take everyone skiing afterward.

In the morning, he spoke to Alicia as she lay in bed, assuring her that New Land was their ticket back to the high life, but reminding her that in order to meet in China with General Manager Wang before year end, he needed to leave for Hong Kong the day after Christmas.

She just looked at him without saying anything, turned over, and crawled back under the covers.

㊅ ㊅ ㊅

The Cathay Pacific 747 banked for its final turn into Kai Tak. Normally, Jack looked forward to going to Hong Kong with Kalin. But this time would be different. She had insisted on bringing her husband Mickey along.

The first time Jack had met him, Mickey had been sitting down and didn't get up when Kalin introduced them. Jack figured out Mickey's behavior seeing him standing next to his wife later. The guy was only about five feet four inches tall; Kalin towered over him. Mickey wore platform shoes, sported a different set of colored contact lenses every day, and tinted the tips of his hair blond.

Mickey had somehow brainwashed Kalin into thinking because he had once been a helicopter weatherman for a local television news station and produced a few television commercials that he was the next best thing to Hollywood royalty. Mickey could be helpful to New Land, Kalin had said, trying to convince Jack. General Manager Wang liked attention, and Mickey could make sure he got it—this was Mickey's métier. They would need to stage state dinners, organize trips, and issue press releases all over China, Hong Kong, and the rest of the world. They needed her husband; Jack would see.

For Kalin, Jack went along with it, but he had no use for the guy. It wasn't his appearance. Mickey treated Kalin like a servant. Worse yet, she accepted it. Kalin was a totally different person around Mickey, playing her devoted Chinese wife role. Whatever Mickey said was brilliant, and whatever she suggested was stupid.

When Jack arrived at the Mandarin Oriental on Wednesday evening, Mickey and Kalin met him in the lobby. Mickey's lens color for the day was purple; his hair was not only freshly frosted but slightly teased and curled. He always wore a pin in his jacket lapel; the current edition was a PRC flag. When Jack learned Mickey and Kalin had already been in Hong Kong for several days on his tab, and Kalin saw Jack mentally counting the dollars, she explained they needed extra time to prepare. Jack just looked at her, she stared back at him dutifully, and then looked away, as Mickey stood next to her, clueless, watching himself in the mirror behind the concierge's desk.

The bellman dropped Jack's luggage off in his room while the three of them went to the Captain's Bar and squeezed into one of the red leather booths. Jack ordered a Mai Tai; Kalin ordered some chrysanthemum tea and so did Mickey. When the tea came, the waiter had begun to pour Kalin's tea when Mickey stopped him to inspect the tea. Announcing the brew needed fresher chrysanthemum buds, Mickey sent it back. Jack made up his mind on the spot: he would never visit the Captain's Bar with Mickey again.

At dinner later that evening, Kalin relayed an announcement from Wuhan: Since deregulating the electric power sector in China was momentous and companies leading the way deserved prominence, the name of their partner-to-be was no longer Wuhan Turbine, but Chang Jiang Energy Corporation, and General Manager Wang was henceforth to be known as President Wang. The way she said it, Jack found himself wondering who she worked for, him or Wang.

President Wang and CJEC had obtained the development rights to five hydroelectric projects on the Min River in Fujian province, Kalin told Jack. There was also the possibility of investing in existing, operating projects if Jack had the capital. For the right deal, President Wang would offer an exclusive foreign joint venture partnership to New Land. When Jack asked what constituted the right deal, Kalin begged off.

Jack knew Kalin better than that. She always got her facts straight, especially when a critical deal was concerned. When she was noncommittal, it simply meant she didn't want to be the messenger. Jack looked her in the eye, but she refused to look back.

As Jack ordered another glass of chardonnay and lit a cigar, Mickey reviewed the trip. Beginning with a meeting the following day with Fong and Fong, President Wang's Hong Kong lawyers, and a dinner that evening, the following day they would travel to Fujian, review the sites on the Min, and return to Hong Kong a week later. After ticking off everything on Mickey's checklist, Jack paid the bill and they took the elevator to Kalin and Mickey's floor.

Kalin wasn't finished briefing Jack, so he got off the elevator with her and Mickey and walked down the corridor toward their room. As she rattled off her checklist of details about the following day, Mickey walked ahead of them and opened the door to their room. It was a suite with a water view on the corner of the building. Jack looked through the door into the rooms that cost a fortune, then back at Kalin, who studied the floor.

He shrugged. Now was not the time. He said goodnight to Kalin, turned back down the hall to the elevator, took it down to his room—a conventional single on the third floor, rear street side—and went to bed.

Waking up automatically at five o'clock even though he was in a new time zone on the other side of the world, Jack dressed in a tee shirt and shorts, took the elevator down to the empty lobby and exited to the streets of the city to jog his daily five miles. Even in the predawn hours of the day, Hong Kong's narrow thoroughfares were jammed with vehicles, bicycles, and people. Running up the steps of the walkway crossing over Connaught Road and back down the other side toward the ferry dock, he swerved out of the way of dock workers carrying bamboo cages of live poultry as he ran along the quay by Victoria Harbor, inhaled the briny air of the surging sea, checked his watch, and returned to the hotel.

Back in his room, Jack showered and shaved, and dressed in a suit. In Hong Kong, business people wore suits, like in New York and London. Especially the lawyers. Hong Kong's lawyers were as stiff as any in the world, even more British than their counterparts in the City of London.

Mickey had procured a Mercedes from the hotel for the day, even though Fong and Fong was in the Hong Kong and Shanghai Bank building less than two blocks away. When Jack pointed out to Mickey they could have walked and spared the expense, Mickey said walking was inadvisable—they couldn't make a proper entrance.

As the liveried driver whisked them down Connaught Road, Jack looked out at the city and the harbor rushing by. It had been less than two years since he and Kalin had last been in Hong Kong, but it was already difficult to recognize the cityscape they had left behind. While the urban areas west of Central still retained the same crumbling concrete buildings draped with laundry, the downtown financial district was dominated by new glass-and-granite-sheathed structures reaching up to the Peak through the morning fog. Even across the harbor in Kowloon, half-built skyscrapers crept up their bamboo scaffolds like stone growths on garden stakes.

After waiting five minutes on the thirtieth floor of the HBSC building in a Fong and Fong boardroom, Felix Fong made his entrance. The Hong Kong barrister was exactly what Jack had imagined: short and trim, English grammatically perfect, yet almost impossible to understand, given his clipped staccato-like Hong Kong delivery of the language. Attired in a worsted wool three-piece suit, Felix's vest sported a gold watch chain, and the cuffs of his shirt were monogrammed.

In the midst of exchanging pleasantries, the door opened again and the management contingent from the newly minted Chang Jiang Energy Corporation arrived. Felix, Kalin, and Mickey jumped up and scurried to the door, greeting the man now to be addressed as President Wang and fawning over him until his coat was removed and he and Deputy Manager Wen were seated at the table. Jensen Chen skulked in a moment later without uttering a word and found a seat in a corner.

As they waited a few minutes for the tea to arrive, President Wang sat silently, his expression indicating his vision ended an inch beyond the surface of his eyes, while Mickey looked at his reflection in the window. The tea service arrived, and another five minutes went by while everyone got involved with the tea. Finally, President Wang had his tea just the way he liked it, everyone else had theirs, and the meeting began.

Even though Felix was speaking in English, his clipped, Hong Kong accent made him incomprehensible to Jack. Kalin leaned close, speaking to Jack where necessary to make sure he understood. President Wang remained motionless. Mickey kept critiquing himself in the window. Bluish smoke collected in Jensen Chen's corner as he chain-smoked. Deputy Manager Wen, who didn't understand English, sipped his tea and stared down at the conference table in silence.

Felix turned his attention to the draft letter of intent, indicating that there were several sections his client could not agree to, at which point Jensen Chen came alive and nodded his head. Felix had prepared a new agreement which President Wang was prepared to sign. When he had finished speaking, Felix took a Mount Blanc fountain pen out of his suit jacket pocket and placed it on the table over the ready stack of draft documents.

It was Jack's turn. He spoke slowly and carefully in complete sentences, stopping after one or two thoughts to allow Kalin to translate every word. He looked directly at President Wang when he spoke, as if Wang were the only person in the room, and expressed his desire to invest with President Wang in the five hydroelectric projects on the Min River in Fujian. He finished in two minutes.

President Wang began his dogmatic response, rambling on for at least half an hour, never pausing so Kalin could translate for Jack. Finally, when Jack had listened long enough to show proper respect to President Wang, the man still yammering away, Jack turned and spoke directly to Felix, sparing Kalin from the embarrassment of interrupting President Wang.

"How are you proposing to change the letter of intent?" Jack asked.

President Wang hesitated and turned and looked at Felix. Felix looked down at the table for a moment. When President Wang remained silent, Felix realized Wang wasn't going to be offended or continue, recovered his composure and looked back at Jack. "Your draft includes an exclusive for all five projects on the Min, and rights to co-invest with CJEC in operating projects. My client has been approached by many internationally recognized power companies larger and more financially powerful than New Land. Out of personal friendship, President Wang will agree to a joint venture, but he wishes to give you an exclusive for only one project on the Min."

"No way," Jack answered. "My competitors may be large organizations, but all that means is they'll take forever to close a deal. President Wang needs money now, and I'm ready to sign papers and start spending, but the economics for one project don't make any sense—the five projects must be done together."

President Wang leaned toward Felix. They put their heads together and began speaking in whispered Chinese. After a few moments Jensen Chen joined them. They kept talking. Kalin said nothing, letting Jack know whatever they were talking about was not worth translating.

They talked and talked and talked some more. Kalin remained stoic, so Jack just sat there looking back and forth at the Chinese men chattering at each other. Finally, Felix composed himself and said, "President Wang doesn't think you have enough money to build all five Min projects."

"I'll be happy to show him New Land's bank balance," Jack said.

"Mr. Davis, your language in the letter of intent locks up my client together with all of his Min River hydroelectric projects. Once we sign that document, you've got control of everything in Fujian, but you could take too much time to come up with the cash." Felix Fong took off his glasses and began polishing them with a paisley handkerchief extracted from the breast pocket of his suit.

Before Jack could respond, Jensen Chen started speaking loudly in Chinese to President Wang. Felix Fong joined in and the three of them harangued one another for another 15 minutes. Kalin didn't translate.

Their chattering ended, and Felix turned to Jack. "My client is very nervous about the money, but out of his profound friendship for you, he may be willing to give you four of the five Min projects. He is reserving the fifth one for Jensen Chen to put in CJEC's Hong Kong subsidiary. I'm sure you can understand."

Jack had them on the ropes. There was no reason to budge, but a shoe still had to drop. President Wang needed money and he hadn't addressed the financial specifics of the joint venture yet. "All five Min projects or no deal," Jack said to Kalin. "Jensen doesn't know anything about the hydroelectric business. The project would be wasted. We need all five to make this deal on the Min work." That didn't take long. Why couldn't they respond the same way?

Kalin translated. Felix and Jensen started chattering again before President Wang brought them up short, speaking loudly, the veins in his neck pulled tight and his brown face turning dark red.

After President Wang had finished, Felix translated. "President Wang doesn't care what the letter of intent says," Felix said. "You can have all five Min projects and you can co-invest in more. He doesn't care whether you are his partner, or it's one of your competitors, frankly. He just cares about the money. He doesn't know whether you have the money or how long it will take you to invest, so he will use a test to decide who will be his partner."

"Which is?" Jack asked. Now they were getting somewhere.

"President Wang requires a certified check for $1 million in 10 days," Felix said. "The balance of the funds for the first project can be paid on installments as it is constructed."

"Absolutely not," Mickey chimed in from out of nowhere, standing up at the table so as to temporarily elevate himself above the others. "Do you take us for a bunch of fools?"

Jack couldn't believe it. He looked over at Mickey, who kept talking. "We've spent hours on this deal. It can't be changed."

Felix Fong translated Mickey's outburst in hushed tones to President Wang, who, looking temporarily glazed and deflated, turned to Jack, hoping for an explanation.

Mickey was starting to say more when Jack stood up himself, reached over Kalin and grabbed Mickey's arm. Mickey looked over at Jack; Kalin's head was down, her eyes staring a hole through the table. Jack kept holding on to Mickey's arm, backed up from his chair, and excusing himself and asking for a short break, dragged Mickey outside. Kalin started to get up and follow them but Jack motioned to her to stay with the others.

When they had gone out into the hallway and Jack had shut the doors to the conference room, he turned and said to Mickey, "I ought to punch those purple contact lenses through the back of your head. From now on, just shut up and handle the press releases."

Not waiting for a response, Jack turned and reentered the room, closing the door behind him.

"Sorry, Felix, I had to make sure Mickey was on schedule regarding our travel arrangements tomorrow. Where were we?"

Everyone in the room remained quiet. Kalin looked at Jack, an expression on her face he had never seen before.

Finally, Felix reiterated, "President Wang's condition for the acceptance of your proposal is the receipt of a certified check for $1 million in 10 days. On a Citibank account."

"I'd just be giving him the money on blind faith," Jack said. "We can't possibly prepare and execute all the documents in 10 days."

"That is correct, I'm afraid. So you are refusing?"

"Why a Citibank account?"

"It is the American bank enjoying the most prestige in China," Felix said in the most clipped language he had issued yet.

"Kalin, may I speak with you for a moment outside?" Jack asked, getting up from the table, helping Kalin out of her seat and heading for the door.

Outside in the hallway, Mickey was gone. Closing the door behind them, Jack turned to Kalin and said in a low voice, "Look, I'm sorry about what happened, but what Mickey did was out of line."

"I know," she said, shaken. "Sometimes he wants to help and it comes out wrong."

He ignored her comment—nothing could dignify Mickey's performance—and moved on. "I don't mind the $1 million. It just confirms my thinking."

"Which is?"

"President Wang's broke. CJEC has no cash. None. For $1 million, he'll give us everything not nailed down."

"But Jack, how can you prevent him from just taking your money and leaving you high and dry?"

"That's where Mickey is going to earn that expensive suite he booked for himself," Jack said to Kalin as she averted her eyes. "I want him to plaster press releases about the joint venture in every newspaper in China—in Wuhan, Beijing, even Hong Kong and Singapore. Getting a bunch of dollars from an American company is a big deal in China—think about all the articles in Wuhan a few years ago when we bought the turbines. Once the central government knows about our deal, President Wang will be a hero, but he'll be joined at the hip with us. He won't be able to back out."

Kalin was quiet. "It's a lot of money. What will you tell your board of directors?"

"I'll schedule a meeting the day I get back. They'll debate the pros and cons, but in the end I think they'll see the deal in its proper light."

"Which is?"

"For $1 million in cash, we're CJEC's exclusive joint venture partner for all of their hydroelectric projects anywhere, not just in Fujian but all over China and the rest of the world. It's the cheapest corporate takeover I've ever heard of."

"Do you really think President Wang will agree to all that for $1 million?"

"What do you think?" Jack asked.

Kalin stood quietly in the hallway, her long black hair framing her sad eyes as she stared past him at the wall. Then she turned and looked Jack in the eye, nodding her head up and down as she opened the door to go back into the conference room.

Back inside, Jack told the group at the table he would agree to President Wang's condition, but at a price. President Wang hemmed and hawed but in the end, he agreed. It was just as Jack had thought—Wang had no choice.

After taking two hours for lunch and continuing to negotiate the details of the deal through the remainder of the day, President Wang began clamoring for dinner at half past five o'clock. Jack shook his head. His new partner was extremely predictable as far as one thing was

concerned—food. Three full meals every day, with all three sessions—
breakfast, lunch, and dinner—timed as precisely as a train schedule and
lasting hours, the amount of food consumed staggering. If Jack ate like
his Chinese counterpart, he would be as big as a horse.

Mickey arranged for the signing dinner to take place in a private
room at Man Wah, on the top floor of the Mandarin Oriental and one
of the best Cantonese restaurants in the city. The space was elegant,
with walls papered in red satin, trimmed with dark ebony, and high-
lighted by large framed Oriental tapestries. When Jack walked in,
everyone one else was already seated in the conversation pit in one
corner of the room. Felix, Kalin, and Mickey were studying the documents, while President Wang and the others were arguing over what
dishes to order from the menu.

A runner from the hotel's business center arrived with 20 copies of
the joint venture agreement, 10 in Chinese and 10 more in English.
The joint venture had to file papers in Beijing and at the provincial
and local government levels in Fujian; since most Chinese governmen-
tal authorities thought copied papers were fraudulent, originals were
required.

After inspecting the papers to confirm they were in order, Felix
handed his Mount Blanc pen to his client, who began signing the
multiple signature pages. Mickey snapped his fingers at the black
sheathed waitresses, who scurried around pouring *baiju* for everyone.
In a few minutes they were done—the joint venture between New
Land and CJEC was official. Everyone around the room raised their
shot glasses, President Wang said a few words in a toast and exclaimed,
"*Gambei*," and they tossed down the firewater. Deputy Manager Wen
snapped pictures, and a waitress took a group photo.

Kalin held Jack's arm as he started to leave the conversation pit on
his way over to the dinner table. "President Wang has a surprise for
you," she said.

President Wang bent over rooting around in a paper bag in a corner
of the room, stood up and presented Jack with a clear Plexiglas cube
containing a duplicate of Wuhan's famous orange man-monkey. "What
do I do now?" Jack asked Kalin, holding the cube and feeling silly.

"Look at the monkey and admire it for a moment, so he knows it
means a lot to you," Mickey said without being asked. "Then put it

down on the table, and still looking straight into his eyes, shake his hand with both of yours to show him affection and respect. We have something nice for you to give him in return."

President Wang seemed satisfied with Jack's performance. The waitresses hurried around the room replenishing everyone's glasses with more *baiju.* Jack looked over his shoulder at Mickey and Kalin. Mickey handed him a small box wrapped in a bow. Jack looked at the box for a moment and Mickey said, "It's all right. It's a New Land lapel pin."

Jack presented the box to President Wang, who put it down without opening it—he didn't want to embarrass Jack by opening it and viewing the gift with any disappointment, so he would open it later in private. He took Jack's hand in his, thanking him in Chinese, and lifted his shot glass a second time. They all raised their glasses. "*Gambei,*" President Wang said again, emptying his and turning it upside down to signify he had drank it all while keeping his eye on Jack, who did the same thing, the firewater scalding his throat.

They sat down to dinner. According to *feng shue,* the seat at the rear of the 10-person dining table was the special one since it looked south toward the door, and was accordingly assigned to President Wang. Everyone ate Chinese food except for Mickey, who ordered filet mignon.

A few hours later, full of food and *baiju,* the group slowly staggered out to the elevator and down to the lobby. After saying their goodbyes to President Wang and the others, Jack, Kalin, and Mickey stood in the lobby reviewing the next day's events.

"Thanks for covering me with that gift, guys. I didn't know New Land even had lapel pins," Jack said.

He instantly regretted his statement when Mickey responded, "There's a lot of things we do to support you behind the scenes."

Jack changed the subject. "Well, the pomp and circumstance is nice, but President Wang doesn't really want a partner, just money. That really makes me nervous."

"That's why we've got to follow everything he does carefully," Kalin said. "No Chinese walls this time."

"Yes, but we don't just have a Chinese wall problem with President Wang," Jack said. "We've got a Chinatown problem too."

"What do you mean, a Chinatown problem?" Mickey asked.

"It's what the movie *Chinatown* was all about," Jack said to Mickey, with no intention of elaborating.

"You mean the movie with Jack Nicholson?" Mickey asked.

"Yes."

"Wait a minute" said Mickey, "Chinatown's not about China."

Jack sighed. "Listen to me, Mickey. It is. Or the Chinese people who live in Chinatown, if you require me to be more precise."

"Look, I'm from the industry—I know what the movie's about. It's a detective movie that takes place in Los Angeles. It's not about Chinatown."

"It's all about Chinatown."

"Why do you say that, Jack?" Kalin asked, trying to referee between the two of them as best she could. "I've seen the movie, too."

"Remember the last scene of the movie? Remember Jake Gittes, the detective character Jack Nicholson played, standing there in the street, looking down the block to where he knows the love of his life, Faye Dunaway, is slumped dead in her convertible? Remember what he said?"

"No," Mickey and Kalin both answered together.

"'As little as possible.' That's what he said. When he was a cop on the beat in Chinatown, his sergeant told him to do as little as possible because as a *laowai* there was no way he was ever going to make sense of what the Chinese were up to. That's what the movie was about, and that's what this deal will be all about if we're not careful."

"Are you saying we should do as little as possible?" Kalin asked.

"No. That's the advice Jake Gittes's sergeant gave him. But Jake was a *laowai* just like me, and he couldn't help himself any more than I can. Jake Gittes tried to do more, with disastrous results. I just hope things go better for me."

Chapter 15

A Date with a Monkey

The Land Rovers Mickey organized for the Fujian trip waited down the block from the Mandarin Oriental. Their Mainland drivers, cruder and darker than the hotel's uniformed counterparts, stood next to the cars, smoking and talking on their cell phones. Standing in front of a Hong Kong police department sign warning "No Hawking," one of the drivers, wearing a counterfeit sweatshirt inscribed *University of Southern California Trojans* with a picture of a husky-like dog below the label, issued a prolonged guttural sound and spit on the sidewalk.

As the cars left Hong Kong and made their way to the border, Jack suspected Mickey had intentionally rigged the transportation arrangements. During the first hour of their trip, Jack's driver would not fasten his seatbelt, his warning signal blaring every three seconds. And even though it was sweltering inside the car, the guy made no attempt to adjust the air conditioning—it didn't appear he knew how.

At the Guangdong border police station, a long line of Chinese, looking as if they had been there for days, waited to obtain clearance to exit the Mainland for Hong Kong. PRC army cadets barely out of high school stood at attention in their olive green army coats, watching over everything as if they could actually contribute.

They parked the Land Rovers behind a line of buses standing with their engines running. Kalin got out, and together with Deputy Manager Wen, took their papers inside the station, reemerging 10 minutes later accompanied by a man in military garb. Older, his uniform was blue, not green—a customs official. He and Kalin walked together over to the car, and she asked Jack and Mickey to get out. The customs official looked them over, speaking to Kalin as he stared at them, looking at their passport pictures and staring back at their faces. He said something to Kalin, handed her their papers, and walked back inside the station.

"What's his problem?" Jack asked.

"You and Mickey are *laowai*, and they don't see a lot of you here. They like an excuse to look powerful. Besides, if we stayed inside, there would be no way for him to get his cash," Kalin said.

"You bribed him?" Jack asked.

She gave Jack a look admonishing him for being so naïve.

They got back into the Land Rovers and drove through the crossing gate into the Mainland, turning up the highway on their way to the Guangzhou Airport. It looked like any other road Jack had taken in Guangdong, a dusty, two-lane thoroughfare, choked with bicycles, carts, people, and animals.

If Mickey had intended to ruin Jack's trip, his plans backfired. Mickey became ill, griping profusely about the dust, the bumps in the road, and the driver's breath.

After 20 minutes, the driver turned sharply left on a dirt path through a construction site and up an incline. They shot out onto a vast, empty highway with three lanes going in each direction, separated by a median planted with flowers. The road's concrete was still white from lack of use, the drains and curbstones were still being installed, and there was no signage.

The cars gathered speed and breezed down the road past the Guangdong neighborhoods. They would be at the airport in 10 minutes—the old way through the city would have taken hours.

"Kalin, what's this road we're on?" Jack asked.

"It's a toll road. Some foreigners got a concession from the provincial government to build it," she answered. "Americans, I think."

"Are we breaking the law? There's no one out here but us."

"No, it's open."

"Then why aren't more people using it?"

"They would have to pay."

"How much is the toll?"

"Two quoi."

"Two renminbi? That's 20 U.S. cents. People will crawl through that city traffic for an extra hour to save two quoi?"

"They're Chinese, Jack."

"Penny wise and pound foolish."

"What?"

"My new Chinese mantra."

Flying from Guangzhou to Fuzhou, the capital of Fujian province, they took a taxi to the Fuzhou train station and boarded the train for the eight-hour ride up the Min River valley to Nanping, the closest city to Wuhan Turbine's projects.

Every seat on the train was full. The first-class car was chaotic; Jack wondered what second class was like. Passengers wandered the aisles, dragging bags of food, wares, animals, and clothing, and bumping everyone's heads as they passed. Everyone smoked, and when they weren't smoking, they were eating and talking at the same time.

Mickey got worse.

In Nanping the next morning, the country air was warm and tropical. After breakfast, Jack and Kalin went with the CJEC men upstream 10 miles to Xiayang, the village at the site of the first hydroelectric project the joint venture planned to build. Jack wore a tee shirt, jeans, and work boots, and packed his fly rod.

It was the dry season, the CJEC men told him as they drove along the Min—the *Minjiang,* they called it—a good time to be on the river. They laughed and joked about what it was like during the rainy season. Jack liked the men. Their faces brown from being outdoors in the sun, their hands were strong, their fingers gnarled and scarred, fingernails broken and split and filled with oil and dirt. Laughing and smiling, their teeth appeared generally intact, but brittle and yellow-brown around the edges.

At Xiayang, the middle fork of the *Minjiang* ran green and clear through a series of rapids. The water was low. Men stood on the riverstone banks alongside the rapids throwing fishing lines from bamboo poles into the shallows below. Farther downstream, others in flat-bottom boats cast lines into the deeper pools below the rapids. Each boat required two men: the one in front did the fishing and the one in the rear propelled the boat using a bamboo pole.

Beyond them across the river, a rambling, green mountain loomed up above the south shore of the *Minjiang*. Where the river swept along-side the village, there was a bund, a high rock wall, and deck, which served as a marina and market area. Farther upriver where Wuhan Turbine had established the project's base camp, whole families of workers were erecting long lines of tents using blue construction tarpaulins, ropes, and flotsam and jetsam hauled out of the river—old boards, bamboo, corrugated metal and even broken bits of Styrofoam. Women tended a fire underneath a three-foot-high iron vessel that served as the rice cooker for the makeshift camp.

"I like this part of the business the best," Jack said to Kalin as they got out of the car and stood on the bank surveying the scene.

"What part?"

"You know; being outside in the sun, no phones, with people doing their work."

"The sun feels good," Kalin said, taking off her sunglasses to let the sunshine bath her face. Jack had noticed that many Chinese women avoided the sun, but not Kalin; she always looked healthy. Birds chirped from perches in the jungle-like bush off-river; the *Minjiang's* rapids ruffled in the background.

"Where are you going?" she called after Jack as he headed down a narrow path snaking along the riverbank.

"Let's see what those guys are catching," he replied over his shoulder, eyeing the fishermen on the river where the rapids formed.

"Crayfish," he said to Kalin when she caught up with him along the shore. He scanned the air for signs of a hatch, but didn't see many bugs; nothing was coming off the water.

"Crayfish?"

"Bait. That's what's on their lines. And they're casting below the rapids, back in the pools, going down deep. Probably after carp."

"How do you know?"

"Bait's heavy. It sinks to where the carp are, sucking stuff off the bottom."

"Are carp good?"

"What do you think?" Jack said as he assembled his fly rod, selected a sinking line, and tied on a yellow-white streamer. "The good fish are up in the moving water, where there's more oxygen and the food is clean. That's why they taste better."

"How come the carp aren't there, too?"

"Too much work fighting the current—that's why they're so fat and oily." As the village men looked up at him but kept fishing, Jack stripped 30 feet of line off his reel onto the bank. "I like this place; the water looks good," he said, absorbing the earthy smell of the *Minjiang*. "Not perfect, but clean enough." He cast across the rapids, dropping the sinking line toward the end of the rapids so the current would carry the streamer down the food lane at the top of the shallows. "Let's see if I'm right," he said as he repeated his cast.

On his second attempt, he felt a nudge, but couldn't react in time. On the fifth cast, something hit. He set the hook, reeling rapidly to keep the line taut as he waded across the gravelly bank to get to the fish quickly. Laying his rod down and pulling some ferns at the water's edge, he pulled the silvery fish out of the water and set it in the ferns. "Here, take a look," he said to Kalin who had come up behind him and was looking over his shoulder. "I have no idea what it is—if I had to guess I'd say a herring running up from the sea—but it looks a lot more appetizing than a carp."

Kalin didn't say anything. Jack glanced up at her, and saw she was continuing to look down the river at the village fishermen. They had stopped fishing and were watching Jack and Kalin.

"Do me a favor, take them the fish," Jack said as he bundled the fish up in the ferns and handed it to her.

Kalin nodded, and walked down the river bank to the men. Stoic as she approached, the men broke out in smiles as she presented them with the silvery fish, chatted with Kalin for a minute, and returned to their work.

"What'd they say?" Jack asked when Kalin got back.

"I have no idea—Chinese in Fujian sounds to me like a foreign language."

After spending the remainder of the morning reviewing the technical details of the Xiayang project, Jack used the afternoon to study the project's construction plans, procurement schedules, and payment arrangements. Returning to the guest house in Nanping, he and Kalin had a light dinner and some cold beer and went to bed. Mickey didn't make an appearance.

During the following days, Jack and Kalin inspected the four sites they would construct once Xiayang was completed, bumping and slogging down everything from blacktop highways to muddy paths as the countryside of northwestern Fujian tumbled by. Every mile or so, Jack saw brick kilns and drying sheds producing piles of bricks and cement blocks, while along the highways, men were busy building stone curbs, retaining walls and drains, digging China out of a century of calamity.

㊄　㊄　㊄

Arriving after midnight in Hong Kong a week later, exhausted from the physical, mental, and environmental onslaught of rural China, they checked back into the Mandarin Oriental, and were asleep in their rooms five minutes later.

The next morning, Kalin was excited when she met Jack for breakfast.

"I've got great news," she said. "Last week after we signed the letter of intent, Mickey contacted the U.S. Chamber of Commerce to tell them about the deal. Yesterday they called back. They've organized a big U.S. trade mission to China next week, and we're invited. Hazel Johnson, the Secretary of Energy, and a group of U.S. electric power executives are coming to Beijing for a big ceremony at the Great Hall of the People. Everyone who's doing power projects in the PRC will sign their joint venture agreements in front of Johnson and China's Minister of Electric Power. You and President Wang will be celebrities."

"That's killing two birds with one stone," Jack said.

"What do you mean?"

"President Wang's receipt of our $1 million will be out in the light of day—we'll make it part of the signing ceremony. He'll be forced to go through with the joint venture," Jack said, feeling strong, like he did the first day in Wuhan when he had realized Wuhan Turbine's products were going to make Catapult Energy millions.

水 水 水

He caught the afternoon Cathay Pacific flight out of Hong Kong to New York. Less than a week later, having briefed his board of directors on the deal, Jack was back, the $1 million certified Citibank check in his briefcase.

The next morning, Jack, Kalin, and Mickey met at Felix Fong's to work on the definitive documentation for the deal.

"Do you have the check?" Felix asked.

Jack produced the unsigned check without a word. Felix held the paper up to the light. "I can't believe it. President Wang will be ecstatic."

"What can't you believe?" Jack asked Felix.

Felix had produced a magnifying glass and was using it to analyze the check. "I can't believe an American businessman is actually doing this. Most of you are so conservative."

"I wonder about that myself," Jack said under his breath, looking out the window.

His examination complete, Felix put his magnifying glass away and turned to Jack and Kalin. "I would appreciate it if you would let me to keep this overnight," Felix said.

"What on earth for?" asked Jack.

"They examine checks for forgery here in Hong Kong," Kalin explained.

Jack shrugged. "Fine with me, I guess. I just need it back by the ceremony in Beijing."

"Beijing? But surely, you will give the check to President Wang tomorrow," Felix said, his teethed bared in an obsequious grin.

"I'm afraid not. President Wang gets his check when we sign the papers at the ceremony in Beijing."

Felix pouted. "President Wang expects to get the check tomorrow. The joint venture papers are very complex. They could take days to finalize."

"Look, I've done my part," Jack said. "You better get to work. Finish the documents, and President Wang gets his check when we sign at the ceremony."

"So is that your board's rule, Mr. Davis?"

"It's the Golden Rule, Felix. You know about the Golden Rule, right?"

"It's from the Bible, isn't it?"

"That's a different one. Mine's the Wall Street version: 'He who has the gold rules.'"

㊌ ㊌ ㊌

Blue sky gave way to a murky shroud hanging over the land as their plane from Guangzhou coasted onto the Beijing runway. The sun was up there, but once on the ground, the only way for Jack to see it was to look straight up. The smell of burning household garbage assaulted him.

Squeezed into their taxi—no one had told the taxi company *laowai* existed, or they didn't care—Kalin told the driver to take them to China World, the big new convention hotel located in the middle of Beijing's Central Business District, where they would meet President Wang, who was flying in from Wuhan.

Of course, Wang wasn't staying at China World. Like most Mainland government heavyweights, he preferred to stay at government guest houses, the ones with the Mah Jong tables in every room, so he and Felix Fong had booked rooms at the Bamboo Garden, a state-owned hotel tucked off a Beijing hutong that had previously been the quadrangle home of a nobleman in the Qing Dynasty.

China World was part of a complex taking up several city blocks. The hotel lobby was the size of a football field. Kalin stood in a long line to check them in. When she had organized their rooms, they left their luggage with the bellman, walked through the public rooms, and took a look around. While the hotel's owners had bribed enough officials to get their five stars, China World was garish and cheap. The lobby swarmed with people, bags lay in piles near the door, and customers stood in line arguing with the desk clerks. Half the visitors had just come to gawk at the place.

They walked around a corner and Jack changed his mind—China World would be given a reprieve. The hotel had a cigar bar. Not just a secluded nook, but a posh, two-story affair connected by a spiral staircase. While not a commercial idea, Jack was happy Chinese developers had gone to great lengths to present Chinese consumers with what they imagined Western people demanded. The place was packed, mainly with *laowai*. Girls in sequined dresses served drinks and cigars. Clouds of cigar smoke rolled toward the ceiling, to be inhaled by an industrial-strength recycling system.

Camped out in the cigar bar, Jack ordered a Cohiba and a bottle of Pinot Noir. Mickey ordered a Punch cigar, saying he had always wanted to smoke one because he had heard they were Winston Churchill's favorite.

Felix Fong arrived and briefed them on the next day's events. The signing ceremony would be at the Great Hall of the People, right down the road. Mr. Li Peng, the premier of China, would give the keynote remarks shortly after nine o'clock, followed by the Minister of Electric Power, who would address China's progress in the power sector. Hazel Johnson, the U.S. Secretary of Energy, would speak next. Finally, Chinese and American representatives of 26 Sino-foreign joint ventures would march up to the dais and execute their formal agreements.

The total amount of deals approached $10 billion. The joint venture between New Land and CJEC was the only hydroelectric deal, and the smallest; all of the other projects were coal-fired power plants. Being the smallest deal on the stage had never bothered Jack. At the moment, he was more concerned about President Wang. No one had seen him or even spoken to him. He should have been there by now to hear the details about the next day's events. But he had always demonstrated a casual attitude toward punctuality. And why not? Everything in President Wang's world revolved around him.

Tomorrow would be different. Wang didn't have any clue—he probably thought he was still going to be the star of the show. His advisors, who knew better, weren't going to tell their client he would be an insignificant part of the ceremony: 25 other joint ventures, all larger than his, would come first. But somebody should. The ceremony meant more to President Wang than the $1 million check.

Early the following morning, Jack started the day with a visit to the China World gym, did his exercises, went outside and ran five miles, showered and dressed in a suit, and took a taxi up the street to the Great Hall. Arriving before eight o'clock, he grabbed a row of seats for his group.

Eight-thirty. The Great Hall was filling up rapidly. Still no President Wang. They were in trouble. A few minutes before nine o'clock, Jack looked around nervously; none of his group had showed up—not President Wang, not even Kalin and Mickey.

The Great Hall was a mass of people. Photographers hovered, aiming their cameras at targets in the crowd. Teams of newscasters and cameramen with technicians holding lights and screens set up in the aisles, blocking traffic while makeup people retouched the faces of the newscasters. Phalanxes of bodyguards squired important-looking groups of officials up to the dais. Most of the Chinese ministers were already seated, looking like the lumps of coal they burned in their power plants, all in dark suits, their hair dyed jet black and their eyes shifting to and fro, red-ringed from last night's *baiju*.

Up at the front of the Great Hall, the crowd issued a hushed gasp— Secretary Johnson had arrived.

A striking woman of mixed racial descent, Secretary Hazel Johnson was statuesque, towering over her shorter, older Chinese counterparts. But it was her demeanor that set her apart. While the Lumps of Coal sat quietly, saying and doing as little as possible, Johnson worked the crowd and appeared to enjoy doing so, moving around the front of the Great Hall, meeting and greeting and selling the Chinese people on doing business with Americans.

The crowd surged around her as Johnson moved slowly toward the dais, stopping every few moments to speak to an official or business executive. It was after nine o'clock. Jack kept looking toward the rear of the Great Hall. Still no President Wang.

The dignitaries reached their places on the dais, the guests took their seats and a spokesman announced that the ceremonies would begin momentarily. Jack turned to look one last time at the rear of the Great Hall.

At last, there was President Wang, a little, wizened old man, standing in the doorway quivering, holding a Plexiglas case half as tall as himself containing a model of the orange man-monkey. Kalin and Mickey stood partially hidden behind him. People streamed by, jostling and knocking President Wang; it looked like either Wang or the man-monkey would crash to the floor momentarily.

Jack looked over at Hazel Johnson. She was still talking to someone on the floor of the Great Hall, and not yet on the stage. He made his decision. Sprinting from where their group had been sitting, he pushed through people down the aisle leading toward the rear of the building where President Wang was standing. Reaching President Wang and ignoring Kalin and Mickey, Jack grabbed the box containing the man-monkey with one arm and President Wang with the other, and turning back toward the front of the Great Hall, dragged the old man through the tide of humanity toward Secretary Johnson.

Pushing and shoving up the aisle, Jack towed President Wang toward his destination, leaving jostled, angry guests in their wake, until they arrived at the ring of officials, admirers, cameramen, and photographers surrounding Hazel Johnson. As they approached, Jack saw her warily spy them out of the corner of her eye; from far away, he had not realized how heavily her face was made up. He pushed through the last protective ring of people. Standing eye to eye with a flummoxed Secretary Johnson, he turned and, putting the man-monkey in President Wang's two flimsy hands, pushed him up to her.

The top of President Wang's shiny head came up to the middle of Hazel Johnson's chest. Wang came alive and began yammering in Chinese. In front of Johnson's black, surprised eyes, Wang offered up the cube containing the orange man-monkey in his outstretched hands. As President Wang rattled on, Jack spoke in English, explaining the man-monkey's provenance to the stunned secretary. As Jack's words began getting through and Ms. Johnson realized neither Jack nor Wang intended to do her bodily harm, the politician in her grasped the significance of the public relations moment at the same time the media's cameramen and photographers saw what was happening and began pointing their lenses toward the group, filming and clicking away.

Everyone else had already taken their seats. Standing up in front of a throng of people, President Wang, Secretary Johnson, and Jack were the entertainment of the moment; thousands of eyes trained on the spectacle, and every camera in the house followed. Show business instincts intact, President Wang and Secretary Johnson eyed each other over the plastic top of the man-monkey's home, turning and posing for pictures.

The moment was over as quickly as it began. Secretary Johnson's handlers guided her up to her spot on the dais together with her gift, and Jack led President Wang through the chattering, appreciative crowd to their seats.

The events began. Felix and Mickey were silent. So was Kalin, a tight smile across her face. President Wang was blissful. Photographers were still taking pictures of him. For one persistent follower, Wang raised his hand and waved. One of the Lumps of Coal began reciting how many new megawatts of power projects would be completed in the fiscal year. Having survived the speeches, an hour later the audience watched as 26 joint venture teams tramped up to the dais and signed their deals into PRC law. Jack pushed his pen across 20 copies of their agreement. After the ceremony, he handed President Wang his check. Wang barely looked at it. After delivering Secretary Johnson, Jack could have shown up empty-handed and Wang still would have signed.

The next morning, featured on the front page of both *China Daily* and the *South China Morning Post* were stories accompanied by color photographs of President Wang of CJEC handing his orange man-monkey to a grateful, dazzling Secretary Hazel Johnson.

Chapter 16

Once Burned, Twice Stupid

On the strength of the deal with CJEC, New Land raised $20 million of additional equity to help pay for the Xiayang project in early 1989, solidifying the company's balance sheet. The problem was the income statement.

Jack and his management team were building a worldwide renewable business for the New Land shareholders. But Richard Abderman had been right—renewable technology was flaky, and electricity from renewables remained expensive. The company's wind farms suffered through a bad winter. Storms pushed maintenance costs higher than projected, and downtime lowered power production. Solar sales ran below expectations as well. Technology improvements were slower than anticipated and the cost of solar-generated electricity remained too high to attract customers.

The company wasn't making enough money. The stock price, once heading upward in the aftermath of the IPO, stalled. Surveying New Land's numbers with Lee, Jack saw difficulty ahead. The first quarter would be profitable because the wind farms in California and Grizzly's hydroelectric projects both performed best in the spring. But as far as the second and third quarters, when the water in Michigan slowed to a trickle, the projected numbers looked grim. Unless something miraculous happened in China, New Land would lose money for the year.

In China, the Xiayang project's construction was on schedule, and due to be completed in the summer of the following year. The issue was cash. President Wang kept calling and asking for money. The New Land engineers and accountants couldn't get a scrap of paper as to where it was all going, but that didn't prevent Wang from asking for more every week, as if New Land was nothing but his personal checkbook.

The engineers at CJEC estimated Xiayang would cost $50 million to build, so New Land's one-third stake meant a financial obligation of $16 million. So far, New Land had already spent $10 million—the initial check for $1 million; another $4 million Jack had wired CJEC when Wang contacted him frantic for funds soon after the Hong Kong signing ceremony; and $5 million more right after they signed the definitive joint venture agreements in Beijing. Jack was determined not to send another dollar Chinaside until he got satisfactory documentation.

But even if things went well at Xiayang, it couldn't solve New Land's earnings problem in the current fiscal year. There was no way for New Land to earn profits from a project under construction. The only way for the company to generate incremental profits in the hydroelectric sector in China was to buy into an operating project and book earnings based on its profitability.

The good news was, the best deals in the hydroelectric world were right there in China. If the company could acquire a good operating project on the cheap, it could pay a little for a lot of earnings. And those earnings could solve New Land's profitability problems for the rest of the year.

The bad news is he had to cut a deal with President Wang.

Kalin called. "I'm afraid to ask—do you have President Wang's funding request?" she asked.

"Yes. Subject to certain conditions."

"Thank God. The man is calling me three times a day. Mickey is walking around the house screaming."

"Mickey's screaming? What for?"

"He says we can't treat our joint venture partners this way."

"So we're supposed to just let them steal from us? Do me a favor, tell Metternich to leave the diplomacy at the door and concentrate on his press releases."

"What conditions?" Kalin asked ignoring Jack's comment.

"Listen to me. I'm going to do President Wang an enormous favor. I'll send him the cash he needs, but based on three conditions: first, he sends the construction drawdown schedule our guys have requested; second, we go over there and complete a site inspection; and third, Wang provides me with an investment opportunity—a good operating hydroelectric project I can buy into cheap. Immediately."

"I understand the first two items—that's all I've been telling him for three weeks. What's the deal on the investment project?"

Jack explained how New Land needed to buy earnings. China was their only chance.

"Did you hear me?" Jack asked her when the phone went quiet.

"Yes, why?"

"You're not saying anything."

"You said it was important—I'm taking notes."

Kalin normally didn't take notes, even for important things, but for some reason this time was different. She kept writing, asking Jack several times to repeat himself until she was sure she knew exactly what he wanted. Finally satisfied, she rang off to make arrangements for the trip.

寀　寀　寀

Jack and Kalin arrived in Hong Kong the last week in May, and flew out the next day for Wuhan.

The usual bowls of fruit were on the table in President Wang's apartment, and President's Wang's wife again served tea in her stoic demeanor. But behind President Wang's desk, things had changed: large, framed copies of the *China Daily* and *South China Morning Post* articles were prominently displayed.

And President Wang acted like a different man. Sipping his tea, he was animated and smiling, fussing over Kalin and urging his wife to make sure Kalin had enough tea. He seemed relaxed around Jack.

"President Wang seems like a different guy," Jack said to Kalin.

"Do you see those photographs over his desk?" Kalin said. "Those and the $10 million you've given him are why. He has no more doubts about you. To him, you are a *dalaban*."

"What's a *dalaban*?"

"You don't really have a person like a *dalaban* in America. A *dalaban* is an all-important person, a big boss, the guy in charge whether with just a group of people, a family, a big company or even the government— the city, the province, whatever."

"So does that mean you're going to laugh at my jokes now?"

"You laugh, but you have no idea how important that event with Secretary Johnson was to President Wang," Kalin responded. "He didn't gain prestige just because he got his picture in the paper with the U.S. Secretary of Energy. It was also due to his association with you, his American partner. Not only are you a rich guy, but you have extensive political connections. That really surprised President Wang. He had no idea you were such an influential person, but it became obvious when he saw firsthand how close you were with Secretary Johnson. And the best thing is, all his contemporaries in the central government know it now too, and are envious of his relationship with you."

"You're kidding me, right? I don't know Hazel Johnson. You know that."

"Of course I do," Kalin said, "but that's not what President Wang thinks. Let him believe what he wants."

Jack didn't like to hear Kalin saying such things. He asked what was keeping Deputy Manager Wen, who usually joined them. Kalin told him Wen was not invited; investments did not concern him.

Jensen Chen arrived, and he and President Wang regaled them with a description of a thermal power project deal they were completing in Shenzhen. Jack nodded his head and smiled and tried to play along. All of President Wang's topics had the same theme—money. Not making money, or earning money—just having it, possessing it. He was obsessed with it, and who had it and who didn't. Looking around the ramshackle apartment, it was difficult to conceive how such a man could live there.

Finally, President Wang stopped his monologue. Jack saw the opening and steered the conversation to his primary topic.

"Kalin, please tell President Wang and Jensen I am delighted to learn about all the investment opportunities at their disposal. And while we really need to spend some time later discussing our project on the

Minjiang, I want to speak about something new. I would like to invest in a profitable, operating hydroelectric project."

Kalin translated as President Wang and Jensen listened, acting as if they had never before considered this subject. They asked Kalin several questions.

After about five minutes, they finished speaking and Kalin turned to Jack. "They asked how much you have to invest," she said.

"This is where you warn me to be more Chinese, right, Kalin?"

"I won't tell them exactly what you say, but give me a range, just so I know myself," she said.

Jack did some calculations in his head. "Between what New Land has on hand, and what we could raise in another secondary round of equity and some project debt financing, I would say $50 million."

"$50 million. For projects in China? That's a lot of money," Kalin whispered.

"Why are you whispering?" Jack asked Kalin, looking at her face, satin-finished with a sheen of perspiration.

"It's a habit when I'm speaking about money, I guess," Kalin said, resuming a normal tone. "It's a lot of money," she repeated.

She turned back to President Wang and Jensen and spoke to them in Chinese a while longer.

President Wang took Jensen to a corner and spoke to him for a minute. When they were finished talking, they came back to the table and sat down.

Jensen did the talking in his cryptic English. "No problem for operating projects. But must have earnings this year, yes?"

Jack nodded.

"Project in Philippines number one for you. Earnings in U.S. dollars," Jensen said through his crooked smoky grin, holding his thumbs up.

"I'm all ears," Jack said.

㊌　㊌　㊌

With Kalin translating, President Wang began to describe the Baguio hydroelectric project. After five minutes, Jack could see Jensen was right. The project was a perfect solution for New Land.

The Baguio project was located outside of Baguio, a large city north of Manila on the Philippines' main island of Luzon, and had been built by the U.S. Army Corps of Engineers in the 1930s when the Philippines had been a Commonwealth of the United States. The civil works of the project consisted of an earth-filled dam containing two water tunnels, or penstocks, that conveyed water from the reservoir down approximately five hundred feet to the powerhouse at the base of the dam.

For the past few decades, while the Baguio project had been owned by Napacor, the Philippine national electric monopoly, its maintenance had been severely neglected. The penstocks, which needed periodic cleaning to prevent debris from clogging up the water flow to the powerhouse below, were ignored, and their water flows had slowed to a trickle. Capable of generating one hundred megawatts of capacity when the water crashing down the penstocks was unimpeded, the Baguio project was now only generating a small fraction of its designed capability.

Napacor solicited international bids for a 30-year BOT proposal. The lowest proposal to rebuild the Baguio project won the right to rebuild and own it for 30 years, after which it would be transferred back to Napacor. Bids were tendered by specifying the price per kilowatt hour Napacor would be required to pay for the project's electricity; payment would be in U.S. dollars.

A dozen of the world's largest and most prestigious construction firms bid on the Baguio Project, as did CJEC, the mystery bidder.

The big firms—Bechtel, Morrison Knudson, Harza—all tendered proposals assuming a total reconstruction of the Baguio project. Baguio's old penstocks, powerhouse, and dam would be torn down and rebuilt from scratch; the proposals averaged $300 million each.

CJEC's bid was counterintuitive, and brilliant. Instead of expensive new equipment, cheap Chinese labor and ingenuity would be used. CJEC would scour the debris out of the penstocks by firing water cannon up from the bottom of the tunnels and rinsing the pipes of 50 years of debris. Once the penstocks were cleansed, and substations and switchgear replaced, the Baguio project would work like new.

President Wang, a proud look on his face, told Jack the CJEC team had outfitted a seagoing barge in Wuhan with water cannon similar to those used on fireboats in the New York City harbor, and had floated it across the sea and up the river to Baguio several months ago. An army of Wuhan coolie laborers and electrical components were their only other costs.

Then all they had to do was substantially underbid the international competition—not so low as to be disqualified—and find the right officials to bribe when credential issues inevitably arose about a Chinese company no one had ever heard about.

"Who does President Wang know in Manila?" Jack asked Kalin.

"Are you kidding?" she said. "All the business there is Chinese, just like Singapore."

"You learn something new every day. So am I going to have Filipino partners?"

Kalin didn't say anything, and President Wang continued before Jack could press for an answer.

CJEC's winning bid was $175 million, but their total cost was only $5 million. The balance, or $170 million, would be paid out to the owners of the project over time, in the form of the difference in the tariff they would receive over 30 years compared to their cost per kilowatt hour of operating the project. CJEC would be selling electricity to Napacor for $.06, but it was costing them less than $.01 to make it. And they had the right to do so for 30 years. The Baguio project was a gold mine.

"The story sounds great," Jack said to Kalin, "but I'd be surprised if the water cannon idea works—probably too good to be true."

"You're a little late," Kalin said. "It's no story. The project's finished. The water cannon worked like a charm." She looked at Jack with the strange expression he had first seen on her face after he chastised Mickey for his outburst at Felix Fong's.

"You're kidding me." Jack looked at the back of Kalin's head as she turned away. She had already known all about the Baguio project, that much was obvious. His antenna should have been raised, but at the moment, Jack was too intoxicated by the Baguio deal. He looked back at Kalin. She just stared at him, her face blank. Distracted, he wondered why she wasn't happier. "It's done already? And everything works? President Wang's right. I've got to see this for myself. It sounds like the hydro deal of the century."

Jensen confirmed Baguio had been successfully completed. All that remained were the tag ends of the construction punch list. The project was already generating electricity.

When Jack asked what it took to close the deal, President Wang laughed and shook his hand back and forth, saying Jack had to see the project for himself. Then they could talk about terms. They should fly to Manila as soon as possible. Wang was getting hungry. Did they have any more questions before dinner?

"Only one thing comes to mind," Jack said, as much to Kalin as to President Wang. "What does he need me for? Why share Baguio with anyone?"

㊌   ㊌   ㊌

Before dinner, there had been no discussion of the Xiayang project. But President Wang had offered Jack the opportunity to be a partner in the Baguio project. Now he wanted payback. After dinner was served and several rounds of *baiju* consumed, President Wang finally dropped the other shoe. Or rather, Deputy Manager Wen did. President Wang would not mar his relationship with Jack, his new *dalaban* friend—Wen could do that.

Citing intense construction activity at the Xiayang site, Deputy Wen told Jack he would need the entire balance of $6 million New Land still owed for its joint venture interest. As Wen spoke in Chinese and Kalin translated, Jack looked across the table at President Wang and Jensen Chen. They were practically falling asleep. The subject of obtaining capital for the Xiayang project was a nonevent for them. The *laowai* would just send more.

Jack turned back to Deputy Manager Wen. When Wen finished, Jack responded by laughing and saying, "So I do something crazy like write out a certified check for $1 million on a handshake, and then wire another $9 million with no construction plans or permits in place, and now you guys think you've got a sucker for life, is that it?"

Deputy Manager Wen, who couldn't comprehend a word Jack said but understood his tone, just sat there saying nothing, his bug eyes blinking rapidly. President Wang acted like he hadn't heard Jack's response and didn't care. Wen would clean up the mess. Jensen remained busy lighting his tenth cigarette.

"Kalin, please offer my apologies to Deputy Manager Wen. I don't mean to sound sarcastic—I'm sure it's wasted on him in any event—but I have yet to see a construction drawdown schedule or any other normal paperwork for the Xiayang project. These guys don't think I'm going to fund all the rest of our joint venture activities the same way I invested the initial $10 million for Xiayang, do they?"

Her silence was his answer.

Jack asked Kalin to take notes to help convey what he was about to say was serious information. He started to speak in a loud voice; Wang and Chen began to pay attention. "Please inform our joint venture partners if they want the balance of New Land's cash for the Xiayang project, we need to prosecute the remainder of the construction according to international standards. For starters, I have no idea what has happened to the $10 million New Land has already invested. After the $10 million of expenditures are documented and I have a complete drawdown schedule for the balance of the project and submitted all the papers to my engineers—and they have visited the site and corroborated the information first-hand—I will consider sending the remainder of the $16 million. In the meantime, I would also like to know what my other partners in the Xiayang project, starting with CJEC, have invested so far."

Reading from her notes, Kalin recounted this information to the group. Deputy Manager Wen was taking notes as well. When Jack finished and Kalin had translated, there was general silence around the table. Jack could see President Wang recalculating. This *laowai* was a typical Western idiot. Having him as his partner was going to be easy. Right? So what was all this commotion?

Kalin sat in her chair quietly.

Jack had hit a nerve. Jensen Chen was their weak link, Jack figured, so he turned to him, laughing to appear casual. "You're in the financial community, Jensen. You know my situation. I run a public company; I've got shareholders and auditors. I broke a few rules in the early going to help out, but going forward, we've got to be professional. It'll be good for everyone involved. If we want to get in the habit of accessing the international capital markets for funding, we might as well start now."

Jensen took the bait. After some unctuous commentary indicating he understood the rigors of the capital markets as well, he turned to President Wang and Deputy Manager Wen. The three of them spoke for several minutes. Deputy Manager Wen turned to Kalin and Jack. He said they agreed to give Jack a full set of construction drawdown documents showing the expenditure of the Xiayang project's funds to date.

Now they were getting somewhere. If they agreed to this, they couldn't say no to Jack's next request.

Deputy Manager Wen started to describe the details of the construction drawdown paperwork.

Jack interrupted him. "We can sort that out in due course. But I've still got to have a solid grasp of the project's current, physical status. As they say in America: a picture's worth a thousand words. Before we fly to the Philippines, Kalin and I would like to go up to Xiayang to see the project for ourselves. That would go a long way toward making me feel more comfortable about spending the balance of the money."

As Kalin interpreted, the three Chinese men bent their heads together and devolved deep into conversation, droning back and forth for at least 30 minutes. Jack asked for a cigar, lit it, and leaned back in his chair, waiting them out. Kalin was lost in her own thoughts.

When conversation across the table concluded, the CJEC group told Kalin halfheartedly not to worry about going all the way up to Nanping. "They're giving you the 'Just trust us' message," she said to Jack.

Jack tried to smile, but really didn't feel like it. "Please tell them sorry; I want to go fishing on the *Minjiang* one more time."

㊌ ㊌ ㊌

Jack and Kalin slept for most of the morning flight from Guangzhou to Fuzhou. Once on the ground, they met a group of CJEC managers and engineers and boarded the train up the *Minjiang* valley to Nanping.

Jack woke early the next day; it was still dark outside. The meeting with the CJEC officials wouldn't begin until noon, an eternity to spend in his grungy hotel room.

He walked down the hall to the room where Kalin was bunked and knocked on the door. "Kalin, are you up?" Hearing a muffled response, Jack spoke through the door. "Please tell the driver to meet me in the lobby restaurant. I want to go up the river to Xiayang."

Somewhat to Jack's surprise, Kalin showed up downstairs, still half asleep, saying she couldn't leave him alone with the driver. The driver appeared about 10 minutes later, smelling like an ashtray. Jack and Kalin finished their breakfast, packed some tea in a plastic thermos, and the three of them headed north up the highway in the Land Cruiser, bouncing up and down on the same bumpy, muddy roads to Xiayang they had traveled months earlier when they visited the region for the first time.

At first, everything looked the same. Jack saw the same brick kilns every other mile. The hills above the *Minjiang* were covered with the same bushy tea gardens. But the landscape betrayed small differences too. The rainy season had started. The sky, blue for their first visit, was now filled with swollen rain clouds. The river, once green and clear, was gnarly. The innocent, storybook life on the riverbank had vanished.

It was still too dark to see anything at the site. Jack had hoped it would be swarming with men and machines—clear evidence of a major construction effort, and validation of his investment. But he would have to wait an hour to find out.

Kalin directed the driver to pull in at the head of the path leading from the bund down to the river. When they parked, she indicated to the driver smoking his fifth cigarette he should stay put. Jack got out, removed his rod case, and started down the muddy slope to where he remembered the rapids had been. Kalin stayed in the car.

Walking down the construction road behind the temporary coffer dam, Jack got to the riverbank and evaluated the water. Maybe he was pushing his luck. He had liked the feeling he had before on the *Minjiang,* and didn't want to ruin it. The river was running too high, at least in the rapids. The fish would tire themselves out there, and they couldn't see anything anyway. The air was humid and moist—bad for aquatic bugs, like trying to fly fish in Mississippi.

He looked downstream of the rapids; the backwater pools were calm. He tied on a wooly bugger, and thought about adding a weight to the line. He didn't want to push his luck, go too far down, where the carp lived. The last thing he wanted to do was tangle with them.

He added a light shot weight to the line, stripped 20 feet out of his reel, and cast down to the bottom of the rapids. Weighted down, the wooly bugger sunk below the surface, bounced along the stone bottom of the shallows, and drifted into the upper reaches of the pool below.

Jack let the wooly bugger sink down for a few seconds, and then repeated his cast. He didn't want it to go too deep.

When it sank down in the upstream reaches of the pool, Jack stripped the line in, pulled the slack off the water as he clocked his rod back and forth once, and threw the line and the wooly bugger back onto the water at the bottom of the rapids.

He turned his head and gazed over along the back of the coffer dam. Men were starting to trickle through the fog out to the construction site. He tried to count them. It was just men, though; men were dirt cheap in China; where was all the equipment? Where had President Wang spent Jack's money?

He was watching the men pounding their picks against the ledge when he felt the tug on the line. He looked back at the pool and realized the wooly bugger had drifted too far—back toward the dead water and into the depths—and he had snagged something. Probably a stump or a tire.

It moved. A carp. Just his luck. It was the last thing he had wanted to happen. Now he would lose the wooly bugger, and maybe his tippet. He hadn't brought spare tippet. He raised the rod skyward, reeling in the line. The surface of the water in the back of the pool swirled. *Jesus.* The lunking fish was enormous. Jack jerked the tip of the rod again— he just wanted to pull the wooly bugger free before the goddamn carp swallowed it—and heard his rod snap.

Back at the car a few minutes later, he didn't tell Kalin.

Standing on the bund as daylight broke an hour later, Jack craned his neck, scanning the project site.

His initial cursory glances gave him a few false seconds of comfort. Underneath the sleeping green mountain, the river was partially dammed up. A ramshackle iron cofferdam stretched out to the midpoint of the river, creating a moonscape of barren, craggy river bottom between where Jack stood on the north bank and the water channel flowing on the far side of the *Minjiang*. A rickety construction crane tottered over the cofferdam. The sight of the crane was comforting. At least there was equipment there. He looked across the river. There were men out there, and they were working. Material sat mobilized in piles on the riverbank: thousands of bags of cement, and tons of rebar. A long line of laborers trudged down along the trail between the bund and the river bed, the ones going down shouldering tools and those coming up loaded down with rocks to be crushed for concrete production.

But as Jack looked closer, he could see the problem. The crane was the sole piece of heavy equipment at the site—there were no excavators or front end loaders or cement mixers to be seen anywhere. The men scattered out across the exposed river bed were as ragtag a throng as Jack had ever seen at a construction site. Those armed with picks and shovels were the lucky ones—many were working with their bare hands. The scene reminded Jack of a clip from the movie *Moses*—a thousand frail-looking wretches wrapped in thongs and turbans braving the wrath of a body of water looming over their heads. How much did the spindly crane cost? It couldn't have been much. And even an army of these men—and there was a least a battalion down in the rocky plain of the riverbed—couldn't have set CJEC back much. Where the hell was the rest of his $10 million?

Jack turned back away from the river and confronted another surprise. On the banks of the *Minjiang* upstream of the village, at the depot where the train tracks ran north and west of Xiayang and the small camp of migrant workers had previously erected tents, was a major refugee encampment—Jack estimated there were at least 2,000 people camped there.

"Jesus Christ," Jack said to Kalin as he returned to the car, "where did all these people come from?"

"Wuhan."

"That must have been expensive, right? Why not just hire locals?"

Jack waited but Kalin didn't answer. What the hell was wrong with her? This had been going on for the better part of a week.

"Look, Kalin, are you all right? I'm sorry if you're feeling tired, but I'm getting alarmed. This activity looks staged, like these people were swept off the street corners of Wuhan yesterday and deposited here to pick up rocks. You've got to snap out of it and help me get some answers."

Back at the hotel in Nanping for breakfast, they corralled Deputy Manager Wen. Jack explained they had been to the project site and could see from a simple visual survey little of Jack's money had been spent there. Where was the rest of it?

Jack pressed Deputy Manager Wen for information. Wen grudgingly gave up data: an admission here; a number there. But as he slowly divulged the facts, Jack's fears hardened. He couldn't quantify how much of the money was unaccounted for, but his guess was at least $5 million, and probably closer to $6 million.

Jack and Kalin left a day later, taking the train back to Fuzhou, flying to Hong Kong and checking into the Mandarin Oriental at midnight. He needed to get Pete and Whitey to Xiayang immediately. He tried to rationalize the situation, but it was difficult. Money was missing. Maybe it was only $3 million, not $6 million. Did that make it any better?

In any event, how could he make another investment with the same guys in the Philippines? On the other hand, if he didn't buy into the Baguio project, New Land's stock price would probably collapse by autumn.

Once, he was just burned, but twice would make him stupid.

Jack and Kalin left Hong Kong for Manila the next day. Several hours later, bumping down through the swollen, gray rain clouds hanging over the Manila Bay, the city appeared as many had described it— the armpit of the world. Everywhere he looked, Jack could see nothing but slums. The entire city looked like one big corrugated metal roof.

Exiting Philippine immigration for the taxi line, the heat hit them with the force of a hammer. At 95 degrees Fahrenheit, with humidity also 95 percent, Manila was a sweltering inferno. Jack was drenched with sweat in less than a minute. Kalin's face was covered with a permanent sheen of perspiration, rivulets gathering on her temples and cutting shallow streams down the makeup on her cheeks.

They stayed at the Manila Hotel. Grand, but threadbare, its best days faded away along with General MacArthur, the building's rickety infrastructure was sagging under the weight of age, its antiquated ventilation and air conditioning system no match for the oppressive heat.

That night, Jack and Kalin had a drink on the rooftop terrace bar overlooking the Manila Bay. The floor of the terrace was covered with ancient green indoor-outdoor carpeting. No longer properly glued down, the carpet's edges curled up in the air, threatening to trip the few customers that braved a crossing.

"So, are you going to tell me what's been bothering you, or do I still get the silent treatment?" Jack asked Kalin as they sat down.

She made a big deal of pulling her chair leg out of a carpet hole and avoided answering him.

Jack lit a cigar, surveyed the view headed west, and changed the subject. "What's that village out in the middle of the harbor? Is it on an island?"

Kalin had no idea, but to avoid any other subject of conversation, she flagged a waiter and asked. Bending over to hear her request, his brow furrowed, the waiter straightened up and peered to the west.

His face cleared, he smiled and explained. "That no island. Just Pontoon City."

"Pontoon City? You mean those lights we see out there are all just boats?" Jack asked. "There must be a quarter million of them."

水　　水　　水

Jack woke up late. The long trip over from Hong Kong, going into the dark against the time zones, had been tiring, but Kalin's demeanor was the real culprit. She hadn't been herself for weeks. The last few days had been the worst. Quiet, even sullen, Kalin wouldn't speak unless spoken to, and seemed angry with Jack. Whenever he had tried to ask what was bothering her, it had only made things worse.

At breakfast, Kalin told Jack they would meet with President Wang outside Manila. She arranged for a driver, and they left the hotel a little before noon. He had no idea where they were going; Kalin did, but she wasn't saying. He held his tongue; he didn't want a confrontation early in the day if he could help it.

Making no attempt to cheer up, over the next two hours of the car trip Kalin was polite but otherwise glued to the window, saying nothing and looking out toward Manila Bay as they headed north. They kept heading up around the curve of the Bay for the next 30 miles, foghorns blaring warnings to travelers foolish enough to venture out on the scummy sea.

Gradually, the city's smoggy environs slid away behind them. The air became clearer, but remained steamy. The sun was bright and hot. Off to Kalin's side, Jack could see Pontoon City. It was indeed an island, just a landless one, made up of tens of thousands of water craft: sampans and junks, barges and rafts, all lashed together in a patchwork connected by ropes and gangways, garbage lapping around the perimeter.

The highway devolved into a two lane mishmash of people, vehicles, animals, and debris. There were no traffic lights. Jitneys, the chopped-up, garishly decorated American buses that had survived the war and been left behind by the armed forces, stopped and started at every corner and roadside stand, dropping people off and letting others jump on. Passengers swarmed over the open air vehicles, choosing to stand inside jammed between people and baggage or cling outside to the roof or side rails.

After another hour of tedious negotiation by their driver through scores of hamlets, with Manila Bay still hard to the left, they veered off west down a sandy, pockmarked lane. In a quarter mile, the driver slowed and pulled in beside a rambling, wood frame house. Ringed by a ramshackle array of porches and balconies, the dwelling perched on stilts at the edge of the shore of Manila Bay. Down where the stilts stood in the sand, muddy waves lapped at the garbage-strewn beach.

"Whose house is this?" Jack asked as he got out of the car.

Kalin's face registered no surprise at her surroundings; she knew where she was. "President Wang's," said Kalin. Grimfaced and saying nothing more, she guided Jack up the stairs of the house and into the front door.

Once inside, Jack found himself in a cramped, moldy living room crammed with dark green velour-covered furniture with the plastic wrappings still on. A large wicker fan spun in the center of the ceiling, but had no effect on the swamp-like air hanging in the room like a fog. Noise from people talking and pots and pans clanking streamed out of the entryway to the rooms beyond.

With Kalin leading the way, Jack passed through the gloomy living room and entered the true living area of the house, a collection of large rooms along the sea side of the dwelling. Exposed to the breeze coming off Manila Bay, in normal circumstances the rooms should have been more comfortable. But with no wind, and the activity in the kitchen off to Jack's left, it was as if he had stumbled into the kitchen of a Chinese restaurant in Kowloon.

Off to the lee side of the room, an older woman stirred two huge, steaming aluminum pots on a stove while a girl ladled shrimp from one of the cauldrons onto white plastic platters. The girl was Chinese, but appeared to Jack to have a little Filipino in her. She looked over at Jack as a cloud of steam from the shrimp cauldron wafted up and bathed her face.

"Who's the girl?" Jack whispered to Kalin.

"She's President Wang's, too," said Kalin.

Seaside, two dozen men gathered around two large round tables covered with grimy plastic table cloths, plates of food, dishes, teacups, utensils, and wads of spent paper towels. Eating and talking and yelling and laughing, most of the men were minimally dressed in white tee shirts—the younger men wore the regular kind with sleeves, the older ones sleeveless tees—and pants or boxer shorts.

Everyone was Chinese; they were all drenched in sweat. Rivulets of perspiration trickled off the men's scalps down their heads and bodies. Their clothes looked as if they had been standing in the shower.

As Kalin and Jack entered, no one in the room paid any attention to them.

The men bent over the table using their hands to tear and pick at plates of shrimp with the intensity of a pack of hyenas fighting over a carcass. They ate greedily, yelling and laughing as they did so and spitting stray shrimp shells onto the floor, or better yet, out the window.

At the table to the right surrounded by the others sat President Wang, dressed in a sleeveless tee, boxer shorts, dark socks, and sandals. Jensen Chen sat next to him. Wang was speaking, intermittently and loudly, aiming his comments at the table in front of him and looking at no one in particular. After interjecting a staccato phrase or two, he would return to picking at his food and then repeat himself a moment later. Whenever he spoke everyone else would momentarily stop talking and listen, laugh at whatever he said, and resume eating and carousing. Although Wang was looking down as he picked at his shrimp, he lifted his head when he saw Kalin and Jack standing there.

"*Ni hao, Ni hao, Ni hao*," President Wang said in their direction, cleaning off his hands with a paper towel and standing up, brushing the food and shells off his lap and pushing through the sweaty humanity surrounding his table to greet the visitors.

Kalin shook President Wang's hand; Jack did the same. Wang's underwear hung on him. His wizened and wrinkled head glistened with sweat; perspiration poured off his face.

While thinner, Wang had been outdoors in the island sun—his skin was shades of dark brown and red—and he looked healthier than he had sitting in his dark office apartment in Wuhan. He seemed to be enjoying himself and pleased to see them. Smiling and speaking in animated tones to Kalin, he turned to point across the room.

Over at the far table, two men pushed back their chairs, stood up and walked around the others toward Kalin and Jack. One of them was Mickey; the other was a fat, doughy man. They were the only men in the house not wearing tee shirts. Both of them wore *barongs,* the type of shirt favored by Filipino politicians and businessmen. Mickey was wearing white tennis shorts and turquoise colored contact lenses. The other man was wearing dress trousers and black shoes with no socks. His shoes had the silly brass buckles they put on shoes for people who think their shoes have to do something other than to be things to walk in.

Jack and Mickey said hello to each other but nothing else.

Kalin spoke, a tremor in her voice. "Jack, this is David Jieh. David is a good friend of President Wang's."

David shook Jack's hand and introduced himself in English. He looked like the type of Chinese guy about whom everyone said, "Oh, he's a Taiwanese guy," and everyone nodded their head except Jack, who still couldn't figure out exactly what the comment meant. But the Taiwanese guys all really did look that way.

David was glib and self-assured, although Jack could discern no reason for him to be so. With no encouragement, David launched into a rambling exegesis on himself. His father was a general under Chiang Kai Shek, he said. Waxing on about the generalissimo, he caught himself and came back to the subject of his speech—himself— explaining he was a businessman from Taiwan, did a lot of things with President Wang, and also had interests in the Philippines.

David kept droning on, speaking as though he had already met Jack and they had already had a conversation and agreed on things, and that yes, he had discussed the subject with President Wang and the two of them had agreed David and President Wang together with Jack could do business together as partners in Asia. Be partners with him? The hairs on the back of Jack's neck rose. He took a closer look at the speaker.

David Jieh's skin was soft and fatty. The perspiration on the surface of his face didn't run, but collected in oily little beads above his lip and on his bulbous nose and chin. His hair was long but thin on top and held in place by some kind of sweetish pomade Jack smelled standing four feet away. Where David's hair was thick around his ears, it was too long and gave him the appearance of having a ring around his head. His sideburns ran too far by half down his temples. The sweat from his scalp ran off down his neck and slicked back the hair on the rear of his head like a duck's tail.

The racket in the room continued unabated. Jack strained to hear David over the din. The hot, wet air hung over him like a heating pad. His head throbbed. He looked around the room at the women bathed in steam working the pots and pans on the stove, the men cackling and gnawing on their shrimp, President Wang nodding his head at David, Mickey staring back at Jack like he wanted to say something, and Kalin miserable and trembling standing next to Mickey.

He had no idea who most of them were, who David was, or why Mickey was there. Turning to Kalin, Jack said, "I'm going in the other room and sit down under the fan for a while."

She looked at him with uncertainty.

"No big deal," he said. "I'm just tired from the drive. It's mainly the heat, I think."

"Do you need me to be with you?" Kalin asked.

It was the first nice thing she had said to him in days. "No, no. Thank you, though. Really, I just want to sit down for a minute."

Jack went into the dark interior of the living room and squashed down on one of the plastic couches. He tried to comprehend the events of the day, but didn't get very far. One thing he wasn't going to do was agree to anything—not here, not with any of the people in the other room. The Baguio project was looking like a dream, a bad one, the people involved an oily collection of misfits, mirroring the ominous atmosphere of Manila.

Of all people, Mickey came in to find him.

"Jack, President Wang and David would like to discuss some things with you," Mickey said.

"How's life, Mickey? I didn't get a chance to ask in there. No, I don't think I'll be discussing anything today. Not here. Not with these guys."

"What do you mean? That's why we're all here. That's why we drove four hours to this rat hole."

Jack looked at Mickey and stayed calm. "No one has explained anything to me about coming to this place—I have no idea why we're here. I just went along with the plan. I guess that'll be the last time I do that for a while. I have no idea who most of those people are. And what are you doing here?"

Mickey looked like he didn't know where to start, and didn't say anything.

"But I digress," Jack continued. "I'm happy to have toured the environs of northern Manila Bay—but there's just no way I'm going to talk with that group out there about anything. Especially that guy David. He looks like a thug masquerading as a flabby baby."

"You're talking about Kalin's brother, you know," Mickey said.

Jack just sat there looking at Mickey, his head throbbing. "Kalin's brother? She never told me she had a brother. She talked a lot about her home and family in Taiwan but never mentioned a brother."

"David is Kalin's stepbrother. Her father was the general David was describing in there. He had David on the Mainland and then fled with the Kuomintang to Taiwan in 1947. Kalin was born 15 years later."

"To whom?"

"General Jieh married again, obviously."

"What about David's mother?"

"I guess David's father left her on the Mainland," Michael said. "They couldn't get everybody out."

"That was convenient," Jack said. "I suppose David favors his father?"

Mickey started to try to answer, but Jack waved him off. "Let's talk about more important things. David's in there talking like a deal's already done, and he's in it. Not if I'm involved. I don't want anything to do with that guy."

"I guess you don't want anything to do with the Baguio project then," Mickey said, looking at Jack through his snake-like turquoise eyes.

"What do you mean?"

"President Wang has already sold David, Jensen, and some of those other guys in the room a big interest in the project. That's why they're all here," Mickey said. "The rest is for us."

Jack sat still, not saying anything and absorbing the news. Then he looked over at Mickey. "Why are you here?" Jack asked.

"David's getting his share. We want to get ours."

"We?"

"Me and Kalin. Me and your girlfriend."

"What are you talking about?"

"I know how you feel about my wife. But she's mine, not yours. She's broken her back for you. Now we want what's fair."

Jack stood up. "You and Kalin have spoken about this?" Jack asked, walking out of the room and heading back toward the eating area.

"I don't have to speak to Kalin about anything."

"You're the one using Kalin. I never did," Jack said as he turned his back on Mickey and made for the others. He was going to get to the bottom of things. And then he was going to get back to Manila and stand in a shower for at least a day.

David, Kalin, Jensen, and President Wang were sitting down at one of the two tables. The others had left. The girl came over and cleared off the table in front of Jack. He heard her speaking to the older woman in Tagali, the Filipino native language spoken by Lydia and Romeo, his former housekeeper and driver. She brought him a big plate of steaming shrimp and a Tsingdao beer. As she was leaving, President Wang grabbed her rear end and said something in her ear. She laughed and kissed the top of his sweaty head.

Jack was hungry—he hadn't eaten all day—so he peeled a few of the shrimp. At least the beer was ice cold. He drank from the bottle and finished half of it in one swallow. President Wang's girl brought him another bottle and smiled at him when he thanked her in Tagali. Jack looked over at President Wang and saw him looking back. Jack turned his gaze toward Kalin and looked back and forth between her and David. She looked nothing like her stepbrother. David was drinking *baiju*—Jack couldn't comprehend how anyone could drink firewater in the heat they were enduring.

David had returned to bragging about his father being a general with Chiang Kai-Shek. Jack looked back at Kalin, who had turned and was looking out the window. Miserable and distracted, it didn't seem she liked her brother much, more like she was just stuck with him and wishing she were somewhere else. She paid no attention to Mickey, who was trying to participate in the general conversation now that he had appointed himself a businessman.

Jack ate a few more shrimp and pushed his half-filled plate away, took a long pull on the fresh bottle of beer, paused to feel it run down his throat, put the bottle down with a thud and faced the group.

"Okay, let's do this. What's the deal?"

President Wang had been waiting. He stopped talking to David and pointed at Jensen, giving him instructions.

Jensen leaned over to Jack and said in a low tone, "First condition: President Wang need visa. You help him, please."

"Excuse me?"

"You ask your good friend Ms. Johnson. President Wang need visa, please."

Jack looked over to Kalin sitting standing alone in the corner. The look on her face told him she knew everything.

"Did you hear that?" Jack asked her.

She just stared at him.

"Look, Kalin, he just asked me to get President Wang a visa. I can't do that, so please tell him so and let's get down to business."

With a vacant expression on her face, Kalin leaned over and spoke to President Wang, who listened, betraying no emotion, and then instructed Jensen.

Jensen stood up from the table and went in the other room. Returning with a crummy valise, he took a sheaf of papers out of the bag and spread them on the table.

"What am I looking at?" Jack asked, pulling his chair up to the table.

David had a short conversation with Jensen in Chinese and then said, "These are the stock certificates of Chiang Jiang Energy Corporation, Philippines, Ltd., the corporation that owns the Baguio project."

"What exactly is Chiang Jiang Energy Corporation, Philippines, Ltd.?" Jack asked.

"I just told you," David said.

Jack sighed. "What kind of corporation is it—Chinese, Philippine?"

David and Jensen both repeated the question to President Wang, and the three of them embarked on a 10-minute conversation. Jack looked over at Kalin, who had sat down in a chair in the corner and was staring out the window at the muddy expanse of Manila Bay. She wasn't going to be any help.

Finally finished, Jensen turned back to Jack. "It's a Philippine corporation."

"Who owns it?" Jack asked.

Jensen said, "President Wang is offering you 50 percent of the corporation for $17 million. And one visa."

"One visa. Jesus Christ. That's not what I asked, Jensen. Who owns the corporation?"

Jensen turned back to President Wang and David and they began again in Chinese. This time they took almost as long as the previous discussion. Again Jensen turned to Jack and spoke for the group.

"President Wang says he will tell you once you buy the shares."

Jack laughed to himself. It was over. He had hoped Baguio could answer New Land's prayers, but there was no chance of that happening.

He could never invest money with these people—they were thieves. He looked west out over Manila Bay as the last of the sun slid into the ocean halfway to China. There was no one—no one—to trust in Manila; the place might as well not exist.

He took another long pull on his beer, finishing it. The girl brought him his third. She smiled at him again. Jack felt bad for her. Twenty years old and stuck with an old goat for life. For Wang's life, anyway.

Jack was already past the bad part. At least for now. Tomorrow, and the day after, and the day after that, he would be depressed. But for now he was past it. Past it enough to think it was funny to watch these guys in front of him try to play games, like trained animals on the bars at the circus.

They were all looking at Jack, waiting for an answer.

"What's the City of Wuhan going to say when they find out they've been cheated out of this project?" Jack asked, wanting to get the discussion over with so he could get out of the swamp he was in and go home.

"What you mean?" Jensen asked.

"Come on, Jensen," Jack said. "What kind of a fool do you take me for? We all know Chinese state-owned enterprises can't have foreign subsidiaries. The City of Wuhan and CJEC don't own any part of the Baguio project, do they? You guys ginned up this corporation, put in the bid using it instead of CJEC, and then bribed any local officials who asked questions. And because the project cost very little money, you got some cash elsewhere, and avoided having to tell CJEC what was going on down here."

Jensen was silent. Jack looked at Kalin. She was still looking out the window, but now she was crying, her cheeks wet with tears and streaked with mascara.

"David, you want to tell me the rest, or do I have to keep explaining things to you guys?"

David pulled a cigarette out of a gold package and lit it, looked at Jack and smirked. "You've got a good handle on things. Who cares? What difference does it make? This project generates $12 million of pure profit every year. You get your $17 million back in less than three years. There's not a hydroelectric project anywhere in the world that comes close."

Jack looked back at David. "Being Kalin's brother, I would have thought you were smarter than that." The girl brought Jack another cold Tsingdao. He took a long pull on it and looked at the group staring at him. He couldn't believe it. They all thought he was somehow still going to invest in the deal. Except for Kalin; she had known all along the session would be a disaster for everyone involved.

"So Jensen, tell me, why should I have to pay twice for shares in this project?" Jack asked, turning back to Jensen.

Jensen did his best to maintain a blank expression.

"I've already paid for the project once. Right? Why should I have to buy into it again?"

No one was saying anything now. The room was silent. Jack could hear the fan whirring in the living room.

"This is where my $6 million from Xiayang went, didn't it?" Jack asked. He was speaking in English but he was looking right at President Wang. "The money sure isn't up on the *Minjiang*. The money isn't even in China, is it, President Wang? It's right here in Baguio, isn't it? And you bastards are so greedy, even that isn't enough. You stole my money from China and used it here, but you can't even have the patience to wait to generate profits over time. You want cash now, so you're trying to swindle the dumb *laowai* again."

Sobbing, Kalin finally broke her silence. "Jack, what's done is done. But you're going to have half of the Baguio project. Who cares where the money came from and where it went? New Land's piece would be the best thing that's happened to the company. You would be set for years."

"We all would be set," Mickey said. "We deserve this. We've worked hard. All we want is a little piece."

"Sure. What's wrong with a little squeeze," Jack said. "Who cares who did what to whom? Who cares about right and wrong? Right?" Jack asked, standing up.

No one said anything.

"Here's all I care about—who's going to ask the driver to take me back to Manila?"

He walked out of the room convinced he would never see any of them again.

Chapter 17

Tell Me Something I Don't Know

Leaving Manila the next morning, Jack started drinking before the plane even took off, draining several glasses of champagne, asking for more and alarming the flight attendants, then slept until they were in the skies over New York.

As soon as he cleared customs at JFK, he called Grace. After asking her to schedule a board meeting for Tuesday afternoon, he asked to be put through to Whitey and Pete. Jack briefed them on what had happened, and told them to meet him at the office Monday morning.

Home in his study Sunday night, the telephone rang. The crackling noise on the line told him it was an overseas call; the caller identified himself as Mr. Liu, an attorney representing the City of Wuhan.

"How did you get my number?" Jack asked.

Mr. Liu ignored his question. "Where is Mr. Wang?"

Jack's first instinct was to hang up. He had had enough of China, especially President Wang, for a lifetime. But he knew better—don't make a *laowai* mistake and overreact. He needed Wuhan's cooperation if he was to have any chance of getting his money out of the Xiayang project.

"I last saw him in Manila two days ago. Hasn't he returned?"

"We haven't seen Mister Wang in Wuhan in over three weeks, Mr. Davis. When you see him, you must tell him to come home."

"I doubt I'll be speaking to him anytime soon. If you need President Wang, I suggest you try to find him yourself. Is the matter urgent?"

"Urgent? I should say so, Mr. Davis. Mister Wang is a fugitive. He has abandoned his wife and family and his co-workers at Chiang Jiang Energy Corporation. And he has stolen a large amount of money and property. If he is apprehended, he will be executed. Maybe you could have your good friend Secretary Johnson tell him."

Wang a fugitive? My good friend Secretary Johnson? Jesus. He shouldn't say anything more.

"Where is Mister Wang?" Mr. Liu repeated.

"I've already told you I don't know."

"Given the nature of the matter, I assumed you might change your answer."

"I don't think I could find President Wang if I wanted to, Mr. Liu."

"Please don't address Mr. Wang by his former title, Mr. Davis. He is no longer the president of CJEC. He is a criminal and a fugitive."

"I heard you the first time, Mr. Liu. How much did he steal?"

"I am not at liberty to say," said Liu.

"Can you give me any information about my company's investment in the Xiayang project?" He felt he had to ask.

"I have no information on that matter," said Mr. Liu.

"Does that mean you don't know or you're not going to tell me?"

"I'm sorry, Mr. Davis. I can't comment further."

"Why should I continue to have such a one-way conversation with you, Mr. Liu?"

"Where would Wang be in Manila?" Mister Liu asked.

"You didn't answer my question. I'm telling you for the last time, I have no idea where he is," Jack answered. "If I were you, I'd call down to the Baguio hydroelectric project in Luzon. They ought to be able to locate him for you."

"What do you know about the Baguio project?" Mr. Liu asked.

"Not as much as I should," Jack answered, and hung up the phone.

Jack tried to contact Kalin. She had checked out of the hotel in Manila, and didn't answer any of her phones. He had thought as much; Kalin was gone.

After a poor sleep, he woke early the next morning, and left before Alicia and the boys awoke. When he arrived at the office, Whitey and Pete, as haggard as Jack, were already there. He told them about his conversation with Mr. Liu. No one said much.

Jack passed out copies of an outline he had prepared. The three of them drank their coffee silently and stared at the words. They knew what had to be done. Jack spent the rest of the morning writing a summary of events for Tuesday's board meeting, while Whitey organized their return visit to Wuhan and the Xiayang project, and Pete got on the phone with his engineering counterparts at CJEC to review the Xiayang project's status of construction and related expenditures.

By the afternoon he was ready to clear out of the office but didn't want to go home and face Alicia. Standing outside in the office driveway by his truck, he looked west toward the Lime Rock ridge and its hemlock mantle. There was no wind. It would be quiet in the snow up there.

He drove home, went through the back door into his gun room and called Ritchie, his English setter, from his favorite spot in front of the kitchen fireplace. Jack put an electronic monitor on the white-haired dog; without it, he would run off and Jack wouldn't be able to see him past 10 yards in the snowy forest. Putting on a sweater and his tin coat and taking a 12-gauge off the rack, he grabbed a handful of shells, opened the outside door and let Ritchie run.

Not particular whether they got into birds or not, Jack took the path up the mountain to the rocky glens where the grouse lived in the trees. It would be peaceful up there in the deep snow, and maybe Ritchie would push up a bird. But instead, the turkeys in the barberry thickets confused the dog. Ritchie would pick up a grouse scent and move to point, but then hear a turkey scurrying through the bushes, forget the grouse and veer off after the turkey, his monitor sounding every few seconds. No dog could point a turkey—they didn't freeze like upland birds, but ran instead—but you couldn't tell Ritchie that.

Chasing after turkeys was worse. The damned things were too fast. All Ritchie got for crashing through the prickers was a bleeding head knotted with burrs. As smart as the dog was, Ritchie couldn't learn when it came to turkeys.

Sounds familiar, Jack thought to himself as he stood in a grove of hemlocks waiting for Ritchie to return, the dogs' monitor sounding a quarter mile off—just like the fog horns on the shores of Manila Bay futilely warning a confused *laowai* traveler about the perils awaiting him.

禾   禾   禾

Tuesday's board meeting was excruciating. In the beginning, when some members told Jack he was being too pessimistic about China, he brought them down to earth by describing his call from Attorney Liu.

Their partner in China was a fugitive. And they were helpless— Kalin, their best connection to China, was missing too. As a publicly held company, New Land would be obligated to make disclosures. And while news in China was closely controlled, Wang's transgressions were crimes against the state; there would be public pronouncements there as well. The stock price was sure to plummet.

As he let his board digest the news, Jack looked out the window at Virginio's sculpture, the pile of leaves at its base confirmation that the season's best days were gone. The board members were crushed. Geoffrey Roakes kept terming the situation a "disaster," not looking at Jack.

禾   禾   禾

Like every other shit detail in Jack's life, he knew the return trip to Fujian would be a miserable one, but it was worse than he had expected.

Trying to save money even though they needed a new agent and translator, Whitey roped Mr. Zhang, New Land's wind farm meteo-rologist, into the job. Zhang was Chinese, had a PhD in renewable energy from Tsinghua University, and spoke decent English.

His performance in his new position shouldn't have surprised anyone. Boarding the flight to Hong Kong, Jack, Whitey, and Pete found themselves in the rear cabin with Zhang in four seats jammed across the middle of the last row by the lavatories. Zhang proudly explained he had never paid more than $500 round trip for a plane ticket to China, and the trip to Hong Kong would be no exception.

At the end of three days of cramped air and ground travel, rolling into Nanping late on a rainy evening, Zhang informed Jack he was happier with their hotel accommodations than the Hong Kong air package. He had managed to obtain their rooms for the week for only $300—for all four of them. Arriving at their hotel, its entrance marked by a single fluorescent tube, the lobby mud-soaked from ripe tenants tracking in the weather, they encountered two lines: one for people checking in, and one for something else.

"What are those people doing in that other line?" Pete asked as they queued up to check in.

"Waiting to use the telephone," Zhang answered, indicating a booth housing a single telephone.

"What about the phones in their room?" Pete asked.

"No room telephones in this hotel."

"There's only one telephone available in this entire building?" Pete barked.

"Penny wise, pound foolish," Jack muttered.

"What did you say, Mr. Davis?" Zhang asked.

"Don't worry, Zhang. You wouldn't understand."

When he got home to Lime Rock, Alicia was waiting for him at the door, just like she had been the day of the stock market crash. He hadn't called to tell her the results of the trip, but she had learned to sense disaster.

"What's New Land's stock price?" Alicia asked him.

"You mean now or when we announce our write-down of Xiayang?"

She just stood in the doorway, and didn't speak.

"Are you going to let me in?"

She pushed the door open and walked out of the kitchen.

"Don't you at least want to know what happened over there?"

Alicia came back into the kitchen, her once marvelous face abused with scorn. "How much have you paid Kalin?"

"What?"

"You heard me. How much did you pay that witch?"

"Come on, Alicia, don't be silly. What are you talking about?"

"Come on, nothing, Jack. If you hadn't been so taken with that Chinese whore, none of this would have happened. You've just been a damned fool."

He shrugged. He loved Alicia anyway; he always had.

Chapter 18

False Starts

When the company announced the fraud and related write-off in China, New Land's share price plummeted. The company's cash account was almost depleted. Without new capital, New Land would go under.

And so would Jack. His salary at New Land had never been enough to live on. In the past when he had needed cash, he had just sold some shares—at least he had learned not to margin them. But with the stock price in the basement, selling was out of the question.

When Geoffrey Roakes proposed a new financing for the company, Jack was thankful until he reviewed the punitive terms. The deal was scheduled to close before the company's board meeting in New York the following month. When it did, Jack would remain the chairman and chief executive officer, but his majority stake in the company would be significantly diluted—Geoffrey and his new investors would control New Land.

At the closing, the investors from Hutchinson Flanders, the big Hong Kong trading house Geoffrey had lined up to lead the round, were tightlipped. Given their firm's historic presence in Hong Kong, Jack had been looking forward to their insights on New Land's situation in China, but they barely spoke to him.

As soon as the papers were signed, Jack convened the board meeting. The first agenda item was China. Jack reported on the disappointing findings from their return due diligence trip to Fujian. No one asked any questions; everyone kept looking at Geoffrey.

"Jack, as a result of the financing just closed, Hutchinson Flanders and I control the company now," Geoffrey Roakes said. "And we want to sell. Despite the company's recent setbacks, we have found a buyer: Dominion Construction Corporation of Montreal, Canada. They are very interested in the Chinese market and are willing to pay a premium price."

Jack wasn't surprised. The first instinct of most passive investors was to run. But they weren't all thieves like Geoffrey.

"But Geoffrey, Foreign and Colonial and Hutchinson Flanders already control Dominion Construction. This is rigged deal," Jack said, watching as the eyes of his adversaries tried to avoid his.

"It's a valid third-party transaction, Jack," Geoffrey said. "We have commissioned a fairness opinion."

"Sure Geoffrey. Look, there's no reason to drag this out—tell me the rest of it."

Geoffrey protested, Jack insisted, and Geoffrey finally relented and launched into his prepared remarks. "The first option is to sell to Dominion Construction," Geoffrey continued. "Speaking for the preferred shareholders, we are all very much inclined to pursue the sale, since pursuant to our liquidation preference, we'll receive a nice return on our original investment. Or, at your suggestion, we could consider pressing on. But if we do, I anticipate major changes to New Land's business plan. It's your decision."

There was really no choice. "Sounds like we're going to sell," Jack said, getting up from the table.

"I had expected you might have an alternative plan in mind," Geoffrey said, doing a pathetic job of playacting as if he really did.

"Look, I'm not going to stand in the way of New Land's shareholders getting out at a premium," Jack said to Geoffrey, who couldn't look Jack in the eye. "Besides, what's the point? You've obviously already made up your minds. Very nice to meet you," Jack said to the investors from Hutchinson Flanders, offering his hand to them as he came around the table on his way out. "Have the people at Dominion Construction call me," he said to Geoffrey.

Geoffrey tried to clear his throat. "There's, ah, just one more thing, Jack," Geoffrey said, his voice becoming close to inaudible as Jack reached the door. "As far as the sale of New Land, the effect of our liquidation preference on your common shares is to …"

"I'm having trouble hearing you, Geoffrey," Jack said, lingering in the doorway.

"Don't you want to know Dominion Construction's acquisition terms?" Geoffrey stammered.

"You know Geoffrey, you've got such a knack for the obvious. You're about to tell me Dominion Construction's purchase price enables the preferred shareholders to make a fat return, but there's nothing left for my founder's common equity, leaving me with no salary, no shares, and no prospects. Right?"

Geoffrey and the others just stared at Jack.

"Well, even though your behavior is scandalous, I'm pleased about one thing—you may have wiped me out, but no New Land shareholder will be able to say I didn't make them money."

The New Land sale to Dominion Construction was scheduled to close at the end of 1989, one year after the company's IPO.

The day the deal was announced, Jack sat alone in his office, staring out west over the cornfield at a flock of Canadian geese chewing at the stubble of stalks left after the threshing machine had done its job. The winter sun was going down behind the Lime Rock ridge, and the arc of a partial moon hung in the apex of the eastern sky.

He watched two black crows fly across the land. Who was less trustworthy, he wondered, Chinese or *laowai?*

Chapter 19

The Worst of Times

When it came to bad news, Jack's telephone had eyes.
Especially if a New Land shareholder was on the other end of the line. Duncan Leeds, a shareholder married to one of Jack's Harvard classmates, called to complain Jack hadn't done right by him—he should have negotiated a higher price for the company. Duncan had purchased his shares in a private sale before the IPO at a tenth of the price paid by Dominion Construction in the buyout, Jack pointed out. "But I had to hold them for two years," Duncan whined. "Factoring in the time value of money, I barely made 20 percent." It was all Jack's fault.

Or employees. Some wanted to quit, but wanted severance, too; others asked for personal loans. If the company wasn't in a position to do so, Jack could pony up himself, they suggested helpfully.

But no one called about buying the house or the farm. Putting his house up for sale, just like after the end of Catapult Energy, the difference was the location of the property: Buyers of country real estate wouldn't show up until after spring arrived, still months away.

"Sometimes you can't make a nickel, Jack." His father had always said that to him. He was always saying things like that.

But folksy statements weren't any help—he needed to generate some cash immediately.

Convened around the dinner table a week after the sale of New Land, the family ate in uneasy silence. None of the boys was anxious to give their parents an opportunity to start another argument. Forks capturing the last of the mashed potatoes scraped against empty plates. Outside the dining room window, the interminable snow thundered down in the stillness.

"We're going to have to do something about money," Jack said.

The boys all looked at him wordlessly.

Thankfully, Alicia was in a matter-of-fact, collaborating mood. "The boys and I have insulated the windows and doors. I'm making their lunch at home now."

"Well, that's a very good start. Thank you, everyone. But it's not going be enough to just save money; we're going to have to start making some, too."

"You mean you're going to have to get a job," she said.

"We can generate some cash right around here," Jack said, ignoring Alicia's hundredth attempt at career advice.

"We could have a tag sale," Alicia said.

He was relieved. Maybe this was going to be easier than he had thought. "That's an excellent suggestion. Not just here at the house. All the stuff from New York in storage down at the barn, too—sell it all."

The table was quiet. The boys fidgeted, hoping the discussion would conclude quietly; Alicia waited. "What else?" she said.

"What else?"

"What else, Jack?"

"The cars. We don't need three vehicles."

"I'm not selling my car."

"I can make do with the pickup. Sell mine."

"All right."

"And the tractor."

"And the tractor. Good. I hate that tractor. You should never have bought it," Alicia said.

"Well, I guess you were right. Does that make you feel better?"

"Is that all?"

The gloom hung over them like a lead blanket. The snow kept piling up outside.

"No."

They all looked at him.

Jack cleared his throat. "I'm going to take my pickup and go up the highway collecting bottles. There's got to be a lot of them."

Alicia stared at him. "You do that." It was his concession, she knew; there had to be more.

"I was speaking to the real estate agent today," Jack said, resigned to completing his miserable task. "We could make a lot of money by renting out the main house for the summer season."

The boys couldn't have expected it, but to their credit, they didn't say anything.

"And where would you propose we live?" Alicia asked.

"We can move down to the woodcutter's cottage; Alex and Helena will have to move to the rooms in the barn for the season."

"Just what I've dreamed of, a Hansel and Gretel summer," Alicia said, staring at Jack as if he were a murderer.

When they had come back from church, the car had been parked down White Hollow Road from the entrance to their driveway with its engine running. It sat there for close to an hour, exhaust curling up from the tailpipe, before the driver put the car into gear and edged it slowly up the driveway. Jack saw it coming; he had just gotten up from his desk in the parlor to check on it for the third time. Might as well get it over with.

In his shirtsleeves, he opened the front door of the house and crunched down the snow-covered steps to the idling Ford coupe.

The driver of the car opened the door and stepped out. "John E. Davis?"

"Just give me the papers."

"Mr. John E. Davis?"

"Yeah, yeah, yeah. Just give me the papers. You've done your job; you can go in a second."

"Are you Mr. Davis?"

"Yes, for Chrissakes. You've got your man; give me the god-damned papers, and you can be on your way."

"Litchfield County Sheriff, sir. I'm serving you on behalf of …"

"Look, Mr.…?"

"Walcott."

"Mr. Walcott. I could sneak out the back door and you'd have to chase me for another six months. So do me a favor and don't make this any more difficult than it has to be. You've served me. Now I'd appreciate it if you could turn that car around and leave us in peace."

The man stared at Jack, started to say something, but then took the signed papers from Jack, opened his car door and got in, backed up, and drove out of the driveway.

Jack walked back inside the house. As he stamped the snow off his boots, Alicia was waiting for him.

"Who was that?"

"Just someone about some things at the office."

"On a Sunday morning?"

He looked at her—when was this going to stop? "All right, Alicia. He was a process server. What do you want from me?"

"A process server? What for?"

"Nothing."

"Don't tell me nothing. Does this have anything to do with the boys and me?"

"It all has to do with everybody and everything, Alicia. Just don't make it any worse. Please."

"Don't make it any worse? Jack, you don't know how bad it is."

"I don't know how bad it is. How could that be, Alicia? I deal with this stuff every day. And whenever possible, I try not to bother you with any of it."

"You think you're the only person under pressure? What do you think about your sons' grades, Jack?"

He looked at her. "What are you talking about?"

"You heard me," Alicia said. "What do you think about your sons' grades?"

He stood there thinking. He hadn't seen their grades. He should have, he realized; it was over a week past the end of the marking period. "I haven't seen them yet," he said finally, waiting for what was coming.

"Do you know why, Jack?" Alicia asked, a churlish look of triumph ruining her face.

"No," he said, preparing to feel really bad.

"Because we can't get their grades until we pay the school what we owe them in unpaid lunchroom fees."

And that was the worst part of it—he couldn't keep it away from the boys. It would have been one thing if it was just him in the crossfire. They hadn't done anything to deserve what was happening: being hungry; the electric power being shut off; or having to go outside to get wood to keep the fires going because there was no more oil in the tank.

But the boys were staunch. Truthfully, he hadn't expected as much. When the holidays came and there was no money for Christmas gifts, he wrote each one of them a poem about their play in sporting events. He had wanted to give them something valuable, more special than the toys he couldn't afford. They couldn't be expected to understand, but maybe they would later.

But he had been wrong. They took their poems out of their stockings, sat down and read them quietly, and then all four of them came and put their arms around him.

As far as how it affected him personally, he didn't feel it anymore. If he had, the notice in the HBS Alumni magazine notes on his class would have hurt more: "Whatever happened to Jack Davis? If anyone's seen him, please contact the editor."

"Bad things aren't always someone's fault—sometimes they just happen." His father had always said that, too.

Chapter 20

Seven-Year Itch

"There's nothing more unattractive than a jealous woman." That was another one his father liked.

It was the dead of winter, cold and bleak—they had already had over a dozen major snows, and the one outside looked to be another big one. Jack didn't have anywhere to go. He didn't like going to the office anymore; it just reminded him of his failures. Pacing around the main house, he stopped to look out the parlor windows. The snow was really coming down. Up by the pagoda, a family of deer picked their way down the mountain to forage for food.

Alicia sent him for groceries. Happy to get out of the house, he took Ritchie in the truck up to Shagroy's Market in Salisbury.

Standing in line at the checkout counter, the cart half full, it was Jack's turn to pay. He automatically reached in his pocket for the roll of bills he always carried. He was out of cash. He pulled a credit card out of his wallet and handed it to the clerk.

She ran it through the machine.

"I'm sorry, Mr. Davis," she said. "Want to try another one?"

Jack wasn't as surprised his card had been denied as he was the clerk knew his name.

He stood there, holding up the line, trying to figure out what to do next. He looked at the people standing behind him. He didn't recognize anyone, but they were all staring at him with knowing eyes. He glanced at the magazine rack next to the checkout counter. On the cover of the current edition of *The Lakeville Journal* was a headline article on New Land's forced sale featuring his photograph.

He fought the temptation to just push the grocery cart to the side and walk out, and asked the clerk to borrow the telephone.

He dialed home. Alicia answered.

"I'm up here at Shagroy's, out of cash and my credit card was denied. You're going to have to come up and pay them."

"I really can't. I'm busy. Besides, I'm running short of funds myself. There's a cash machine inside the store. Just use that."

"That's a great idea—I wish I had thought of it. Better yet, I wish there was some cash in my bank account."

The clerk was trying not to stare at Jack. He looked over at her and smiled.

"You don't have any cash in your account?" Alicia asked. "How could you do this to us?"

Jack didn't say anything. What was the point?

"I'll be up when I can," Alicia said and hung up.

Standing to the side of the checkout line, the village idiot on display, he waited until Alicia showed up, wordlessly turned the cart over to her, apologized to the clerk, and left.

He and Ritchie drove down to the farm. Parking his truck behind the barn, he let the dog out and followed him. The white English setter blended into the snowfall, his nose leading him back and forth across the path that wound down to the banks of the Housatonic. The snow was coming down hard. It was quiet in the sycamores along the banks of the river, as if the snowflakes were absorbing any bits of sound hanging in the air and pulling them down to the ground.

Ritchie wandered wherever his nose took him. Jack was content to follow the dog. Usually he had had a plan. Not this time.

When the sale of the company to Dominion Construction closed in December, Jack received a small balance of cash for his shares and put the money in the bank. On Alicia's birthday, he arranged to take her to dinner at the White Hart, their favorite restaurant up the road in Salisbury. At first, she refused to go, saying that they couldn't afford it. He insisted, and she relented when Helena, their Polish caretaker's wife, pushed her out the door.

She had a lot to drink. They were just finishing when it happened. He had been recounting how Geoffrey Roakes's fear and greed had doomed New Land before the company could turn the corner, how things were bad and were going to get worse, and how there wouldn't be any money, at least for a while, and how sorry he was.

Alicia wasn't saying anything. He hoped she was listening to him like the old days when he had told her the bad news, when she would say he would think of something, when he told himself how much he loved her, and when she still had loved him.

She had had way too much to drink. He had had a lot to drink too, enough so he didn't realize what was coming until he looked up and saw the look on her face. And then she told him. She couldn't understand him, she said; how it was he could gamble with their livelihood and their lives. He had made mistakes, she said, leaving his family high and dry. How could he let such a thing happen, she said. She said she had tried to help him, to talk to some of New Land's board members, but it was too late. Maybe he had been lucky before, but now he wasn't. And it wasn't just that he wasn't lucky, anymore; he wasn't any good. He didn't make enough money. He traveled too much, especially with Kalin. He wasn't home to help them. He wasn't a good father. He was a loser.

She couldn't hold it in anymore, and wasn't going to be satisfied until she let it all out. He knew she had been angry and saving it up, but still, he was surprised she said what she did. She had to know there was no turning back after saying things like that to him. He would always love her, but there was just no turning back.

He got up from his seat and walked out of the dining room, stepping through the front door of the inn outside onto the long front porch, and looked up at the gossamer chandelier of winter stars. The Big Dipper hung in the northern sky where it always lived in December. He thought about the days in his childhood when finding the Big Dipper had been the only thing he cared about on a winter night. He looked back inside the restaurant, then out again across the snowy lawn frosted by the full moon. Turning away for good, he walked down the stairs, his boots crunching through the snow as he crossed the road running from the inn down into town, and started the long walk home.

He walked down the backcountry roads in the frigid moonlight, stepping behind trees when headlights appeared, like he had done on his way to his first lover's house years ago. She would come after him but wouldn't be able to find him. He was walking home, but not to her. That life was over. He wasn't going back. He would sleep in the barn in his clothes and leave with his things at first light, while he could still get his life back.

The next morning he awoke and walked over to the main house to get some things before going down to the city for a few days. The house rattled. There was no one there. Alicia had left a note saying she had taken the boys and gone to her parents' house in Washington.

He sat down in the parlor and watched the snow bury the place. The fireplaces gave off the smell of charcoal from old fires, dredging up memories of when they had been there on the holidays and they were happy, the smoke finding its way into his clothes and saturating the fabric of his being with a snuff of sorrow he could not burn out.

A month later, she telephoned. He was expecting to be lectured unmercifully, but when she told him about the colon cancer, he was speechless. She came back then, of course, and he stayed with her until the end late that winter. And then he regretted that night, and the way things had ended badly for them, and for her. He loved her very much; he really did. It would be better for her if she didn't have second thoughts about her life. He told her he hadn't meant to leave, and he didn't hold it against her for calling him a loser, but he knew she didn't believe him.

The truth was, at the time he had accepted what she had said. His luck had been bad. But maybe it wasn't just about luck. Maybe he had been good once or both good and lucky, but now he was returned to his fundamental self, something less; maybe even a loser like she said.

Ritchie died at the winter's end, too. He was the best hunting dog Jack had ever had.

In the days and weeks that followed, he spent every day after school with his sons, making them dinner and helping them with their school work, the five of them trying desperately to convince themselves that their current life wouldn't be that much worse than the one they had had before.

At the end of the evening he tucked them into bed and helped them say their prayers and answered their questions about why their mother had been angry with him at the end and why everything had gone wrong and how it was he had no money now but would make some later, but at the moment he didn't know how he was going to get it. They would all put their arms around one another in a circle and hold each other and weep. He told them he felt like he had slipped into a crevice and every time he tried to climb out he would get almost to the top and someone would stomp on his fingers and he would slide back down and then climb up once again but he just couldn't crawl out.

China was at the bottom of the crevice, he knew that. He had been able to handle the everyday things in China. The food, the garbage, the crush of humanity and the smells—that had been one thing. But the treachery—that was something else. He had gone to China for all the right reasons—it was the right thing for his business, and it had been an adventure, too—but the treachery was something he hadn't bargained for. Life was too short for treachery, and now that he knew what they truly thought of him—a stupid *laowai* who the men just wanted for his money and the women viewed as a hairy, smelly ape—he never wanted to go back.

So forget her; forget China. It wasn't important anymore. What was important was to be good at something. More than ever. Before it was too late. His children were watching—they needed him to be good, to succeed. And he didn't have a lot of time left.

He would live the rest of his life for them. Not for him; for them. He would show them.

And there couldn't be any women involved anymore. He used to think he understood them; what a joke. Besides, he wouldn't have any time.

And he was never, ever going back to China.

Book Three

HAINAN JACK

Chapter 21

Rather Be Lucky than Good

"Isn't it time for you to go out and get a job?"

Lots of people felt free to offer their advice. The topic usually came up when Jack made the mistake of speculating about his future plans. He would confide in someone—thinking it smart to get their opinion, just needing to talk to them—and once allowed inside, they delivered the question, always with the same lame facial expression intended to convey heartfelt words.

The first few times it happened, he tried to explain. He was not employable; he was too entrepreneurial and intimidating to a potential employer. He had really never worked for anyone but himself. No one was going to give him a job.

And he couldn't afford to take a job anyway. A pay check would be nice, but it wouldn't be enough to service his unpaid obligations, and in the meanwhile he would lose any upside associated with his efforts.

Most people couldn't understand his predicament. When he said he couldn't work for someone, they thought he was being arrogant. After a while, he learned to avoid the subject. When it came up anyway, he listened, let the speakers express their thoughts, thanked them, and switched the subject.

But it was on his mind every day. Everyone had a high water mark, Jack was sure of that, a point where life peaks and starts heading downward, like Waterloo for Napoleon or Gettysburg for Lee. Where death becomes convenient.

Maybe Catapult Energy had been his, with New Land a way station on a path spiraling down toward complete failure at the bottom. He couldn't let it happen. He needed to be good at something, really good. And he had little time left to experiment.

But maybe he couldn't be good; maybe he just wasn't. There were people like that. Perhaps thrashing around was useless; he should just accept his fate. He could work at the Post Office. Kalin would laugh if she heard that one.

And the truth was, while he wanted to be good, he needed success more—he would take it any way he could get it.

It was unclear if being good and being successful were connected. As he looked back on Catapult Energy, he was prepared to believe its success didn't have much to do with him, just events. So maybe it was true what they said: successful people were simply in the right place at the right time. All he had to do the next time was figure out where to stand.

But if the chances of two successes—of "lightning striking twice"— were rare, then the likelihood of a third winner was all but impossible.

But what else could he do? However he parsed it through in his mind, the conclusion was always the same—he just had to keep going.

He was going to have to start another company. With no money. And it couldn't be small or inconsequential. It had to be big and profitable enough to pay his bills, and more importantly, get the monkey off his back. Thinking about it was a mistake—he just had to do it.

Chapter 22

Monkey on His Back

He couldn't start another power company—he didn't have the capital. And he didn't have the time. He needed cash right away.

He would have to go back to being an investment banker. He possessed the two natural elements any investment banker requires—experience and contacts—and it was the only business he could afford to be in. Dusting off the Davis Brothers shingle—he had maintained the firm's regulatory certification—he borrowed some seed capital from his younger brother Greg and Sam Sheppard, his best friend from Harvard, and made plans to go back to work in New York City.

He allowed himself to be optimistic. Things had a way of happening on the Street. Even though a tiny participant, Davis Brothers looked over the same runway of people trying to cross over from middling life to affluence as Merritt Partners and Goldman Sachs. Between those seeking money to finance their opportunities—real or imagined—and others representing financial institutions burdened with billions to spend, something was sure to rub off.

After settling Alicia's affairs and spending most of the late winter with his sons, he sublet a small one-room office in the Graybar Building from an attorney friend. With mahogany paneling and high ceilings, the rooms provided a view of Park Avenue South from 20 floors above Grand Central Station. He could kiss the boys goodbye in the morning while they slept, take the Harlem Line to midtown, get on an elevator, and never have to go outside.

Early on a spring Monday in 1990, leaving the boys with Alex and Helena, he caught the six o'clock train out of Dover Plains, becoming a commuter for the first time in his life.

The trip wasn't going to be pleasant—from Lime Rock, it took two hours one way—but he was happy to be working again. Taking a seat, he opened up the morning's papers. For the first hour, his energy remained high. But when he looked out the window and saw the outer suburbs with an hour still to go, the length of the sojourn began to register—two hours was forever. He looked around. The other passengers dozed or snored, gray and lifeless.

Jack looked closer.

Losers.

As the train lurched into Grand Central and wheezed to a stop, he took his briefcase and coat off the rack and stepped off the train onto the platform. The waking humanity trudged by, ghosts hovering by night in the exurbs after failing the challenge of the City, their cadaverous brown shapes floating through the pathetic remainder of their lives, aging a week every day.

As he turned toward the terminal, he looked to the left and caught his reflection in the window of the train. Unless something happened, he would be one of them soon.

A week later, Jack unlocked the office, hung up his coat, straightened the blinds to let the sun wash away the weekend gloom, opened a window, poured a bag of grounds and some water into the coffee pot, turned on his computer, and started scanning the night's e-mail.

Taking a gulp of the day's first cup of coffee, the effects of the caffeine reminding him of his circumstances, he looked up as the telephone rang. It wasn't even eight o'clock. No legitimate person would call so early. He ignored it, and the ringing stopped. Thirty seconds later, it started again. Maybe he was wrong; his expectations lifted as he picked up the receiver.

"Jack Davis."

"Mr. Davis, I own ten million bearer bonds," the voice on the other end of the line said. "I need a million in cash; can you handle it?"

"Who gave you my number?"

"A person who told me you're very creative."

"They must have been talking about someone else."

A malodorous swathe of miscreants wandered through the one-room Davis Brothers office. Taking the seat across from Jack to sling their pitches with Hollywood-like sincerity, the line of scumbags, hucksters, deadbeats, fraudsters, and deviants seemed endless. Most of the popular scams perpetrated across the globe slithered under Davis Brothers' door: bearer bonds hidden by Army generals in a Vietnamese temple; letters of credit issued by the defunct Bank of Crete; cooperation proposals from trust company officers looting unresolved estates. The line of honest but misguided fools whose business plans would never generate a dime was much larger.

Jack made calls all day. He rarely got through; most of them were answered by secretaries or voicemail. Few got returned.

At six o'clock, collecting the garbage in a plastic bag—he couldn't afford a cleaning service—and putting on his coat, he turned out the lights and locked the door. The train got him home by eight thirty, in time to ask the twins how their day went, review homework with his older sons, tell them all a story, kiss them goodnight and lay down for a while before getting up the next day at five in the morning to do it all over again.

"Close any deals?" Bobby asked six months later, on the line from the Coast, saying he would be in New York the following week, why didn't they have a drink.

"I've got a few things lined up."

"How's the rest of your life?"

"About as bad," Jack admitted.

"You're not going to solve anything sitting around that farm; you've got to get out a little."

"I don't think so."

"What about what's her name, the skier?"

"Suzy?"

"That's the one."

"I haven't spoken to her. She wanted to have children."

"You've already got children."

"No kidding."

Jack stood alongside the bar at Bice, waiting for Suzy and Bobby and the others.

Jack had forgotten about Suzy until Bobby mentioned her. Suzy worked for Dominion Construction's office in Dallas, and Jack and Bobby had met her during the sale of New Land. After the end of things, when Bobby had taken Jack on a spring skiing weekend to Colorado to cheer him up, they had run into her again in Aspen at the bar of the Hotel Jerome. She was not Jack's type, more a fit for Aspen's rhinestone cowboys, but she had been fun, laughing at his lousy jokes. It had been way too early for him to have any interest in anyone and he had not thought to call her, but later Bobby told him she had followed up to ask about Jack.

Bice was a lot like Aspen and Suzy had said it was her favorite New York restaurant. She had sounded glad to hear from him, and not too serious. Maybe they could just spend an easy evening together the next time she was in the city.

Jack ordered a gin gimlet and looked around. Most of the women in the place were blondes and wore designer clothes and diamonds, and exhibited evidence of cosmetic surgery. The men were packaged similarly: open, Italian shirts, gold neck hardware, and eye jobs. Jack finished his gimlet and ordered another.

Suzy and Cynthia, Bobby's hard-edged wife, walked in with Bobby. Suzy looked better than most of the women in the room in spite of her streaked blond hair and leopard-skin tights. But she was just not his type. He should have known better, he thought as the group approached him across the dining room, getting the same queasy feeling as he did being pitched by someone with tattoos on his knuckles.

Jack said hello to Suzy, kissing her on the cheek, said a guarded hello to Cynthia and followed Bobby to their table.

As they sat down, Jack exchanged a few words with Bobby while Cynthia was already quizzing Suzy.

"What does your father do in Texas?" Jack heard Cynthia ask Suzy, beginning with a leadoff question that was, to Cynthia, perfectly natural.

"All," Suzy said, flashing an expression designed to let Cynthia know she was speaking to a Texas insider.

"I'm sorry?" Cynthia asked.

"Daddy's in all," Suzy said again, saw Cynthia's lack of comprehension, and looked over at Jack for help. She really was a nice girl, and she meant well.

"I think she means oil,'" Jack said to Cynthia, getting a look of thanks from Suzy.

"Well, all right then," Cynthia said, moving to the more important topic of the designer responsible for Suzy's leopard-skin tights.

Turning back to Bobby to finish catching up, Jack tried to ignore the rest of Suzy's interview, but it was impossible.

"What does Jack do these days?" Cynthia asked Suzy loudly, not caring if he heard.

"Honey, Ah don't know; Ah was going to ask you that. But tell me something: is he as rich as he looks?"

Now that he thought about it, other than Alicia, he couldn't remember the last woman he had admired. Kalin, maybe. In a perverse way. She had worked so hard. Despite what she had done, she cared about him; he knew she did. And after everything that had happened, he still cared for her, too.

Looking around at the blue eyes framed by bleached blond hair, diamond earrings, and gold chains, he sure didn't see anyone remotely like Kalin. He shouldn't have let Bobby talk him into the evening. Suzy was all right if he was just having a drink at a bar, but he cringed at the thought of bringing her home to meet his sons.

As soon as the dessert course was over, he excused himself and caught the late train home, sitting alone in the stale coach, the day's spent newspapers swirling around his feet, listening to the wheels clacking up the lonely Harlem Line. A heavy rain coated the train with cold gloom. He was glad the train was empty—he didn't want to have to talk to anyone. Especially a woman.

The following day was as disappointing as the previous evening. Closing a small equity financing for a private company, the lead investor, Sasquatch Capital, told Jack they were cutting his fees by 50 percent— take it or leave it.

Forget U.S. private equity deals, he thought as he drove home. He would do anything to avoid another one.

And forget women, especially women in blond hair and tights. They were just a complication. He didn't need any more complications, just a little certainty and the chance to make some money. He would go anywhere, even back to China, for that.

Chapter 23

Hearts and Bones

A month later, a knock on the door interrupted his telephone call. A woman Jack had never seen before walked in, carrying a sheaf of manila folders.

Elizabeth Krupp had called earlier and introduced herself. She worked for Hartford Insurance, Dominion Bridge Corporation's property and casualty carrier, and needed to come by his office to get his signature on some documents overlooked at the sale of New Land.

He asked her to sit down and give him a minute to review the materials. She made herself comfortable and looked out the grimy, rain-streaked window at the taxis queuing up on 42nd Street.

Jack looked up, followed her eyes, then came back to take her in.

Elizabeth Krupp was definitely German, possessing all the dominant features—wide set, intelligent blue eyes, reddish blond hair, a freckled face, and creamy white skin—that make German women so desirable. Sitting on the couch looking out the window, she gave Jack the vague impression she preferred to remain disengaged, almost as if she didn't approve of him.

"This New Land sale has dragged on forever," he said. "Is there anything else I need to do after this?"

"I'm just part of Dominion Construction's financial advisory team, so I really don't know, but if the attorneys have anything else, I imagine they can send it to you by overnight mail. Your signatures today are the only ones I need to notarize," she said, taking her notary seal out of her bag.

"What department at the Hartford do you work in, Elizabeth?"

"Mergers and acquisitions."

"What's that like?"

She raised her eyebrows slightly, and Jack felt her eyes focus in on him. He had been correct; she had purposely not looked at him directly before. Now that he was asking her questions and wasn't going to just sign the papers, she was forced to decide if she wanted to involve herself.

"Instead of working on deals, I'm just supervising a lot of people," she said, "and I don't know if I want to do that."

It was his turn to be surprised; he hadn't expected such a candid response. Maybe he could talk to her after all. "So, Elizabeth, what *do* you want to do?"

She laughed. "They didn't tell me you would ask me questions like this."

"What did they tell you?"

Now she was really flustered, the pink tone of her cheeks giving way to red. It seemed to matter to her that he took an interest in her, almost as if someone had told her he would not.

"Would you like to see some pictures of China?" he asked. "I'm sure you've heard about New Land's business over there. It might give you a better sense of what the company was all about."

"Why . . . yes, I would love to. If you have time, of course."

"I have time."

Jack took out the photographs of the Xiayang project and spread them out on his desk. She leaned over to look at them.

"Fascinating. It looks a little . . . wild."

"It wasn't so bad. But that's over now." Jack tried to phrase the next words as best he could. "Is it me, or do I sense some type of, I don't know, reticence on your part?"

"What do you mean, reticence?" she asked, her face turning pink again.

"It just seems like you had some opinion formed about me before you came in here, that's all. I was just curious."

"Oh, I don't know," she said, looking away.

"Come on."

"You're not what I expected, that's all."

"What did you expect?" Jack asked.

"Someone less capable."

"They told you I wasn't capable?"

"No one told me. I determined that for myself. Your company didn't make any money, so I just assumed it must have been run by a jackass."

"Wait a minute. We made money—maybe not a lot, but we made money."

"Not as much as you would if I were involved."

Jack just stared at her, a grin etched on his face, checking to make sure he had just heard what he had just heard.

"Okay, Elizabeth, what would you have done?" Jack asked, still smiling.

"Why? It doesn't matter. You sold the company."

"Did you see the sign on the door when you walked in? Davis Brothers' business is helping people finance theirs. I know it doesn't look like much, but with the right people, it could be."

She sat in her chair looking at him. "Give me a week and I'll let you know."

㊌ ㊌ ㊌

Elizabeth stopped by his office the next day.

"I'm going to join you," she said, standing in the doorway.

"You going to join me?"

"Davis Brothers. You said you needed a partner. I'll do it."

"Well, that's not exactly how I remember our conversation," Jack said to her. There was no way he was ready for another mouth to feed, and he hardly knew her. "In any event, I can't afford you."

"You haven't got a choice. You can figure out how to pay me later."

"But you don't know anything about me, and I don't know anything about you."

"That's not true. I was up all night reading news releases on Catapult Energy and New Land."

He looked at her looking back at him, yesterday's disapproval gone.

"First, I should apologize," Elizabeth said, blushing as she looked down at the floor for a moment, then back into his eyes. "I shouldn't have said the things I did yesterday; I had no idea you're the guy who started Catapult Energy."

"Don't worry about it," Jack said.

"No, really. Catapult was an incredible accomplishment," she said. "I don't know anyone else who started a company listed on the New York Stock Exchange by the time he was 30."

"Well, you're nice to say that, but I've made my share of mistakes, too."

"Who hasn't? Anyone who's done what you have and says they haven't is a liar. Like that reprobate Geoffrey Roakes and those horrible people at Hutchinson Flanders."

"Well, I don't want to make a mistake now, especially where your career is concerned. I have no idea where my first deal is coming from," he said, wondering if she was going to come into the office or just stand in the hallway.

"You'll think of something," Elizabeth said, backing out of the door and shutting it behind her.

❀　❀　❀

She was waiting at the office door the next morning when he arrived.

"Jesus, I'm sorry," he said, fumbling with his keys. "I wasn't sure you were really going to come."

"I don't say anything I don't mean."

Jack unlocked the door and let Elizabeth in. While she hung up her coat, he started the coffee machine and turned on his computer. She sat down at his desk and waited for him. He took a seat at the table and looked over at her.

"Let's not start off with you looking at me like that," Jack said. He didn't know why he was nervous. "I haven't had time to prepare anything."

"Prepare anything?"

"Yes; like what we're going to do; that type of thing."

"What were you working on when I came in yesterday?"

"I was talking to a man in Denmark about putting together a fund to invest in wind farms." It had sounded more interesting yesterday.

"A wind fund."

"Something like that."

"Do you really want to be an explorer again? Out on the point, where no one can teach you anything?"

How could she know that much about him? "So you don't think it can be done."

"No; I think you can probably do anything you want to. That's your gift—and your curse, too."

"My mother used to tell me that; at least the first part," Jack said laughing as he turned from looking out the window to look at Elizabeth and realized she had not been joking. "What do you mean, it's my curse, too?"

"I'm just saying, the next 35 years, don't waste as much time."

"On what?"

"Exotic ideas and ineffective people. Like I was saying," Elizabeth said, "I never heard of a wind fund."

"Well, it is a little adventurous, I'll admit, but you know what they say—the early bird gets the worm."

"Look, I'm not joking. That's all you were left with at New Land—a bunch of worms," she said.

"I don't think the wind fund would turn out that way. Soren's a good guy."

"Just make sure he's not another user like most of the people you did business with at New Land."

"What are you talking about?"

"You heard me," Elizabeth said. "Look, when I heard about New Land, my first thought was, 'What a great concept—a worldwide renewable power company. I wonder who came up with that?' I looked further, read the early releases, said to myself 'So far, so good,' and then bang—your deadbeat investment partners lost their nerve and killed it. People you thought were your friends. They weren't friends—they used you. Especially those thieves from China. If you know what's good for you, you'll never go back there again."

"Look, if it wasn't for China, New Land wouldn't have even completed its IPO."

"All I'm saying is don't do anything more with them; let them go. And that goes for all the women I've heard you've been running around with, too."

"What are you talking about?"

"I know all about Suzy in Dallas. Blondes in leopard-skin tights and diamond earrings? That doesn't sound like you, from what little I know."

"I don't know what you're talking about."

"I'm not saying anything more. Just thank God you've got me. A few more sessions with the others and you'd be broke or dead or both."

Jack stood up to get a cup of coffee. "Some people I know don't do well on criticism early in the morning."

"You know what the New Land people at Dominion Construction told me about you?"

"Like who?"

"Like Judy in accounting."

"I don't want to hear it."

"I asked her how New Land worked."

"I don't want to hear it, I said."

"Judy said, 'Everyone sat around figuring out how to spend the money in the bank and maybe collect some insurance proceeds, and when the cash ran out, we told Jack and he went out and raised some more.'"

The telephone rang and Jack almost dove for it.

Maybe her scolding was the reason it took him time to realize he needed someone like her. When he traveled and left the business with her, things were in better shape upon his return than when he had left.

And he could come up with ideas, but someone had to make sure things behind the scene got done—manage the people, pay the vendors and the taxes, say no when the plans were too grand—and do so with a smile.

Her expression was more winsome than most, but behind it, she was a watchdog, a special breed, genetically devoted. She encouraged him, believed in him with a ferocity little short of his mother's, but was dubious of everyone else—potential clients, employees, advisors, or partners—unless she vetted them first.

Jack suffered fools for the sake of potential opportunity, but she looked at the process as wasting precious resources. "Why do you talk to these jackasses?" she asked at one point.

"I like talking to jackasses," Jack said, getting a glare in return. "Look, Elizabeth, if you watch carefully, you'll see I don't waste time on deals that from the outset looks truly hopeless."

"But so many of these guys are just pretenders. Why do you need to even speak to them? Nothing they ever do or say will amount to anything—at least nothing legal."

"Listen to me; the investment business just isn't that cut and dried. Most deals aren't obviously good or bad at first glance, and the people promoting them aren't clear-cut, either. It would be one thing if we were Morgan Stanley. But we're not. We're Davis Brothers. So we can't be picky. We've got to scrutinize everything coming our way that looks even mildly interesting. Sooner or later, if we're just in the mix every day, something good will happen."

"It's your choice, but do you realize what you're going to have to go through to get there? Another New Land will kill you."

Jack kept pushing, stealing hours at both ends of the day, working seven days a week. Things wouldn't be able to keep him down much longer.

Walking up Park Avenue in the spring of 1991, he felt it. The days had gotten longer, and the first smells of cut grass were in the air. And something else, too. Surprised when he finally turned the corner, his Chinese friends told him he shouldn't have been—with their country involved, they would have predicted his change of fortune much sooner.

Chapter 24

China Fortunes

Jack was on the phone with a brokerage customer when Elizabeth took the incoming call shortly after nine o'clock in the morning.

"Good morning. Davis Brothers."

"Good morning, Madam," said a man's voice on the other end of the line. "Some told me Jack Davis was back in business in New York. Is it true?" The man sounded old, his voice frail but enthusiastic.

Elizabeth answered. "Yes, it's true. Jack is back in the City. You've reached Davis Brothers' New York office."

"Well, that's great news. And who are you?"

She gave the caller her background.

"Thank you for the introduction. The best of luck to you," the caller said. "My name is Cyrus Polley; everybody just calls me Cy. Please remind Jack I'm the guy who used to do a lot of business with Charley Allen. Jack will remember."

"I certainly will, Mr. Polley. I'm sure Jack will remember you. He's on the other line—may he call you back?" Elizabeth said, Jack nodding his head to her as he heard Cy's name, still glued to his phone.

"Oh, sure," Cy Polley said, and kept talking to Elizabeth. After a few minutes more, he ran out of small talk. "Well, please give Jack my best," the old man concluded. "He should remember me. We've missed him."

"I will indeed. Before you go, one last thing. You didn't tell me what you are doing now."

"Same thing I've always done—putting deals together."

"Are you working on anything we could help you with? I'm sure Jack would love to do more with you—for old time's sake."

Jack, listening but still on the other phone, nodded his head up and down.

"Let me think about it and get back to you. But don't you worry yourself, young lady. Jack's a survivor—he won't be down and out for long."

"Oh no, Mr. Polley. I know that. I'm not worried when it comes to Jack."

"Say, what's the matter with me?" Cy said to Elizabeth. "I've got the perfect deal for Jack. I've been sitting on it for a few months, not knowing where to turn. But it's right up his alley. It's a Chinese deal: a power equipment company called Haikou Transformer. My client, Madame Ling, lives in New Jersey; she's the company's president. The company is located in Haikou, on Hainan Island, south of Hong Kong. They were a state-owned enterprise, but Madame Ling and her husband Mr. Li bought the company and privatized it. I think Jack might know the company."

Still talking on the other line, Jack kept nodding up and down to Elizabeth.

"Charley Allen and I gave them their first equity a few years ago," Cy continued. "Now that they're coining money, I handle Madame Ling's stock portfolio here in the States."

Elizabeth remained silent.

"Are you still there, young lady?"

"Yes, I'm here," she answered, hesitating as she looked at Jack, who was looking back at her. "Jack's luck in China hasn't been too good lately, Mr. Polley," Elizabeth said as Jack stared at her, his eyes narrowing.

"Oh, come now," the old man said. "I know all about what happened to Jack in China with New Land, if that's what you mean. But that's ancient history. Two years ago, there were no private companies in China. Jack had no choice but to try to deal with a bunch of government crooks. Things are different now."

"But you said you've been sitting on the deal for months," Elizabeth objected. "Why?"

Cy laughed. "I told you," he laughed. "It's a Chinese deal."

"See?"

"But young lady," Cy said, sounding a little impatient. "No one knows China like Jack. And the buyers know that. The company's in the power business, for God's sake. If anyone can get this deal done, he can."

"What does the company want to do?" Elizabeth asked.

"What does the company want to do? Same thing every Chinese company these days wants to do—an IPO. They're too small for the Shanghai exchange or the Hong Kong, and the wait is too long at those places anyway. So they've got their eye on doing a $20 million reverse merger IPO and listing on the American Stock Exchange. Come on, what do you say?"

Elizabeth hesitated. "Mr. Polley. You know Jack. Of course he can do it. I just don't know if I want him to."

"Young lady, it's nice you want to protect him, but it's Jack's decision, don't you think? Talk to him. In the meantime, I'll courier over some paperwork on the company this afternoon. Have him call me as soon as he's reviewed the documents. I can't imagine Jack won't want to get involved."

㊌　㊌　㊌

When Jack got off the phone, Elizabeth told him about her call with Cy. "He's a very nice man," she said.

"You have no idea. What a great guy. Do you know who Charley Allen is?" Jack asked.

"No idea."

"He's a legendary Wall Street investor. Before Warren Buffett, there was Charley Allen. He and his family started an investment bank. The two of them—Cy and Charley—are money. So what'd he call about?"

Elizabeth told him what Cy had told her about Haikou Transformer.

"Haikou Transformer; sure. We used their equipment in the Xiayang project."

Jack switched subjects and tenses, and started talking about institutions who might be interested in buying a piece of a Chinese transformer company. She just sat there looking at him, waiting.

"What's the matter?"

"Jack, it's China," she said.

He saw the look in her eye, came over to the couch where she was sitting, and took a seat on the other end.

Elizabeth just sat there; she wasn't planning on saying anything more.

Jack looked out the window. It was early afternoon and rainy. The skies were a dark shade of pewter. Smudges of white condensation floated up from midtown's chimney tops and dissipated in gauzy banks of fog around the spire of the Chrysler Building across the street.

The two of them sat in silence in the dark office, the sepia light bathing the mahogany walls and casements brooding over the two of them.

"So what do you want me to say, Elizabeth? In a way, I dread the thought of going back. But I dread the thought of selling deals to American private equity guys more. And we can't turn up our noses at a $20 million IPO just because the company's in China."

"No. But you're just getting back on your feet. You can't afford to stumble."

As they spoke, a light wind lashed tiny beads of moisture against the window pane looking out over the roof of Grand Central. On Park Avenue South below, a flock of yellow cabs moved in and out of the flow of traffic, their tail lights flashing a red, rain-washed light show on the shiny street.

"Wrong response. We can't afford not to do this deal," Jack said. "Besides, if I get stiffed by another domestic private equity firm, I might commit a felony."

They both sat there looking out the window and not saying anything.

"Okay, okay," she said finally. "Enough of the silent treatment. It's your decision. And we both know what you're going to do. It's just that you've got to learn to say no to things," Elizabeth said.

"How do you know what I'm going to decide? You haven't even told me the details," Jack said, trying to laugh to take the edge off.

He wasn't worried. As soon as she had started telling him about Haikou Transformer, he had sized things up. Maybe it was crazy to go back to China again, but he couldn't ignore the money. A $20 million IPO would yield over a million in fees. One deal would mean the difference between living hand to mouth and prosperity. He had to do it.

The courier dropped Cy's package off around one o'clock in the afternoon. Elizabeth signed for the package and handed it to Jack without saying a word. Jack took the envelope, went to his desk, spread the contents out in front of him and spent the next hour studying the information.

He skimmed the glossy promotional materials, but read the financial statements cover to cover. Haikou Transformer appeared to be everything Cy had claimed. On sales of $50 million, the company was generating after tax earnings of over $6 million. Their auditor was internationally recognized.

Finished, he was day dreaming about China when he caught Elizabeth sitting at her desk staring at him.

"So?" Elizabeth asked.

"What?"

"Are we going to do it or not?"

"We could if we wanted to," Jack said, smiling but trying to be serious.

Not play acting, she said, "I don't see how you can afford it. We can't make new business calls in China."

"We don't have to make any new business calls. Cy wouldn't be referring the deal to us unless he had it locked up, and Madame Ling lives right here in Englewood Cliffs."

"But even if we land the deal, how are we going to pay for the travel costs? It's at least ten grand a person to get to Hong Kong and back these days."

"Elizabeth, this is a Chinese company from Hainan trying to do an IPO on the Amex. Think about it. They've got to be desperate. They'll pay our expenses in advance," Jack countered, waiting for her next objection.

"We're going to have all kinds of out-of-pocket costs beyond travel. I just don't see it."

"I'll get them to pay us a $25,000 nonrefundable retainer."

Elizabeth kept looking at Jack, but she wasn't saying anything more.

"Do me a favor," Jack said, getting up from the couch and turning on his computer. "I'll start preparing the proposal and the pitch book. You pull together the engagement agreement. Make it a six-month agreement with a two-year tail upon success. And back up the truck on the fees—an upfront retainer; a documentation fee when we've finalized the offering materials; a cash shell fee when we find a clean backdoor vehicle; a 10 percent cash placement fee; warrants; and exclusive investment banking rights for two years when we close."

Scribbling Jack's instructions into a notebook, Elizabeth looked over at Jack as he picked up the telephone. "I'm going to get a hold of my friend Lee Fu, New Land's CFO," he said. "He can scrub the company's numbers and review their Chinese documents to make sure they match the English versions."

She returned to the notes she had just taken. "Do you really think they'll agree to all this?"

"The only issue we'll have to argue about is the upfront retainer," Jack said. "They could care less about the rest as long as we raise the money."

"So how are we going to pry a $25,000 retainer out of them?" Elizabeth asked. "We can't do an IPO on the come."

"Cy."

"Cy?"

"Cy. His reputation with them is on the line. They've asked him to deliver them an IPO, and now he's doing it. He'll get them to pay us the retainer."

"Do we really have to go to China?"

"No; we could deliver milk instead if you'd like."

水 水 水

Two weeks later, Jack and Elizabeth left for Shanghai on the morning Northwest flight out of JFK.

When Elizabeth had organized the trip, Madame Ling made a halfhearted attempt to suggest they fly economy, but Elizabeth just laughed. Everyone knew working *laowai* flew business class. Since she would meet them in Shanghai as well, Madame Ling was less reluctant regarding good lodging, and agreed they would reserve rooms at the Peace Hotel, one of Asia's finest.

Jack had only been to Shanghai once, five years earlier, and retained a fuzzy memory of the place. As their plane dropped through the late afternoon haze on their final approach to the runway, he looked down to find an unexpected scene. The Shanghai airport he had remembered was an untidy urban airfield tucked in a crowded city neighborhood. Below was something totally different—a brand new airport in a rural setting, with the city nowhere in sight. Cruising over the intersection of the Yangtze and the ocean, the plane glided down over a web of canals and rice paddies lacing foggy agricultural land. Gargantuan landing strips appeared out of the mist; off to the northwest, an elevated monorail ran above miles of parking lots.

Inside, the terminal was gleaming, light and airy, boasting promenades lined with stores selling Prada and Versace luxury goods. Collecting their luggage, Jack and Elizabeth set out for downtown Shanghai to meet Madame Ling. Where once Jack had meandered city bound on a two-lane road, they now whisked along an eight-lane freeway.

In 30 minutes, the downtown skyline came into view, looking like a giant bird's nest thatched with hundreds of cranes. The buildings along the bund appeared as impressive as they had in the famous scenes of Spielberg's *Empire of the Sun*. Across the river, the gleaming new city of Pudong poked up into the smoggy mist, the profiles of its buildings almost cartoonish, as if Jack was looking at an artist's rendition of a Chinese Oz airbrushed onto a canvas backdrop.

He checked his bearings, looking down the streets and alleyways perpendicular to the bund. They remained gritty; the same old men in sleeveless tee shirts sat playing Mah Jong under laundry hanging from the porches. He looked back across the river—the spires and needles of Pudong hadn't gone away. Compared to the scene across the river, Los Angeles looked like a small town from the 1950s.

㉗　㉗　㉗

They checked into the Peace Hotel. Jack forced Elizabeth to accompany him to the lounge for a nightcap, the hotel bar still offering its famous ensemble of African-American jazz musicians playing the smoky Memphis blues that had dazzled patrons for decades.

The next morning, Jack rose early, called his sons, checked with Helena on what she had served for dinner, told them he loved them and would check in with them same time tomorrow, did his exercises, showered and shaved, dressed and packed, and met Elizabeth and Madame Ling for the drive to Haikou Transformer's Mainland sales office.

At the office, Jack and Elizabeth satisfied themselves that the company offered competitive products, but they were more impressed with the cell phones. In the Catapult Energy days, Jack had been one of the first of his contemporaries to own a cell phone, a Motorola device as big as a brick. As the technology advanced, he bought a smaller device, but didn't use it much—the service stateside was terrible, and he couldn't afford it anyway. The idea of making a call in China never crossed his mind. But sitting around the table with the managers from Hainan Transformer, everyone had at least two cell phones, and were using them to call customers around the world. Jack looked around the office for a landline and didn't see one.

After lunch, they grabbed a taxi to the airport, caught the three o'clock flight to Hainan Island, and two hours later crossed the Hainan Straits and coasted down over Haikou, the capital of the province. White cumulus marked the edge of the departing Mainland, while up ahead tropical thunderheads loomed over the South China Sea. From the air, Hainan Island reminded Jack of a poor man's Hawaii—the sea was not as blue, the mountains mere gum drops compared to the towering grandeur of Mauna Kea and Mauna Loa—but the land was green, soft, and pleasantly undeveloped.

They landed and rolled up to a shoddy airport terminal constructed of white cement block streaked with brownish green mold. Disembarking, they cleared customs, found their driver and their bags, and headed out onto the highway toward Haikou.

The route to their hotel took them through the middle of the city and then out along the coast. It was a gray, dusty evening, the wind sweeping up rude clouds of crud. Their car whooshed by small groups of people standing or sitting around poorly lighted shops at the intersections. The islanders appeared darker than Mainlanders, their hair longer and unruly; men walked down the roadways in sarongs.

Even in faraway Haikou, stark evidence of China's construction boom surrounded them. Dozens of half-constructed towers, ribbed with bamboo scaffolding and dotted with nightlights flickering like fireflies, lined the roads. It was after eight o'clock in the evening, but the walls of gray concrete laced with webs of rebar itched with human activity, men crawling persistently through the structures, oblivious to the night.

Their hotel, a Parrot Courtyard posing as a resort establishment, was on the Straits a mile outside the city. Checking in, they filled out their forms at a lanai facing a grubby beach 30 yards beyond. Across the water, they could see the Mainland lying low in the gray, smoggy distance.

Jack changed quickly and waited for Elizabeth in the lobby bar behind the reception area. A salty tropical breeze washed over him. The place was slightly frayed and ratty, but serviceable. If they were lucky, Haikou Transformer would be a similar vintage, and they would have a chance at a closing.

Jack ordered a watery Mai Tai and a cigar made in Vietnam. He stretched out in a rattan chaise lounge, drained half of the Mai Tai in one gulp, and took a long pull on the cigar.

Elizabeth arrived a few minutes later, dressed in white and flushed from the subtropical heat.

"What are you drinking?"

"A Mai Tai," Jack said. "Ever had one?"

"No. And I've never been to an island."

"Well, celebrate and have a Mai Tai," Jack said. When Elizabeth nodded her consent, he held up two fingers for the waitress. "But I must tell you, I've had much better. There are two ways to make a Mai Tai, the way this place makes them, with too much ice and cheap light rum, or the way they make them in Hawaii—four kinds of rum, two dark and two light, in a big glass with pineapple juice and a lime. But I'm not complaining," he said, taking a long pull on his cigar as the last of the sun expired below the smog of the Mainland.

The waitress brought the Mai Tais. Elizabeth took a sip of hers.

"What do you think?" Jack said.

"It's all right; a little strong."

"No, I meant everything; the island, the hotel."

She sighed and raised her eyebrows.

"It's not Hawaii," Jack said, "but it's not bad."

"You think so?" Elizabeth wrinkled her nose. "Did you see the beach? I wouldn't go in that water if you paid me."

"Look at it this way Elizabeth—it beats sitting at our desks in the Graybar Building making cold calls," Jack said, looking out across the Straits.

❀   ❀   ❀

Mr. Li was not what Jack had expected. In marked contrast to Madame Ling, who was plain, wide, and slightly frumpy, Mr. Li was tall and handsome, his face dark like the other islanders, his physique trim and athletic. Giving him an invitation to play golf next time, Jack was sure Mr. Li did so expecting to more than hold his own.

Mr. Li spoke English—not as well as Madame Ling, but passable, and spent most of the evening telling them about his other businesses: a software company; a hotel; and his favorite endeavor, his yacht business. For some reason, the majority of Mainland Chinese businessmen Jack had met over the years felt it obligatory to own a hotel. As Mr. Li kept talking, Madame Ling kept trying to steer the conversation back to Haikou Transformer. Spending as much time as she had stateside, she knew American investment bankers and investors got nervous when executives had divergent interests.

But Jack had already decided he didn't care about Mr. Li's distractions, which probably included a collection of mistresses as well. Madame Ling ran Haikou Transformer. At dinner, she not only provided all the company's facts and figures off the top of her head, but addressed their questions on the strategic direction of the business as well. And her English was very good. He could put her in front of any institutional investor.

The next day, whatever fears Jack still harbored about Haikou Transformer vanished soon after they pulled into the driveway of the company's headquarters. Assembled behind Madame Ling and Mr. Li were hundreds of smiling employees standing at informal attention, identically dressed in white tee shirts, gray trousers, and blue hats with the company's logo. The company's office building was a modern structure, spotless and decorated throughout with flowers and plants. A team of engineers escorted them through a gleaming research and development laboratory lined with Chinese patent certificates. The marketing department looked no different from the bullpen at Salomon Brothers, technical personnel on their telephones assisting customers across China. The factory floor was dominated by German tooling and assembly equipment, while spools of cast resin transformer cores were wound and then sequestered in an inventory cage monitored by a computer system.

Jack had allocated all day for due diligence, but after 30 minutes the conclusion was obvious—the company was eminently financeable.

Haikou Transformer could sell anything they could produce. The missing ingredient was capital—equity capital. Manufacturing businesses like Haikou Transformer required lots of money. While the company had access to debt from the Chinese banks, it could borrow only so much. They needed equity desperately. Anyone who could deliver it would be handing Haiku Transformer a license to print money.

In the hiatus since Jack had been gone from China, her business climate had changed. Private ownership and wholly owned foreign enterprises were being encouraged, and companies like Haikou Transformer were bursting at the seams, while rivers of foreign investment remained stalled outside the country, trying to figure out how to get in. The only thing missing was someone to point the way. He could make a fortune there.

At the end of their visit, sitting in the cafe at the airport waiting to catch the plane to Hong Kong, Jack turned to Madame Ling.

"Are there any more companies like yours in China?" Jack asked.

"You kidding?" she asked, curious but not smiling.

"It's probably a stupid question, but no, I'm not."

"Thousands," she said, looking at her husband who nodded his head and went back to slurping his noodles.

徐 徐 徐

Once back in New York, Jack, Elizabeth, and Lee scrunched around the table in Davis Brothers' one-room office, assembled the offering papers for the Haikou Transformer deal, dialed up potential investors, organized the road show, and started putting Madame Ling and her team in front of one-on-one appointments. Mr. Li could stay at home and play golf; Jack didn't need him.

Things went smoothly compared to an American deal. Even though no financial institutions had yet financed a Chinese company in a reverse merger, they read Davis Brothers' offering materials and decided China didn't scare them quite as much after all. Few turned down road show appointments.

Three months late, the deal closed. Davis Brothers earned more than a million in cash fees, plus warrants, and not one institution griped about the compensation. But the money he earned wasn't Jack's source of greatest satisfaction. He felt a sense of accomplishment, doing a professional job for a grateful client, and delivering a good deal to investors at the same time.

"How nice is this," he said to Elizabeth at the closing dinner. "Not only do these guys pay us top dollar, but they actually respect our thoughts and listen to our advice."

"You think so?" Elizabeth asked, looking at Jack.

"You're too cynical," Jack said.

"Maybe I should be."

徐 徐 徐

The money in the bank and Jack's immediate financial pressure easing, he sublet more space in the office next door and hired a controller and a receptionist.

The day the furniture arrived and people settled into their new quarters, Jack took them to celebrate over lunch at Tao, a Chinese fusion restaurant in midtown. Everyone ordered Chinese food, even Elizabeth. At the end of the meal, Jack asked for the bill; the waiter brought it over together with a basket of fortune cookies.

Jack handed the waiter his credit card, passed the basket of cookies around the table, took the last one for himself, and opened it. "Your fortune lies in the Middle Kingdom," the small rectangle of paper read.

Jack looked around the table. Elizabeth was reading her fortune, Lee and Robert Gander, his compliance director, were commiserating over the Giants' draft picks, and Will Francis, the new receptionist, and Sarah Gimbel, his controller, were discussing how to make a bank deposit over the telephone. Jack didn't show his fortune to anyone— that would be a mistake. Bad luck. He folded the tiny piece of paper and tucked it into his wallet.

The waiter returned with Jack's credit card paperwork and one more fortune cookie. Jack opened it. "True love waits in China at the end of a long walk home."

There wasn't a doubt in his mind—the pieces of paper had his name on them.

If being good was really only luck, maybe lightning in China would strike again. The issue would be the storm.

Chapter 25

Killing Two Birds with One Stone

"Who's Paul Chin?" Elizabeth asked, when she saw Chin's name on the Davis Brothers appointment calendar.

"He's that Chinese guy who wandered in a few months ago trying to peddle some research on PRC companies," Jack said to Elizabeth.

"Was his research any good?"

"Terrible."

"I don't get it," Elizabeth said.

"Look, we need Chinese deal flow," Jack said. "Forget the research; the guy said he was connected over there. We've got to talk to everyone."

"Deal flow is one thing, but we can't operate over there without a trustworthy partner," Elizabeth said.

"It sounds like you're getting more comfortable with the place."

"I wouldn't go that far."

Paul Chin arrived at Davis Brothers' offices the next day. Overdressed in a snap brim hat, an English tweed jacket, and brown suede oxfords,

Chin's baleful expression accented by his long black eyelashes reminded Jack of his dog Ritchie.

Chin produced business cards from a silver case and made a great show of walking around the table presenting his card with two hands to Jack, Elizabeth, and Lee.

"What's Mainland Advisors?" Elizabeth asked Chin, eyeing the card.

"One of the best financial services firms in China," Chin said.

Jack, Elizabeth, and Lee just looked at each other.

"Here are some examples of our work product," Chin continued, opening his leather valise and extracting a sheaf of research reports. He tried to pass them around the table.

"Thanks, Paul," Jack said, putting the pile of reports on the table, "but we have a different topic in mind."

Chin looked confused.

Jack explained. "We've just finished a $20 million IPO for Haikou Transformer. We wondered if you might know where in China we could find some similar companies."

"A $20 million IPO? My goodness. Where did you get the money?"

"Financial institutions," Jack shrugged.

"I know some rich Chinese guys who might be interested in investing in IPOs," Chin said.

"We don't deal with individual investors," Elizabeth said. "We're not looking for money, just companies."

"I'm in touch with lots of Chinese companies," Chin said.

"As good as Haikou Transformer?" Elizabeth asked.

"Yes, I believe so."

"Do you know the company?" Jack asked.

"Yes, I think I may have done some work for them in the past."

"So they paid you to write a research report," Elizabeth said, testing him.

"At some point, perhaps. I would need to speak to my contacts in Hong Kong and get back to you."

"So it was someone in your Hong Kong office who really dealt with the company," Elizabeth said, looking at Jack for a moment before pressing ahead with Chin.

The air conditioner in the office drowned Chin's voice. The three of them sat watching Chin squirming in his seat, his chair's leather cushions groaning and squeaking.

"Yes, I believe so. I must check our firm's relationship with the company. As you know, *guanxi* is so important in China."

"*Guanxi*?" Elizabeth asked.

"Relationships," Paul answered. "Relationships are everything in China."

"As opposed to the rest of the world," Elizabeth said.

"What?" Paul's eyes opened wide and blinked several times in rapid succession, like Ritchie when he got a gnat in his eye. He slid lower in his seat and looked down at the floor for a moment. His hair was closely cropped, exposing his skull's contours and bumps.

"Let's get back to Mainland Advisors," Jack said. "How many employees does your company have?"

"Oh, I don't know," Chin said, rubbing the side of his face. "Twenty to 30, perhaps?"

"Twenty to 30 people?" Jack asked. "Well, that's not enough to be one of the best financial services firms in China, as you put it, but still decent size. All Chinaside?" Jack looked at Chin's face as he averted his eyes.

"Yes," Chin said.

"Except you," Lee said. "You're not over there. It says you're stateside," Lee said, holding up Chin's business card and reading it.

"Well, yes."

Lee said something to Chin in Chinese. Chin looked back at him with a blank expression, offering no response. Lee looked over at Jack and said, "I was just asking him what part of China he's from."

Paul still didn't answer Lee, and instead squirmed more, punishing his leather seat.

"All right, whatever," Jack said. "Do you have any deals in your pipeline now?"

"Yes," Paul responded, exhaling and obviously relieved to be able to change the subject. "Sino Solar," he said, taking three reports on the company from the pile on the table and handing them around to the group. "The company sells solar hot water systems; they're top 10 in China."

"Do they need money?" Jack asked as he, Elizabeth, and Lee all leafed through Chin's report.

"Yes, of course," Chin said. "They want to do a $10 million reverse merger. Just like Haikou Transformer," he added.

"What's your relationship with the company?" Jack asked.

"Sino Solar is a Mainland Advisors' deal," Chin said. "The company has given me exclusive authorization to find an investment banker in the United States. We could collaborate immediately. We've done all the legwork Chinaside; you raise the money stateside, and we split the fees down the middle," Chin proposed.

Elizabeth and Lee rolled their eyes in unison, looking at Jack.

Paul looked across the table at the three of them and stammered, "This is just the first deal. I've got a dozen more."

A dreamer, Jack thought. He was about to call the interview to an end when Chin added, "One more thing; Sino Solar's sponsor, my colleague Dr. Yu, is very well connected in China. He provided the company with their only outside equity capital, and is very anxious to see it successfully complete its IPO. Making Dr. Yu happy could be very important for Davis Brothers."

"Tell us about Dr. Yu," Jack said.

"He is from a very prominent family. His grandfather was one of the founders of the PRC. His father was with the Ministry of Electric Power, and Dr. Yu has a vast network in China's power industry—he has been personally involved in the financing of Three Gorges."

Jack looked at Lee, who was nodding his head. Even Elizabeth seemed to be paying attention. "All right, Paul. We might take a look at this Sino Solar deal, meet your friend. Why don't you give us a few days to look at what you've prepared, do some homework. Then, if we want to talk further, we'll give you a call."

"Okay," Chin said, pushing back from the table with a satisfied look on his face, standing up as the others did and gathering the rest of his research reports off the table.

"One more thing, Paul," Jack said, looking across the table at Chin. "There's a chance we may raise money for Sino Solar and help your friend, so I don't want to appear too harsh when we're just getting to know each other—but there's no way we're splitting our financing fees with you or anyone else. If raising money were easy, everyone would be doing it."

Jack kept looking at Chin, who stood shuffling uncomfortably, his long eyelashes blinking up and down as he looked down at the floor, then out the window. "That sounds all right," Chin finally stammered. "But you'll change your mind when you see Mainland Advisors in action. We'll be your feet on the street."

㊍ ㊍ ㊍

Jack showed Paul Chin out and returned to the office, where Elizabeth and Lee remained sitting at the table.

"You realize that guy's useless," Elizabeth said.

Lee laughed. "He's a finder, Elizabeth. He's got the deal, and that's all he's got, but it's enough. There's a thousand guys like him in China. It's just part of doing business over there."

Elizabeth looked at Lee and said, "Are there any good finders, or are they all the same?"

Lee shook his head. "They're all the same."

"I don't know how else we're going to get access to deal flow sitting here in New York City," Jack said.

"You're right," Lee answered. "If you want to do business in China, you've got to hold your nose and use finders."

"Finders like him?" Elizabeth asked, exasperated.

"They're all like him," Lee said.

"Well, there is one difference with Paul Chin," Jack said. "He's got an important friend, remember? If this guy Dr. Yu is for real, we could kill two birds with one stone. It's worth a shot. Let's take a look at the company. In the meantime Lee, why don't you follow up with Chin, see if you can get him and some other people from his firm back here in a few days."

㊍ ㊍ ㊍

The following week, Jack and Elizabeth and Lee assembled in their conference room at 10 o'clock as Will Francis ushered in Paul Chin and two other Chinese men.

Everyone introduced themselves; the two new Chinese guys handed out business cards.

Before Jack had time to look at the cards he had been given, Elizabeth sat down next to him, leaned over, and whispered, "That guy's business card says he works at Merritt Partners."

"Which guy?" Jack asked.

"That guy over there talking to Lee; the one who looks like a human Pez Dispenser."

Elizabeth was referring to the tall skinny Chinese man with rectangular glasses whose bony head was too large by half for his body. His voice deep and booming, he stood at the other end of the long table, nodding and laughing with Lee, speaking Chinese.

Jack looked at the business cards; both of them said Merritt Partners. The Pez Dispenser's name was Kerry Chew; the other guy's name was James Zheng.

The group spent an hour reviewing Mainland Advisors' exclusive agreement with Sino Solar and the Davis Brothers' engagement agreement. Chin barely spoke, and the remarks from his two colleagues were gratuitous; it was clear none of them had ever closed a deal.

At eleven, they took a break. Kerry Chew and James Zheng went down the hall to the men's room.

"So, Paul," said Elizabeth to Chin, "Why do your colleagues have Merritt Partners business cards?"

"Ah, yes. Just a temporary thing; their new cards are coming any day."

"They've left Merritt Partners to join Mainland Advisors?"

"Yes."

"And they work for you."

"Why yes, of course."

The group reconvened, and the meeting concluded an hour later. Citing another engagement, Paul Chin dashed for the door.

Kerry Chew and James Zheng lingered, chatting in Chinese with Lee. Chew couldn't help himself; it was obvious to Jack he would network with a wooden Indian if given the chance.

"What's it like working for Paul?" Elizabeth asked Kerry Chew.

"Working for Paul? Oh no, no, no," Chew laughed. "I don't work for Paul. He works for me."

Kerry Chew and James Zheng left a few minutes later. Jack made sure the door closed after them, waited a moment, and then turned and looked at Elizabeth and Lee, and started to laugh. "You're right, Lee," Jack said. "They've got an exclusive, and that's all they've got."

"I told you," Lee said, laughing as well.

"You guys think this is funny? We're in bed with a bunch of incompetent liars who don't even know who works for whom," Elizabeth said. "They're not finders; they're losers."

Chapter 26

The Man to See

Jack told Paul Chin Davis Brothers would accept Sino Solar's IPO engagement subject to due diligence, an advance retainer, and most importantly, meeting Dr. Yu during a initial due diligence session to occur in Beijing, all expenses to be paid in advance. The following Monday, Jack delivered Chin a package of documents containing Davis Brothers' proposal to Sino Solar for its IPO; the firm's standard engagement agreement; and a separate agreement between Davis Brothers and Mainland Advisors regarding a proposed fee split.

Paul Chin couldn't do much right himself, but someone at Sino Solar had the lights on: Davis Brothers' engagement agreement was signed and returned a week later, together with two Sino Solar check drafts, one representing the retainer and the other an expense allowance.

Cash in hand, Elizabeth booked flights for them to Beijing. Jack had no idea what kind of name cards they would see from Chin's people in China; he just looked forward to meeting Dr. Yu.

Jack, Elizabeth, and Lee left JFK on Sunday afternoon and arrived overnight on Monday evening in Beijing. Lee had booked their rooms at the Bamboo Garden, the state-owned hotel in the hutong President Wang of CJEC used whenever he stayed in Beijing. While Jack could do without the Mah Jong tables, he had learned to love the Bamboo Garden, especially the garden with its moon gates and terrace restaurant.

Before leaving New York, Jack had asked Paul Chin if Tuesday's meetings would convene at Mainland Advisors' offices. Chin had been vague, mumbling something would be worked out by the time they arrived. When they checked in to the Bamboo Garden, a message indicated their meeting would convene at the offices of Redstone Investments, the financial services firm headed by Dr. Yu.

Tuesday morning, after Jack called his sons and had breakfast in the hotel's garden restaurant, the Davis Brothers group took a taxi to Redstone's offices. Dr. Yu came to the door to greet them, and they all traded business cards and chatted while waiting for Paul Chin and his people and the Sino Solar management to arrive. Redstone's staff was small—less than a dozen—but friendly; they all spoke English.

Dr. Yu was not a medical doctor—Jack had learned many Chinese men with PhDs used the appellation "Doctor"—but he possessed an equivalent bedside manner. He looked solid, but his persona was that of someone seeking to avoid attention. His frame was neither thin nor heavyset, his face clear and forehead high. He wore glasses, and was well dressed in an understated way. His demeanor and mannerisms were not Mainland Chinese—he could have been from anywhere in the world.

Jack found it difficult to get Dr. Yu to utter even a few words about himself, but when Jack asked him questions about China's electric power industry, Dr. Yu spoke enthusiastically, and the information wasn't anecdotal.

Dr. Yu introduced Jack and Elizabeth and Lee to Kevin Tong, his lieutenant, and Kitty Ji, Redstone's analyst who would also handle the translation for their meetings. From speaking to them, Jack could tell they were under the impression Redstone was somehow doing the IPO with assistance from Paul Chin. They had little idea what an American investment bank did or why Davis Brothers was there.

Chin showed up next—by himself, sans "feet on the street." By the end of the day, Jack was convinced Mainland Advisors was just Paul working out of a telephone booth.

The Sino Solar management team arrived last. Mr. Hu, Sino Solar's founder and CEO, was exactly what he appeared to be—a Chinese peasant from Bazhou, a county in Hebei, the province surrounding Beijing. With a fireplug physique, buzz-cut black hair, gray long johns showing under his white socks, Hu's low social beginnings would have been obvious to anyone from China, but the clincher was the inch-long, tapered nail on his left pinky finger.

Hu brought his wife with him. Squat, dark, and identical to her husband at 20 yards, she controlled the company checkbook. That Hu and his wife were peasants was of no concern to Jack. He hadn't expected anything different—peasants were China's biggest consumers of solar hot water systems. But Sino Solar's provincial management would be part of the challenge of the deal, and Hu's wife, if anything, would be a tougher problem. Hiring a chief financial officer with English language skills and a certified professional accountant accreditation would be a minimum requirement; Ms. Hu would have to go back to Bazhou.

At ten o'clock, the collected group filed into Redstone's crowded boardroom and the company began its presentations.

When it was time for questions, Jack opened with a lob pass. "Mr. Hu, what's your gross margin?"

Kitty translated.

"*Shi*," Mr. Hu said.

"Yes," Kitty said. Jack, Lee, and Elizabeth looked at each other. "*Yes?*"

"Okay, there must be a translation error," Jack said. "Kitty, I was trying to ask Mr. Hu about his profit margin after his cost of goods sold—his gross margin."

"I know. That's what I asked him," Kitty said.

"All right, then; maybe he doesn't understand. Why don't you just ask him what his cost of goods sold is, and we'll try to get to the same place."

Kitty posed the question to Hu.

"*Shi,*" Hu said.

The challenge of financing a company whose management team lacked an English-speaking member started to set in.

"Jack, some of these terms don't have direct translation in Chinese," Lee said. "Let me pry it out of Mr. Hu," he said as a look of relief passed over Kitty's face.

Lee and Hu had a conversation that must have lasted 10 minutes. "Forty percent," Lee said finally.

At 15 minutes per easy question, it was going to be a long day; having Kalin around would have helped a ton. "Okay. Maybe we should stay away from the numbers for now," Jack said. "You can discuss it with him later, Lee. Kitty, please ask Mr. Hu to tell us in his words the best thing about his company."

Kitty dutifully repeated Jack's request to Hu.

"He says they are Number One," Kitty said.

"Okay …; is that by units sold, revenues—what?"

Kitty repeated the question in Chinese to Mr. Hu. Ten minutes later, she sighed, knowing what she was about to say was not acceptable. "He just says they are Number One."

"All right, who's their competition?" Elizabeth asked, trying to get to the bottom of things.

Kitty translated. "He says they have no competition," she said, her face betraying her dissatisfaction with being connected, even through conversation, with Mr. Hu.

"No competition," Jack repeated. This was going nowhere. "What does he worry about, then?"

Kitty translated, and couldn't keep the smile off her face. "He only worries whether you will get the money."

"Jack, it's almost lunch time," Lee said. "Add that to the other topics I'll review with Mr. Hu."

The group broke for lunch and went around the corner to a restaurant. Dr. Yu, who took his host role seriously, waited for them at the entrance to a private room. As the guests arrived, Dr. Yu seated everyone according to their role in the deal, placing Mr. Hu, the most important guest, between Jack and Paul.

Mr. Hu would do nothing at lunch without checking first with Dr. Yu—probably a peasant class thing—except once when, in a fit of exuberance, Mr. Hu had Kitty ask Jack whether he wanted *baiju* or beer with lunch; Dr. Yu defused the transgression, telling Hu lunch would be a working affair.

Sitting next to Mr. Hu, who was expecting conversation, Jack turned to Paul and asked, "Could you please ask Mr. Hu how many patents his company holds?"

"Uh, yes; of course. Excellent question," Paul replied. "Let me see if Kevin can get Mr. Hu's attention. Kevin. Say Kevin; a moment, please. Kevin," Paul persisted, calling across the noisy table, trying to attract the attention of Kevin Tong, Dr. Yu's lieutenant.

After waiting a minute more, Jack said, "Kevin's talking to someone, Paul. Just ask Mr. Hu the question yourself, for God's sake."

Paul ignored Jack for another moment, tried again to get Kevin's attention, and then finally, with Jack staring at him and Mr. Hu waiting for someone to speak to him, said "I can't."

"You can't? Why not?" Jack asked.

"Mr. Hu speaks Mandarin, and I speak Cantonese."

Jack laughed even though he was stunned. "You've got one of the best financial services firms in China and you don't even speak the language? What am I missing?"

"I speak to our Cantonese clients."

Jack had heard enough. "Oh, come now. Cantonese clients. Everyone in China north of Kowloon speaks Mandarin, even the taxi drivers. Speaking Cantonese might suffice if you are financing a restaurant in the New Territories, but that's about it." He didn't say another word to Paul Chin for the rest of the day.

"What do you think of what you've learned so far?" Kevin Tong asked Jack after lunch as they walked from the restaurant back to the office.

"About what I expected," said Jack. "Certainly fewer surprises than those I've received from our colleague at Mainland Advisors," he said.

"What do you mean?"

"How well do you know Paul Chin?"

"Not well. I just know he's a friend of Dr. Yu's, but that's all. Why?"

"I'm just trying to figure where he's coming from."

"I think he's a banana. If he's not a banana, he's ABC. He's not a sea turtle—he doesn't even speak Mandarin," Kevin said, looking at Jack.

"Banana?"

"Oh, sorry," said Kevin. "I forgot; these terms are probably not familiar to you. A banana is a Chinese guy trying to masquerade as a foreigner."

"Why a banana?"

"Yellow on the outside, white on the inside," Kevin said, grinning at Jack through his glasses.

"I've got to remember that one," Jack said. "And a sea turtle?"

"That's someone like Dr. Yu; a person from the Mainland who goes overseas periodically, but then migrates back."

"Right. ABC?"

"American-born Chinese, of course," said Kevin, raising his eyebrows.

"So what are you?"

"Oh, I'm nothing special—just a Mainland Chinese guy trying to make a buck together with the fruits, animals, and alphabet soup."

㊌ ㊌ ㊌

When it came time to take the Sino Solar IPO on the road, Jack had planned to schedule all of the meetings stateside, but Kerry Chew insisted they also schedule one meeting in Hong Kong. One of his whale accounts, according to Kerry.

It took Jen Koo, a new institutional sales person Jack had hired, to provide him with the last word on Kerry Chew.

Jen was efficient and perpetually pleasant. Jack put her in charge of organizing the stateside road show for Sino Solar, including booking the one-on-one appointments, and asked her to coordinate with Kerry, who had implied he had a great network of institutional accounts—after all, his day job had been at Merritt Partners. A few weeks later, Jack asked Jen how things were working out.

"We're getting there. It's a small deal, and solar hot water is not well understood, but my book so far is 15 meetings in four cities. It'll happen."

"Is Kerry pulling his weight?" Jack asked. "Other than the guy in Hong Kong, who else has he lined up?"

Jen just stared at Jack for a moment like she hadn't heard him. "Kerry? Are you kidding? I haven't heard from him since the kickoff meeting a month ago."

"What? Are you telling me he hasn't helped you at all?"

Jen smiled at Jack. "I could tell you so many things," she said, laughing. "Your problem is you're not Chinese. We know the Kerry Chews of the world as soon as we see them coming."

"Meaning?"

"Kerry embodies what every Mainland Chinese guy thinks a good Chinese investment banker from the United States represents—a Merritt Partners business card, fancy clothes, funny stories, and most importantly, lots of alleged Wall Street relationships. I'm sure Kerry's already dazzled Mr. Hu, to the point where Hu's convinced all he needs to do to get his cash is make sure Kerry's involved—exactly what Kerry wants him to think. So Kerry's locked in. He's already cut a deal with Hu, trust me. He's just waiting to put his hand out at the closing. If he doesn't get what he bargained for from Mainland Advisors, he'll get some more from Mr. Hu directly."

"Without doing a shred of real work."

"Are you kidding? Real work? Kerry wouldn't know real work if it bit him in the ass," said Jen.

"Well, he's not going to get away with it. If Kerry doesn't execute, he's not getting paid."

"Oh no, don't do that to me," said Jen.

"What do you mean?"

"Having to cooperate with Kerry Chew is a recipe for chaos. He won't do anything himself—he can't—so he'll just ask me to do his job and then buzz round and round until it's done. He's a headless fly."

"A headless fly?"

"Think about it," Jen said, and turned back to her phone.

Chapter 27

Original Sin

"May I speak to Chairman Roo, please?" Jack asked the person in the Red Bank investment department who answered the telephone.

"Whom may I say is calling?" the woman replied. Her voice sounded familiar.

"My name is Jack Davis. I believe my colleague Kerry Chew may have mentioned I would call. My firm, Davis Brothers, represents Sino Solar, a Chinese company doing its IPO in the United States. Mr. Chew said Chairman Roo might be interested in hearing the story." There was a long pause at the other end of the line. "Hello?" Jack said.

"Yes, I'm sorry, Mr. Davis; I was just checking the schedule. Chairman Roo is looking forward to seeing Sino Solar here at our offices in Hong Kong next Tuesday afternoon at four o'clock."

"All right; I'll let the people at Sino Solar know; thanks again."

"Quite all right, Mr. Davis."

"Goodbye," Jack said.

"Mr. Davis?"

"Yes?"

"Will you be attending the meeting?"

Kerry Chew's whale was Chairman Roo, the head of Red Bank, the gargantuan financial services organization controlled by the Chinese Red Army. Red Bank's tentacles extended throughout the Chinese financial and industrial complex, mainly due to the leadership of Chairman Roo, one of China's most respected leaders who, before becoming head of the bank, had been the PRC Army general responsible for harnessing the ethnic areas of western China for the majority Han Chinese.

As Jack walked with Kerry and Mr. Hu off the elevator of Hong Kong's Shun Tak Centre into Chairman Roo's offices, they entered a supple and elegant space, not so much a place to do business as the personal quarters of a tasteful, powerful person.

The afternoon sun was streaming over the purple ridge of the New Territories as the receptionist opened double mahogany doors and ushered the three men into a small vestibule at the end of a boardroom the size of a bowling alley. A large floor-to-ceiling decorative screen depicting a water scene of lotus flowers stood 20 meters away at the far end of the room.

Kerry and Mr. Hu excused themselves to visit the washroom. The receptionist turned to Jack. "You must be Mr. Davis," she said.

"Yes."

"Chairman Roo is will be with you shortly, Mr. Davis. You will have tea?"

"Green tea would be fine, thank you."

The receptionist retreated out of the vestibule for a few moments, returned with a tray holding Jack's tea service and backed out again, shutting the double doors behind her. Jack stood looking out the windows over the harbor, idly watching the Star Line ferries coming and going to and from the terminal below.

A side door opened and Kalin walked in.

Jack stood stock still, wordlessly staring at her. She appeared taller, standing before him in high heels and a figure-hugging silk skirt and jacket, her dark, mournful eyes staring at him, her face quivering slightly. She had never worn heels before—in deference to Mickey, Jack was sure.

"You're not surprised?" Kalin asked, her voice dusky.

"I had a feeling it was you as soon as I hung up the telephone," he said after a pause.

"I was so surprised to hear your voice, I just didn't know what to say. I'm sorry." She shut the door behind her, and when she turned around to face him again, he saw she was crying. "Jack, I'm so sorry. For everything. Really." She walked to where he stood and put her arms around his neck.

There was a first time for everything. Jack didn't move as Kalin hung on him, her tear-stained cheek touching his, the wet smell of her lily perfume taking him back to Manila. "Don't worry about it, Kalin."

"Don't worry? How can you say that? It's all I've thought about every day for two years."

"I'm sorry."

"Oh, Jack, don't make me feel more miserable than I already do. There's no reason for you to apologize to me. It was all my fault. David and Mickey made me do it. I shouldn't have listened to them."

He wanted her to let go, to pull away, but didn't want to hurt her feelings. "Kalin, that was a lifetime ago. I'm still not sure exactly *what* you did, but at this point, I know I don't want to find out."

"I just wanted to be good for you; if not for anyone else, at least for you," she said, finally unwrapping her arms from around him, backing up and looking at him, her pleading eyes set in mascara-stained cheekbones. "I didn't mean to hurt you. Can you ever forgive me?"

"Where are you doing here?" he asked, wiping her tears off his face.

"Here, let me," she said, rubbing his cheek with her fingers, her eyes still looking for an answer. "My father was a general, remember?"

"I thought he was on the other side."

"China's a general's club, Jack. Sometimes they change the rules here, but not for generals."

"Was President Wang a general, too?"

"President Wang," Kalin said as she rolled her eyes. "Are you staying at the Mandarin Oriental?"

"Why?"

"We've got a lot to talk about. I asked the receptionist to take Kerry and your client into another room, but Chairman Roo is very busy, so I must go brief him now on your deal before your group meets with him—we'll have to finish later."

Jack just looked at her. She looked incredibly good. She had always been good to look at.

"Yes, we are, but it was a struggle." When she looked at him with a puzzled expression, he added, "Kerry Chew wanted to stay at the Mansion."

"Kerry Chew." She rolled her eyes. "Of course, the new, nouveau Mansion. Perfect for Kerry. What are you doing with him? Never mind, tell me later. I must get back to Chairman Roo; I'll come get you when he's ready."

"Okay."

"Captain's Bar at six tonight?"

"Well, I'll be there with Duncan Leeds then," Jack said.

"Duncan Leeds? What are you talking to him for? I'll join you, then. It'll be just like old times," Kalin said, looking at him for confirmation.

"The more the merrier," Jack said, feeling like he had taken a wrong turn on a back road.

"Oh, I almost forgot. How much of the Sino Solar deal would you like us to take?"

水 水 水

Once Kalin left, it was as if the air was sucked out of the vestibule. Jack walked through the open doors to the boardroom and slowly down the carpeted chamber. Discombobulated, he looked absentmindedly out at the harbor. As he surveyed the view, he heard a scratching sound from behind the screen painted with lotus flowers at the other end of the room. He walked a dozen steps on the thick carpet toward the noise.

Coming around the edge of the screen, he was greeted by a vision from ancient China.

An elegant Chinese woman was painting the back side of the screen, her brush guiding daubs of paint across the woven reeds in quick but controlled strokes. Dozens of plump, avocado green lotus plants with pink and purple flowers had already found their place on the screen's surface, transforming it from an innate two dimensional piece of furniture into a languid portrait of summer life.

Wearing a floor-length linen gown and holding her brush in her right hand, the artist moved between the screen and a table holding her palette like a Degas dancer, as if she were doing so to music. Her long black hair, except for tresses that dangled down alongside either temple, was piled high on her head in a bun held with a tortoise-shell hairpin.

She was finishing the pink bud of a lotus flower when she saw him.

"Oh. Oh, I'm sorry." Her brush fell out of her hand onto the canvas drop cloth beneath her slippered feet. "I didn't hear you. You have business. I will stop."

She spoke very precisely and carefully. Jack could see her concentrate as she talked. She had an odd, elegant accent, with a slight British inflection, but different. She looked at him through calm, black eyes; her skin was lustrous. She appeared young, but it was difficult to discern her age.

"No. It's my fault—I surprised you. Don't stop. The painting is beautiful."

She stood looking at him, not moving.

He stooped to pick up her brush. "I hope I haven't broken your concentration."

She was shaking her head back and forth when Kalin reentered at the other end of the room.

"I see you've met Ms. Lian, our artist in residence," Kalin said, walking toward them.

"Interrupted her is more like it, I'm afraid," Jack said, looking from Kalin back at the painter who stood silently, but smiling, looking down at the floor, as if she didn't know what to do next.

"Chairman Roo is waiting, Mr. Davis," Kalin said.

"Yes, all right. Well, I hope I see you again—what did you say your name was?" Jack asked the painter as he looked at her, trying to see her eyes, Kalin by this time standing next to her, an impatient look on her face.

"You may call me by my Buddhist name," the painter said. "Lianhua."

"What a nice name," Jack said. "What does it mean?"

"Lotus flower." Lianhua smiled and looked directly at Jack for the first time.

"Ms. Lian," Kalin said, "works for us."

"I can see why. I hope I see you again, Lianhua. I enjoy your painting very much," Jack said, handing her the brush.

She smiled wordlessly as he followed Kalin out the door.

Chapter 28

Living Large

Although there was no place where Jack would rather be on a Friday afternoon in Hong Kong than the Captain's Bar, Duncan Leeds was not his ideal choice for company.

Duncan, a New Land shareholder who Jack hadn't heard from in over two years, had recently called the office, having heard Jack was back in the fundraising business. Duncan had a Chinese deal that needed funding—would Jack be in Hong Kong any time soon? Guys like Duncan came with the territory, Jack reminded himself as he descended down the stairs into the cave-like bar.

"Mr. Davis," the bartender said.

"Hey Billy, it's been awhile," Jack said to the bartender, who was standing alone at the bar in the quiet, the cigar humidor humming in the background. In the late afternoon, except for Billy manning his post, the place appeared deserted. Maybe he was off the hook.

"Good to see you again, sir. What may we offer you?"

"I'm not sure," Jack said, peering around the dark room and spying Duncan and another man holding down a table in the corner. Jack leaned against the bar railing opposite Billy for a minute, looking over at the two men, the specter of their faces trying to encroach on the receding vision of Lianhua and the lotus flowers floating just inside the inner edge of his mind. "Duty calls, I'm afraid. I'll just have some sparkling water."

"We have your favorite white Bordeaux on ice."

"No thanks. Maybe when the sun's over the yardarm. In the meantime, do me a favor and drag me out and shoot me if I spend more than an hour with these guys."

Jack walked over to where the men were sitting, slid onto one of the red leather banquets opposite Duncan, and said hello.

"Jack," said Duncan, "I asked after you at the concierge desk; it seems everyone in the hotel knows you."

"Not really. A few of them have had to roll me out of their saloon late at night, is all."

"It's been a few years, hasn't it," Duncan said, peering across the table at Jack in the dim light of the room. "You certainly seem to have landed on your feet."

"Well, I've been using them to stand since I was born—no sense in stopping now."

"Meet my friend Mr. Soo," Duncan said. "He is head of the publicly traded Red Bank subsidiary here in Hong Kong."

"How do you do, Mr. Soo."

Before Mr. Soo could respond, Kalin walked down the stairs from the lobby and sat down on the red leather stool next to Duncan.

"Kalin Gao: Duncan Leeds and Mr. Soo," Jack said. "You remember Kalin, Duncan."

"You do look very familiar, Ms. Gao," Duncan said.

"I was wondering if you would recognize me. I used to work for Jack at Catapult Energy."

"Quite so. You look … different," Duncan said.

"I was married then," Kalin said.

Jack looked over at Kalin, but she was still watching Duncan chuckling at his seat next to her.

"Well, I hope you and I have some time to catch up on the old days. Meanwhile, Jack," he said turning his attention back to Jack, "I'm here in Hong Kong to participate in an Asian Society convention on

China-U.S. business relations. You should attend; the topics are fascinating."

"Yes, I guess I should."

"No, really. I can get you in. I'm very influential with the people running things."

"That's very kind of you. But I don't think so."

"Why not?"

"No time, I'm afraid."

"What are you doing here?"

"I'm raising some money for a deal we're financing."

"What kind of deal?"

"Oh, I don't think you'd be interested."

"Why?"

"Solar hot water; pretty boring stuff for you, I'm sure."

"Come now, Jack. Nothing you're involved with is boring."

Kalin didn't say anything; she was just looking at Jack. Mr. Soo finished fussing with his tea, took a sip, and lit a cigarette.

"Jack and I have known each other many years," Duncan said, turning to Mr. Soo. "Jack, you've been coming to China for a long time, right?"

"Quite a while, yes."

"My friends tell me you've been very successful in China recently."

"They weren't always saying as much, were they? It's probably a temporary phenomenon, I assure you."

He looked back over at Kalin, who was still looking across the table at him.

"Do you know Red Bank, Jack?" Duncan asked.

"Sure, who doesn't?"

"No, really; they're a very important player here."

"I'm very aware of Red Bank's presence in China, Duncan."

"Just ask if you want to meet them."

"Well, we do know someone there."

"Who?" Duncan wouldn't drop it. He needed to know comparatives: where he stood; where Jack stood. It was important to some people.

Jack looked over at Kalin.

"I introduced Jack to Chairman Roo earlier today," Kalin said.

Andrew Soo began paying less attention to his tea.

"So you work for Chairman Roo at Red Bank?" Duncan asked, looking first at Kalin and then at Mr. Soo.

"No, I don't work for the bank; I manage the U.S. side of Chairman Roo's personal investments," Kalin said.

Duncan nodded his head up and down, looking at Kalin more carefully. "Do you have a business card?"

Kalin reached into her bag and handed a card to Duncan and another to Mr. Soo. "Chairman Roo is retiring next year. I'll probably be out of work after that," she smiled.

"In that case, you can come and work for me," Duncan said, now hunched over the table on the edge of his seat. "And what are you doing with Chairman Roo, Jack?"

"As little as possible," Jack said, grinning as he looked up at Duncan and Kalin peering back at him in the dark corner of the bar.

"I beg your pardon?"

"Sorry, Duncan; that's not fair. It's just a line from a movie about China."

"What movie?" Duncan asked.

"*Chinatown,*" Kalin said, staring at Jack.

"What happened in that movie?" Duncan asked. "I can't remember."

"It's about foreigners who stray into places they don't belong," Jack said, Kalin still staring at him.

"What kind of places?"

"Chinese places." Jack looked at Kalin's eyes as he spoke; it was as if they had never left Manila.

"Oh, look here Jack, you're just playing with us," Duncan said. "You really should get to the Asian Society conference. I'll be one of the speakers."

"I wish I could find the time. What are you speaking about?"

"The keys to success for U.S. business people in China," Duncan said.

"Well, now I'm really sorry I won't be there. So what are these nuggets of wisdom?"

"Well, it's not simple, of course. If I had to pick one thing, I'd suggest getting a good local partner."

"I thought at least three guys had already wrote books with that title," Jack said, grinning again across the table at Duncan and Kalin.

"I beg your pardon?" Duncan asked.

"Nothing," Jack said, turning to Mr. Soo to change the subject. "Tell me Mr. Soo, in which areas of the PRC do you typically invest?"

"I concentrate on the major deals. In Hong Kong, Shanghai, and Beijing; that sort of thing."

"I see—deals in Fake China."

"Fake China?" Duncan asked.

"Yes, the three big cities," Jack said.

"Why do you call them Fake China?" Duncan asked.

"It's just not real China, that's all."

"So what's real China to you?" Duncan persisted.

"Pretty much every place else."

Mr. Soo finally stirred. "Very interesting, Mr. Davis, very interesting indeed. I would like to learn more about your investments. In fact, Duncan and I were discussing an investment in a Hong Kong electronic game board manufacturer—we're here today to offer you a piece of it."

"Well, thank you very much for thinking of me, Mr. Soo," Jack said. Duncan hadn't offered him one of his deals for years. He probably just couldn't get this one funded.

"Not at all," Mr. Soo continued. "You see, the Chinese game board market is exploding. As I've explained to Duncan, due to my extensive contacts with the family that owns the subject company, the deal is locked up. We should easily make 10 times our money. I assume that type of return gets your attention," Mr. Soo said, blowing a huge plume of cigarette smoke Jack's way, peering at him through gold wire rim glasses and grinning the way most people do in Hong Kong any time the conversation turns to money.

"Oh, thanks again. But it sounds high tech. I'm not much for high-tech deals."

"Jack, come on. I really had hoped to bring you into this one. Why not participate?" Duncan asked.

"It just doesn't sound like my kind of transaction, that's all."

"What types of deals do you do?" Mr. Soo asked.

"Well, we're very involved in an alternative energy company right now, but generally the business has to smell before we'd finance it, Mr. Soo."

"I see. Basic businesses."

"Very."

"Cash flowing?"

"I should hope so."

"And the nature of most of these businesses?"

"I'd describe them as businesses where owning one takes as little as possible."

"There's that phrase again," said Duncan.

"As little as possible? Why so, Mr. Davis?"

"Well, Mr. Soo, I tend to think we foreigners don't really understand how things work here, and we probably never will. So if there's a business requiring a lot of thought, when we add up all the uncertainties, we're in too deep before we've started."

It was dark and cool in the corner where they sat. Billy came out around from behind his bar, picked up the empty bottles and glasses, and refilled the trays of potato chips and pretzels. "Sure you wouldn't like a drink, Mr. Davis?" Billy asked Jack.

"Thanks, Billy," Jack said. "I'll hold off for now."

"How about a Cohiba?" Billy offered.

"Would anyone mind if I smoked?" Jack asked. Duncan and Mr. Soo shook their heads.

"I love it when you smoke cigars," Kalin said.

Jack looked at Kalin, her eyes not leaving him, turned and nodded at Billy, and the barman turned to fetch the cigar box.

"Kalin, would you like another one?" Jack asked, seeing her half-empty drink.

"Call me Lin."

Jack and Kalin kept looking at each other as if no one else were there, prompting Duncan to try to get his conversation back on track. "So Jack, how are you spending your social time here? These beautiful Chinese girls turning your eye?" Duncan asked, looking sideways at Kalin as he spoke.

He was definitely interested in her, Jack thought. "Well, you've got to be careful there, Duncan. It's Chinatown."

"What does that mean?"

"Just another line from the movie."

The hotel had given him one of their better rooms, a mahogany paneled mini-suite high up on the twelfth floor on the water side with a good view of Victoria Harbor. Although August in Hong Kong, the temperature in the room was cool. The king-size bed was turned down, and a bowl of fruit sat on the coffee table. The bellman had already unpacked his bags and hung up his suits.

Traffic from the street below thrummed like white noise in the background. He plugged in his computer and sat absentmindedly waiting for the machine to power up, thinking about Kalin, then Lianhua, then Kalin, then Lianhua some more as he looked out over the traffic heading west on Connaught Road.

The setting sun, its orange orb warping as it slid down behind the Mainland ridge, washed stripes of red and purple across the dark slick of the harbor. Just like Jack, the Star Ferries meandered in and out of their terminals, no firm connection to either destination or port of call, laboring back and forth across the darkening stretch of Pacific water, ebbing and flowing with the tide, trying to find a place to land.

Chapter 29

Jack, It's Chinatown

Kalin was sitting right there waiting for him, like she knew where he had been and where he was going.

On the mezzanine floor of the Mandarin Oriental the next day around noon, Jack had dropped in to place an order at Mayer Shoes, checked the price of a Ferrari drawing hanging in the window of an art gallery next door, and was just finishing with Patrick at James Chen Tailors down the hall.

Coming out of the tailor's, he spied her sitting in the Clipper Lounge across the way waving at him. The stores were on the mezzanine level in the rear, out of the way of the hotel's main foot traffic, but there she was.

She waved at him again.

He turned and gave a few last instructions to Patrick, and crossed the marble walkway to the restaurant's dining area. A young waiter in a gold jacket and hat and striped morning pants scurried over, pulled out the table and helped seat Jack as he tossed his suit jacket on one of the empty seats and slid in on the brown leather banquette next to Kalin.

"Hello again."

"Still using James Chen's for your clothes?" she asked.

"You know me, Kalin. I hate to shop. One stop here and I'm good for a couple of years."

"But can't you get someone at home to do that for you?" Kalin asked.

"There isn't anyone."

"Still?"

"That's the way it is. Anyway, I haven't needed to do much shopping lately."

"Why is that?" she asked.

"I've been broke."

"I'm so sorry, Jack," she said, looking away.

He caught her out of the corner of his eye looking him up and down, trying to figure out how threadbare he really was. Just like Suzy. "Don't worry about it, Kalin. New Land was my company; I was responsible for what happened. And I gave up thinking about that stuff a long time ago." He looked over his shoulder and flagged the waiter. Hearing the faint rustling of her dress, he turned back around to find her closer and facing him directly on the banquette next to him, her skin flushed, the pearls around her neck lustrous as her body temperature turned them a soft shade of pink. "I'd like a Tom Collins," Jack said to the waiter. "Kalin?"

"You can call me Lin," she said.

Jack looked at her, hesitating. "I heard you yesterday. All right, Lin. What would you like to drink?"

"Two of those would be lovely," she said to the young waiter who bowed his head and hustled off to fetch the drinks. "I'm sorry about Alicia, Jack," she said, trying to get Jack to look her in the eye.

He gave in, and looked back at her without saying anything. She had always been good to look at. He liked sitting there just gazing at her, imagining he wasn't sitting next to her at all but afar for a few more years, until the pain of Manila subsided, no longer marring his view of her beautiful face and ebony hair and the straps of her dress drawing lines across the skin of her bare shoulders.

He still hadn't responded when the waiter returned with their drinks. As the boy made a show of arranging the drinks and some nuts on the table in front of them, Jack drained off his Tom Collins without even putting it down, and asked for another. Kalin sat next to him, waiting for him to say something.

"Yeah; that was tough. But it's over now." He hadn't thought of Alicia for at least a day. China did that for him.

"I left Mickey, Jack."

"I heard you say that. I always envied that guy."

"You envied him? Why? I thought you hated him."

"Well, I didn't hate him; I don't hate anyone. I didn't like him very much, that's for sure," Jack said as he took his second drink from the waiter and drank half of it in one swallow. "But I definitely envied him."

"Why?"

"You treated him like a god," he said, looking at her.

"Oh, Jack." She moved closer to him on the seat.

"So how did you go from working at New Land to managing Chairman Roo's U.S. investments?" Jack asked, finishing his second drink and signaling the waiter for a third.

"I don't know if the correct answer is 'With great difficulty' or 'Predictably.' You decide. After New Land and Mickey, I moved to Vancouver. I was walking down the street one day and a photographer offered me a modeling job. That was followed in short order by my ill-fated acting career."

"Your acting career. My goodness," Jack said.

"My *ill-fated* acting career," she laughed. "And then, when I was on a grade B movie shoot in Hong Kong, I met the man financing it—Chairman Roo, who had known my father. The rest, as they say, is history."

Jack didn't want to know anything about what had happened with Mickey, or what the deal was with Chairman Roo. He didn't have any time for that.

Jack lifted his Tom Collins and thought about ordering another. Kalin's was half full.

"Would you like another drink?"

"I'd rather just go to your room."

Chapter 30

What Happens in China Stays in China

A half dozen institutions led by Red Bank committed $10 million to Sino Solar, and the deal closed two months later in New York. Jack breathed easier. Between Haikou Transformer and Sino Solar, Davis Brothers had already grossed over $2 million in revenues in 1991, and the year was only half over. A few more deals and he could pay down some of his obligations and move himself and his sons back into the main house.

The most troublesome issue in his business was the Chinese managements. Mr. Li at Haikou Transformer was one thing—thank God for Madame Ling—but Mr. Hu at Sino Solar was quite another. Three months after the Sino Solar closing, Mr. Hu used a half million of corporate funds to buy a massage parlor.

At least the latest miscreant, Mr. Liu of the Brightway Corporation, sitting across the table from him in the dinner tent in Mongolia, was Lee's problem for the moment. Lee had joined Davis Brothers full time and brought the Brightway deal with him.

"Mr. Liu's taking his host role seriously," Lee said, sitting next to Jack in the tent and laughing as girls cleared the table and dinner wound down.

"What do you mean?" Jack asked.

"Well, he's hosting this dinner, and in Mongolia, that means he must get drunker than everyone else."

"I'd say he's being overly considerate then," Jack said, as Mr. Liu strained to raise himself to a standing position from his seat across the table. Jack had never been comfortable with either Mr. Liu, a blowhard, or his shady steel business, which sold specialty materials to Chinese defense contractors.

At least Mr. Liu spoke English, having worked at Groton's submarine base for 10 years. "Bottoms up," Mr. Liu exclaimed, prompting Jack to throw down his tenth glass of *baiju* as the three men stood and looked at each other across the expanse of the banquet table. Mr. Liu contemplated his own glass, raised it slowly and tried to down it, swallowing half of the firewater and spilling the other half off his chin and down his neck, and slumped back in his chair.

"I'd like to see any investment bankers stateside match this soiree," Lee said to Jack.

Sitting in a tent made of skins, Jack and Lee were a hundred miles northwest of Daqing on the edge of the Mongolian steppes. Smoldering in the center of the tent, the fire that had roasted two spring lambs on a spit was reduced to a heap of glowing coals. The pretty girl sitting next to Jack all night was now attending to Mr. Liu in what appeared to be a role closer to her full-time occupation. The troupe of costumed performers, having required their guests to fulfill various Mongolian activities like eating lamb's eyes and dancing, were tired and ready to go home.

But Mr. Liu wasn't done yet. Stirring, he managed to stand up yet again, and pointed a finger at Jack and Lee. "What did you do with all our money?" Liu yelled at Lee and Jack.

Lee looked over at Jack, a silly grin on his face, shook his head, saying "I'll handle this," and turned back toward Mr. Liu. Looking across at Liu but speaking in a low tone to Jack, Lee said, "If he's so angry with the U.S. government, why'd he hire American investment bankers?"

"He's your client. Ask him."

"What money?" Lee, laughing nervously, yelled back at Liu.

"Chinese government buy all your Treasury bonds," Mr. Liu said. "You waste on defense; that's what you did."

"That's not true," Lee said, seeming more agitated he had to argue the stupid point than anything else.

"What did you spend it on? Planes? Tanks? What?"

"Sit down," Lee said, his patience with Mr. Liu exhausted.

"Tell me what you spent it on."

"Stuff," Lee yelled back at him.

"What?" Mr. Liu was standing at the table burping, the Chinese lady trying unsuccessfully to hold him up wearing a disgusted look on her face.

"We spent it on *stuff*," Lee yelled louder across at Mr. Liu, who, as if the words had smote him, slumped over onto the table, his face sliding across a platter of grease.

Jack took one last look at Mr. Liu and glanced over at Lee; he was ready to leave.

"At least we don't have to put up with this guy back home," Lee said, standing up from the table in agreement.

"Why's that?"

"You know what they say: What happens in China stays in China."

Chapter 31

Finders, Keepers

O ther than clients like Mr. Liu, Jack's biggest business challenge Chinaside remained finders.

Davis Brothers was closing Chinese deals with regularity. The firm was growing. They moved to a larger suite of offices in the Graybar Building. When the building agent told Jack there was a larger space on the eighth floor—Suite 860—he signed a lease the same day, telling Elizabeth they had to do it—stacked on top of each other in their old sublet, the suite number clinched matters—the number 8 in any address signified good luck to their Chinese clients.

Jack agreed with Dr. Yu to begin subletting a small corner of Redstone's Beijing office and paying a portion of Kitty Ji's salary. But while Davis Brothers now had an address, telephone, fax, and human voice at the receiving end of an inquiry in China, it still did not have senior, knowledgeable employees on the ground. Until he could afford to hire and train some, Jack remained captive to the finders.

Who were all the same. They knew nothing about their clients' businesses, and even less about the basics of the investment business.

The services they brazenly proposed to perform—represent a Chinese business in all aspects of its fundraising—were tasks they were completely unqualified to provide. It didn't matter to them. Their existence wasn't based on their professional skills, but their exclusive agreement with their Chinese clients. No matter how they persuaded the client to sign up, once the agreement was executed, the deal went through them.

In a way, everyone in China was a finder. It was second nature in the PRC, something done by every Chinese who took pride in himself, like washing one's face in the morning.

As the chairman of the San Francisco conference on financing Chinese companies finished his closing remarks and thanked Jack and the other speakers for their participation, Jack stood on the dais calculating what plane he could catch back to New York when a man moving on a bee line from the audience blocked his exit.

"Mr. Davis, Brad Starch of Boxwood Capital," the young man said. "I truly enjoyed your insightful remarks on China—couldn't agree more with what you had to say, although I'm not sure the audience caught the nuance. Of course, I think we both know most of these attendees are unschooled where China is concerned."

Another Chinese finder—they were everywhere. Starch looked the part, wearing a boxy suit made of a chemically derived fabric, a tie as wide as a board crossed with multicolored stripes on a chalky background, and shoes with extra thick soles and squared off toes, the kind favored by public servants. He had a wild look in his eye and the appearance of a religious zealot.

"Well, I'm not smart enough to communicate a nuance to a dog, Mr. Starch, and I know for sure I'm not capable of insightful remarks. So I must have something you want. What's on your mind?"

"My firm has client relationships with several attractive Chinese companies. Mr. Cao, our second-in-command, would very much like to meet you; he'll be in the City next week. Any chance we can make an appointment?"

Jack looked at Starch and reminded himself it all came with the territory.

And so it was Starch and a boyish, slight Chinese man arrived at Jack's office the following week.

"Mr. Davis, good to see you again, sir," said Brad Starch. "Allow me to present the president of Boxwood Capital, Christopher Cao. Chris is a Chinese national who has been educated here in the States. He is from a very prominent family—his father is a general in the Chinese army."

A boy trying to do a man's job, Jack thought as he waited for Cao to begin speaking. Chris Cao was indeed young, although it was usually unproductive for foreigners to guess the age of Chinese men. His frame and stature were slight, and together with his full head of carefully coifed hair and long eyelashes, gave Cao a decidedly effeminate air. He wore a silk suit, a hand-crafted shirt that was more of a blouse, with drooping pointed collars hanging loosely around his neck, and patent leather shoes. His hair fell into his eyes as he sat looking down at the table between them, trying to compose himself.

"Mr. D_D_Davis, a r_r_real p_p_pleasure, sir," Chris Cao said to the table.

"How about some coffee or tea," Jack offered, trying to do something to make Cao feel more comfortable. "Say Will, can you take an order from Mr. Cao here?" Jack called to his receptionist. "We have Chinese green tea, Chris."

"Thank you very m_m_much, Mr. Davis," said Chris Cao, breathing deep and slow, and starting to get adjusted.

Jack sat looking at Cao a minute more. He wasn't as young as he looked, based on several strands of long black hair spooling out of his cheeks below his ears, defiling the face of a man who was old enough to shave but since he didn't have much to do, didn't. Jack looked over at Brad Starch. To give Chris some more time, he said, "Brad, you guys must have some specific business you'd like to discuss—why don't you take a shot at laying it out?"

Brad bounded like a puppy into the subject as Chris Cao's mournful eyes lifted from the table in relief.

"That's good to know," Jack said after Starch had recited Boxwood's full service propaganda. He reciprocated with a hypothetical description of Davis Brothers' ideal Chinese business target, and asked, "Anything that fits?"

"Y_y_yes," said Chris. "The company's name is Xushi Wire and Cable Corporation. They are located in Dalian, make bimetallic wire for the cable communication and electric power industries, and are the Chinese counterpart to Copperwire, the American company which is the worldwide leader of the bimetallic wire industry. William Dickle, our Chairman and CEO, and I would like to host you on a visit to Dalian; we think you're really going to like the company, Mr. Davis."

"I'm sure I will. Just do me one favor, will you, please?"

"Sure. What is it?"

"Close the deal with Xushi before I get there, okay?" Jack said.

"What do you mean, Mr. Davis?"

"I don't want to fly all over China doing your job for you. You guys say Boxwood is full service, and you've got this deal. Terrific. So if I provide you with a copy of Davis Brothers' engagement agreement in advance, by the time I visit the company in China next month—if you guys really do control the client—the agreement should be signed. Right?"

㊍ ㊍ ㊍

Jack's Air China flight floated down toward the runway at six o'clock in the evening. The airport lights winked and flickered. Another smoggy, muggy evening in Beijing.

He could see Kitty standing at the railing outside of immigration. Getting picked up at the airport ranked as one of his favorite Chinese customs—never, going all the way back to the old days, had he ever arrived at an airport in China and had to fend for himself.

In those days, it had always been Kalin waiting for him, and it had felt like coming home. Not with Kitty. The expression on her face let Jack know picking him up was just part of her job; there were a million places she would rather be. Like most people in China, Kitty was an only child. Even though she was just under thirty, until she took the job with Dr. Yu and earned a decent salary, she had lived at home with her parents. After signing on with Redstone, she had moved out and gotten her own place—a unit on the floor above theirs.

Her name fit perfectly, that was for sure. Her feline body—all one hundred pounds of it—and her Cheshire facial features gave her the most cat-like aura Jack had ever encountered in a human. And like a cat, she betrayed no hint as to what she was thinking. Jack had attempted several times to joke and make her laugh, to no avail. But no matter; she spoke excellent English—she had received a master's degree from a university in Great Britain—and was good with numbers.

Kitty shook hands with Jack and tried to take his luggage cart until he insisted several times on pushing it himself. They drove to the Kunlun Hotel, an SOE hotel near the Sanlitun nightlife area, and Kitty took Jack's passport and went to check him in, while Jack headed to the lobby bar looking for Cao and Dickle. Entering the room, Jack spied Chris and some others at the rear booth, including a *laowai* looking like he was from the Midwest who had to be Dickle.

Dickle saw Jack, got up from where he been sitting and walked over. Dressed like someone trying to look like a Wall Street investment banker who doesn't really know what Wall Street investment bankers wear, Dickle was still 10 feet away when Jack smelled the stench of stale cigarettes rising from his woolen three-piece suit.

Heavy tie hardware was always the clincher, Jack thought as he looked at Dickle's tie encumbered with both a tie clip and a stick pin. Plus diamond pinky rings. Sure enough, a gold pinky ring with an encrusted diamond chip appeared as Dickle reached Jack and extended his hand.

"You must be Jack," said Dickle. "I've been looking forward to this."

"Thanks for referring Xushi to us, William," answered Jack, shaking Dickle's outstretched hand.

"My friends call me Bill," Dickle said as the two of them joined Chris Cao and the others at their table in the back. "If it's all right with you, we'd like to give you a presentation on Xushi Wire and Cable." He pulled his chair back so Jack could see everyone around the table and addressed Chris Cao. "Do you have the books?"

Dickle was trying hard. At least he was organized and making an effort to be professional, which was more than most of the Chinese finders were prepared to do. He might be teachable, Jack thought. "Guys, I'm looking forward to your presentation," Jack said, "but before we get into discussing the company itself, can we cover a few preliminaries? Did you receive the Davis Brothers' engagement agreement I sent?"

"Yes, we did," Dickle said.

"Great. And you sent it on to the client?"

The Boxwood group became silent. Chris Cao looked out of the corner of his eye at Dickle.

"Well, we wanted to speak to you tonight about that first," said Dickle.

Jack took a breath and told himself to be patient. "Sure, we can talk all you want about it. But I don't see how we can go to Dalian tomorrow."

"Why not?" Chris Cao blurted out. Jack's comment had sparked a pained expression on Chris's face, reinforcing Jack's sense of his inexperience. Disappointing Xushi by not showing up in Dalian tomorrow was hardly the end of the world, but no one looking at Chris's face would have known that.

"Chris, we went over the ground rules when you were in New York. Davis Brothers doesn't do deals on the come. I'm not going to spend a whole day with the company on their business plan without a signed engagement agreement. Otherwise, they've gotten a lot out of us for nothing and we're out the airfare, too. If the company is still unsure about going forward with Davis Brothers or if they have some questions about our firm, I'd be happy to meet with them here in Beijing at our mutual convenience."

"M_M_Mr. Davis, there's no way Xushi will sign the Davis Brothers' engagement agreement," Chris Cao said as Dickle unsuccessfully motioned to him to keep quiet.

"Well, if they won't sign the engagement agreement, what are we all doing here? You told me Xushi was in the bag. If they're not, how do you guys at Boxwood justify your fees? I'm not here to talk them into working with us; that's your job." It was a good thing he had insisted on meeting at the hotel to smoke things out before going to Dalian.

"Jack, Chris is very close to Mr. Xu, the head of Xushi," Dickle said. "Mr. Xu told him the company's been burned in the past, signing engagement agreements with firms and paying up-front retainers, then feeling like idiots when their checks get cashed and no one raises any money. So Mr. Xu has sworn off engagement agreements and retainers."

"Well, he'll have to swear off IPOs too, because he's not going to list his shares in the United States without a good firm to help him, and no decent firm—not Davis Brothers nor anyone else—is going to take Xushi public without a standard engagement agreement in place. And I'm not going to spend my money on a plane ticket to convince him otherwise."

"I'll tell you what," Dickle said. "I'll make it easy for you. I'm so confident we can land this deal, Boxwood will spring for your airfare tomorrow—first class seats."

They had to be desperate—he would never do that. "Well, I hate to take your money, but I might take you up on that," Jack said. "But don't worry about first class; it's only an hour flight. And I'm still going to be out a whole business day if Mr. Xu wastes our time."

"Not if you get them to sign the agreement," Dickle said. He motioned to the waitress and ordered Jack another drink. Jack let him.

Amateurs, Jack thought as he finished his drink and stubbed out the last of his cigar, but at least with the appearance of being honest and teachable. If he could talk some sense into Mr. Xu, maybe in the bargain he could pick up some guys to represent him on the ground in China.

水 水 水

Jack called his sons, dressed, got down to the café in the lobby of the Kunlun at six in the morning, and ordered a pot of coffee and some orange juice. He was leafing through the morning's edition of *China Daily* when Dickle walked in and sat down a few minutes later.

"*China Daily?* You don't pay any attention to that rag, do you?" Dickle asked.

"Oh, I do," said Jack. "It's nice knowing what the Chinese Communist Party thinks is important enough to try to influence our thought, don't you think?"

They finished with their coffee. Dickle paid the bill. Walking out of the lobby, the group started climbing into the van Boxwood had organized to take them to the airport. Dickle barked out instructions, showing Jack who was boss. "Chris, make sure whenever Jack rides with us he is seated immediately rear of the shotgun seat," he said to Cao, dutiful if slightly sullen. Jack guessed Chris barely tolerated Dickle, especially when he behaved this way. "Jack, you're the *dalaban*," Dickle continued, sounding like a guide on a cultural tour. "The big boss always rides behind the shotgun seat. It won't do to have you ride in a lesser seat. We'd all lose face."

Somehow Jack couldn't imagine that was totally true, but he kept quiet and took his assigned seat.

"I read your bio from the investment conference," Dickle said when they got under way. "Very impressive."

"I've made my share of mistakes, but we don't put that in there," Jack said, trying to laugh; he got uncomfortable when people tried to flatter him.

"I could learn a lot from you, Jack; all of us at Boxwood could. And that's what we'd like to do. The more you can teach us, the better we can help you here in China."

"That would be worth doing," Jack said, meaning it. At least Boxwood's rube-like but earnest leader was not impressed with himself, as far as Jack could tell.

"Tell me a little about yourself," Dickle said.

Jack knew better than that. "Oh, there's not much to tell," he said.

But Dickle didn't need an opening to tell Jack more about himself. With a guy like Dickle there was always at least one such session, where Jack would hear more than he wanted to know. Better to let him talk now and get it out of the way.

"Myself, I'm a three-legged dog."

Jack knew what a three-legged dog was, but if Dickle was determined to go that direction, Jack would indulge him as far as he could.

"An orphan," Dickle explained.

"I know." Everyone Jack knew who was an orphan told him so during the first hour they knew him. Them, and men who had lost children.

Dickle went on to say he hadn't gone to a fancy college like Jack; he only had lasted a year at an undistinguished university for day students outside of Detroit. And he hadn't been the captain of his college football team, although he did play some basketball. After that, he had sold industrial equipment, got bored and divorced, and was in the process of becoming an alcoholic when his company had asked whether he would consider going to China to help establish the Asian office. So he had pulled up stakes, and here he was.

Jack was always sucker for an underdog story. "And how did you get from selling industrial equipment to the investment business?" he asked.

"There's more money in investments, and besides, all business is the same—don't you think?" Dickle asked.

"Not really," Jack answered. He wouldn't have answered unless he felt strongly about it. To be continued, he realized with relief as their van pulled into the airport.

A few minutes later, they boarded and looked for their seats. Jack, Dickle, and Cao were in first class as Dickle had promised. Invariably, the first class seats in China were always empty unless a *laowai* took one. Only rarely would a Chinese person pay the first class premium, even though it wasn't that much and the scrum in steerage could be brutal.

"You really didn't have to pay for first class seats, Bill. It's only an hour flight to Dalian. I'll be happy just to get there."

"Nonsense," said Dickle. "Investment bankers don't sit back there."

"I always take coach inside China."

"Well, you don't strike me as the typical American investment banker, that's for sure."

"Maybe that's because he's not," Chris Cao said to Dickle.

"All I know is what I've read," Dickle continued. "It sure sounds like you're a big-time investment banker. And by the way, on that subject, you should think about switching hotels."

"Why is that?" Jack asked Dickle.

"All the big-time investment bankers stay at the Grand Hyatt," said Dickle. "Especially the Americans. The Kunlun is too Chinese. There's a lot of SOE types there; no one you can really rub elbows with."

"What about the Bamboo Garden?" Jack asked.

"The what?" Dickle laughed. "Jiminy Christmas. I like someone with a sense of humor, Jack. The Bamboo Garden. You make that up or is there really a rat hole named the Bamboo Garden?"

"I made it up."

Chapter 32

The Future of China

Flying east from Beijing out over the Bo Hai, the semi-circular body of salt water west of the Yellow Sea, they had barely finished their coffee before the seat belt light signaled their descent into Dalian. On the western tip of the Liaodong Peninsula, Dalian was an international melting pot of Han and Manchu Chinese mixed with Japanese, Koreans, and Russians. Its streets were wide and European in flavor, the onion domes of Russian Orthodox churches marking the oldest parts of the city.

The car carrying them to the company's factory sped through the outskirts of Dalian for several miles and turned into an industrial section. On the right sat squat, nondescript manufacturing buildings, while to the left their counterparts had been razed to yield a barren landscape, piles of bricks and rubble all that remained while the scraped, raped land waited for its new masters. Beyond the piles, a squatter's town of tents and ramshackle tenements sprawled across the dusty plain, children, dogs, and old men and women picking through the trash.

A few blocks later, they pulled into an alley alongside a dilapidated industrial relic: Xushi Wire and Cable's manufacturing facility. Mr. Xu, the owner of the company, stood waiting for them at the entrance, smoking, as were all the men around him. There was one woman in the group; probably the company accountant.

Mr. Xu looked younger than Jack had expected, probably no more than 45, although many Chinese men looked younger than their *laowai* counterparts. Overweight, with an overfed physique and a dimpled, freckled face, Mr. Xu was dressed typically for a Chinese business man, in *nouveau couture:* all of his clothing was branded, with a heavy reliance on Tommy Hilfiger; his belt sported a shiny, useless clip of hardware; and his shoes were patent leather, accented with ineffective buckles.

Jack got out, and Dickle hustled him over to meet Mr. Xu and his team. Xu's eyes were clear and intelligent, and didn't betray three shots of *baiju* for breakfast. A conversation with him might actually be enjoyable. Ms. Cheng Hang, who was indeed the company accountant, spoke serviceable English.

Xushi's factory was ancient. On a packed dirt floor 50 yards long, two dilapidated wire manufacturing lines pulled, stretched, and clad raw materials into finished bimetallic wire. Fifty or more Chinese men, some in greasy overalls, others in nothing more than shorts and flip-flops, wrestled with the wire during its manufacturing process and rolled the finished product onto wooden spools.

Jack had a camera with him, but didn't take any pictures. No one back in the United States would believe such a decrepit manufacturing facility actually functioned, and if he tried to explain he wanted to raise $20 million in an IPO for the business, they would laugh him out of the room.

After a half hour inspecting everything observable in the company's production lines, the group left the building through the back door, passing by the loading dock. Alongside spools of wire stacked 30 feet into the air, a man with a clipboard in one hand and a big roll of bills in the other released spools to drivers paying cash on the barrelhead for the Xushi product. The line of trucks snaked down the alley and around the corner—Jack counted 30 of them.

Xushi made bimetallic wire, aluminum or steel wire covered with copper and used in the electric utility and cable television industries. The component costs of bimetallic wire were basic: commodities including copper, aluminum, and steel—the costs of which were the same all over the globe—and men, who were dirt cheap in China. A Chinese bimetallic wire manufacturer had a huge cost advantage over Western manufacturers, subject to only one thing: capital to buy the manufacturing lines to make the wire. And it had to be equity capital— Chinese banks would make loans against a building, but equipment was another story.

Xushi's new facility was supposed to be the key aspect of the tour. A half mile away from the old facility down a road lined with piles of construction rubble, Dickle, who had filled the morning with gratuitous comments about the potential of the company's expansion, raved about the building as Mr. Xu and Ms. Cheng Hang preened through the new space.

Jack was supposed to be impressed. But he knew better. The new building was just a big, empty box of metal and concrete. Its newness alone couldn't make money. There wasn't a single piece of productive equipment inside. The building had sponged up all of the company's cash, and all the funds it could borrow from the banks besides. Xushi had run out of money, construction had halted, and the company's dreams were on hold until they found someone to finance them.

"Okay, Bill, please tell Mr. Xu I've seen enough," Jack said a few minutes later.

"But Mr. Xu wants to show you the site for the new office building and workers' dormitory," Chris Cao interrupted.

"Please just thank Mr. Xu for the tour, Chris."

"So you're not interested?" Dickle asked, a deflated look on his face.

Jack looked back at Dickle but didn't say anything. He gazed around the floor space from where they stood in the new building. Mr. Xu stopped kibitzing with his men; he and Dickle lit cigarettes. They all stood there looking at Jack.

Jack turned and looked at Mr. Xu. Speaking to Dickle and Cao, but continuing to look Xu in the eye, Jack said, "I'm sure this deal has been shopped, so I need to know how many foreign investors have come through here. Not investment bankers; investors. And please tell Mr. Xu I don't want to listen to a discussion of the subject in Chinese for 20 minutes. It's a simple question."

Cao spoke in Chinese to Mr. Xu, who smiled to himself, his cheeks dimpling and the fat around his eyes crinkling.

"He asked why you want to know," Chris said, almost whispering.

Jack kept looking at Mr. Xu. "Listen to me, Chris. Tell him I want the answer, and if he says anything like that again, I'm leaving," he said. "Tell him," Jack repeated, as Cao stood there mute, afraid to utter such a direct statement to a Chinese boss. "Tell him."

Chris finally spoke to Mr. Xu. Xu's eyes widened; he looked closely at Jack who kept looking at him with no expression. Faint traces of a smile flecked Xu's pupils and curled the corners of his eyes. He said something to Chris.

"Four," Chris said, exhaling.

"Who were they?"

Chris repeated the question in Mandarin to Mr. Xu, who gave him a short answer. Chris told Jack the names; none were institutions Jack did business with.

"All right, so let's see if Mr. Xu agrees with my analysis of his problem," Jack continued. "When he showed the four foreign investors the hell hole of a factory we just toured, they all ran for the hills. Have I got it right?"

Chris repeated Jack's statement to Mr. Xu in Chinese.

Mr. Xu looked at Jack again. This time he wasn't smiling. He nodded his head.

"Now we're getting somewhere," Jack said. "Brand new, how much does one of those bimetallic wire manufacturing lines cost?"

"Around $650,000," answered Cheng Hang, who had been listening as she stood next to Mr. Xu.

Jack turned to face them both. "And how many lines can you fit into this new building?"

Cheng Hang deferred to Mr. Xu. For a question that should have received a two-word answer in as many seconds, there was the usual 10-minute discussion, and then Chris translated in English, "Twenty-six."

"Ms. Cheng, this question is for you—we Americans get very nervous when CEOs answer profit-and-loss questions," Jack explained. "How much profit can Xushi make per assembly line per year?"

She knew exactly where he was going. "Over $300,000; each line has two year payback," she said. She was proud of herself. She should have been.

"And if all 26 of the lines were operating, how much of their production could you sell?"

Her eyes widened, and she didn't respond, but repeated Jack's question to Mr. Xu. After five minutes, she explained that Mr. Xu felt she hadn't heard Jack's question correctly: could he repeat it? Jack did, and the Chinese discussed things for another 10 minutes, arguing back and forth.

Finally, Cheng Hang waved at everyone to quiet them down, and turned to Jack. "You ask if we can produce this wire or sell this wire."

It was a question.

"Sell it."

"Yes. We can sell it."

"All of it?"

"*Duai*—Yes."

"From all 26 manufacturing lines, right?"

"Yes."

"And if you had *126* manufacturing lines, you could sell everything you could produce from all of them as well, couldn't you?"

Cheng Hang hesitated, looked at Mr. Xu, and then looked back at Jack. She knew as well as he did they didn't need another 10-minute conversation in Chinese. Besides, she knew the answer.

"*Duai*."

"Just like Copperwire, right?"

Cheng Hang translated for Mr. Xu and he grinned and raised both thumbs.

"Okay. Please tell Mr. Xu I'll raise him the $20 million he needs. It will take 90 to 120 days."

Dickle was looking at Jack as Cheng Hang told Mr. Xu what Jack had said. A big, toothy smile bloomed on Xu's pasty face. He grabbed Jack's hand and shook it, not letting go.

As they turned and walked away from the building, Dickle sidled up to Jack. "I'm just trying to learn here, Jack. But I'm confused. That decision took you less than an hour. But when everyone else looked at the old factory, Xushi struck out," said Dickle.

"It's the trucks lined up at the company's loading dock, their drivers armed with cash to pay for wire," Jack said. "You're talking about some highly motivated buyers. With China's demand for infrastructure, together with Xushi's cost advantage, this deal should be a home run."

Dickle was making notes as they walked.

"One other thing," Jack said. "I asked about the other foreign investors to determine how shopped this deal is. I didn't recognize any of the names. We should be all right; we need to portray this deal in the right light for institutions or it won't happen."

Jack looked away from Dickle back to where Cheng Hang was bringing up the rear. She looked at Jack and smiled. She was pleased for the company. She knew she was doing a good job.

"Ms. Cheng, what do I call you?" Jack asked.

"Me?" She answered, pointing to herself with her thumb.

"Yes. I need a name to call you; what would you prefer?"

"Oh, Hang is okay," she said, smiling.

That wouldn't work.

"How about Ms. Cheng?" he asked.

"Ms. Cheng fine. Good," she answered, smiling more.

㊟   ㊟   ㊟

The first thing they were required to do in Mr. Xu's office was admire his fish. Together with his aquarium, Mr. Xu's office had all the accoutrements of a successful Chinese businessman: fiberboard furniture made to look like European fruitwood antiques; cabinets stuffed with unopened bottles of American scotch and bourbon the way someone had seen on the *Dallas* television series; and a bag of golf clubs in the corner.

Xu's fish were Red Dragons, a rare species of freshwater fish found in the Amazon. The fish were striking, their upper bodies shimmering neon blue across the crowns of their backs, and undersides devolving from a red swath around their middle to an orange-yellow underbelly. According to Dickle, the fish cost $100,000 each. For good luck, the tank held eight of them.

Everyone ogled the fish for a few polite minutes, and then got down to business, Xu and Dickle lighting new cigarettes. The obligatory haggling began immediately. Jack listened to the group go back and forth in Chinese, watching the fish rise and fall with the air bubbles in the aquarium. After three hours, Jack and Mr. Xu executed the engagement agreement, and Jack, Dickle, and Chris got in the car to go back to the airport.

"Two last things," Dickle said to Jack when they were in the car, "and you're not going to like one of them."

Jack looked at Dickle. "You just didn't want to disappoint me, right?"

Dickle looked at Jack with a confused look on his face. "Jiminy Christmas, Jack."

"Never mind," Jack said, "go ahead."

"If you want the Xushi deal, I'd like you to agree to do two more deals with us," Dickle said.

"What's objectionable about that?" Jack asked.

"That's the good news. Look, we're low on funds," Dickle said. "Could you see your way clear to paying us a small nonrefundable retainer?"

"Why are you guys always broke?"

"What's that supposed to mean?" Dickle asked, but Jack had turned and was looking out the window. He would pay the retainer; he was happy to get the business, but he hated being held up.

㊌　㊌　㊌

The next step was the preparation of Xushi's offering documents. According to the agreement between Davis Brothers and Boxwood, Dickle and his people would take the lead on the documents, and Jack would edit the final versions.

When the papers arrived from Boxwood the following week, Jack found the materials predictably abysmal. He shouldn't have gotten his hopes up, he said to himself as he dialed up Dickle from home that evening. They went over some housekeeping items, and then turned to Xushi.

"Did you receive our initial drafts of the executive summary and the PowerPoint presentation?" Dickle asked.

"Yep."

"What do you think? Not bad, right?"

Jack didn't say anything. He didn't know what made him feel worse, agreeing to a fee split with Dickle that presumed Boxwood would accomplish what Jack now knew they could not, or having to tell Dickle the materials were awful.

"Jack?'

"Yeah."

"I've got a thick skin. If there are parts you don't like, just tell me. We can change it."

"Bill, listen to me. When you're writing a description of Xushi Wire and Cable for institutional investors, you don't take 30 pages to tell them about the worldwide wire industry. They want to know about Xushi Wire and Cable."

"Wait a minute," Dickle protested. "I've made a living doing technical presentations. We're really proud of our writing skills here. And we knocked ourselves out researching the wire industry. Your investors are going to love this executive summary."

Jack sighed. "They don't care about wire, Bill."

"If they don't care about wire, why would they invest in Xushi Wire and Cable?"

"Now you're catching on. That's what you need to tell them."

"What?"

"Why they should invest in Xushi Wire and Cable. That's what they want to hear."

Dickle exhaled. "I guess I don't know what you mean."

"The company makes a huge gross margin on each spool of wire and they can sell everything they can make."

"So?"

"That's all you have to say."

"That's all we have to say?"

"That's all you have to say."

In the draft executive summary of the next deal Jack did with Boxwood, Dickle located the line at the end of the first paragraph: "The company can sell everything they can make."

It wasn't true with the other company, but Dickle didn't care.

The road show began on the first day of October, and was well attended. They started in New York, visited Boston, crossed the country to Dallas, and hit the West Coast. The California trip began in San Francisco and finished in Los Angeles, where they had a half dozen one-on-ones culminating in a meeting with Torrey Grove, a hedge fund on the northern edge of San Diego.

Mr. Xu was disengaged throughout the trip, regarding the road show portion of his IPO as a travel lark and delegating all the presentation duties to Chris Cao and Ms. Cheng. And where many Chinese entrepreneurs made their subordinates drill through the presentations, including memorizing the PowerPoint, Xu was casual. He was much more interested in toys.

In New York, Xu asked Jack to take him to Tourneau, the famous watch store on the corner of 57th and Fifth, where he dropped $100,000 on a watch with a black quartz face encrusted with diamonds that matched his black quartz diamond-encrusted cell phone. He asked Jack if he wanted one. Jack laughed and said he liked his stainless steel watch just fine, but maybe he'd reconsider after the closing.

Mr. Xu loved cars, especially the exotic ones stateside that weren't on the road back in the PRC. He had a Porsche and a BMW in Dalian, but the trip to America whetted his appetite. He had Jack take him to the Rolls Royce dealership along 2nd Avenue, thought about ordering a new Bentley, left, thought about it some more, went back together with Jack, and then decided to wait until after the closing.

But he had no use for New York's Chinese food. The low point of Mr. Xu's American trip occurred when Jack took them to David J's, the most upscale Chinese restaurant in New York. From the time he opened the menu and saw the atmospheric prices, Mr. Xu was on his guard, and after a round of appetizers, he waved his hand at Chris Cao.

"J_J_J_aack," Chris said, his black eyes apologetic, "Mr. Xu wants to go to a New York steakhouse instead."

"All right; sure. What's the matter, Mr. Xu see someone from the tongs?"

"No," Chris said, afraid to smile in Xu's presence. "Mr. Xu doesn't want you to pay for this expensive Chinese food. He says it's terrible."

"But this is David J's, the best Chinese restaurant in New York," Jack said.

"In my opinion, it's terrible, Jack. The food's not fresh; don't waste your money. Tell your friends."

The highlight of Mr. Xu's trip to the United States occurred in San Diego. Their three o'clock meeting in Pasadena with Wilshire Partners went well—they were interested in leading the deal—but finished late. Walking out to their car, Jack looked at his watch. They had exactly an hour to get to the northern suburbs of San Diego, 90 miles down the interstate.

Jack started the car, a big Ford sedan, and checked his fuel level. Chris Cao sat next to him in the shotgun seat. Jack looked over his shoulder at Mr. Xu and Ms. Cheng in the back.

"Okay, listen up everybody. We're very late for the Torrey Grove meeting in San Diego. To get there on time, I've got to drive very fast, and I don't want you to be alarmed when we're rocketing down the highway. We probably don't even have to go to Torrey Grove; my guess is the deal is sold already."

Ms. Cheng translated to Mr. Xu. They stopped talking and sat in the back seat, just looking at Jack.

"What's it going to be?" Jack asked them.

Mr. Xu said something in Chinese to Ms. Cheng.

"What'd he say?"

Ms. Cheng giggled like a schoolgirl. "Mr. Xu say, 'What you wait for? Let's go.'"

Jack told everyone to check their seatbelts, gunned the gas to blow out the carburetor, and headed for the entrance ramp to the highway.

On the interstate, he kept the big Ford in the left lane most of the time, seeing no cops and cruising at over 100 miles an hour for long stretches of road, winging to the right when an idiot hung out there doing 70, swooping around the slow traffic to the right and pulling back out to the left, gunning the car up to as much as 120, and cruising south, his hands tight around the wheel. As Jack looked in the rearview mirror from time to time, Xu kept grinning all the way, looking like a kid in a bumper car.

They pulled into Torrey Grove's parking lot with five minutes to spare, got out, stretched, and walked into the office at noon on the button.

After the interview, they were standing on the sidewalk next to the Ford when Mr. Xu grabbed Ms. Cheng's arm and asked her something in Chinese. She turned to Jack and said, "Mr. Xu ask where you learn drive like that."

Jack said something about learning to drive when he was 13, before he was legal, and kept standing there looking west, the warm San Diego sun beating down on his shoulders, looking out over the brown land to the cliffs dropping to the azure Pacific less than a mile away.

"Mr. Xu says when we close, he sponsor car in NASCAR. He want you be his driver."

Too much money too fast did that to everyone.

Once the road show began, Jen's subscription book filled up fast. Wilshire Partners did indeed want to lead, and designated a guy named Ben Jackson to work on the deal. Jack was not impressed with Jackson, a blowhard former stockbroker who insisted on talking about stock market trends. Never trusting stockbrokers who thought they knew about the market, Jack asked Robert Gander to run a U5 on Jackson, and learned Jackson had moved to California when he had been barred from practicing the investment business in Florida.

Elizabeth took the committed investors to Dalian for follow-up due diligence, and gave Jack a report on the trip when she returned a week later.

"Did Dickle remember he's not an investment banker, and stay the hell out of the way?" Jack asked her.

"You mean Dickle the Pickle?" She couldn't help herself.

"How was Mr. Xu?"

"You mean the future of China?"

"The future of China." Jack laughed. "What does that mean?"

"You didn't know Mr. Xu represents the future of China? That's what the mayor of Dalian told us."

"Really?"

"Really."

"How did he behave?"

"He was okay. I had to set him straight on a few things."

"Like what?" Jack could just see Elizabeth lecturing the doughboy.

"I guess at first Mr. Xu thought he had another *laowai* sucker on his hands. But by the end of the trip, he said he liked me so much he would sell me one of his Red Dragon fish."

"What'd you say to that?"

"I asked him how much, of course."

Jack waited for the punch line.

"He said $120,000, and I said only if the fish could sing and dance."

Jack wished he could have seen the look on Mr. Xu's face.

"And does Ben Jackson realize he's met his match?"

"What a jackass."

"Ben Jackass. That's got a nice ring to it."

"That's what I thought."

The Xushi Wire and Cable deal closed at the end of October. At the end, other than Chris Cao, who took the deal as seriously as Jack and Elizabeth did, the Boxwood people were predictably absent. It was too late for Jack to change his deal with Boxwood. He had already agreed to the fee splits on Xushi, and would have to honor the arrangement between the two firms, not only on Xushi, but on the second deal Dickle had found.

But Jack had made up his mind. As soon as he had closed the next deal he did with Boxwood, Davis Brothers wasn't going to do any more transactions with finders—not with Paul Chin, not Bill Dickle, no one. He was ready to install his own people on the ground in China.

The initial Xushi Wire and Cable board meeting took place a month later in Dalian. Jack and Ben Jackson from Wilshire Partners were appointed to represent the investors; all the other board members were affiliated with Mr. Xu. At the beginning of the meeting, Mr. Xu and Ms. Cheng thanked Jack for taking Xushi public, telling the other board members Jack was a great investment banker, and everyone got a good laugh as Mr. Xu repeated his NASCAR offer.

An hour into the meeting, the agenda turned to mergers and acquisitions. Now that Xushi had a war chest and publicly traded stock to use as currency, Mr. Xu wanted to acquire Xushi's Chinese competitors.

Jack listened to the discussion on the subject. Finally, when he had given the other board members face and the opportunity to speak before him, it was his turn. "I agree with the acquisition theme—it's one of the main reasons we wanted to do Xushi's IPO—but I disagree with the targets."

Ms. Cheng, interpreting for Mr. Xu, repeated Jack's comment and then leaned over and said, "Mr. Xu no understand."

"Merger and acquisition transactions are complex, and take a lot of time and resources. Don't waste time on the small fry in China," Jack said. "Go right for the prime target."

After Ms. Cheng translated, they all sat there looking at him.

"Copperwire," Jack said. "Xushi should buy Copperwire. Acquire Copperwire, and Xushi controls the world market for bimetallic wire."

"But Copperwire huge American company," protested Ms. Cheng, not waiting for Mr. Xu's reaction.

"You mean huge *money-losing* American company," Jack said. "Xushi would be doing Copperwire's shareholders a favor. It could move all their conventional wire production to Xushi's Chinese factories, and convert their U.S. plants to high value wire for computers and electronics."

Mr. Xu said something, and Ms. Cheng translated. "Mr. Xu ask how much Copperwire cost."

It was always a good sign when they start asking about price. "Less than you think," Jack said. "I spoke to the CEO of Copperwire when we did our due diligence on Xushi. I think he'd jump at the chance to merge."

When Jack's answer was translated, the board all started speaking in Chinese. Jack sat there, waiting for them to get it out of their system. Ben Jackson leaned across the table and said, "Great idea, Jack. I'll support this, but first you have to promise you'll cut your fees."

Jack looked at Jackson for a moment. Elizabeth was right—he was a jackass. "I'll send you a copy of our engagement agreement, Ben. Take a look at it; you might learn something," Jack said, turning away and ignoring Jackson for the rest of the meeting.

A few minutes later, Ms. Cheng signaled to Jack the board had finished its discussions. "Mr. Xu say you board's strategic thinker. If you think Copperwire say yes, you do."

水 水 水

The board meeting had been over for an hour. Most of the members of the Xushi group had left or gone up to bed. Jack, Ms. Cheng and some other Chinese managers from Xushi sat in the lobby of the hotel. Jack was having a cognac and a cigar—wine wasn't served in most hotel bars in Northeast China, since the Russians, Japanese, and Koreans living there were more partial to hard liquor.

Ms. Cheng looked over at Jack and said, "IPO over, so I think I leave Xushi soon."

That wouldn't be good. Jack spent the next several minutes explaining to her she was a big reason investors had put money into Xushi Wire and Cable. She knew, she said, and had identified some acceptable replacements, but felt she couldn't stay, especially if there was any chance the Copperwire merger would go through.

"Why does that make a difference?" Jack asked.

Ms. Cheng wrinkled her nose and forehead, and squinted her eyes. "Mr. Xu not what we say about you at board meeting," she said.

"What's that?"

"Strategic thinker. He no strategic thinker. Now Xushi very good. Later, I think maybe not so good," she said, shaking her head back and forth.

"Why?"

"Too many men; no pay much."

"What?"

"Not much money now to pay men."

"I see. Slave labor. You're saying Xushi is taking advantage of slave labor."

"Yes. Xushi pay very good—maybe $3 per day, almost double what men get in other jobs in Dalian."

"So?"

"Still very cheap; much less than U.S. That only reason Xushi good. One day soon, Dalian men expensive too, like U.S. Then Xushi no good."

"But that could be years away, Ms. Cheng."

"Yes, but I young girl. I no want to sign."

"Sign what?"

"I CFO. I must sign SEC documents. I sign now, shareholders sue me later. I no want to sign."

Ms. Cheng was every bit as smart as he had thought.

"Anything else I should know?"

"Mr. Xu nice. He honest. No steal money. But he just like his cars."

He looked at her. "What will you do now?"

"I no know. What you think?"

"I think you should go to work for me."

"I like that," Ms. Cheng said, a big grin on her face.

A month later, at the same time as Ms. Cheng stepped down from her position at Xushi and Chris Cao moved over from Boxwood to replace her, the Xushi board and management team reconvened in Dalian to hear Jack's presentation on the Copperwire acquisition. Jack's Davis Brothers team had finished due diligence and lined up the financing to pay for the deal. Once the board approved the transaction, it could close immediately. Jack had finished his presentation and was answering tag-end questions from board members when Mr. Xu told Jack he was going up to his room but wanted to discuss some important company matters the next morning on the way to the airport.

The next morning at breakfast, Chris Cao seemed distracted and depressed. Jack didn't ask him what was wrong, as he would do if a friend in America was distraught—Chris would never say anything anyway.

"So what's this meeting with Mr. Xu all about?" Jack asked, stirring his coffee.

"Oh, I don't know. Really," Chris said.

"You don't know."

"No. I really don't."

He was lying, but Jack didn't push it, seeing Mr. Xu walking toward them across the lobby, carrying a bag and wearing a big smile on his face. Xu looked at Jack as he took his seat, checking him out, said something to Chris, and before Chris could stop him—he tried—Xu handed the bag to Jack and made hand motions indicating he should open it.

Jack looked at Mr. Xu, who continued to smile back at him, and then at Chris, whose face was a mask of concern. "Chris, are you all right?"

Chris looked down at the table, his long hair hanging over his brow, his eyelashes fanning up and down. He didn't speak at first, and then, still looking down, said, "Mr. Xu brought you a present. You should open it so Mr. Xu doesn't lose face."

Jack turned his attention to opening the gift. It was a large veined piece of jade, carved as a half dog-half dragon animal. Grotesque, it still must have been expensive.

"Thank you, Mr. Xu. What did I do to deserve this?"

Xu wasn't paying attention to Jack. He was speaking to Chris. "Lehman Brothers" fell out of the Mandarin words.

Jack looked over at Chris. "What's Mr. Xu want to know about Lehman Brothers?"

"J_J_Jack. W_W_We gotta talk." Chris looked miserable.

Mr. Xu was looking at Chris, too. Xu grabbed Chris's arm and yelled at him in Chinese. Chris kept looking down at the table, and shook his head back and forth, his long black hair whipping across his ashen face. Mr. Xu raised his voice more, and issued a sharp command. When Chris didn't respond, Xu screamed the command again.

Finally, Chris raised his head slowly, and stared over Jack's shoulder. "Mr. Xu thanks you for your service. He knows as a Xushi shareholder you'll be happy he has hired Lehman Brothers to be the company's new investment banker." Chris exhaled, nodded, stealing a glance at Jack's eyes and then looking down again, his long black hair hanging down over his face.

Jack felt a rush of warm blood surge to his face, and an itchy, tingling sensation under the skin of the top of his hands and forearms. He looked at Chris, who kept staring down at the table, and then over at Mr. Xu, who sat looking back at Jack with a stupid grin on his face. "When did the company retain Lehman Brothers ?"

"About a week ago," Chris mumbled.

Jack forced himself to go slow. Looking at Mr. Xu, who was just sitting there, his grin now stale and lopsided, Jack said, "You can tell Mr. Xu he's right, Chris—as a shareholder, I agree having Lehman Brothers as the company's investment banker is a positive step. He's just handled it poorly. What normally happens is the company tells us they've gotten a larger firm involved, and we move to the right."

"What do you mean, move to the right?" Chris asked.

"It's a Wall Street expression. As companies grow, small investment firms like Davis Brothers that launch organizations like Xushi know big firms like Lehman Brothers will pitch their clients one day. So they agree to be co-investment bankers—when there's a deal done, the names appear on the front of the offering documents in order of size, and more importantly, compensation. In this case, the next deal Xushi does, it will be advertised showing Lehman Brothers on the left and Davis Brothers on the right. It's good for everyone. Davis Brothers doesn't make as much money, but the company prospers, and that's what matters most."

It was already a fait accompli, he could see that. So he couldn't understand why Chris remained so miserable, the hangdog look still covering what Jack could see of his disconsolate features through the tangled mess of his hair. He looked like he was starting to cry.

"It won't work, Jack."

"Why not? I'm saying Davis Brothers is willing to move over. There's nothing left to talk about."

"Mr. Xu has been advised Davis Brothers is too small a firm to continue to be involved with Xushi Wire and Cable. Xushi will lose face on Wall Street if you continue, we have been told."

"That's ridiculous," Jack snapped. "What do you mean 'you've been *told*'?"

Chris said something, but Jack couldn't hear him.

"What?" Jack said. "Chris? I didn't hear you. Look, I'm about to lose my patience."

"It was Ben."

"What?"

"Ben told us."

Ben Jackass. He should have known better. Ben had practically lived in Dalian since the closing. In addition to the company, the blowhard probably had a side deal with Lehman Brothers, too.

Jack slumped back in his seat, thinking about what to say. "Mr. Xu, Chris," he said, looking back and forth at them slowly, "look at me."

Chris lifted his head up and looked at Jack. Xu had been staring at Jack the whole time.

"Ben doesn't know his ass from third base. I'm only going to say this one time. It's all right for Xushi to retain Lehman Brothers. Davis Brothers will modify its agreement with the company; we'll move over to the right. But that's it. You can't dismiss us. Our contract with the company has a two-year tail. If you try to terminate us, I'll sue in U.S. court. My damages will be large. And I'll win."

Jack got up to leave.

Mr. Xu said something to Chris as they all stood up.

Jack looked at Mr. Xu, then at Chris.

"Mr. Xu said he just wants to be friends," Chris said.

In the car on the way to the airport, Chris tried to make small talk with him, but Jack ignored him.

He had been wrong about them. All of them. So wrong. They didn't respect him. They didn't value him. A "great investment banker"; their "strategic thinker." What a joke. They just wanted the money. As long as Jack represented the shortest distance between them and cash, they were willing to listen to him, do what he advised them, and generally behave. But the minute they had other funds, he was no use to them.

"Let's be friends." Jesus. What an idiot he had been. After everything he had done for them, they were dumping him out on the street. Right before Thanksgiving, for Chrissakes. But he had an ironclad contract. They might be heartless, but they couldn't be so stupid. Could they? If they terminated him, he would have no choice; he would be forced to sue.

Part of life for most people in the investment business, Jack never sued anyone. He didn't believe in it; it wasn't worth the headaches. And the Street was a very small place. Many times he had been advised by lawyers he should sue the party on the other side of a dispute. But he always formed the same opinion listening to the earnest but unfeeling experts. They did not share his view of the world. A deal was a deal, even if he didn't get exactly what he bargained for. If he made a promise, he was going to stick with it no matter how difficult.

Unless he was defrauded or cheated. And he was about to be cheated in spades. By the guys sitting in the car smiling at him. "Let's be friends." Jesus Christ.

They arrived at the airport, checked in, got Jack's tickets, and passed through customs. Jack was too numb to speak. Mr. Xu kept talking to Chris about something else, doing his best to let Jack know the issue they had discussed at the hotel was behind them, being businesslike, moving on to more important things.

First in Chinese and then English, the voice on the loudspeaker announced the Beijing flight. Mr. Xu and Chris stood up. Mr. Xu turned and said something to Chris, looking up as he spoke and grinning at Jack, his cheeks red and puffy.

"Mr. Xu asked if you want a girl here in Dalian," Chris said.

What a bizarre thing to say. "No thanks. I haven't needed to pay for it yet."

Chris didn't understand Jack's response, and Xu was waiting for an answer. Chris tried to be helpful. "Dickle has one."

The termination letter was waiting on his desk when Jack returned to his office in New York. Happy Thanksgiving. As soon as the lawyers prepared the papers, he filed suit against Xushi in Connecticut federal court.

Chapter 33

Chinese Coverage

"**W**hat's Chinese coverage?"

It was Dickle on the telephone, forwarding a question from one of the Xushi shareholders about a convertible bond financing proposal Xushi had received from a big hedge fund.

"Next question," Jack said. Xushi wasn't something he wanted to spend time on, and after his lackluster performance on the Xushi deal and the way the deal had gone down, Dickle wasn't high on his list either.

Still, *Chinese coverage*. Another China riddle. He should have thought of this one himself, though; it was a term from the bond business.

"Jiminy Christmas, Jack. You don't have to be like that."

"Look, what do you want me to say? You made all these grand statements about how you were going to do your part on Xushi, but as soon as the agreements were signed, you disappeared. And now, in spite of your 'blood brother relationship' with Mr. Xu, they've terminated us."

"What are you talking about? I was involved on the deal right to the end; we were just working on different things," Dickle blathered, stupidly trying to explain to an eyewitness how he had been there the whole time when they both knew he hadn't been.

Jack scoffed. He didn't know what Dickle thought he was accomplishing; it was all just talk. "Whatever; let's get this over with. Why don't you tell me about your second deal."

"Please just tell me about Chinese coverage first," Dickle said.

"What do you want to know?"

"Well, first of all, what is it?"

"It's a term used in the bond business."

"That doesn't give me very much to go on, Jack."

"All right, I'll tell you—but there's a condition. Coverage is when a lender requires a reserve to be funded to pay off debt in an emergency— the coverage describes the additional payments to be collected to fill the reserve. So 1.25 times coverage means the issuer must set aside cash equal to 125 percent of debt service, with the extra 25 percent going into the reserve after the debt service for the period is paid."

"Okay." It sounded like Dickle was having trouble following him.

"The point is, that's expensive. So Chinese coverage is when the reserve funded in the first year is used in the calculation for future years. Once the issuer funds the reserve in the first year, he doesn't set aside any more money. It's really false security."

"So the reserve never builds up; the company covers its risks on the cheap."

"Not bad, Bill."

"So what's your condition?"

"For bonus points, why do they call it Chinese coverage?"

"I have no idea."

"I didn't used to know either, but now I think I've got it figured it out."

Dickle's second deal was going to be even better than Xushi, he said— Baoqing Bioengineering, a soybean company that wanted to do a $30 million IPO. Demand in China for soybeans, a fundamental staple of the country, was way up, and the company was profitable. The transaction was all teed up—Jack just needed to visit the site and give the word.

"Where's it located?" Jack asked. A $30 million deal would be Davis Brothers' biggest yet.

"Baoqing," Dickle said.

"Where the hell's that?"

"The closest big city is Jiamusi, up in the far northeast corner of Heilongjiang—the heart of soybean country."

"Jesus, that's only a hundred miles from Siberia. And it's December. It'll be cold as hell up there."

"We'll be fine. The company's got one of those big green army coats with your name on it."

"I've got a coat. So how do we get there?"

Dickle cleared his throat. "There's no flights in the winter; we have to take the train from Harbin."

"For Chrissakes." Jack needed this like a hole in the head. But it was a $30 million IPO. "How long's it take?"

"The plane to Harbin takes two hours."

Dickle had lived in China too long. "The train ride, Bill."

"Ten hours one way."

"Jesus Christ." Jack didn't say anything else; he wasn't going to pass on a $30 million deal over a little cold weather.

"I'm going to book the tickets—we good to go?" Dickle asked.

"I guess so, but get three. I'm going to ask my Chinese friend Dr. Yu to come along."

"Sure. Christmas in Siberia, Jack. What could be better?"

㊌　㊌　㊌

After flying in the previous day from JFK, Jack met Dr. Yu in the airport in Beijing at six o'clock Monday morning for their flight to Harbin. It was still pitch black, and where they were going was so far north dawn wouldn't break until nine.

Dickle was waiting in front of the Harbin station when they pulled up in a taxi from the airport. Jack wore khakis—it was just a due diligence trip—and Dr. Yu wore casual clothes too, but Dickle was in his full business regalia, still trying to look like a deal guy.

Standing inside the maw of the train station, Dr. Yu questioned Dickle about the deal and their agenda. Baoqing Bioengineering wanted to use the proceeds of its IPO to acquire a large state-owned competitor, Dickle said; the plan was to visit both companies.

"We should eat here," Dr. Yu said. "There will be no decent food on the train."

"Okay with me," said Jack, looking around the big crowded station for some place that looked warm. The building's only source of heat was human bodies, and while there were probably a thousand or so milling around inside, the double doors of the station gaped open, the wintry air whipping through the crowd.

"You sure?" Dickle asked.

"Why not? Lead the way, Dr. Yu, but we should be quick. We don't want to be stuck here overnight."

They filed into a small cafe jammed with people off the main floor of the station. Its windows were steamed opaque, rivulets of moisture perspiring down the glass. Inside, half the people were standing and waiting, the other half sitting and shoveling food into their mouths with their chopsticks. Everyone was in a hurry. Jack and Dickle were the only *laowai* there. Jack could see the kitchen through a doorway at the rear of the restaurant; a half dozen cooks were jammed into a cubicle the size of a telephone booth. Something smelled good, though; he hadn't eaten breakfast.

They looked around for a table. Some travelers pushed back from the table where they were sitting and the men behind them tried to push their way through, but Dr. Yu was quicker and grabbed it. The losers were about to start yelling, but then they saw Dickle and Jack and clammed up. The *laowai* win another round, Jack thought; it wasn't right, but the convenience was undeniable.

Dickle's cell phone jangled. Mr. Wong, the head of Baoqing Bioengineering, and Mr. Tsi, the General Manager of the state-owned target, would arrive in five minutes.

"What would you like to eat, Jack?" Dickle asked.

"Whatever Dr. Yu's having."

Dr. Yu ordered *congee* and fish stew for them. A few minutes later, two large steaming bowls of food arrived at their table. Dr. Yu ladled the *congee* and fish onto tin plates and passed them around. Dispensing with conversation, they wolfed down their breakfast; the train was leaving in 10 minutes.

With a few minutes to spare, Mr. Wong and Mr. Tsi pushed into the restaurant. Between Dickle and Dr. Yu, introductions were made; neither Wong or Tsi spoke English. The two men didn't sit down; they were going to have to run to make the train.

Leaving Dickle to pay the bill, Jack headed for the exit, Dr. Yu walking next to him.

"Tsi's stealing money, I believe. You should be careful with him," Dr. Yu said as they hurried along.

"Why do you say that?" Jack asked, walking fast to keep up with Dr. Yu as they knifed through the crowd toward the train platforms at the rear of the building.

"His clothes," Dr. Yu said. "He's too well dressed for a general manager of a Heilongjiang SOE."

They breasted the wide doors at the rear of the station where the trains fanned out along platforms jammed with scrambling passengers and luggage carts. Jack felt the cold outside air hit his face like a board as he made his way with Dr. Yu, who had spotted their train. Waiting on Platform One, the train to Jiamusi was electric powered and consisted of 10 boxy cars painted a drab olive green, a mustard yellow stripe the only concession to visual design.

Dr. Yu led them to the first class car, and they mounted the stairs into the coach hallway as the conductor cranked up the steps after them and prepared to leave.

The air in the cabin was a fogbank of cigarette smoke. His eyes tearing up immediately, Jack could barely see the other end of the car. There were no compartments, just a long boxy room with rows of bench seats facing each other. As a concession to the first class fare premium, the seats were cushioned. Every seat was taken, including theirs. Dr. Yu spoke tersely to the men camped in the bench of seats reserved for them, showing them his ticket number. The men uttered a half-hearted protest, eyed Dickle and Jack, and slunk off without another word.

It seemed as if every person on the train was smoking. Jack took a seat next to the window, and pushing the rusted metal sash up for all he was worth, managed to create a small sliver of airspace. As the train lurched out of the station, a funneling stream of whitish smoke from the cabin began escaping into the Manchurian sky.

Jack sat back, kept his head close to the air valve, let the others keep talking in Chinese, and looked out the window. The train rocked back and forth as it slowly rolled out of Harbin, the onion domes of the city's Russian churches fading in the early morning haze.

A half hour later, on the flats outside of town, the train gained regular speed. It was a little before nine, and dawn was breaking. Looking off to the right, Jack could see the white-gold edge of the eastern sky, clear and unfettered by the polluted haze hanging over the old city to their rear. Grayish pink tufts of clouds absorbed the first sun of the day. To the left, the remains of what had been a stormy night retreated angrily.

As the train glided on its tracks along the silvery ripples of the Songhua River, Minnesota-like vistas opened up. Hilltops covered with dark green pines framed agricultural valleys, low villages of tan-colored mud houses dotting the plains.

The smoke billowed in the cabin as someone opened the door between them and the next car. Jack looked back out the window. He wondered if they were going to see any wildlife. If it were a train crossing Minnesota, they would have seen herds of deer, maybe even a moose, by now, but after traveling across Heilongjiang for over two hours, Jack hadn't even spotted a squirrel.

It was time to check out Mr. Wong. Jack turned from the window and eyed the older, sweater-clad man across from him. "Are any of the soybeans in Heilongjiang genetically modified?" Jack asked Mr. Wong.

Mr. Wong raised his eyebrows and turned to Dr. Yu, who repeated Jack's question in Chinese. As Dr. Yu spoke, Mr. Wong began nodding his head confidently. Jack hoped he would deliver a succinct answer. But as Wong began to speak—and kept talking and talking for 10 minutes—Jack shrugged to himself. It was going to be a long ride.

Dickle tugged on Wong's sleeve, and he stopped talking long enough to allow Dr. Yu to translate.

"Mr. Wong was explaining he is one of China's leaders in the soybean industry," Dr. Yu said, looking at Jack as he spoke.

"That's not what I asked him."

"I know," Dr. Yu said, his face not changing expression.

"Why don't you try again, if you don't mind. I know China is very protective of its non-GM soybeans; I'm just curious if they allow any genetically modified beans to be planted in Heilongjiang. I would think it could contaminate the organic crop."

"I'll ask him again."

Dr. Yu turned back to Mr. Wong and said something in Chinese to him that sounded more terse. Mr. Wong began to speak again in Chinese. After a few sentences, Dr. Yu interrupted him—Mr. Wong getting a surprised look on his bespeckled face—and restated the question. Wong continued, a little less self-assured, until Dr. Yu turned back to Jack with a resigned smile crossing his face.

"You see, I know what you want, but Mr. Wong is not used to this. It's very difficult to make him answer directly."

"Don't worry about it, Dr. Yu. Thanks for trying. Why don't we stick to the most direct questions. How about revenues and earnings? For the current fiscal year."

Dr. Yu turned back to Mr. Wong and spoke to him briefly in Chinese. Mr. Wong smiled, his brown stained teeth lining the crooked opening on his face; he liked this question.

"He says they'll generate $50 million of revenue and $8 million of earnings," Dr. Yu said.

"That's more than the projections you gave me, isn't it, Bill?" Jack asked Dickle.

"Mr. Wong's the man," Dickle answered. "My guess is he's having a bang-up finish to this year."

"But are those results really from soybean oil sales?" Jack asked. "Based on the figures he's produced at the end of the third quarter, I don't see how he can get there. That's a huge amount of crushing and processing to do in three short months; he doesn't have the capacity."

"He's saying he does," Dickle insisted.

"Dr. Yu, if you wouldn't mind, ask him again," Jack said. The smoke in the cabin was getting thicker, causing the skin inside Jack's nostrils to dry and crack.

Dr. Yu turned to Mr. Wong and spoke to him again in Chinese. Wong started to speak, got about a dozen words out, Dr. Yu stopped him and spoke, and Wong began again.

Dickle looked over at Jack. "I'm telling you, he's having a hell of a year," Dickle said. "This is going to be a great deal, Jack."

As the dialogue kept to its pattern, Jack asking basic questions, Dr. Yu interpreting and asking a few of his own, and Mr. Wong pontificating, it would have been easy for Jack to get exasperated. But his headache had begun to divert his attention.

It was a monster. He never got headaches. The pain, low and dull at first, massed across his forehead, throbbing against his cranium.

He looked at Wong and Tsi across from him, turned his head and looked at Dickle and Dr. Yu. They all appeared blurry-edged. He begged off further conversation, saying he didn't feel well and needed to rest for a while. He slumped down in his seat, leaned his head back on the top of the bench, and closed his eyes. The throbbing expanded, pushing out against his eye sockets and his temples.

Four hours into the trip, the pain was pounding his head to bits. He had to get out of the smoke; it felt like it was going to choke him. He looked across at Mr. Wong, who was talking animatedly to Mr. Tsi. Dickle was asleep. Dr. Yu's kind but puzzled eyes looked back at him. Without a word, he got out of his seat, lay down on the floor, and put his hands on his head. Everyone stared at him—Mr. Wong, Mr. Tsi, the other Chinese passengers nearby—while Dr. Yu came down next to him on the floor.

"Jack, you're hurt. What is it?"

"I don't know, Dr. Yu. I've got a horrible headache, and at least there's no smoke down here. It feels like there's something pushing at my brain—it's killing me. As crazy as it sounds, I think maybe it's a tumor."

"Just stay down here and close your eyes. We'll arrive in Jiamusi in a few hours, and I'll get you to a doctor."

Jack heard Dr. Yu call ahead on his mobile phone to the local hospital in Jiamusi and arrange his admittance. At six o'clock in the evening, the train slid out of the foggy gloom of the Manchurian plain into the Jiamusi station. The hundred captives caged in Jack's coach bolted for the exits, clogging the narrow doorways as the smoky cabin air and people exhaled from the drab green car at the same time.

Jack sat on the bench, conscious, his head numb and pulsing, while the crush receded. When everyone else had left the coach, Dr. Yu helped him climb down the stairs and walk along the loading platform out through the grimy station.

The Jiamusi train station sat on a moor-like, misty square. Across the stone cobbled expanse of the square, small bonfires burned alongside vendors hawking food and staples. A black pile of coal six feet high sat in one corner of the plaza. Several small wagons pulled by tiny, bedraggled ponies stood alongside the coal pile, their drivers shoveling fuel onto the cart beds.

"Do you know how cold it is?" Jack asked Dr. Yu.

"Twenty five degrees below zero—your temperature; Fahrenheit."

"Jesus," Jack said, but it was just a reflex; he couldn't feel a thing.

At the bottom of the front steps of the train station, two police cars waited, their flashers rotating. Why two cars briefly crossed Jack's mind, but he was too involved in the instructions Dr. Yu was translating from the policeman standing next to the first car.

The man spoke precisely, Dr. Yu translating that they knew what was wrong with Jack. It was an emergency; he should get in the car, lean back, and close his eyes. Dr. Yu clambered in after him. Disoriented, Jack looked around. Behind their car, another passenger from the train was being loaded into the second police car. Dickle, Mr. Wong, and Mr. Tsi had disappeared.

Even though he had been told the hospital was a short distance away, it seemed to take forever to get there. The driver navigated methodically through the crummy, trash-strewn streets of Jiamusi, making no attempt to hurry. Jack looked behind; the second police car was following them.

When the two cars stopped alongside a cinderblock, clinic-like building lighted with a blue neon sign, everyone got out and shuffled through the front door. Jack looked around the well-lighted space. It was painful to open his eyes. The lights were fluorescent; they seemed to be circled with fuzzy orange halos. Other than that, the place looked just like any hospital. And the inhabitants looked just like their counterparts in a facility stateside—the doctors in white coats, the nurses blue scrubs—except they were Chinese.

Jack sat down and waited while Dr. Yu, standing up at the reception desk counting out dozens of hundred yuan notes, paid in advance. When he had settled Jack's account and exchanged a few words with the desk clerk, a man in a white coat and a nurse pushing a wheelchair came out of another room down the hall, approached him and engaged in a whispered conversation.

The three of them finished talking and walked over to Jack. "This is Dr. Chen," Dr. Yu said. "He seems quite good. Very professional. He will be treating you."

"For what?" Jack asked.

"We take picture of your head," Dr. Chen said to Jack.

"That sounds like the right thing to do," Jack said, "but what do you think is the matter?"

Not answering, they pointed him to the wheelchair and, walking past the other train passenger slumped in a ball in the corner, wheeled Jack down the hall into an X-ray facility. Helping Jack to lie down on the bed in the center of the room, the two men left him in the hands of the nurse. She positioned a camera-like device above his head, covered his body with a lead blanket shield, and snapped several shots, moving in and out of the room each time.

The nurse finished and left; human activity around him ceased. He lifted his head up; he was alone. He closed his eyes. He lay still, losing track of time, wishing he could sleep, his head throbbing, the pain long ago having progressed from sharp points to a massive, white numbness. He was sure it was a tumor; he had just never heard of one killing someone so fast, with so little warning.

Dr. Yu, Dr. Chen, and the nurse walked back into the room, carrying some black and white pictures and talking in Chinese. They looked down at him on the bed.

"Did you find anything?" Jack asked the group.

Dr. Yu hesitated. "Cerebral hemorrhage," Dr. Chen said, nodding his head up and down.

"A cerebral hemorrhage?" He couldn't believe it. "From what?"

"The fish," Dr. Yu said. "In the Songhua. Upstream from Harbin, there was a chemical spill in the river—benzene. The other man on the train was poisoned, too."

"You lucky. Television say two hundred people die," Dr. Chen said, trying to be helpful. "That means maybe two thousand dead."

"But not me?"

"No; just big headache," Dr. Chen said. "We fix you."

"They will give you traditional Chinese medicine," Dr. Yu said. "Some black mushrooms for your blood. And some new things—organisms—to eat the benzene."

"To eat it?"

"It can't dissolve, so the headaches will remain otherwise. The organisms eat the petroleum."

"This no TCM; from America," Dr. Chen said proudly.

Christmas in Siberia came and went. Jack remained in the hospital in Jiamusi for two weeks. Dr. Yu insisted on staying with him. On Christmas Day, he brought Jack a miniature Christmas tree with some makeshift ornaments. A week later, on New Year's day, Dr. Yu hired a car and driver and drove Jack from Jiamusi all the way back to Beijing—no more trains full of cigarette smoke. At the end of the week, they booked Jack on a flight from Beijing to New York.

Dr. Yu came with him to the airport. "I called some people in Bill Dickle's office," Dr. Yu said. "You were right. Mr. Wong lied. Baoqing Bioengineering didn't even process soybeans this fall; they bought the fall crop in September and flipped it for a quick profit on the Dalian commodity exchange. The person I spoke to said Dickle told everyone it didn't matter; as long as the company was profitable the *laowai* would finance it. No one would find out how the company made its money until next year, and then it would be behind them."

"Jesus; I'm sorry, Dr. Yu. I should have known."

"No, no. That's all right. We must be careful, though. You just can't trust those guys."

"Which ones?"

They looked at each other, hesitated, and started laughing. They never had to say anything to each other after that.

Chapter 34

The Fish Will Die

Kerry Chew burst into the lobby of the Kunlun Hotel around 10 o'clock in the evening, his oversized head bouncing on the top of his skinny neck, bug eyes scanning the lobby and spying Jack and Dr. Yu in the lounge having a drink with Paul Chin. Scurrying through the lounge toward them, Kerry stopped a few tables away to speak to a Chinese guy, and then resumed his trajectory.

As Kerry navigated the room, the two female Brazilian entertainers were just ending their set, performing from a small stage next to the waterfall dominating the room. The Brazilians had been the entertainment at the Kunlun since Jack had begun staying there, but it couldn't be because anyone liked the music. Maybe it was their blond hair, but more likely it was because they were cheap. A couple hundred quoi and free drinks per night, enough for two Brazilian girls to see the world and the hotel management to get their fifth star.

Until Kerry had called a day earlier, Jack hadn't heard from either Kerry or Paul since the Sino Solar closing, when they picked up their checks and faded back into the Mainland, as invisible as their performance during the deal. Five minutes after Jack had hung up with Kerry, Paul had called. Jack had told them each of them he would be in the Kunlun lounge that evening having a drink with Dr. Yu.

Paul had arrived first, joining Jack and Dr. Yu, ordering green tea and making small talk, not giving any hint what was up.

Arriving at their table, Kerry pulled up a chair. "I trust you had a good day, Jack," Kerry said; "Dr. Yu," he added, nodding to Dr. Yu, and ignoring Paul, who didn't acknowledge him either.

"You're sounding a little formal, Kerry, which if history is any guide warns me you're about to spring something on us," Jack said.

"Maybe," Kerry laughing loud enough so people across the room looked up.

"Does that Chinese guy across the room have anything to do with why you're here?" Jack asked.

"Maybe twice," Kerry said, laughing some more as he studied the menu.

"Please, Kerry, have something to eat," Jack said, looking at Dr. Yu as they both chuckled. Kerry couldn't sit in a restaurant without ordering something, especially if someone else was picking up the check.

Kerry flagged the waitress, ordered an iced coffee and some dessert, and perched on the edge of his chair as he wound up. "Jack, the guy I just spoke to works for Chairman Roo. He's got a perfect situation for us—I mean you. Chairman Roo's company owns waste-to-energy plants in China. They burn garbage and make electricity. Garbage and power in China? Gold mine!"

"Kerry," Jack said, "Not that you'll listen to me, but operating waste-to-energy plants isn't just rolling off a log."

"Yes, but surely you have experience with these types of facilities," Kerry said.

"Some."

"See? I knew it; it's a perfect situation for us. You know the business, we have a relationship with Chairman Roo, and I'm good friends with Mongo, the chief executive officer—we went to school together in Hong Kong."

"Mongo?" Jack peered at Kerry, shaking his head. "Does Kalin have anything to do with this?"

"Kalin?" Kerry looked at Jack as if he had inquired about someone who didn't exist, and then focused all of his attention on the iced coffee and cream puff the waitress was setting in front of him.

"Kerry, Jack said the business has technical issues," Paul Chin said, speaking for the first time since Kerry had sat down. Turning to Jack, he continued, "I know about this deal too, Jack. The company in question is in Hong Kong. Let me talk to my contacts and do some investigation."

"You heard about the deal from me on the phone, Paul," Kerry complained.

Jack looked at both of them. "Guys, work this out on your own time, but here's the fundamental ground rule: finders work for sellers. If this is Chairman Roo's deal, get him to pay you; we're not going to," he said, looking at Kerry and Paul as Dr. Yu nodded, listening but not saying anything as he poured hot water from an earthen pot through a strainer filled with green tea leaves into his teacup.

"Sure, Jack. Look, just come over and meet Thomas," said Kerry. "He's the chief engineer of the company. He has a presentation for you."

"Jesus, Kerry, it's practically midnight. Can't this wait until morning?"

"I asked him to fly up here to meet you tonight. He's got to get back to Hong Kong in the morning."

"You told this poor bastard to fly all the way up here tonight just to meet me? You didn't even know I was going to be here."

"You told me you were staying at the Kunlun, and here you are," Kerry said, shrugging his shoulders as he asked the waitress for another iced coffee.

Jack looked sideways at Kerry as he stubbed out his cigar. "Let's go meet him, then; I'm not going to ruin the poor guy's trip just because I'd rather have another drink and go to bed."

Kerry left his food uneaten and jumped out of his chair, heading across the room to the table where the chief engineer sat looking at some paperwork.

Tugging at Jack's arm as he rose to follow Kerry, Paul said, "Jack, be cautious. These are Hong Kong guys; very shifty."

"Paul, you're a Hong Kong guy."

"Let me talk to my contacts, do some due diligence. My father's family is connected in Hong Kong, and we know several highly placed people at Red Bank."

"I'm just going to say hello to the guy."

"You should keep me alongside you; things could get very delicate."

"Look, it's late. You need your beauty rest. I appreciate it, but really, I'm just going to say hello for a few minutes. If anything interesting happens, you'll learn about it in due course. Dr. Yu, do you want to join us?"

"Oh, no thank you," Dr. Yu said. "I'll just stay here with Paul." Then, as Jack started to walk over to Kerry's table, Dr. Yu stood up with him and whispered in his ear, "I know the Roo family. If anything bad happens, they won't protect you."

"Are you saying I shouldn't do the deal?"

"No, but be careful; Hong Kong people only invite *guilao* into a deal when something's gone wrong."

㊀ ㊀ ㊀

Kerry's friend stood up as Jack approached the table and took off his glasses. "Thomas," Kerry said as Jack reached out and shook Thomas's hand, "this is Mr. Davis, the expert I've been telling you about. Take him through your presentation. Chop chop. He doesn't have much time."

Thomas opened up a plastic PowerPoint flipchart, stood it up on the table, and began his presentation. "China Waste Power is a company that ... thousand ton waste-to-energy project ... capital cost of 36 million ... fluidized bed technology...."

The Brazilian girls had started back up and were going through a loud version of *The Fool on the Hill*. Jack could barely hear Thomas over the din.

"Thomas. Thomas; hold it. I can't hear a word you're saying. You don't have to go through everything. I know the technology and the business—I owned waste-to-energy projects stateside. The thing is, there are issues with these projects: you've got to get the waste hauler to pay tipping fees to dump the garbage at the plant, and a utility to purchase the electricity; the construction is complex; and there's the ongoing issue of the water content of the Chinese waste stream."

Thomas tried to answer, but the Brazilians kept whacking their marimbas.

"What?"

Kerry cut in. "Jack, he agrees these can be major problems. But they're solved. The project is built and operational. Now they want to finance and build 10 more, and they need your help to attract institutional capital."

"Okay, okay; why didn't you say so? What size is the operating project?"

"A thousand tons per day," said Thomas.

"Jesus."

"Is that big?" Kerry asked.

Jack just looked back at him and nodded.

"I told you. Gold mine!"

❀ ❀ ❀

"Kalin, why didn't you tell me about Chairman Roo's waste-to-energy deal?" Jack asked on the telephone when he called her later that night.

"It's Lin, remember?"

"Lin."

"Who told you about it?" Lin asked.

"Kerry."

She sighed. "He would."

"Didn't you want me to know about it?" Jack asked her.

"I'm not really involved; I only handle Chairman Roo's U.S. investments," Lin said. "Did Kerry say what they want?"

"I have no idea. I just heard about it tonight; Kerry brought the chief engineer up from Hong Kong to brief me."

"Will you be coming down here soon, then?"

"I might be," Jack said. He hadn't seen her in a month. "What do you know about this guy Mongo?"

"Stay away from him."

"So don't do the deal?"

"No, I'm not saying that," she said. "I don't know anything about the waste-to-energy deal. Mongo can't be trusted, that's all."

"Can Chairman Roo?"

"When are you coming?"

The next day, Kerry contacted Jack again. Chairman Roo wanted to fly Jack down to Hong Kong to meet with China Waste Power and its key management. They had an important role for Jack; there was going to be a lot of money involved.

Because it was to Chairman Roo's account, Jack left the trip arrangements to Kerry, and regretted it as soon as they stepped off the plane in Hong Kong. Arriving late in the evening, he had presumed they would go to the hotel and retire for the evening. Not with Kerry in charge.

Two cars met them at the airport: the first took their luggage to the hotel, and the second, a shiny black 500 Series Mercedes, took Kerry and Jack to Kowloon. Fifteen minutes later, the Mercedes slipped past people and rickshaws as it navigated down old Kowloon's cobblestones, shiny under a putrid film of waste and rain.

Pulling up to a dark storefront, the car let Kerry out and Jack followed him through a nondescript doorway and up a steep, narrow stairway to the second floor. The upstairs landing opened onto a wide, dim lobby covered entirely with black onyx. Behind a long reception counter, female attendants sheathed in tight silver gowns greeted them. Without a word, one floated out and led them down a hallway past closed doors to an open entrance on the right.

Inside, the room was well lit and smoke-filled, decorated in wood and ochre. A pudgy little man with a crew cut over a sweaty scalp sat behind a dining table on the opposite side of the room, a roll of skin bulging over the collar of his white tee shirt. Held hostage by three cell phones on the table in front of him and a microphone clip hanging from his ear, he didn't look up.

To his right, a thin, ascetic Chinese man, dressed in white sailor pants, a blue blazer, and a white collared shirt sat smoking passively, his young face prematurely wrinkled with guile, the skin around his yellowish eyes lizard-like, his eyelids opening and closing periodically.

"Hey, Mongo," Kerry said, speaking loudly to get Mongo's attention. "This is Jack Davis, the guy I told you about." Kerry turned toward the second man. "Jack, that's Anthony, the CFO."

Mongo kept talking on his phone, staring across the room to a spot on the wall to the right of Jack. The reptilian CFO blinked, looked up at Jack, and blinked again. Slowly, he pushed his chair back, got up, and extended his hand.

"My pleasure, Mr. Davis," he said, a thin smile crossing his face resignedly. "I'm Anthony, Anthony Chow, CWP's chief financial officer. This is Mister Ho," Anthony said, pointing to the squat butterball sitting next to him, still jabbering into the air on the microphone clip. "He's always on the phone."

It was supposed to be an apology, but it didn't make any difference to Jack. He had already seen enough. Kalin was right; there was no way he was getting involved with these guys. The trip was over as far as he was concerned. All he wanted to do was get to his hotel, go to sleep, and leave Hong Kong the next day.

"What's he doing, talking to his mother-in-law?" Jack said, sitting down. Making a point of ignoring ceremony, he helped himself to a potsticker. A waitress rustled behind him in her silver sheath, whispering a choice of drinks. He ordered some fruit juice. He didn't want to get comfortable there; he'd have a drink at the hotel with Kalin later.

The CFO blinked again. He had taken Jack's comment seriously. "No, no; it's not his mother-in-law. Of course not. It's a shareholder. The stock was down a dollar today."

Perfect. Not only is the CEO a thug, but he's a Hong Kong stock jockey, too. "Doesn't he know any better than that?" Jack said out loud, picking up another potsticker with his chopsticks, then deciding against it and putting it down. He was ready to leave.

Kerry was in the midst of helping himself to the desert tray while Mongo kept yapping on his phone.

Anthony took a cigarette out of a red package, removed a cellophane wrapper, and lit it. "What do you mean, Mr. Davis?" Anthony asked.

"No one can run a company that way," Jack said. "Everyone knows that. If you let them call you at midnight one day, they'll call you at two in the morning the next." Jack shook his head. "Hey Kerry, is that car still downstairs?"

Kerry looked up from the stuffed creampuff he had selected. "I'm sure it is; why?"

"I'm taking it to the hotel," Jack said, standing up. "You booked us at the Mandarin Oriental, right?" As he spoke, Jack slid around the table to where Anthony Chow sat. "Mr. Chow, nice to meet you," he said, shaking the CFO's hand and turning from him back toward Kerry.

"No; I thought we'd try the new Mansion," Kelly said, pushing back from his dessert with surprise in his eyes and trying to get Mongo's attention.

"The Mansion? For God's sake; I told you before, not in Hong Kong," Jack said, shaking his head as he slid out from behind the table and walked out of the room.

Mongo, finally realizing what was about to happen, was negotiating to get off the phone as Jack reached the door. "Oh my goodness, oh my goodness, I'm sorry, Mister Davis. Such a long phone call," Mongo cried at Jack's back as he went out the door.

"Tell me all about it some other time," Jack called behind him as he walked down the black hallway.

㊌ ㊌ ㊌

Jack woke early the next morning, turned over, tried to remember where he was, and read the telephone message pad: "Mansion Hong Kong." An empty wine bottle and two glasses sat on the table in front of the window looking out over Statue Square. He looked across the bed; Lin had left hours earlier.

He got into his running clothes, let himself out of his room and walked down the hallway to the elevator, passing Kerry's room. Outside the door on the floor was a tray filled with half-consumed items: a sandwich with a few bites chewed from a corner; another dessert tray filled with leftover cookies; and a half-eaten plate of French fries.

Jack jogged for several miles along the Wan Chai waterfront where groups of old men and women were doing tai chi, and returned an hour later to Statue Square. It was the weekend, and hundreds of

Filipino maids working in the city were gathered there, meeting with their friends and relatives. A long trailer festooned with yellow flowers carried a group of Filipino priests playing guitars and singing hymns to the clapping, participating audience.

The music from the square lapsed as he got into the elevator, went back up to his room and dialed Lin.

"How are you this morning?" he asked when she offered a muffled hello.

"Much better now."

"Listen, the last thing I was going to do last night was talk shop, but how much would I insult your boss if I got on the plane this morning and went back to Beijing?"

"You would do that?"

"After meeting Mongo? Sure. You were right about the guy."

"What about me?" Lin asked after a moment.

"Well, we had last night, didn't we?"

"Don't leave, Jack. Everyone knows Chairman Roo invited you down here. He would lose a lot of face. Listen to what he's going to say—he's prepared to pay you a lot of money, you know."

"The money doesn't matter if those guys are involved."

"Mongo's not so bad."

"Are you kidding? He's a scumbag." Jack waited for Lin to respond. When she didn't, he asked, "So do you get hurt?" He could hear the sheets of her bed rustling as she rolled over.

"Yes," she said. The sleep was gone from her voice.

"Well, why didn't you say so?"

"So you'll stay?"

He didn't answer.

"Thank you, Jack. You won't be sorry. See you at the office later."

＊ ＊ ＊

After telephoning his sons, he showered, donned some casual clothes and took the lift to the dining room for breakfast. He ordered some coffee, and was reading the headlines of the *South China Morning Post* when Kerry came in.

"Mongo feels terrible about last night," Kerry said, not waiting to sit down.

Jack didn't look up, and kept scanning the headlines. "He should, but it's no big deal. We wasted only one night, and they paid for it. How soon can we get out of here?"

"Jack, you crazy? We can't leave. You know what's behind this deal?"

"Not me, that's for sure," said Jack, putting the paper down and spreading some marmalade across a slice of his toast. "I just want to get back to Beijing."

"Jack, you can't leave, man. This is Chairman Roo's deal. He's installed his daughter as the family placeholder. And when he retires from Red Bank next year, the company will become his personal platform. You know what they say: in Hong Kong, it doesn't matter what the company does, only who owns the shares."

"Why's Mongo involved?"

"He owned the shell they used to backdoor the deal," Kerry said. "He's just small fry."

"He's dangerous, is what he is," Jack said. "Why don't they just get rid of him?"

"Because they've been waiting for you," Kerry said, bringing his head over the table to focus on Jack's face, his eyes bugging out.

"What am I going to do?" Jack said, ignoring Kerry and focusing on his breakfast. "It sounds like it could be a great business, but I can't raise money for any company when guys like Mongo are involved."

"You can tell Chairman Roo and his daughter that yourself. We've got a noon meeting at the company's offices with them. They're going to make you a proposal you're going to like. Please, Jack."

Jack looked up at Kerry, and then turned back to his newspaper. In a panic, Kerry got up from the table and walked over to the corner, talking on his cell phone. By the time they arrived at Chairman Roo's office, Jack figured the package they planned to offer him would double.

水 水 水

Lin was waiting in the reception area for Jack and Kerry when they arrived at China Waste Power's offices. "I thought you weren't involved," Jack said to her as she escorted them down a hallway past the boardroom. Her sad eyes glanced back at Jack in mute response, her heels clattering down the ebony floor until they submerged into carpet as she and Jack entered an oval drawing room. Chairman Roo and a young woman stood next to a table and chairs arranged in front of a broad window overlooking Victoria Harbor.

"Jack Davis, you remember Chairman Roo. And this is his daughter Karen," Lin said.

Chairman Roo just smiled and bowed his head. He didn't talk much, and when he did, Jack had only heard him speak in Chinese. During the Sino Solar transaction, Lin had done most of the talking. Jack had no idea if Chairman Roo knew English or not, but from the man's eyes it looked like he absorbed everything.

They all sat down, and Karen spoke in English, delivering what seemed like prepared remarks about China Waste Power. Jack had expected a hard, businesslike woman, but Karen was soft and kind. Slightly plump, she had a social, pleasant demeanor. Karen spoke uncertainly for five more minutes about the company's mission of bringing renewable power and a cleaner environment to China. At intervals, Kerry murmured agreement. Karen started to run out of script and began to drift, Kerry threw in additional platitudes, and the pace of Chairman Roo's nodding and blinking picked up considerably as the conversation went nowhere.

Jack glanced over at Lin. She sat at the end of the table, her chair turned off to one side, looking out the window at Victoria Harbor, as if trying to distance herself from the discussion. Jack turned back to the group, and saw Chairman Roo looking at Lin, too. The chairman stared at her a moment more, and then interrupted his daughter's monologue, speaking sharply in Chinese to Lin, who appeared startled as her boss's comments brought her back to the room.

Nodding up and down to Chairman Roo, with the same subordinate expression on her face as she wore with Mickey in Manila two years ago, Lin reiterated to Jack she knew little about the deal, and then proceeded to describe the company's situation in a way that underscored the opposite. Just like Manila.

The company had a bright future, Kalin said, if they could solve three problems: first, the inadequate management held over from the company's original shell; second, ownership was typical for a Hong

Kong company—no institutional shareholders; and third, they were in a very capital-intensive industry.

When she was finished, she looked over at Chairman Roo. Her boss and Kerry were nodding their heads up and down, tight grim smiles on their faces. "I'm a little out of my depth on this, Jack," Kalin said. "You know I'm only speaking on behalf of the Roo family." She looked back at Chairman Roo, who nodded and blinked his eyes.

"I don't think I've ever seen you out of your depth, Kalin. All the same, it sounds challenging," Jack said, turning from her after a moment to look at Chairman Roo, Karen, and Kerry, who just looked blankly back at him. "What do you all have in mind?"

The three of them remained silent. Jack looked back at Kalin. "They thought you could tell us," she said, sighing and looking at Jack through her mournful black eyes as she glanced over at Chairman Roo, who imperceptibly nodded his approval, and then started speaking forcefully to Kalin in Chinese.

Kalin translated, her demeanor telling Jack she wanted to be anywhere else. "Chairman Roo says China Waste Power needs to raise capital. Each project costs $40 million, so not including debt, to build 10 additional projects the company needs to issue at least $200 million of equity."

"All right," Jack said, looking at Kalin and ignoring Kerry, who was enthusiastically nodding his head.

"And the Chairman says to do that the company's shareholder base must change," Kalin said.

"Agreed," Jack said.

"So this is where you come in," Kalin said, zombielike as she looked over the table at Jack, repeating her boss's words in English. "Chairman Roo proposes you join the company's board of directors and take charge of all the fundraising efforts, and in exchange for doing so, you will not only receive a 7 percent placement fee for the money raised, but a 10 percent equity stake in China Waste Power." She kept her eyes on Jack the whole time she spoke. By the time she had finished, she was barely audible.

Chairman Roo and Kerry nodded their heads up and down, while Karen Roo looked at Jack blankly. Kalin had shifted her gaze back to the harbor.

"Let's set aside the numbers until we see if the other parts of this deal make any sense," Jack said. "We're replacing Mongo and Anthony, right?"

"That's difficult," said Kalin, now looking even more miserable. "Chairman Roo knows he has to do it, but he can't until after you raise the initial institutional money."

"Why, for God's sake?"

"Chairman Roo has convinced Mongo a management change is in his best interest, and he's agreed to go, but he's not willing to leave until after your institutional investors buy at least $50 million of the company's shares."

"So Mongo knows about all this?"

"Yes."

"No wonder."

"No wonder what?"

"Mongo's demeanor last night," Jack muttered. "Look, I don't know if I can raise $50 million with those two involved."

Kalin repeated Jack's concerns to Chairman Roo, who responded briefly to her in Chinese.

Looking like she was going to cry, she repeated his words in English to Jack. "It's just temporary, Chairman Roo says. You can tell your institutions we intend to initiate an executive search for a proper CEO and CFO as soon as we close on the $50 million. He wants to make you an executive director of the company immediately," said Kalin, "and head of the finance committee, with complete authority for fundraising."

"Look, I'm not worried about raising the money. I'm worried about what happens after the company gets it," said Jack.

Finished a few minutes later, Jack looked into the boardroom as they were leaving. The lotus flower screen stood at the other end of the long room, completed but a world away.

㊡ ㊡ ㊡

Jack got back to the hotel shortly before six. Figuring it wouldn't be long before Kalin showed up to explain things, he put on a pair of jeans and a tee shirt and went to the bar to have a drink.

Furnished as if the decorator had tried to duplicate the feel of a Ralph Lauren advertisement, the Mansion bar was jammed with people, some having casual conversations and just as many conducting business meetings.

The crowd was mainly foreigners. Most of them looked like investment bankers. Jack looked around; it was a comfortable bar, the hotel was conveniently located in Central, and he liked the decor—well, appreciated it, anyway—but he would never be able to get used to the place. The pushy *laowai* clientele embarrassed him, as if a competition had been organized between the American and British expats to determine the rudest guests.

Jack sat in an upholstered chair in the corner and ordered a glass of Chablis, a Cohiba, and the papers. The young Chinese waiter returned with Jack's drink and cigar, and a copy of the *International Herald Tribune*. Jack's eye contact was all the excuse the young man needed to launch into English.

"What do you think about the American elections?"

Jack looked up at him, grinned, and gave him a short, polite answer. The waiter was in Hong Kong to work on his English. He needn't have been concerned; it was excellent. A few more months and instead of serving drinks to the *laowai* investment bankers, he could be running models as one of their analysts.

Across the way in a circle of small couches and chairs, a group of American investment bankers surrounded some Chinese businessmen. The Americans were young and dressed in Wall Street costume, as if they hadn't left New York City. Randomly firing bullets of information toward their audience, they were all interrupting each other. The businessmen, Mainland SOE guys, appeared cagey, drinking their tea as they looked over the Wall Street types through black eyes rimmed with *baiju*-stained red circles, their coppery faces splotched with dark patches, hinting of provincial upbringing and too much alcohol, tobacco, and stress.

Jack was wondering if the Americans had any idea they didn't have a prayer of landing whatever transaction they were pitching to the SOE mossbacks when Kalin walked in and slumped into the armchair opposite him. She had been crying.

Jack signaled the waiter for two more glasses of Chablis and waited for Kalin to compose herself.

"It's no use Jack; I can't do it."

"What are you talking about?"

"Chairman Roo's deal. Chairman Roo. Me."

"What about you?"

"I'm his mistress, Jack. But you knew that," she said, looking at him through wet eyes ringed with dark circles.

He looked at her a moment before speaking. "I told you I didn't want to talk about other people."

"But you knew, Jack."

"It doesn't matter, Kalin. It was none of my affair."

"It doesn't matter," she said, mimicking him. "You just don't love me, Jack."

He just looked at her.

"I know you don't," she said, the tears running down her face.

"What's this got to do with what happened today?"

"I just couldn't do what he wanted."

"Which was what?"

She sat in an armchair opposite him, crying quietly. "The $50 million. Ten million off the top would have gone to him and Mongo; they were going to split it."

Jack sat in his chair staring out at the crowd in the bar without seeing them, shaking his head back and forth as he downed his second glass of Chablis and signaled the waiter for another. "Can't stay out of that dirty water, can they?"

Kalin looked at him blankly.

"Just an expression."

"I know what it means, Jack," she said. "You're right. Some of us just can't avoid it."

She took a sip of her wine and sniffled. "There's one more thing," Kalin said, sitting up straight on the edge of her chair and looking him in the eye. "My cut would have been a million," she said, her game face on. "And I told him no and walked out." Her eyes were welling up again as she stood up. "Don't ever forget that, Jack," she said as she turned to leave. "I told you—you didn't have to find out for yourself."

Jack stood up and grabbed her shoulders. "Kalin, wait a minute." He put his arms around her. "You didn't have to say that," he said as he held her, kissing her temple and breathing in the sad, sweet smell of her hair.

"Just remember, Jack. They're not all like me."

"Who's not?"

"China. I just wanted to see your face one last time, and tell you that."

Chapter 35

As Little as Possible

Dennis was saying something to him.

"Sorry, Dennis; I was daydreaming."

They were in New York City, having lunch at the Sea Grill.

"No problem, Jack; I won't ask about who. I was wondering how long you've been doing investment banking deals in China."

"Too long."

Dennis ignored Jack's ennui and plodded ahead on his topic, investment banking business in China. Jack listened idly; he could mislead Dennis and brag, saying the fees Davis Brothers was generating had solved most of his difficulties, but he didn't. Because the fees only solved his financial problems—the other issues over there were more fundamental. As long as his work involved raising money for guys like Mr. Hu or Mr. Liu or Mr. Xu or Chairman Roo, being an agent in China wasn't sustainable—the exposure to human indiscretion left his psyche too raw and abused.

"So what's your deal of the month?" Dennis asked him.

Jack considered what he should say. He wasn't going to try to fool Dennis to glamorize his own endeavors, to offer a falsely enthusiastic answer about a subject that at the moment filled him with pessimism. To change his sentiments would require good people. And so far, Chinaside had provided few of them.

Lianhua was one, a brief glimpse of Chinese light—if she wasn't just a dream—surrounded by far too many dull letdowns. And his only means of finding her had been Kalin.

"I don't know, Dennis. We just closed a deal for a company that makes bimetallic wire," Jack heard himself say robotically. "Something we were doing in the waste-to-energy business didn't pan out. My Beijing office told me when I get back Chinaside they've got a small Chinese hydroelectric company that might be interesting. But I'm not sure I'm going to continue on the investment banking side of things."

"So what will do you do in China?"

"As little as possible."

Dennis looked at Jack with an expression indicating he didn't know whether he should laugh or be serious. "What does that mean?"

"Nothing—sorry, that's not fair. It's just a line from a movie."

"What movie?"

"*Chinatown.*"

"The one with Jack Nicholson?"

"That's the one."

"So what's it mean?'

"Jack Nicholson's a *laowai* detective in Chinatown who always turns right when he should go left. The movie's message is when it comes to China—Chinatown in the movie—*laowai* are better off standing still. Doing 'as little as possible.'"

"Well, we're not standing still at Morgan Joseph. We're committed. They've put me in charge of the international banking effort, and I'm building up our business in China. So if you see anything interesting over there, let me know."

"Sure, Dennis," he said, trying to remember Lianhua's face. "Good luck."

"Why so cynical, Jack?"

"It's Chinatown, Dennis."

"What does that mean?"

"Just another line from the movie."

Walking down Fifth Avenue on his way back from lunch, he had to admit he hadn't been totally candid with Dennis—doing as little as possible wasn't really in the cards. He was in China up to his earlobes, too deep to turn his back on the place like he had after Catapult Energy and New Land Power. Doing business there posed problems, but the prospect of greater opportunity continued to beckon. And China was no longer just about business. There were people there who depended on him.

That wasn't honest either, he told himself, crossing 47th Street against the light. It wasn't just them depending on him—he depended on them, too. And then there was Lianhua—wherever she was.

As far as his business was concerned, he was just going to have to devise a better formula. He turned out of the sun streaming down Fifth Avenue and crossed east on 44th Street, the flags over the Cornell Club snapping in the April breeze, came to Madison Avenue and decided to turn south again.

The epidemic problem Chinaside was the sense, mainly among the men, that shortcuts—lies—were permissible, as long as the crime led to wealth. And especially if the victim was a *laowai*.

So, he reasoned, walking down Madison, if most of the men were liars, he would just hire women. And if being an investment banker raising money for dishonest ingrates wasn't workable, he would start investing money himself, but only in businesses he could control.

Where he would get the money was secondary. And it never occurred to him that agents could remain uninvolved—what many dislike about them—while principals, if they're not careful, can get hopelessly entangled. He would have to learn those things the hard way.

He kept going down Madison Avenue, dodging the lunch crowd coming the other way. Looking into people's eyes as they drifted past him, he didn't see anyone he knew. He didn't come this way very often; he usually walked down Park.

Off to his left, he glanced into the display window of the Gagosian Gallery, the venue for several of Virginio's one-man shows of small sculptures and works on paper. The poster advertising the current works caught his attention. "Tibetan Portraits and Landscapes."

In the past, when reading the *New York Times* and coming across an article on China, he had usually just turned the page. Not his territory; not enough time. But in the recent years since he had started to finance companies there, he had forced himself to stop and read everything on the subject. Looking in the window, something told him to do the same thing.

As he studied the featured painting hanging in the window, he didn't need any special impetus to continue to pay attention. He had seen the work before. Focusing, he scanned the details printed on the poster.

"Tibetan Portraits and Landscapes. By Lianhua." Jack's heart jumped, then slumped, as he read on: "November 1992." The show had ended five months ago. Jack tried to look inside. The gallery was closed. He peered closely at Lianhua's photograph on the poster. The Chinese vision he had seen in Chairman Roo's Hong Kong boardroom stared back at him, dressed in the same classic Chinese costume, holding her brushes and palette and standing in front of a pond covered with lotus flowers.

No wonder her English was so good. Gagosian was a big-time gallery. She probably had shows all over the world. He looked back at the poster one last time to remember her face. Demure as she appeared in the picture, the imagery was probably only his naive idealism at work. She was an international artist; practically a celebrity. She probably had an entourage. Forget it.

Forget all of them; Kalin, Lianhua, China; all of them. He had no time anyway, and he had a lot to do.

Still, he couldn't stop thinking about them that night, the trails of their mystery wrapped tightly around him as he slept, dark-haired angels floating across the misty, star-crossed expanse of the Orient, remaining just beyond his grasp, massaging him with hope and exhilaration as the dank air wafting up from the ground threatened to choke him with deception, betrayal, and sorrow.

Book Four

HYDRO KING

Chapter 36

Sand Pebbles

"Jack Davis, how the hell are you?" Richard Abderman said as they crossed the lobby of the Pan Am building on a balmy day in May 1993.

"How's life treating you, Richard?" Jack hadn't seen Richard since the end of Drexel Burnham four years earlier.

"I just got out of an investment conference on China. It's amazing what's going on over there. What are you up to?"

"Well, you may recall that most of my business is in China."

"Really? What kinds of things are you doing over there?"

"Now you ask," Jack said, laughing. "I tried to tell you about China a while ago—Dennis Galileo too—but at the time I think you guys thought I was crazy. I just saw Dennis yesterday; he's come around on China. Maybe you should too."

They had lunch the following Tuesday. Richard invited Dennis Galileo to join them. Richard and Dennis had worked together at Drexel in the old days, and he wanted Dennis involved so his firm could validate whatever Jack had to say. And Morgan Joseph would pick up lunch, too. Richard didn't miss much.

Richard had only a little time, and had talked to Dennis before the meeting.

"Jack, what about the small Chinese hydroelectric company you mentioned the last time I saw you?" Dennis asked Jack.

"What about it?"

"Richard and I thought it might be a good thing to do together with you."

"I like the idea of being in a hydroelectric company with you, Jack," Richard said. "You know the business. Maybe the company needs a little seed money. Any chance we can invest on a venture capital basis prior to you guys going to institutions?"

Some things never changed—Richard and Dennis always liked doing business on their terms. But that was all right. Any type of involvement with Richard Abderman would be good; he knew everyone on the Street.

㊆ ㊆ ㊆

If Jack was going to shift from investment banking deals in China toward transactions in which he was investing as a principal, hydroelectric power was an obvious place to start.

So when Mr. Zhou, a businessman from Hebei who owned toll roads, asked Jack and Dr. Yu to invest in his small hydroelectric company, they agreed. And based on Richard and Dennis's encouragement, they pushed ahead. Mr. Zhou owned a few small hydroelectric projects, and most importantly, in exchange for a small amount of capital, was willing to cede control of the fledgling enterprise to Jack and Dr. Yu. Zhou's negatives were cosmetic. Although his toll road made him worth more than $50 million, he looked like a janitor. Dennis had a thing about nose hair; Jack laughed to himself envisioning Dennis meeting Mr. Zhou for the first time.

Together with Zhou's staff, Kitty assembled a package of offering documents and a PowerPoint presentation on the small hydroelectric company, and Mr. Zhou, Kitty, and Dr. Yu flew to New York, where

Jack and Elizabeth arranged for the Zhou group to make a presentation at Morgan Joseph, preceded by meetings with a few small financial institutions to acclimate Mr. Zhou and the group to one-on-one presentations.

A presentation to financial institutions in New York was a challenge when the entrepreneur didn't speak English, or didn't speak it well. And Zhou didn't know a word, so they followed some basic procedures to get the job done.

Jack designed the PowerPoint to be short and simple. As the key spokesperson, Kitty would take the institutions through the presentation, the audience would get the feeling they were hearing from Chinese management, and in the question and answer period, Jack could steer the dialogue without the institutions feeling like they were getting pitched by the investment bankers. The institutions hated that. After all, they were smarter than the investment bankers, weren't they?

When an investor directed a question to the Chinese management—Mr. Zhou—a standard procedure was used. After the question was asked, Kitty would respond, "That's an operations question, so I will ask Mr. Zhou the answer," and turning to Zhou would repeat the question in Chinese. Mr. Zhou would answer in Chinese and Kitty would repeat his answer in English. While cumbersome and time consuming, the procedure allowed investors to see Zhou handle the question and to discern he was speaking with veracity, even though answering in another language.

And most of the time, it worked. Kitty's role was the most important. She had the most talking to do, but more importantly, she had to manage Mr. Zhou. She knew Jack's 10 second rule—no answer can take longer than 10 seconds—so when Mr. Zhou rambled on like most Chinese businessmen, Kitty told him in Mandarin to get to the point. Furthermore, she knew most of the answers—often better than Zhou did—so when he gave the wrong answer in Chinese, she corrected it in the English response.

After a few dry runs, they were ready for their presentation to Morgan Joseph. Dennis Galileo arranged for a large group of the firm's management to attend, from Henry Morgan and Frank Joseph, the co-chairmen, and John Pickens, the CEO, down to salespeople off the trading desk. Abderman brought a group of private investors as well. More than 30 people convened in Morgan Joseph's main conference room overlooking Fifth Avenue as Kitty set up their presentation equipment. When the cover slide—a picture of one of Mr. Zhou's hydroelectric projects showing a long concrete dam on the downstream side of the spillway—was centered on the screen, they were ready to begin.

Dennis Galileo began making introductions for Morgan Joseph.

"Where's the watta?" Abderman interrupted.

The audience laughed nervously. After all, it was China—who knew what to believe?

"Where's the what?" Kitty whispered to Jack.

Jack leaned over to Kitty. "*Water.* Richard's from Brooklyn." He told her to make sure they replaced the slide with one showing plenty of water.

"Where's the watta?" Richard repeated.

"Richard. Listen to me," Jack said. "You're looking at a dam. The water's there, believe me—right behind the dam where it belongs. But we'll replace the picture."

"I should hope so."

The session continued. Frank Joseph said some kind things about Morgan Joseph's long friendship and business association with Jack, and the floor was turned over to Jack and Dr. Yu.

Jack asked Dr. Yu to introduce himself. Dr. Yu's cosmetics, especially with the Morgan Joseph crowd, were critical. Jack could tell the audience everything they wanted to know about hydroelectric power in China, and while it would be comforting coming from one of their own, they wanted to hear about China from a Chinese person. And not just any Chinese person. Hopefully, someone fluent in English and credentialed, a Western-like person to whom they could entrust their money who would employ the same sense of fiduciary responsibility beaten into their souls over the course of their lives by their parents, teachers, religious leaders, and superiors.

And Dr. Yu didn't disappoint. From his impeccable English to his doctorate in economics from the Australian National University to his experience financing Three Gorges, the cosmetics were perfect.

But it was Dr. Yu's substance that captivated the group. He didn't answer questions in the manner of a promotional entrepreneur. When a question addressed a difficult area, he didn't offer: "No problem," or "You've got to be more flexible in China." Instead, he provided thoughtful, objective information. In some cases, he served up an answer Jack rarely heard in Chinese presentations: "I don't know."

As Dr. Yu wound down to the end of his remarks, Jack looked around the room. Dennis was glowing. Richard looked over at him and arched his eyebrows in a salute. Mr. Morgan, Frank Joseph, John Pickens and the other senior officials of Morgan Joseph were rapt. They ran out of questions on the hydroelectric sector, and turned to inquiries about the general Chinese economy. The first part of the presentation was clearly a success.

But as good as Dr. Yu's performance was, Mr. Zhou's was equally bad. The size of the group must have been intimidating to Zhou, but even a yeoman effort by Kitty could not disguise his mediocrity. At the end of the presentation, as the questions and answers on the business started in earnest and Zhou flubbed them, Jack was forced to play a more active role than he had intended. Gradually, he began punctuating Mr. Zhou's answers, until by the end of the session, in an effort to make sure the audience received the full message, he was reluctantly doing most of the talking.

The presentation ended shortly thereafter. As the attendees filed out, Dennis and Mary Lou O'Malley, Morgan Joseph's head of investment banking, told Jack they'd be back to him the following week.

In the meantime Jack took the group to Dallas for a one-on-one with Peak Capital, a hedge fund managed by Perry Winer. Making do with an on-the-run breakfast, which the Chinese hated but tolerated without complaint, they had just taken their seats in the conference room at Peak Capital's offices when Perry swaggered into the room. Jack had warned everyone about Perry.

Looking at Kitty, Perry walked over to where she sat preparing her notes. Standing behind her in his silly cowboy boots, Perry asked in a loud voice, "What's this deal about?"

Shy and quiet like most Chinese women, it didn't take much to intimidate Kitty—just the way Perry asked the question was enough. Her face flushed as she shuffled her papers. Jack watched at first, not wanting to intervene, willing Kitty to handle Perry's degrading "Welcome to Hedge Fund Investing Texas Style" ritual.

But Perry was just getting started. "Why should I waste my time talking to you about a shitty little Chinese hydroelectric company?" he said to Kitty.

She stammered trying to provide him an answer, looking over at Jack, her expression like that of a trapped animal.

Things were just going to get worse.

Jack stood up and starting to disassemble the overhead projector. "Tell Mr. Zhou to pack his things," he said over his shoulder to Kitty.

His back to Jack, Perry didn't comprehend what was happening at first. But as the presentation screen went dead, he turned to Jack and said, "What the hell do you think you're doing?"

"I just got a call," Jack said. "We've got to go see a man about a dog." As he spoke, Jack kept breaking down the projector, unscrewing the lens, unplugging the wires, and stuffing the components into their black canvas bag.

"It's just a shitty little Chinese hydro company, Jack. Don't do this. It's not worth it; we go back together," Perry said, sitting down at the end of the conference table, as if his getting comfortable was going to make Jack change his mind.

Ling, Perry's Chinese analyst, was mortified. She got up to open the door for Dr. Yu and Kitty, who had packed her briefcase and was walking around the table toward the exit, her head down, staring at the carpet. Stuffing his cigarettes into his pocket, Mr. Zhou followed them through the door, his eyes wide open, the whites showing.

"You going to be sorry, Jack. I'm going to make your life difficult," Perry said, sitting alone at the end of the table.

"Not on this deal, Perry. We'll be oversubscribed," Jack said over his shoulder as he left the office and joined the others in the hall waiting for the elevator.

Once in the parking lot, Jack unlocked their rental car, waited until everyone threw their bags in the trunk and got in, backed out of the garage, jammed the car into gear and careened out onto the street. The airport was an hour away.

No one spoke while he gunned the vehicle up the entrance ramp of the freeway and joined the morning traffic. Finally, Kitty said, "You didn't have to do that. I could have taken his insults. I'm a professional."

Jack didn't say anything. Mr. Zhou, sitting in the back seat, lit a cigarette and opened the rear window. The hot Dallas wind blew in and scattered his ash all over Dr. Yu sitting next to him.

After a few minutes, Kitty felt like talking some more. "He was mean," she said, looking out the window and watching the United States roll by. "But you said he manages a lot of money," she said, turning back to look at Jack. "No one in China would have done what you just did. Will it be bad for you?"

"It's a great country, isn't it?" Jack kept his eyes on the highway in front of him.

æ æ æ

Thirty minutes from the airport, Jack's mobile phone rang. He looked at the caller ID display: Mary Lou from Morgan Joseph.

Jack opened his phone. "Well hello Mary Lou," he said, warbling the opening line to the Everly Brothers classic.

"Hello Jack; I'm on the speaker phone with Dennis."

"Hey, Dennis. How do you like my singing voice?"

"Hello, Jack. Do you want the good news or the bad news?"

"You didn't like it."

"Seriously; good news or bad news?"

"You know me, Dennis; bad news first."

"The hydroelectric company's too small, Jack. And we're not impressed with Mr. Zhou. If you hadn't taken over, the meeting would have been a disaster."

"That's not very original, Dennis. A jerk down here in Dallas just told me the same thing, this time before we even started our pitch," Jack said, looking over at Kitty and winking, hoping to get her to laugh to take the edge off.

"Do you want the good news?" Mary Lou asked him.

"Any news from you is good, Mary Lou. Sure, fire away."

"We don't like the company, but we buy the idea of a hydroelectric business in China. We like Dr. Yu very much. And you know we love you. So we're prepared to back a company led by you with $200 million of financing."

Jack stared in front of him at the highway running out toward Fort Worth. A large green overhead sign indicated it was 30 miles to the airport. The rental car hummed along the interstate highway bordered by ranch homes surrounded by straw-like grass, tiny trees, and wilting shrubbery, the land permanently parched and scrubby.

He wouldn't ever have to live in a place like the ones he watched flying by. Head of a $200 million hydroelectric company in China; running an operating company again—it had been four years.

"All right, Dennis, now that Mary Lou is getting me all excited, you must be getting ready to prick my balloon."

"Jack ... me?"

Jack just waited; there was no point in saying anything.

Dennis paused a moment, and then ticked off a prepared list of requirements: their offer was subject to due diligence; background checks; site visits; and fees, of course. The road show would begin the day after July 4th.

"What else?" Jack asked. With Dennis, there was always something else.

"Counsel—we'll use Wheel Gotcham, and we propose you use Jonathan Katz and the guys at DLA Piper."

"That's fine, Dennis, but come on. Get to the part I'm not going to like."

"What part is that?"

"I don't know. There's got to be something."

"Oh, you mean the 'skin in the game' part?"

"Now we're getting somewhere."

"We'd like to see you put up $5 million, Jack," Dennis said.

"Forget it," Jack exhaled. "I haven't got anything close to that, guys. I knew this was too good to last."

"What can you come up with?" Mary Lou asked.

Jack thought as the car passed under a new green sign saying the airport was 25 miles away. "$500,000 tops," without the slightest idea where he would come up with even that amount.

"That won't work," said Dennis.

"I haven't got it, then. I wish I did, but I don't."

"You know, Jack, I've always wanted to ask you something," Dennis said. "How come you're not richer?"

Jack tried to laugh, but couldn't.

"$500,000 is it?" Mary Lou asked again.

"Maybe $600,000."

On the other end of the line, Jack could hear Mary Lou and Dennis whispering back and forth.

"We need you to have $2 million in the deal," Mary Lou said. "But you don't have to put it all up yourself. As long as you personally invest $1 million, and your management team, including Dr. Yu, puts up $250,000, Richard Abderman's group and Morgan Joseph will invest the balance."

Jack didn't say anything.

"Well?" Dennis said. "Are we a go?"

"I'm almost at the airport. Let me think about it. I don't know where I'm going to get $1 million. And I need to talk to Dr. Yu and Elizabeth, too."

"Call us tomorrow?" Mary Lou said.

"I'll call you tomorrow."

"We need a name for the company," Dennis said. "Think about it."

"Your greatest fortune lies in the Middle Kingdom," the fortune cookie had said. "I don't have to think about that one," Jack said. "Middle Kingdom Hydroelectric Corporation."

"How'd you like to be a Sand Pebble?"

Jack was back from Dallas, attempting to break the news to Elizabeth.

"What's a Sand Pebble?"

"Some people who go up a river in China on a great adventure."

"Just what I need. No thanks."

"Wait a minute," he laughed. "That didn't come out right. You were supposed to react differently." He explained that sand pebbles were the men serving on the San Pablo in the movie *Sand Pebbles* starring Candice Bergen and Steve McQueen about an American gunboat plying the Yangtze, and Morgan Joseph was offering to bankroll them on a similar mission in China, and wouldn't it be great?

"You're doing it again."

"What?"

"As soon as we're making money and paying our bills, you figure out a new way to reach for the moon and make life difficult."

She was right, as far as it went. The practical thing to do was to say no, to keep focusing on their investment banking business, and earn some more fees. But that meant raising money for another Mr. Xu or Chairman Roo, and holding their noses and their breath again. "Sure, Elizabeth. You're right," he lied.

God, he would give anything to be back in charge of a $200 million operating hydroelectric power company; in China, no less.

"So what's the verdict?" Elizabeth asked.

"Why are you asking me? You seem to have it all figured out."

"I haven't got anything figured out. I just know what's practical, that's all. That doesn't mean we're supposed to do it."

"Well, I guess we're supposed to be practical."

"I can't imagine you being practical."

She didn't say anything more. She knew what was coming.

"There's got to be some way to make this work."

Elizabeth rolled her eyes.

Jack got out a pad of paper and asked Elizabeth about the firm's cash balances and what was coming in during the next few months. Davis Brothers and his friend Sam Sheppard could pony up the $1 million if the firm's banks would cooperate.

The other members of the management team would have to invest the rest, and Morgan Joseph's rules meant they had to write real checks—probably no less than $100,000 each, at least for the critical members.

Jack called Lee Fu and offered him the position of chief financial officer. He agreed on the spot, and before Jack could even ask, volunteered to invest.

That left Dr. Yu, the key to the whole deal. Jack saved his call to Dr. Yu until last, when he had everything else lined up. He only had one shot. The conversation couldn't contain anything farfetched, or Dr. Yu would hesitate, and things would fall apart. It was highly unusual for a Chinese guy to invest real cash in a foreign deal—they were usually on the receiving end.

Jack sat in his office at his farm house looking out across the fields as he spoke to Dr. Yu 9,000 miles away, explaining the Morgan Joseph offer. At first, Dr. Yu was excited. This was what they had wanted, ownership of a controlling stake in a Chinese hydroelectric power company. And now the company would be much larger than anticipated.

But when Jack told him about the investment part, he got quiet.

"So how much do you think you can put up?"

Dr. Yu didn't answer.

"Dr. Yu, I don't mean to back you into a corner, but the truth is, that's the best we can do. This type of deal is fairly typical stateside. Morgan Joseph and a group of institutional investors are going to throw $200 million at us, and they want to know we take it seriously. Henry Morgan, Frank Joseph, and their partners are actually going to invest themselves. Yours doesn't need to be a lot. They just need to know you're committed. What's the minimum you can do?"

"I will think about it."

"Yeah, I know. I'd like to think about it, too. But they want to know now. We don't actually need to come up with the cash for a month or so, if that helps."

"I need to think about it."

"Ok, sure. I guess I'll tell them no, then."

"So they will go away now if we don't give them an answer?"

"Unfortunately. Look, I feel really bad about having to press you on this; I wish I didn't have to. And I'd like to put up the money for you. But I can't—they'll want to see your check. You're actually the most important investor, as far as they're concerned. If you're not willing to invest, they'll assume the deal is no good."

"I see." Dr. Yu remained quiet.

Jack sat at his desk in his office. He looked out across the cornfield to the pond. The ice had melted and the willows were sprouting buds. A warm, earthy breeze swayed the branches of the sycamores lining the riverbank. Shoots of asparagus raised bright green tips on the gravely hillside stretching in the distance toward Lime Rock.

"I will invest $100,000."

Jack closed his eyes in relief. "Thank you, Dr. Yu. Thank you so much. You won't be sorry; we will have a very good business."

"No, you don't need to say this. You are the one who arranged this deal. It's a good deal. Don't worry about the money. If we lose it, too bad."

"Well, if it means anything, I worry about my friends' money more than my own. I'll do everything I can to make sure we don't fail."

"But you can't be sure. Just try your best, and we'll have a good chance. When will the road show start?"

"July."

Chapter 37

Chinese Water Torture

When Dennis said the lawyers in London had a problem about the stolen car, Jack thought he was joking.

They had worked into the summer on the Middle Kingdom Hydroelectric Corporation offering. The plan was to capitalize Middle Kingdom as a new type of entity called a special purpose acquisition corporation, or SPAC, and register its shares on the London AIM Exchange.

When utilizing a SPAC, founders' capital, not funds from investors, was used to pay corporate expenses until they acquired the first hydroelectric project. If they couldn't find one, or if the investors didn't like the project, the money would be refunded, and Jack and the other founders would be out $2 million.

The offering documents and due diligence were close to complete when Dennis called.

"You're kidding me, right?"

"I can't help it, Jack. Why didn't you tell them?"

"Tell them what? That when I was thirteen I stole a car and it's relevant to my business credentials?"

"Something like that."

"Because it's not. I was thirteen. This is a business deal—I'm not running for president."

"You know the English lawyers. They dig deep, and they're finicky. You should see Lee's report."

"What'd it say?"

"Well, I wouldn't want to get in a car with him, put it that way. You stole a car, but he wrecked two."

"Jesus. Let me ask you something. Truthfully—do you think this London financing is a good idea?"

"Everybody's doing it."

"That's not what I asked."

"All of the other big SPACs have been London AIM deals. Our international sales desk is saying we'll have the money by the end of the summer."

"Who's on your international desk?"

"A bunch of Brits we just hired."

"Great. How do we know they can sell anything?"

"Not my department. But I've seen their resumes; they come from good British firms."

"But a good British firm could be the wrong entry point. The good firms cover the stodgy old City accounts. The upstart hedge funds are the ones buying the SPACs. Do your new guys do business with them?"

"We'll see when we get out on the road, I guess."

"In the meantime, can't we take Shakespeare's advice?" Jack asked.

"What's that?"

"Kill all the lawyers."

Flying over the Atlantic to begin the road show after the July 4th weekend, all Jack could think about was the cash remaining in Middle Kingdom's bank account. Everything about London was expensive— lawyers, auditors, taxis, hotels, and restaurants—and his $2 million had to pay for not only the road show, but payroll, and costs associated with finding hydroelectric projects in China as well.

By the time they landed, Jack was down to $1 million.

The road show's initial meeting Monday morning was with GLP Partners, a large, London-based hedge fund. GLP's offices were on the edge of Mayfair, on the penthouse floor of a building overlooking Hyde Park.

Waiting for their hosts, Dennis helped himself to his fourth cup of black coffee while a young associate from Morgan Joseph's London office put offering books in front of every chair. Jack sat on the east side of the glass-enclosed conference room, looking out over the street toward the Queen's flower gardens. Beyond the gardens, tall leafy elms swayed in Hyde Park's summer breeze.

Roger and Omar, their hosts from GLP, entered a moment later. Dressed in shirt sleeves, lacking ties and unshaven, their appearance was designed to announce their membership in the hedge fund fraternity, but Roger could not disguise his British schoolboy background, while Omar appeared to be from India.

"Right. Omar, have you received the materials?" Roger asked. "I don't believe they were sent to me."

"We sent both of you the documents a week ago. I've got the e-mail confirmations right here," Dennis said, holding up his laptop computer. Dennis lived on his laptop.

"Right." Caught in his white lie, Roger made no attempt to disguise his irritation, but moved on. "Well, maybe you could tell us something about the deal before we hear the company's presentation. Just so we don't inconvenience anyone."

"Certainly," Dennis said, the combination of four cups of coffee and Roger already causing his face to tick.

Keep calm, Dennis, Jack thought to himself. It was Monday morning, the first presentation of the day on the first day of the road show, with 90 more meetings to go; it wouldn't do to get bothered now.

"Middle Kingdom is offering $200 million of units in a SPAC vehicle that will register its shares on the London AIM," Dennis began.

It was all Roger needed to hear. "We hate SPACS. And the London AIM is a swamp."

Jack just sat there as everyone absorbed the napalm-like remark, recovered, and said, "But other than that, I take it our deal sounds good."

People laughed, but the meeting was over. There was no point in wasting time if their host wasn't interested. Repeating the admonishments he had mentally directed at Dennis a moment ago to himself—don't lose it, at least not now; maybe after this happened another 10 times, he could throw things—he stood, looked at the young associate from Morgan Joseph's London office trying to disappear in his seat, thanked Roger and Omar for their time, and left the others trailing behind him as he took the lift to the ground floor and stepped into the summer breeze bathing Knightsbridge Road.

The audiences they encountered from the United Kingdom through Europe weren't as rude, but were similarly dismissive of the SPAC and its London AIM listing; Jack still didn't throw anything.

He and Morgan Joseph had simply miscalculated: the international buyers were just not interested in their deal. After two weeks overseas, they returned to New York empty-handed. They had taken no orders, and Jack was out another $50,000.

The United States was only slightly more hospitable. After the three-week domestic road show, they had soft circles for $10 million. Jack had spent another $50,000 and was rapidly coming to the conclusion the best thing would be to call the whole thing off, return the balance of the money to the founders, and put Middle Kingdom out of its misery.

But Dennis wouldn't give up. His colleagues at Morgan Joseph served up a new idea: money from the Gulf. A sheik high up in the royal family in Bahrain had an interest in renewable energy in China, and could invest a huge amount in the right deal. The sheik's representative, Georges Polski, was in New York and had requested a presentation.

Dennis and Mary Lou described Georges Polski as a Belgian of Polish background who had worked in project finance for a number of U.K. and E.U. financial institutions, migrated to Hong Kong, married a Chinese wife, and transferred to Bahrain to work for the sheik. He claimed to have interested his superiors in hydroelectric power in China as a hedge against oil prices.

Jack agreed to meet Polski at Morgan Joseph. When he arrived, Dennis, Mary Lou, and Georges Polski were waiting for him in a small conference room.

Georges was pleasant. He was also plump, short, dressed outlandishly, and more interested in details than substance. It was a mild day in early September, but Georges had shown up in a wool tweed suit and spats, carrying a cane and an opera cape. His suit jacket sported a boutonniere in the lapel.

When Jack had started to describe the company, Georges had insisted on spending 30 minutes on the differences between a Pelton wheel and a Francis turbine, even though Jack explained technology was not a key factor in hydroelectric power.

"What do you think?" Dennis asked Jack after Georges had left.

"He's a perfectly nice guy, but it makes no sense to do what he's asking," Jack answered.

"Why not? All he wants to do is visit a few of the hydroelectric sites you're planning to acquire in China," Dennis said.

"Dennis, did you see the guy? His clothes? He wouldn't last a day in China. And he said he wants to fly into Beijing and spend two days visiting half a dozen sites. These projects are eight hours down back roads—one way. Maybe, if we're lucky, we could visit two sites in three days."

"Jack, the man lived in Hong Kong. He knows China," Dennis said.

"Hong Kong is fake China," Jack responded. "He's probably clueless about real China."

"What's the difference?"

"I'll tell you some other time."

"I'll make you a deal," Dennis said. "Take me and Georges to China to see some hydro sites and I'll pay my own way."

"What good is that going to do? I need investors, not lower expenses."

"Jack, he's all we've got. Come on."

Jack looked past Dennis and Mary Lou, past the wall covered with Morgan Joseph tombstones through the window to the façade of Saks on the other side of Fifth Avenue. In another month or two, the building would be covered with Christmas decorations and Jack would be walking by it, having failed again, looking at the display windows on the street level and reminding himself of the good days when he had steered his family through the holiday crowd and everything was right with the world.

"All right, but that's it. If he doesn't invest, and no one else surfaces by the time we get back, I'm pulling the plug."

Dr. Yu confirmed what Jack already knew—Georges's proposed mission was impossible. All the projects their team had lined up to acquire were in the mountains of Yunnan and Sichuan. Including airplane and driving time, it would take at least six days to visit a small group of sites.

Jack couldn't get Georges's foppish dress out of his mind. He was living in a dream world. And then it came to him. He *was*, but that was all right. They just had to play along, and tailor the China visit to Georges, not the other way around. They didn't have to show Georges the actual sites Middle Kingdom intended to buy; all they needed to do was show him hydro sites, and explain the projects he was looking at were similar to those the company would actually acquire. There had to be some sites near Beijing. They could just drive Georges to view them—in a Mercedes, of course. Then he could go back to his sheik in Bahrain and confirm he had seen the subject of Middle Kingdom's intentions with his own eyes. Mission accomplished.

"Dr. Yu, are there any hydroelectric projects near Beijing?" Jack asked.

"Yes, there are," Dr. Yu answered, "but none Middle Kingdom can buy."

"Whose are they?"

"They are large state-owned facilities, some of the most important hydroelectric projects built in the early days of the country's coming out," said Dr. Yu, not sure where Jack was going.

"Great. The bigger and fancier the better," Jack said, and explained his plan to Dr. Yu.

When he was finished, Dr. Yu agreed to arrange for them to visit several large, impressive hydro facilities within a few hours of Beijing, including one dedicated by Chairman Mao himself.

"Good. And lastly, we'll pack him off four hours south of Beijing to see one of Mr. Zhou's projects in Hebei, and explain it's a small one we're buying cheap," Jack said. "Then the story won't be a complete fairy tale."

㊌ ㊌ ㊌

Dennis, Georges, and Jack walked down the jetway to the Centennial 747 tethered to the terminal at JFK.

Dennis had insisted on Centennial, saying he required an international level of service. Settling into the business cabin, Dennis tested his seat—the ancient kind that only reclined a few degrees—punching the cushions, and raising and lowering the headrest. Then he made a big deal of chatting with the head flight attendant, Victoria, who looked as if she had logged as many miles as the plane. Real, English-speaking service, though. Jack always took the Chinese carriers—they were much cheaper, and who cared about the food?

Georges found his seat a few rows back, wrapped himself in a blanket and went to sleep.

As the plane leveled off after takeoff, the flight attendants lumbered down the aisles with their service carts, spreading white table cloths on passengers' tray tables and serving them drinks and small porcelain dishes of nuts. After serving Dennis and Jack, Victoria was two rows behind them when Dennis sampled some nuts.

"Victoria, Victoria," Dennis called, waving to her over the heads of a dozen passengers. "I've got a problem."

Parking her service cart at the other end of the aisle, Victoria appeared next to Dennis's seat. "Yes, Mr. Galileo?" she said, not amused.

"My nuts aren't hot, Victoria."

"I beg your pardon?"

"My nuts. They're not hot. The menu says 'warm nuts,' but they're cold," Dennis said, as Jack looked down at his lap and listened to the surrounding passengers' stifled laughter. "Maybe you could warm them in the oven."

"I'll see what I can do, Mr. Galileo," said Victoria, an expression of thinly veiled loathing cracking the makeup of her overpowdered face.

"I see what you mean about the premium service, Dennis," Jack said. "You better watch out; if you don't behave, my guess is she'll warm your other nuts in the oven, too."

Surviving the flight, they arrived in Beijing 15 hours later to find Dr. Yu, Kitty, and a group of Chinese hydroelectric experts retained by Dr. Yu waiting at the immigration entrance. Georges waddled behind Jack and Dennis, pushing a cart laden with three large trunks containing his wardrobe for the weeklong trip. As one of Dr. Yu's helpers grabbed Georges's cart, introductions were made and they got into a large, stretch Mercedes and headed for Beijing.

Stopping temporarily at the hotel to change before going to the initial project site, Jack and Dennis waited with the others in the cars outside the lobby for Georges. After Dennis checked on him several times, Georges finally appeared, decked out in German lederhosen and Austrian hiking boots. Kitty looked at Jack and raised her eyebrows as if he was responsible for his fellow Westerner's outlandish garb, while Georges plopped into the rear of the Mercedes and promptly went to sleep.

The first day went exactly as planned. The sites Dr. Yu had arranged to visit were only slightly less impressive than the Hoover Dam. Georges couldn't have been more pleased.

After visiting a pumped storage hydroelectric project dedicated by Chairman Mao, complete with a mile-long underground tunnel, a huge storage lake on top of a mountain overlooking Beijing, and a power-house clean enough to eat off the floors, Jack turned from his shotgun seat to look at his two guests in the rear of the Mercedes, Georges resplendent though rumpled in his walking clothes, and Dennis in a checked double-breasted jacket, gray flannels, and brown suede Guccis.

"What do you think so far, guys?" Jack asked.

"Fantastic," said Georges. "The sheik will be very pleased."

"Jack, how much would that one cost?" Dennis asked.

Jack looked at Dennis carefully. He's serious, Jack thought to himself. "A lot."

"Don't worry, Dennis," Georges said. "The sheik has enough."

"That's what I thought," Dennis answered, smiling.

Early the next morning, the group left to visit Mr. Zhou's small operating project in southwestern Hebei. After two hours of driving, Georges and Dennis started getting antsy. Jack had the driver pull over when he saw a decent roadside gas station. Dennis and Georges visited the men's room and returned to the car voicing typical Western complaints. Jack explained roadside rest stops in China had a few decades to go before they would compare with foreign equivalents. Dennis confided he had the runs.

After another hour, Dennis leaned up and whispered in Jack's ear that Georges was hungry. Jack reminded Dennis that the site was four hours from Beijing, they had been on the road three hours, and they needed to get to the site and see the project before they could stop for lunch or they would not make it back to Beijing by dinnertime.

Thirty minutes later, the paved highway ended in a gravel road slightly larger than a goat trail as it wandered up the mountain. Jack stopped looking over his shoulder at his passengers as they started turning green.

Finally, just as Dennis suggested they turn around and go back, their car veered off the main thoroughfare and headed down a precipitous, rutted driveway toward a concrete powerhouse astride a stream a quarter mile down the ravine.

As the Mercedes plummeted down the hill, Jack felt Dennis tugging at his shoulder and turned around as Dennis tried to whisper in his ear.

"Jack, there are broken windows in that building up ahead."

"I see them."

"I'm not sure it's wise to take Georges down there if the project is in such bad shape."

"It's just some broken windows, Dennis."

"I think it's a bad idea."

"Too late now."

The Mercedes approached the site, slowing down at the last moment and pulling up in a cloud of dust at the edge of the facility's parking lot. In front of them was the powerhouse, its whitewashed cinderblock façade stained with stripes of greenish brown mold. The Yi River, a dishwater-colored stream flowing out of the coal fields of Shanxi, splashed into the intake of the powerhouse to the right, and exited over a waterfall to their left as it continued west down to the Baoding plain.

At the bay doors of the powerhouse, a group of approximately 30 men blocked the way, milling around and staring at the Mercedes. The majority of the men were smoking. A few seemed to be joking with one another as they pointed toward the big black car, but the rest frowned and concentrated on the passengers. Most of the men wore canvas shirts tied at their waists; some were shoeless. Two men, apparently the boss and his deputy, clad in dusty wrinkled suit jackets, stood in front of the group. The head man had a broad, brown face, several gold teeth and, incongruously, badly scuffed dress shoes.

Off to the right and up a weed-covered bank was a three-story building with outside staircases leading to balconies ringed with iron railings. Three dozen peasant women and at least as many children lined the balconies, looking down on the car and its passengers.

"Welcome to the Zijinguan hydroelectric project, gentlemen," said Jack.

Dennis and Georges extracted themselves from the Mercedes and stood taking everything in, not moving from the car. "These guys don't look very happy," Dennis said after a pregnant silence.

"They're afraid they may lose their jobs," Jack said, shrugging his shoulders. "That's what happens when a private buyer acquires an SOE project."

Dr. Yu and Kitty explained to the men what was happening: they were there to show the *laowai* a typical small Chinese hydroelectric project. The locals relaxed. The *laowai* were not a threat; they were just visiting. The group of men went back to what they were doing before, and the women and children started to disappear into the doors of their apartments.

Dennis and Georges continued to stare at the crowd and the decrepit façade of the powerhouse behind them.

"This facility is somewhat different from what you saw yesterday," Jack offered.

"I'll say," Dennis said under his breath.

Georges stood blinking in the sun, swiveling his head from powerhouse in front of him to the dormitory on his right and stream off to his left. "Yes, Jack, this one is, how do I say it, more rustic, wouldn't you agree?"

"First impressions can be deceiving in this business," Jack said, trying to be matter of fact to set his two *laowai* guests at ease. "A good hydroelectric project can last a lifetime, and cosmetic problems can be easily altered. I brought you here to give you a sense of the value-added nature of Middle Kingdom's business plan. We don't want to pay top dollar for every asset we acquire; some, like this one, we may buy cheap and refurbish."

Georges seemed relieved. "You mean this one could someday look like the others?"

"Well, it's possible," Jack said, willing to go only so far.

Georges and Dennis kept standing in the same place next to their Mercedes, still too taken aback to move. Dennis's camera was nowhere to be seen. Bringing them to the site had been a calculated risk, and while he didn't think Zijinguan was going to be a factor in Georges's decision making, Jack could see now it would be better to leave Georges in his dream world.

"Just take a look around and let me know when you're ready," Jack said.

That snapped them out of it. Dennis and Georges brightened up, shuffled around the facility for five minutes, the last three for show, and declared themselves satisfied.

Jack and Kitty squired them back to where the car waited. As Georges retreated to the backseat of the Mercedes, Dennis took Jack to one side as they stood outside the car. "How do we get the driver to stay off his cell phone? It's driving us crazy."

Kitty stood there listening to them, a blank expression on her face, undoubtedly thinking they were a collection of *laowai* idiots.

"That's going to be difficult," Jack said to Dennis. "It's like a body part to those guys."

"Talk about Chinese water torture," Dennis continued. "Can't we at least get him to put it on vibrate?"

"I don't think they know that feature exists, but I'll ask Kitty to talk to him."

"Thanks. One last thing. Where's the bathroom?"

"It's over to the left," said Jack, "but I'd avoid it if possible."

"Not possible," Dennis said, a grim look on his face.

Jack told Kitty to ask the driver to turn off his cell phone for the ride back to Beijing. She wasn't happy about the request, but spoke to the driver; a sourer look crossed his face.

Waiting for Dennis, Jack wandered over to the intake facility where the Yi River entered the powerhouse, leaned over the concrete wall and looked down at the river. Practically opaque, its chalky water was saturated with coal mine tailings from upriver. A scum of foam covered the flat, pond-like area that ran the width of the river where it entered the powerhouse. A used condom floated by.

No fish down there.

Kitty walked up behind him. "Your friend Dennis is calling you."

"Where is he?"

"Back at the slit trenches."

Jack walked around to the downstream side of the powerhouse where a door cut through the wall and a path snaked down toward the river, and called down over the roar of the river. "Dennis? What is it?"

"There's no toilet paper here."

"There never is. You're supposed to bring your own."

"Thanks for telling me. Can you find me some?"

"Let me get the driver to bring some down. And Dennis—it's going to cost you."

The driver and Kitty had smiles on their faces the whole ride back to Beijing.

㊈ ㊈ ㊈

"He was just what I expected," Jack said.

Jack, Dennis, and Mary Lou were back in Morgan Joseph's offices after the China trip with Georges.

"So what's your prediction, Jack?" Mary Lou asked.

"No way."

"Dennis?" she asked her partner.

"Oh, I don't know. It's too early to tell."

"No chance," Jack repeated, looking at Mary Lou. "I'm calling Richard today and putting this misguided venture out of its misery."

"Don't do it yet; something could still turn up," Dennis pleaded.

"Impossible. All I'd be doing is postponing the inevitable, and spending more of my friends' money."

"You're probably right," Mary Lou said, "so I hate to ask you this, but Tim Bonny, one of our salesmen, spoke to an institution today who wanted to speak with you about the deal once you returned from China. Would you mind?"

"Why bother? These guys are all the same, Mary Lou."

"Tim says this one isn't."

"Where's his office? I hope at least you're going to say New York."

"54th and Park."

Jack sighed. "Sure, let's go over there. What's another hour or two?"

"We don't even have to go over there—he just wants a phone call," said Mary Lou.

"Mary Lou, a phone call?" Dennis exclaimed. "There's no way anything good is going to happen from a phone call."

"Sounds like my kind of guy," Jack said. "Let's just get it over with."

"I'll go get Tim," Mary Lou said.

㊌   ㊌   ㊌

Tim Bonny, one of the Morgan Joseph institutional salesmen, arrived in the conference room and briefed Jack on Chad Champion, who ran Victor Capital, a large hedge fund. Previously, Champion had managed the derivatives desk of Credit Suisse First Boston after leaving Cravath, where he had been an attorney.

"Sounds like a smart guy," Jack said, as much to be polite as anything else. Jack had never heard of Champion or Victor, but that didn't mean anything. He didn't do that much business with hedge funds.

With Jack, Dennis, and Mary Lou sitting around the speakerphone, Tim dialed up Chad, made the introductions, and turned the call over to Dennis.

At the beginning of every Middle Kingdom presentation, Dennis gave an old-fashioned investment banker's soliloquy describing Morgan Joseph's view of the investment opportunity and their long relationship with Jack; provided some information on Jack and on hydroelectric power in China; and finished up with a summary of the terms of the offering.

As Dennis was starting out, Chad Champion interrupted. "Sorry, Dennis. I've only got a few minutes. If it's all the same to you, I'd rather just hear from management."

Dennis looked over at Jack, raised his eyebrows, shrugged his shoulders, and said, "Sure. Jack, it's all yours."

"Thanks, Dennis," Jack said. "Thanks, Mr. Champion. Before I go ahead, would you mind telling me a little about Victor Capital?" It helped to know his audience before he said too much.

Chad spoke for a few minutes about his firm. They were just speaking over the telephone, but Jack could tell what Chad was made of. He didn't want to be sold; he couldn't be sold. He just wanted to know, in as few words as possible from someone who was supposedly an expert, why hydroelectric power in China was a good idea. And he would expect Jack to serve up the bad news, too. Unsolicited.

So Jack told him. The good news and the bad news. In five minutes. And then waited while Chad didn't say anything.

"Dennis, maybe you could review the terms of the deal," Chad said finally.

Dennis did so, describing the SPAC and its AIM listing.

When he was finished, there was silence again.

Chad said, "I like the business concept, but not the way the deal is structured. How much of the $200 million have you raised?'

"We've got circles for a fair amount," Dennis said.

Jack knew the question was for him, even though Dennis was correct to answer it because it was technically the investment banker's business. But he wasn't going to let Chad hear anything but unvarnished reality.

"Look, I don't blame Dennis for his optimism, but so far we haven't taken in a penny, and I don't think we will," Jack said.

"Not with that structure," Chad agreed. He was silent for a moment more. "$200 million's a lot of money. What's the minimum it would take to get your company under way?"

Jack could give Chad a low, easy number, but that wouldn't do either of them any good. "I don't think it would make any sense to launch this business with less than $50 million," he said, figuring the conversation was now over for sure. Fifty million from one guy? Impossible.

The phone went silent again.

"I'll put up $50 million then," Chad said, "but you've got to throw out the structure, and I've got to be in control of the cash until you find a project. How long do you think it will take you?"

"We can have two projects or more by New Year's."

"That fast?"

"Yes sir."

"Call me Chad. How does my offer sound to you?"

"Terrific."

"How soon before you can get back to China?"

"I'll leave today."

Chapter 38

Soldier of Fortune

Winter was a bad time to prospect for hydroelectric projects in China.

Travel would be treacherous on the back roads of the mountainous country where Jack was headed. In the PRC's northern highlands, the roads were nothing more than brown, deeply rutted ice floes. In the southwestern areas of the country, the late seasonal monsoons blowing north from the Indian Ocean flung rains over the land, swelling the rivers and turning the byways into bogs.

Jack didn't have much time. He had to find $50 million of hydroelectric projects by New Year's. If he couldn't find good ones and execute agreements to buy them, or if Chad didn't like the deals, Jack would be forced to give the money back, plus interest, and Middle Kingdom would be over.

Jack hired Pete and Whitey as the company's operations managers, and Ms. Cheng from Xushi Wire and Cable as the Chinaside controller. Dr. Yu took some additional space in his building for Middle Kingdom's temporary offices, organized a team of PRC hydroelectric engineers to help them find and evaluate suitable projects, and promoted Kitty to be the company's analyst. Lastly, the company hired a squad of English-speaking young Chinese women—Nu Yu, Leilei, Coco, and Xu Xu—to help translate, codify, and analyze information on its pipeline of potential projects.

With their fledgling organization funded and staffed, Jack prepared for six weeks in the mountains of China. He packed one bag containing underwear, socks, and several pairs of khaki pants and shirts. He needed to travel light, and China had plenty of laundries. He didn't plan to return until he had signed up $50 million of projects.

A stiff, biting wind was blowing when Jack, Whitey, and Pete landed in Beijing; the temperature at the airport was 20 degrees Fahrenheit. The most likely spots to find good hydroelectric sites in China were the Tibetan foothills of Sichuan and Yunnan, so after staying overnight in Beijing, and together with Kitty and two hydro-electric engineers, they left early the next morning for Chengdu, the capital of Sichuan.

A mixture of fog and smog hung low across Sichuan, hovering over the land like a gray-yellow film of mold. Knocking about in the drizzly, poor province during the first two weeks of the trip, they looked at two dozen projects. Visiting each project usually meant six hours driving one way to the site, two to three hours of inspection, and another half day returning to their original point of embarkation.

Jack bounced up and down in his seat, holding on to the grip above his head as miles and miles of inner Sichuan's clammy, gray-green acres slogged by. The main highways were modern, rivaling any in the West, but their cars only traveled on them for brief interludes. Most of the time, they climbed up secondary and tertiary roads and rocky, flinty byways, many nothing more than paths and animal trails, rutted and pocked with boulders and sinkholes. Travel speeds should have aver-aged five miles per hour, but their drivers pushed their machines faster, with no regard for the comfort of their human cargo.

They traveled in Prado Land Cruisers. Mud covered, with extra gasoline tanks lashed to their front and rear bumpers, the vehicles were plodding, stout beasts, and the margin of difference between being marooned in the wild or making it back to civilization.

The land was hilly, wet, and sober, its valleys and flatlands littered with a jumble of small farms, duck ponds, irrigation canals, and fields of rice, lettuces, *bok choi,* and taro. Curling through the farm valleys, the rivers were roiling, muddy streams, too dirty to permit any fish Jack cared about to live in them, and with the steamy heat of the Sichuan bowl hanging over the land, too warm as well.

Small villages appeared intermittently along the roadways, looming up around a corner or down a hill, their housing stock consisting of ramshackle farm buildings and mud brick homes, every other dwelling bristling with rebar, the metal webbing together with piles of unused bricks betraying expansion plans. At night, many of the houses appeared completely empty. When Jack asked, someone told him people lived there, but refused to use electricity because of the cost. When he did see light, it was bluish white, the inhabitants content to use cheap fluorescent bulbs.

They stayed in small towns. Since they were important travelers—acquisition of any potential project would be the largest transaction in the county—and because of Dr. Yu's contacts, they were provided accommodations at county guest houses owned by the local governments. Dr. Yu's agents would call ahead, and upon their arrival, Jack and the others would be greeted by a contingent of local party leaders, mayors, utility managers, deputies, and minions.

At the end of a long day, Jack was grateful to collapse into a bed with sheets, the best that could be said about most of the guest houses. No matter the town, the same, fetid aroma hung over the public areas and the rooms of the government-owned hostelries, a combination of improper plumbing ventilation, cigarette smoke, garbage incineration, and farm mud.

In many cases, shortly after his arrival, the telephone in Jack's room would begin to ring. At first, he had not understood the callers, who were always female: "Messaage? Messaage?"

Only when the pattern continued at several guest house destinations did he figure it out. Messaage didn't mean "message"; it meant *massage*. Upon his arrival, the person at the reception desk would notify someone on call a *laowai* had checked in, and a girl proposing service would telephone his room a short time later. Condoms were thoughtfully available in the bathrooms.

After a night's sleep, if he awoke too groggy to remember where he was, the breakfast menu served as notification that he was in the western reaches of the PRC. In China's seaboard provinces, especially in the big cities, foreign influence and wealth meant breakfast was a recognizable meal. The better hotels provided full English breakfasts, complete with sausage, bacon, ham, eggs, and omelets and fresh fruit, as well as Chinese dishes. But beyond Fake China, Western repasts quickly disappeared. The further west Jack traveled, the more vegetables populated the breakfast menu. Instead of meat, eggs, dairy products, and breads, a morning meal consisted of cooked cabbage and multiple varieties of *congee,* China's staple rice porridge: plain *congee, congee* with chives, *congee* with dried vegetables, pickled vegetables, or garlic.

Dinner was worse. Jack experienced whole dinners where every dish was derivative: instead of pork, they made do with pig's knuckles; instead of chicken, chicken feet. The fish weren't even fish. Any time he had ever visited an ocean beach stateside, Jack had been told that the ancient horseshoe crabs piling up by the thousands were inedible and poisonous. But someone forgot to tell them in Sichuan—a school of them floated in the murky tank of a guest house restaurant lobby one evening, waiting for a hungry customer.

Mr. Wu was a perfect match for Sichuan's dreary ambiance.

The owner of six run-of-the-river hydroelectric projects on Sichuan's Dong He, a river in north-central Sichuan, Mr. Wu was a Chinese version of the Cat in the Hat, the famous character from Dr. Seuss's menagerie. Rawboned, long, and gaunt, with stringy oily hair combed over the crown of his skull and unkempt sideburns crawling down his temples, Mr. Wu spoke through movements of his thin, scraggly eyebrows, which constantly arched, then flattened, over devious, squinty eyes.

Wearing the same clothes each day—a greasy flannel shirt, pants with legs six inches too short and a pair of clip-on suspenders that hiked his trousers up around his crotch—Mr. Wu was permanently in a foul humor. His dark countenance the product of swarthy coloring and a constant state of penury, the man was desperate for cash. He wanted to sell his six Dong He projects—one operational, one under construction, and four greenfield—immediately, for $25 million.

In a single transaction, Jack could get not only an operating, cash-flowing project, but a whole river basin development with growth and expansion potential. But Wu's price was too high by at least $5 million.

After negotiating for two days, Wu refused to concede a single point. Jack began to think he didn't know how to. When Mr. Wu telephoned Kitty and proposed yet another "final" bargaining session, Jack told Kitty to send the Chinese engineers to negotiate with Wu. Pounding him into submission, they could bring Jack in to sign the papers when and if they reached a deal.

After beginning the meeting, Jack went into another room and studied maps of Sichuan and Yunnan for several hours. Waiting for what seemed like an eternity, he finally returned to the meeting chamber filled with equal amounts of Chinese humanity and cigarette smoke and asked Kitty for a progress report. She looked at him and slowly shook her head back and forth.

"What does that mean? He's not going to sell?"

"So far, the men are just talking," she said.

"Just talking? About what?"

"They're just talking." Kitty seemed dubious herself.

"So there's no progress at all?"

"I don't think so."

"Why not?"

"I'm not sure."

When Kitty said she didn't know, it usually meant she didn't want to say something that might offend him.

"Kitty, come on."

Her look at him said, "I shouldn't have to tell you this." "There's nothing these men can say. Mr. Wu knows it's your money, and the men just work for you. In the future, you shouldn't be involved in the negotiations at all; just appear at the end to sign the papers."

Jack sighed. Live and learn. But if Mr. Wu thought he could just outlast the *laowai* and get the American price, he was wrong. "All right, so the stupid *laowai* thought he could bargain for himself. Now I know better. So how do we change things?"

"We must leave and give Mr. Wu the idea we're not coming back. Then when he calls us, our men can bargain him down, but in a way that will allow him to save face."

"What if he doesn't call back?"

"Oh, he will."

"What makes you so sure?" Jack wanted the projects. They were the best ones he had seen in Sichuan.

Incredulity crept across Kitty's face. She looked at Jack as if to say, "Don't you get it yet?"

Jack just stared at her, waiting for the answer.

"You're the *laowai*," she said. "Everyone knows you're the ones with the money."

Yunnan and Sichuan bordered each other, but their weather was completely different. Southerly breezes from the Indian Ocean swept Yunnan's sky clean, clearing off precipitation and letting the land breathe. The plane they took south was only an hour out of Chengdu when the clouds opened up and the snow-covered peaks marking northern Yunnan appeared off to the right below.

They flew to Zhongdian, a city in the far northwest corner of Yunnan. On the ancient trade route coming down out of the Tibetan highlands to the west, Zhongdian had recently changed its name to Shangri-La to capture for itself the world's continued fascination with the famous Conrad Hilton novel. At more than 11,000 feet in altitude, the region was above the tree line and much colder than where they had just come from.

As they arrived in the early evening, a stiff wind whipped tiny balls of ice across the dusty brown steppes, buffeting their plane on its approach and chasing the herds of yaks on the surrounding foothills. The Hengduan Shan mountains loomed up to the west, their jagged crags cutting off the remaining light of the day. Patches of deep green fir trees hunkered in steep crevices between the pointed tops of the ridges, while a purple sky settled on the Yunnan hills to the east.

Coming out of the airport, their Prado Land Cruiser rocketed northeast along a silvery road stretched across a barren plain. On the horizon, the last of the sun's rays lighted the way to Shangri-La, high on a hill several miles away. The China of his dreams, Jack thought as he scanned the landscape, the remote magical place he had conjured up in his mind when Yu Cheng first introduced the idea of traveling to the country years earlier.

The farmland along the road was well kept, some parts fenced while other areas remained open wetlands. Marsh grass was cultivated for feed and thatching for fencing and housing. The farmsteads, made of stucco, rock, and timber topped with stone and slate roofs, appeared solid, with multiple floors, housing livestock on the ground floor and people above. Tibetan designs indicating family names and warnings to evil spirits decorated their ochre walls.

They entered Zhongdian through a gate at its southwestern corner. A melting pot of Tibetans, Naxi, and other minorities, Zhongdian teemed with people. The city was clean and neat, its streets laid with rock and cobblestones, and lined with sidewalks and mud brick walls topped with decorative frets. Within minutes, their Prado turned off the narrow route from the airport onto a main boulevard lined with restaurants, hotels, and shops.

Off the main square of the town, an ancient gate of wooden timbers led the way to a tiny inn where they would spend the night. As Jack and his group registered for the night, an old man played an *erhu* on a bench in the cobblestone courtyard. The floors of the inn were crudely cut and polished dark woods. Walls of rock boulders and a roof frame of log timbers covered by reed thatching kept out the cold.

The next morning, Jack opened his window, looked out at a cobalt sky, and felt the sharp, clean breeze flapping the red-and-gold-colored flag of China flying above the inn. After a light breakfast of hot yak milk, toast with fruit jam, and tea, they climbed into the Prado and headed west to China's Three Rivers area, approximately 50 miles distant.

The region should have been called the Four Rivers area, Jack concluded as he studied his map. Within 100 miles of each other were four—not three—of the world's major rivers, including the Yangtze, China's mightiest stream; the Lancang, better known as the Mekong, the principal river of Laos, Cambodia, and Vietnam; the Nujiang, known downstream as the Salween, which drained much of Thailand; and just along the border with Burma, the main branch of the Irrawaddy, the mother river of that country.

Leaving the city, the valley containing the highway narrowed as they drove northwest. Along the two-lane road heating up in the morning sun, the car slowed in the higher elevations, climbing toward the crags of the mountains. Snow appeared along the sides of the road.

At the peak of the pass, leaving the Zhongdian plain behind, they turned west on a smaller, single-lane byway. Splitting a notch in the towering mountain ridge, the Prado plummeted down a narrow, winding trail through a mountain gorge. Through the windshield Jack could see a ridge line 20 miles ahead, and a great airy canyon in between containing the Yangtze.

A mountain freshet crashed over boulders in the narrow chasm paralleling the roadway. The stream, clear and glacial, its water high from snowmelt, crossed back and forth in culverts under the road, dropping hundreds of feet every mile of roadway. Jack was sure there were fish in there—maybe even trout.

The Prado careened downward, as if the driver was racing the water. "Kitty, please tell the driver I don't care when I get home," Jack said. When Kitty spoke to the driver, he smiled apologetically over his shoulder, slowed down momentarily, but soon resumed his breakneck pace. "Once more with feeling," Jack said. "And as long as you're at it, can you ask him if there are any fish in this stream?"

When she spoke to him, the man nodded his head vigorously, as if his affirmation would absolve him of his speeding transgression. "*Zunyu,*" he said. "Zunyu."

"*Zunyu*?" Jack said.

"I think it's what you call trout," Kitty said, appearing as pleased as the driver at the look of satisfaction on Jack's face.

Halfway down the mountain, they came around a curve and Jack saw the Yangtze curling off to the north 3,000 feet below. A thin ribbon of silver, the river was anything but the gnarly, angry trench he had expected, more resembling a trout stream in the American West.

He looked forward to a closer view of the waterway—when and if he could get down to it. He had never been on a more dangerous road. The absence of guard rails looking over 3,000-foot heights was only one problem; at the next corner the driver slammed on the brakes, stopping their Prado feet from the brink, as a goatherd and a flock of goats totally blocked their way.

Ten harrowing minutes later, they skidded to a stop at the intersection of the river road and turned south, paralleling the azure Yangtze, morning mist rising from its surface as it flowed downstream.

"Remember doing this for Catapult Energy, Jackie?" Pete said as the three *laowai* all kept their eyes on the river running in front of them.

"Sure seems like a long time ago," Jack said, Whitey nodding his head up and down where he sat in the back seat.

Along the riverbed, the Yangtze scoured rocks and cliffs as it moved swiftly through narrow switchback canyons, and then slowed, spread out and grew clear and shallow where valley floors opened up. Farming villages filled the lowlands, the houses up on hills, safely removed from spring torrents, rice paddies above them, stacked up the sides of the foothills all the way to the bases of the snowy mountains.

Twenty miles south, they pulled into the parking lot of Mai Di He, a newly constructed hydroelectric project on the left bank of the Yangtze. It was a high-head facility. After tapping into the Mai Di He spring creek miles up behind the cliffs above the Yangtze, the project channeled the creek water into a network of tunnels and canals that ran through the mountain. When the water arrived at a point still hundreds of feet up the hill, it flowed through a gate into two huge penstocks and down to the powerhouse alongside the Yangtze, where after turning the turbines it discharged into the mother river.

Their Chinese advisors introduced Jack and the others to Madame Zhang, the owner of Mai Di He. Jack shook her hand; it was cold. Kitty translated, explaining Madame Zhang had studied hydroelectric engineering at university. The project had originally been developed by her father, but he had died recently, leaving her to complete it with little money.

Madame Zhang seemed distracted and distant as they inspected the site together. Her face, dark and slightly pockmarked, was expressionless. Pete kept trying to get Kitty to help him talk to her. Pete always did that.

"Do me a favor, Kitty," Jack said. "Could you ask Madame Zhang if there are any *zunyu* in the river?"

Kitty asked.

"*Meiyou,*" said Madame Zhang in a clipped tone, shaking her head back and forth once, letting Jack know she was all business, and had no time for small talk.

"Even where the streams come off the mountain?" Jack persisted, but Madame Zhang ignored him; she was speaking to Kitty about something else.

"She wants to talk about money," Kitty said to Jack when Madame Zhang had finished.

"Have one of the engineers speak to her. We're not making the same mistake we made with Mr. Wu," Jack said, standing with Whitey and Pete and looking down off the bank of the Yangtze to see if he could see any dark shapes moving in the flat spots of the big river.

Kitty and the Chinese engineers walked over to the powerhouse with Madame Zhang and had a 30-minute discussion. When they were finished, Kitty walked back over to where Jack, Pete, and Whitey stood.

"She says Mai De He is a 25-megawatt facility, and cost $27 million to build."

"All right, that's how much Pete guessed. So how much does she want for the project?"

"$38 million," Kitty told Jack.

"We're out of here," Jack scoffed, loud enough so that Madame Zhang could hear him and get the message. Jack walked over and stuck his hand out to the surprised seller, thanking her for the visit, asked Kitty, appearing shocked at the abrupt end of the discussion, to get the Chinese engineers ready to go, and headed for his Prado.

Pete was the last one into the car when they pulled away from the site a few minutes later. "Jack, we didn't even get started with that woman," Pete said, looking through the rear window back toward the Mai Di He powerhouse receding in the distance.

"Who, the Ice Queen?" Jack said.

"What do you mean, Ice Queen? She wanted to sell to us. We didn't give her a chance."

"What is an Ice Queen?" Kitty asked.

"A woman incapable of love," Jack said to Kitty, as Pete turned to look at him.

"We gave her a chance," Jack said, turning from his place in the shotgun seat and looking back at Pete, "and she responded with a ridiculous number. This company won't make any sense to investors unless we can get the China price for these projects," he said, turning back toward the front of the car and looking straight ahead down the Yangtze gorge. "We've got to be disciplined buyers. And don't worry—Kitty thinks Madame Zhang will call us back next week, right, Kitty?"

In the back seat between Pete and Whitey, Kitty took his meaning and nodded her head.

"So we'll stay out of it and let the Chinese engineers negotiate her down," Jack said, "and maybe we'll get somewhere—who knows?"

"I really liked that project," Pete said.

"I did too, Pete," Jack said, "but what are we supposed to do? We can't pay $38 million for a 25-megawatt project, that's for sure."

"The next time, let me negotiate with Madame Zhang," Pete said. "She liked me—we're both hydroelectric engineers."

Jack turned and looked over his shoulder at Pete, and then glanced at Kitty who looked like she might actually smile. "That's your conclusion about every woman we meet—Chinese, *laowai*—it doesn't matter."

"For reasons that are obvious, at least to them."

Jack looked over at Kitty again, who was looking out the window so no one could see her grin.

"Why don't any of these women you're talking about give me that feeling?" Jack asked.

"Because I'm the one they're after."

They drove a few miles farther south. In front of them on the road, another goatherd tended a flock of goats.

"So Pete, when we hear back from her—assuming we do— what's Madame Zhang's affection for you going to do for us?" Jack asked.

"What do you mean?"

"Let me rephrase the question. What do you think Mai Di He's really worth?"

"$32 million."

"Come on."

"It's a beautiful project."

"It's not *that* beautiful," Jack said. "But I'll tell you what. You get Madame Zhang down to $30 million, which means she gets a 10 percent builder's profit even though as it stands she hasn't got the money to finish the thing, and we'll buy it. And you'll not only get a nice bonus," Jack continued, looking sideways at Kitty, "but a rich new wife."

Pete didn't laugh; it looked to Jack like he was actually thinking about it.

Chapter 39

Hydro King

"Look at that guy crossing the Yangtze on a wire," Jack said to Whitey.

Small and wiry, the Chinese man lay prone in a small wheeled rack suspended from a zip line. From a take-off point high up on a mountain, the thick wire traversed the river to the opposite bank. As they watched him, the man coasted down the line across the Yangtze, ferrying a payload of cut timber three times his size.

They spent several days visiting hydroelectric projects in the upper Yangtze valleys. All of them were high-head projects. The powerhouses were usually located in villages clinging to the banks of the Yangtze where small valleys carved by feeder streams met the mighty river. At the villages, they could cross the river by the few bridges spanning the upper Yangtze: rickety wooden suspension affairs for foot traffic only, a few rusty iron fabrications suitable for automobiles, and zip lines.

Driving downstream, they took the river road as it paralleled the Yangtze south. The road and the river wound through dark, cave-like gorges carved into mighty rock cliffs, and then straightened and slowed in sunny flatlands. From time to time they drove up out of the river bottom to look at a project or find a village with an inn to spend the night. Immediately above the Yangtze, the road wound through wet and fertile fields planted with rice, celery, watercress, and taro. In the higher elevations, the arable land grew drier and scarce, every flat piece of ground claimed by a network of paddies and irrigation canals.

They were in the land of the Naxi, the largest of the minority groups of northwestern Yunnan. As the visitors blew by the fields, women in brightly colored blouses and straw hats, their bright eyes set above high cheekbones, lifted their heads from where they stood to steal a glance at the strangers. As the Prado came through the villages, dogs trotted along, oblivious to the traffic, while women and children covered the road with grain and beans to be crushed by the tires.

Crossing the Yangtze for the last time, they drove west, up and over the next ridge of the Hengduan Shan to Weixi, where they spent the night in a state guest house and the next morning at first light dropped into the valley of the Lancang.

The weather was big and brisk. High white clouds skidded from mountain to mountain across the Lancang valley. The sun was bright, but it was very cold. Driving down the east side of the river, the road took them through the riverside village of Weideng. It was market day, and Weideng was jammed with peasants.

Hungry, Jack's group parked their cars outside the village, got out, and walked down the main street, looking for a place to eat. In the central part of the village, they found an open air restaurant along the sunny side of the thoroughfare. A Naxi waitress organized chairs around charcoal-fired braziers, and they sat down, stretching their feet close to the fires. When Jack was seated, the waitress gathered a blanket, wrapped it around her *laowai* customer's shoulders, and made him some tea.

Jack poured some cognac from his flask into the tea. The tea tasted warm and smooth with the cognac. Jack felt very good, the charcoal wood smoke from the braziers smelling like the campgrounds of his youth. Wrapped in the blanket, the bright sun beating down on his face, he took off his boots and warmed his feet on the edge of the brazier. Flakes of ash rose in the wind and floated into his hair.

After Kitty ordered chicken stew for all of them, another Naxi woman emerged from the kitchen in the rear of the restaurant clutching a live chicken in each hand. Walking next door to a meat market, she handed the thrashing, squawking birds to a man in a long white apron covered with blood. The man took the birds, raised a meat axe over his head and decapitated both chickens on his butcher's block in one stroke. He quartered the birds and dropped the parts into a sack. The cook took the sack without a word and trotted back past the restaurant patrons to her kitchen.

In 10 minutes, the cook and two helpers emerged from the kitchen with three iron pots of chicken stew and placed them on the braziers. Shortly, the stew began to boil and bubble as chicken heads, necks, wings, and legs floated in a broth together with Tibetan potatoes, carrots, celery, and spices.

Jack was starving. The waitress passed out brown earthen bowls of rice. Taking pieces of chicken and vegetables out of the iron pot with his chopsticks, he put them on top of his rice, ladled broth into his bowl, added some spices and condiments from the table, mixed it all together and ate.

The waitress brought out earthen pitchers of local red wine and glass jars used for canning jam and jellies, and served them wine. The wine was fruity, warm, and musty. It tasted good with the stew. They finished three pitchers of wine, and ordered three more.

As they ate, people shopping passed by in the streets, staring at the *laowai*. Across the thoroughfare, open stalls offered household goods— kitchenware, utensils, fabric, dried foodstuffs, meats, fruits, vegetables, sweets, electronics—even cell phones. Men and women and children moved in tight crowds up and down the street, sampling wares and foods, talking and laughing. Cars and trucks, moving less than a mile an hour, tried to make their way through the throng, their drivers too intimidated by the crowds to honk.

From where Jack sat, he could see a rusty suspension bridge spanning the big, green river. Across on the other side, hills sloped steeply up to the sky. A web of trails and paths coming down the mountain spewed forth a parade of Naxi families, the men in dark clothing, the women and children bedecked in their market day best of red, teal, and yellow sateen.

Jack and the others finished their meal. He handed his empty bowl to the waitress, lit a cigar, and watched the crowd up and down the market street. The wine had made him tired.

He yawned and looked around for Kitty. "Would it be all right if I lie down and take a nap?"

Kitty looked at him. "Where? There is no place here."

"Right here will do," Jack said. Wrapping himself in his coat and his blanket, he put his seat cushion on the floor alongside the brazier where the hot coals had heated the stone floor and lay down, putting his head on the cushion.

Opening his eyes once, he caught the Chinese engineers laughing as they pointed at the *laowai* lying on the floor. He woke an hour later to look at Kitty staring at him. She paid the bill, and they left the restaurant and walked down the main street to the southern edge of the village.

On a promontory looking out over the river, an ancient Catholic church of stucco and rock sat under a copse of trees. A small stream separated the roadway from the parish grounds. A stone bridge arched over the water as it trickled down a mossy, rocky chasm to rice patties along the Lancang below.

Jack told Kitty the church was a good omen. He asked the others to wait, and went inside. The body of the church and the nave were dark, and no one stirred. A small alms box on the wall had a little sign in English that suggested donations. Jack pushed paper money into the slot, knelt down in a pew, spent a few minutes in silence, and left.

"What happens in a church?" Kitty asked Jack when he came out.

"You pray," he said to her.

"What is praying?"

"You try to speak to God."

"I see."

Jack wondered if she did.

"Will you take me one day?"

"Sure."

"Is it lucky?"

"No, it's better than that; it's good."

The Prado pushed south down the Lancang along the border between Yunnan and Tibet, and then turned west over the ridge toward the tributaries of the Irrawaddy, into the Dehong prefecture. The country-side changed. The looming mountains and deep valleys of northern Yunnan gave way to semitropical hills ringed with tea gardens and lush lowlands crisscrossed with sluggish rivers, irrigation canals, fish and duck ponds, and miles of terraced rice patties.

The hydroelectric projects changed, too. From the majestic high-head projects prevalent in northern Yunnan, the southern Yunnan projects devolved back to run-of-the-river facilities similar to the ones they had seen in Sichuan.

In the villages along their route, hibiscus and bougainvillea crawled up the sides of buildings and fence posts. Along the side of the road, men herded water buffaloes, their deep brown eyes wide in a state of alert as the traffic rushed by. Women waded in the patties and bogs, planting rice and vegetables, their babies snug on their backs.

Rolling south on the highway, the traffic began to change from farm vehicles, pickups, and tractor trailers to motorbikes and bicycles. The evening cooled the sweet air of the Dehong plain as they entered the outskirts of Mangshi, a city in the southwestern corner of Yunnan. Located astride the Burma Road, the stretch of highway built by U.S. troops to connect India to Kunming in the War of Japanese Aggression, Mangshi was the capital of Dehong and an agricultural center whose economy was bolstered by smuggling—the Burmese border and the northern gateway to the Golden Triangle was only 20 miles away.

Around the corner, a group of helmeted Chinese border patrol officers and a temporary crossing barrier blocked their way. The driver stopped the car and the head officer peered in. He spotted Jack and spoke in Chinese to him. When Jack didn't respond, the officer continued speaking in Chinese to the driver.

Kitty turned to Jack in the back seat. "He wants to examine your passport," Kitty said.

"Me? What for? We're not at the border."

"Please Jack, your passport." Kitty took Jack's passport from him and gave it to the officer. The man examined it, told the driver to pull over beyond the barrier, and went inside his hut. They sat in the car and waited.

"Because we're near the Burmese border, they're looking for smugglers, and you fit the description," Kitty said.

"Why me? They're letting everyone else through."

"You're *laowai,*" Kitty explained in a low tone. "That's what every-one else who is *laowai* is doing here—smuggling."

"What kind of smuggling?"

"Precious stones and drugs."

"Do you need to give him some cash?" Jack asked.

"I don't think so," Kitty said, peering out her window trying to see what the officer was doing in the hut. "He seems like a senior officer; he's not local. Cash might be taken as an insult."

A few minutes later, with no explanation, the man returned Jack's passport and waved them on their way.

Coming into the central, older part of the city as the evening fell, their Prado passed down well-lighted streets lined with coconut palms, mango trees, and shops. Two-wheeled machines filled the streets and sidewalks, surrounding the Prado like a swarm of insects. The bikes often conveyed two or more passengers, or even a whole family: the father driving; the mother riding behind him; and the baby sitting on the gas tank between the father's arms.

Their muddy, tired Prado creaked into the courtyard of the Mangshi Hotel, whose spotlighted tower stood alone and beacon-like over Mangshi's western hills. Gardens of posies, pansies, and chrysanthemums lined the entryway, and 30-foot columns marked the hotel's entrance.

Kitty checked them in. Too tired for dinner, Jack went up to his room. Opening the mini bar, he poured a small bottle of cognac into a glass, lit a cigar, and sat down in an armchair looking southwest toward the ridge marking Burma and the sun dropping behind the mountains along the border.

Still magenta toward Burma, the sky color above him was a dark indigo. Off to the northeast, the evening star winked. Chants lowed from the temples dotting Mangshi's hillsides.

Jack drank the last of his cognac and took a pull on his cigar. He had been on the road for 40 days.

Roosters crowing in their coops on the rooftops below the hotel woke Jack the next morning. Although dawn was just breaking, China's single time zone was misleading—it was already seven o'clock. After checking in on his sons at home, Jack and his group packed their breakfast and began the two-hour trip west to inspect the Binlangjiang hydroelectric project, a facility on the Binlangjiang tributary of the Irrawaddy.

They were accompanied by the project owner, Mr. Dong, together with his friend, Ms. Li. According to Mr. Dong, Ms. Li was a television star where they both lived in Hangzhou. Dolled up in an expensive white pant suit and flat, delicate shoes, she was not dressed for a visit to a hydroelectric site. Covered with mud within 10 minutes of their arrival at the project, she acted like it was all a lark, jumping across little streams of mud and climbing on rocks as they walked from the vehicles down the riverbank to the site. Jack presumed her behavior was an attempt to convince Mr. Dong that she was still a girl at heart.

Jack addressed her as Madame Li, but Kitty corrected him, saying she and Mr. Dong were not married.

"Well what are they, then?" Jack asked.

Kitty shrugged her shoulders.

"She's his mistress, right?"

Kitty shrugged her shoulders again.

Jack looked over at Kitty. "So Kitty, are you always so discreet, or at some point do you break down and gossip with your friends?"

Kitty looked back at Jack. "Of course I gossip."

"You don't with me."

"You're my boss," she said, looking at Jack as if to say, "What a silly question."

"What's the verdict?" Pete asked Jack when their group was gathered back in the bar of the Mangshi Hotel that evening.

Marking the end of their trip, Jack had asked Pete, Whitey, and the Chinese engineers to prepare a spreadsheet ranking all the projects they had seen.

"Looks like Binlangjiang is the clear winner," Jack said, scanning the data on the spreadsheet.

"Based on EBITDA, I would agree," Whitey said.

"What is EBITDA?" Kitty asked, wedging herself between Jack and Whitey to have a look at the spreadsheet.

"This line here," Jack said, directing Kitty's attention to a line of numbers halfway down the page. "Earnings before interest, taxes, depreciation, and amortization."

"Why use EBITDA?"

Kitty had been remote when Jack had first met her, but she was coming around. He liked her attitude about learning. "It's the project's free cash flow," he explained. "Around the world, people usually use multiples of EBITDA to determine the value of hydroelectric projects."

"How?"

"If you wanted to buy a project in the United States," Jack said, "you would first determine its EBITDA, and then multiply by approximately 12. So if a project in California has EBITDA of $1 million, you would have to spend approximately $12 million to buy it."

"Or said another way," Whitey added, "If you divide the project's purchase price of $12 million by its free cash flow of $1 million, you receive a simple 8 percent return on your investment."

"8 percent doesn't sound like much," Kitty sniffed.

"You're right, it's not a lot, but it's enough for hydroelectric projects because they have few other risks," Jack said as Kitty nodded back at him. "Remember, risk equals reward."

"And we can do much better here in China," Pete chimed in, looking across the room at Mr. Dong and his mistress having tea and waiting for the Middle Kingdom decision. "I've looked at everything—current operations, tariff contract, expected maintenance, condition of the equipment—and I'm confident Binlangjiang will generate those numbers."

"Anything else we need to worry about?" Jack asked his group.

"Mr. Dong upgraded the rotors when he bought the project from the local government in 1992," Pete said, "so my only concern would be the external electric works: substation, transformer, those kinds of things. Small stuff. No big deal."

"All right." Jack turned to Kitty. "So how much does Dong want for his project?"

Kitty whispered into Jack's ear, "170 million RMB."

"In dollars, please."

"About $24 million."

"Why are you whispering?"

"I don't want the men to hear me," Kitty said.

"What difference would that make?" Jack asked, looking at the Chinese engineers sitting next to them, blankly looking back at Jack, unaware of the content of the English language conversation.

"You never want the men here to know things involving money," Kitty said, unsmiling as she looked up at Jack from where she sat.

"All right, then," Jack said, the grin wiped off his face. He continued to study the spreadsheet and made some additional calculations. "Go over there and offer him 140 million RMB. And tell him it's subject to due diligence and board approval, but the offer's only good today. I don't want him leaving here and shopping the deal all over China."

With Kitty shuttling back and forth between the parties, they stayed in the bar all evening and continued to negotiate. "I think this is his last proposal," Kitty said, coming back from Mr. Dong with his most recent terms. "The movie star looks very tired."

"What is it?" Pete asked.

"One hundred forty-five million," said Kitty. She was tired too. She brushed her hair out of her eyes, and stared at Jack.

He was punching numbers on his calculator. Five point three times EBITDA, or about a 19 percent return—more than double the world average. He turned and looked up at Kitty. "Done."

"What?"

"That means yes," Jack said. "Tell Dong we've got a deal, and let's go to bed."

"Can we really trust this guy, Jack? Maybe we're just Dong's stalking horse," Whitey said.

"What does he mean?" Kitty asked Jack.

"Whitey's afraid Mr. Dong's going to shop our deal," Jack explained.

"What does this mean—'shop our deal?'" Kitty asked.

"Whitey's saying now that Mr. Dong has our best offer, he's going to use that as a floor and try to sell to someone else."

"He's not going to do that," Kitty said.

"Why do you say that?"

"He wants to sell to you. You're the Hydro King," Kitty said, breaking into a smile.

She could be his analyst any time she wanted.

About to become the owner of one of Dehong's largest power stations, Jack asked Mr. Dong and Kitty to organize a breakfast for the leaders of Mangshi the following morning.

In the hotel coffee shop, sitting across from the mayor, the general manager of the utility grid, and the local branch manager of the Agricultural Bank, Jack felt relieved as he watched the mayor, a rough-hewn steamfitter type sporting tattoos on both forearms, nurse a mixture of tea and soymilk. Early morning *baiju* would not be required. Chocolate brown eyes betraying his minority heritage, the mayor laughed with his audience as he reeled off local jokes with Kitty and the Chinese engineers. Like all Dehong politicians, he was a Dai, the dominant ethnic minority group in southwestern Yunnan.

Making short work of his free meal, the mayor loaded Jack and Kitty in his Jeep Wagoneer and led their entourage to the airport. A mile from the hotel, the Burma Road's macadam surface crumbled away, revealing ancient cobblestones, and the careful plantings of the city's signature mango trees ended, replaced by sporadic stands of gargantuan banyans, each emblazoned with a sign in Chinese. When Jack asked Kitty to ask the mayor about the signs, he explained the Dai people considered Banyan trees as family members—the signs stated each tree's name and age.

They passed over a bridge crossing the Mangshi River, running high and fast. It looked like there could be fish in the stream—it was clear enough—but they wouldn't be *zunyu*. Too warm.

Along the road, clusters of Dai women walked in bright colored blouses and long chemises with fabric wrapped around their faces to protect against the dust, carrying bamboo poles across their shoulders with containers at either end. More women labored in the fields, some carrying babies in backpacks, wearing pants rolled to the knees as they waded in the rice paddies. As the Wagoneer and the other vehicles blustered by, Jack turned around and looked back through the rear window at the striking Dai women, their brown, friendly eyes peeking out through the gap between their dusters and hats, their skin healthy from the sun.

Passing through a village of mud brick homes with thatched roofs, Jack saw a group of little Chinese men squatted in front of the local store playing cards. "Kitty," he said, "could you please ask the mayor who these men are, and why they're here playing games when the women are out working in the fields?"

Kitty spoke to the mayor, who then rambled on in Chinese for 10 minutes.

When he stopped, Kitty said, "The mayor says the situation is very bad. The cultural history of the Dai people requires the women to perform all domestic tasks, including managing the household, the family, and the farm."

"What's that leave the men to do?"

Kitty laughed. "They're hunters."

"Going after China's abundant wildlife."

"That's the problem," Kitty said.

"So they play cards."

"Right. And the mayor says the Dai women are wising up."

"What do you mean?"

"A lot of them are leaving and going to the eastern provinces to work in the karaoke bars."

Kitty and Jack laughed, and so did the mayor as he directed a grin full of rust-colored teeth at Jack. After a moment, he lost his grin and his face took on a serious expression as he spoke.

Kitty said, "The mayor says some Dai elders have gone to Lijiang to consult a Dongba about the problem."

"What's a Dongba?"

"A sort of combination wise man and priest, the mayor says."

"Tell the mayor I've got similar problems where women are concerned; maybe I'll go speak to the Dongba myself."

Kitty laughed, the mayor started to laugh too, and even the driver joined in.

禾　禾　禾

Kitty's predictions had been correct; Mr. Wu came around, and so did the Ice Queen. With agreements in place to acquire Dong He, Mai Di He, and Binlangjiang, Jack returned to New York in time for Christmas, and arranged to meet with Chad Champion during the week between Christmas and New Year's.

"No seasonal holiday for the Davis family?" Chad asked as he welcomed Jack to his office the day before the end of 1993.

"No," Jack said, inclined to tell the truth—because all his money was in the deal, he couldn't afford a vacation—but thinking better of it. Christ, he would be 38 in a few months, and he was still practically broke. Why tell anyone that?

Chad's office was deserted; the two of them the only ones there. Jack sat opposite Chad's desk and watched his eyes review the Middle Kingdom materials, skimming the PowerPoint and then surveying the numbers in the spreadsheet. Neither of them said anything. Chad pulled out his calculator, punched in a few entries, looked back at the spreadsheet and then looked up at Jack.

"You think there's more out there like these?" Chad asked.

"Hundreds."

"And no other experienced, well-funded competitors."

"None that I know of."

"Because?"

"This job isn't easy," Jack laughed, shifting his position in the chair. "Six hours one way to a site on a bumpy dirt road dissuades most *laowai*, at least the ones with Gucci shoes."

"But not you."

"Not me."

"I guess it starts with being willing to travel 15 hours one way to get to China, let alone spending hours on its back roads," Chad offered.

"There's that, and more, I think."

"Like what?"

"Small things. It helps to speak slowly and look them in the eye when you talk."

"That works where I'm from in North Dakota, too," Chad said.

"And ideally, it's good to be large physically."

"Why is that?"

"Helps hold your liquor. They admire people who can outdrink them."

Chad smiled and shook his head. "As long as you don't have to do it every day, I guess. Anything else?"

"The most important thing is to accept them. Not to like them—that's fawning, that's different—but to accept them, not talk down to them. Meet them and their culture halfway. So I don't insist on doing things the American way. The Chinese way is fine, as long as it's legal."

"Sounds good to me."

"All right. So what would you like to cover next?"

"I think we're done."

"We've only discussed one project. There are two more."

"I've heard enough. Get the papers ready and we'll close. I have only one condition."

"What's that?"

"If you find any other good businesses in China, you'll bring them to me first."

"No problem, Mr. Champion. You can count on it."

"It's Chad; I'm younger than you are."

"Don't remind me."

Chapter 40

Timing Is Everything

"When things are going well, why do anything differently?" Chad had counseled Jack after closing the first acquisitions. Jack didn't need to hear anything else, and returned to China to find more projects to buy.

The best ones they came across were in Zhejiang province. Luosha Group, a big Hangzhou real estate developer, owned four excellent projects in the southern hills. Luosha had been caught in a capital crunch and was a motivated seller—but it was going to take a lot of capital to pull off the deal.

On a spring evening in Hangzhou, surrounded by several members of Middle Kingdom's acquisition team studying Luosha due diligence reports, Jack, Dr. Yu, and Lee camped out next to Luosha's offices in the lobby lounge of the Hangzhou Hyatt Regency. In the West Lake district, the Hyatt sat on the edge of the water, surrounded by hills dotted with the lights of luxury villas. Boats plied the lake, their engines and passengers' voices echoing in the distance.

In the north end of the hotel, there was a large, museum-like art gallery. The three men took a break from the grind and strolled through it, Jack looking at the paintings and trying not to think about Lianhua, Dr. Yu eying the antique porcelains.

"I don't know, Jack," Lee said. "Do you really think we can figure out a way to buy these projects? Luosha's not going to accept less than $200 million, I don't care how desperate they are."

"We're better off trying to raise a lot of money than a little," Jack said, pausing to look at a marble sculpture. "And if we can pull this deal off, after one more private financing we'll probably be in a position to do an IPO next year."

"What did Chad say he was good for?" Lee asked.

"Another $50 million," Jack said.

"So we need $150 million more," Dr. Yu said. "Where can we get that kind of money?"

"Hong Kong," Jack said, taking a last look at the art in the gallery; no sign of Lianhua's work. "Chad gave me the name of the head of Merritt Partners' Asian private equity group there. If Chad's in, there's a good chance they'll get involved too. You guys stay here and finish the due diligence, and don't let these guys drain any of the goddamned water out of the reservoirs before we close. I'll see if I can find some money, and be back in three days."

㊌ ㊌ ㊌

Jack called Chad's contact at Merritt Partners, booked a nine o'clock appointment for the following morning, and made reservations at the Mandarin Oriental.

Flying out of Hangzhou on the early flight, Jack arrived in Hong Kong on time and went straight to Merritt Partners' offices in the Citi Centre on Garden Road, feeling conspicuous in his khakis and work boots. A receptionist escorted him down a long hallway running along the western face of the building to a small conference room, asked what type of tea he preferred, indicated his hosts would be available shortly, and closed the door.

The conference room was quiet. Jack peered west through the teak venetian blinds over Victoria Harbor at the hydrofoils tracing white foam routes to Macao and Zhuhai and the new buildings sprouting up like stalks of bamboo on the Kowloon waterfront.

Each time he revisited Hong Kong after a lengthy hiatus, the stark changes to the cityscape reminded him life was rushing by. When he first gazed on it eight years earlier, Victoria Harbor had been wide and unspoiled, a real harbor, containing hundreds of sampans bobbing up and down, Star Ferries zipping everywhere. There were practically no sampans down there, and the new IFC Tower was going up where the Star Ferry terminal was once located.

He had been unspoiled then, too, dressed in a suit and tie, representing Catapult Energy, youth and innocence. Even two years earlier, looking out over the harbor from Chairman Roo's boardroom, he had wanted to trust people, Kalin in particular, until her confession had forged him a cynic in a furnace of treachery.

He checked his watch.

The door opened and a young Chinese man walked in. Tall for a Chinese and slim, the man's face was clear and open, and framed by a large thatch of black hair and bushy eyebrows set over lively, sparkling black eyes. Carrying a folder of notes, he was dressed in casual clothes, wore no tie, and smiled as he introduced himself as Sam Lu. Sam had an Australian accent.

Jack took a few minutes to tell Sam why he was there. Sam understood, having spoken to Chad, who had contacted him the day before. Sam spent some preliminary time explaining that he and David Ng, who would be joining them shortly, invested Merritt Partners' own money in principal investments across Asia. They had a mandate to find good renewable investments in the region.

Just as Jack was beginning to feel he had come to the right place, Sam took the air out of the room. "Now that we've gotten the introductions out of the way, I suppose I must say I doubt we'll be able to help you," he said to Jack.

Jack didn't know why, but he felt like laughing. "Of course," he said, shrugging his shoulders, looking up at the ceiling and feigning resignation. "Silly me. Why would I think life would ever get easy?"

"No, no, it's not like that," Sam said sheepishly. "We spoke to Chad and reviewed the Middle Kingdom material he forwarded, and we liked what we saw. We'd love to do something with Chad, and with you," he continued. "But the Chinese hydro players we've seen are small; we wonder if any group can gain critical mass fast enough for our exit guidelines. And while we appreciate you dropping everything to come down here," Sam said with an embarrassed smile, "your timing may be a day off. We've just given a term sheet to another group similar to yours. We can only fund one of you."

Jack was in the midst of nodding his head when another man entered the room. He was slightly older, and unlike Sam was dressed in a suit and tie. While Asian, the man did not look Chinese, and felt American. He also was tall, and his head was shaved and shiny.

"Jack, this is David Ng, my colleague and the head of Merritt Partners' principal investment desk for Asia," Sam said as Jack stood and shook David's hand. "David, I was just explaining we are interested in what he and Chad are doing, but may not be able to invest because of the other deal we're pursuing."

David continued Sam's admonishment. "Yes, anything Chad invests in interests us, but we're pretty far along on this other deal."

David was probably just there out of respect for Chad.

"So it looks that good," Jack said.

"What?"

"The other deal."

David looked at him, and without answering turned his gaze to Sam.

"Well, no," said Sam. "Actually, the other deal has some warts," he said, looking at Jack, his eyes checking with David from time to time.

It was the only opening Jack would need. Acting as if he was one of them, Jack said, "So what's wrong with it?"

"The business is all right. Their projects are similar to yours," Sam said. "It's the sponsors. They have shortcomings."

"That happens here, doesn't it?"

Sam glanced over at David, didn't see any stop signs, and continued. "Right. They've never run an institutionally funded company before. Never dealt with institutional investors like us, accountants, lawyers, disclosure; you know the drill. It's all new to them. I don't know if they'll get there."

David added, "We need an exit in one to three years, and even if these guys can learn the ropes, we don't know if they can grow big enough fast enough." He sighed, and looked out the window.

"To jumpstart an IPO," Jack finished the thought.

"Right," they both said to him.

"How big is the company?" Jack asked.

"The other one?" David said, arching his eyebrows. When Jack nodded, David answered his question. "Fifty million in assets. It's small, but so are you all." He shrugged.

"Well, gentlemen, your problems are over," Jack said, looking at them and trying not to smile, instead maintaining a guileless expression on his face.

"Why do you say that?" Sam asked. David just watched him and waited.

"How would you like to do a $200 million deal with a team that's already done two IPOs and is battle tested?"

"Who wouldn't," said David, pulling his chair up to the table and looking directly at Jack. "We know all about your track record, but take us through the $200 million part."

Jack pulled out some photographs of the four Zhejiang projects and a spreadsheet projecting the future financial performance of the facilities. The pictures showed projects that were large, well maintained, and prepossessing. In one of the project photographs, Zhejiang's Oh River, full and green, pounded down the spillways, providing a powerful backdrop that said "Money." David and Sam looked at the photographs, glanced at the model, which indicated Middle Kingdom would earn $15 million annually the following year, and turned and looked at each other.

"How'd you queue these all up at once?" Sam asked. "It's unusual to find multiple sellers of good hydro projects in one place at one time."

"It's the Luosha Group," Jack said. "They own them all and they're desperate for cash."

"Right," David said. "We know Luosha. We heard they were in trouble." He had heard enough. "I take it this situation is ready to go? If we wanted to proceed, I'd want to begin due diligence tomorrow, and fund in 90 days."

"We're ready when you are," Jack said.

"Where are you staying in Hong Kong?" David asked Jack.

"The Mandarin Oriental."

"Sam, can your people run a quick model on these Zhejiang projects in the next hour?" David asked Sam, still looking at Jack.

"I expect they can," Sam said.

Standing up from the table, David put his hand out to Jack. "We've got a committee meeting with New York in two hours. I'm not saying we're going to commit to your deal, you understand," he said, "but if Sam can get comfortable with your numbers, we'd be foolish to do anything else."

"You're right," Jack said. "Thank you, David; you won't regret this."

"I'm not saying yes," David warned. "Only the committee can do that. We'll talk with them, and if things go well, we'll call your room after noon." He shook Jack's hand and turned to leave.

"See you this afternoon," Jack said to David, nodding at Sam as he left.

Jack walked the two blocks back to the hotel, taking the stairway two steps at a time down along the stream that ran off the Battery Path. Escaping the heat of the late morning as he crossed under the covered plaza formed by the lobby floor of the Hong Kong and Shanghai Bank, he entered the lobby of the Mandarin Oriental, stopped at the concierge, collecting his key and arranging for the operator to forward any calls, passed the newsstand where he purchased the international papers, and walked up one flight of stairs to the Café Causette on the mezzanine level.

The restaurant was deserted. Breakfast was over for all but the stragglers or retirees, and lunch wouldn't get busy for an hour. Telling the maitre d' he was expecting a telephone call, Jack took a corner table in the back, and splurged, ordering a cappuccino, two eggs over easy, bacon, whole wheat toast, and a large orange juice. He opened the *International Herald Tribune,* read it cover to cover, switched to *USA Today,* and then the *Wall Street Journal*'s Asian edition. Concentrating on the papers, awaiting his fate, he thought about her again: Lianhua, Lianhua—he was in Hong Kong; where was she? He tried to remember her face, couldn't, and went back to the papers. Finished with the foreign papers, he was just opening *China Daily* when the waitress brought him the telephone.

"Jack, it's David and Sam on the speaker phone. We've got some news—it could be good, depending on your answers."

"Go ahead."

"The committee voted to proceed with your deal. We would want to be the lead investor for this round; we're good for $75 million of the $200 million."

"Sounds good so far. Thank you."

"But Mr. Thune, our chairman and CEO, has three specific conditions."

"Okay." His pulse picked up a beat.

"I doubt you'll have much difficulty with the first one," David said. "Since Merritt Partners will be leading this round, we want the right to do Middle Kingdom's IPO. We're thinking about a $200 million offering next year."

"That's a tough one." He could hear David and Sam laughing. "Next?"

David cleared his throat. "This item is nonnegotiable. Our investment must be used to purchase convertible preferred senior to the company's common stock. If there's no IPO, or if the IPO is delayed or its valuation is less than one billion ..."

"I know all about preferred stock."

"So that's okay with you."

"Not really."

"What's that supposed to mean?"

"I'm just saying, I don't like it."

"So what are we supposed to do about that?"

"Nothing, I guess. You said I haven't got a choice, right? So what's the last condition?"

David sighed. "Hopefully, this is as easy as the first one, but you tell us," he said. "Mr. Thune is a member of the board of directors of the World Wildlife Federation, a position he takes very seriously."

"All right."

"So he needs specific assurances your hydroelectric projects do not endanger any animal species."

No one spoke.

"Jack?"

"Yes."

"Are you there?"

"You're joking, right?"

"Do I sound like I'm joking?"

"I wondered if you were Chinese, David, but now I know you're not, or you would know the saying 'The Chinese eat everything with four legs except tables, and everything with wings except airplanes.'"

"What's the point?"

"These hydroelectric projects are in China, for God's sake. There haven't been animals running loose in Zhejiang province since before the Boxer Rebellion."

"So there's no endangered animal or bird species affected by your projects?"

"None edible, that's for sure."

"Well, if you post a gamekeeper up at your reservoirs and keep us out of the papers, we may have a deal."

They had a good laugh, he hung up, gave the waitress the telephone, and requested his check.

When she returned with the bill, for some reason Jack actually read it—he never did that. Breakfast had cost $40. Jesus Christ. Back to work; at least all he had to do to earn his next dollar was preserve the lives of a few parrots and ground squirrels.

Chapter 41

Who Knows Where
the Time Goes

The Beijing streets were deserted as Tommy, the Middle Kingdom driver Jack had hired, guided the Audi 800 down Gongren-tiyuchang Beilu past the Worker's Stadium. It was seven o'clock Saturday morning. A couple left over from the night before stood in the parking lot next to the Regal karaoke club arguing, their car running, its driver sitting in the front seat smoking a cigarette, paying no attention to the commotion behind him. The man was grabbing the woman's arm, trying to persuade her to get in the car. She was pulling the other way, struggling to free herself and flag a taxi at the same time.

Crossing over Sanlitun, another weekend's worth of bottles piled into huge clear plastic bags on the street corner, the driver put the city in the rearview mirror, pushing down the rain-slicked streets, taking Jack, Lee, Kitty, and Nu Yu to the airport.

With the Merritt Partners deal closed and the $200 million in the bank, Middle Kingdom was an enterprise under full sail. If Jack could find a half-dozen good projects to double the company's size, an IPO was in reach. He staked out a handful of promising locations around the PRC and made plans to stay in China through the summer.

It had been simple to determine where his group should travel next—Fujian, the part of China's hydroelectric geography he knew best. They would fly to Fuzhou and take the roads up into northern Fujian to look at the Banzhou project, a hydroelectric project on the Minjiang that was for sale. If they had time, Jack hoped to drive over to visit the Xiayang project, the one he had built years earlier with Wuhan Turbine.

Fifteen minutes later, the Audi swept up the long ramp approaching the departure terminal. Tommy dropped them off, Jack and Lee gathered pushcarts for their luggage, while Nu Yu and Kitty collected their passports to present to the ticket agent. Ticketed and baggage checked, they headed for the gate, joining dozens of others funneling into a line to run the procedural gauntlet of air travel in the PRC: showing their passport and boarding pass at the first security checkpoint; going through the medical detector; passing through the baggage scanning device; and then showing their passport and boarding pass again when they boarded the plane. Why the government required passengers to show passports and go through the rest of the international security rigamarole on a domestic flight remained a mystery to Jack.

The line at security was huge.

"We're going to be lucky to make our flight," Jack said to Lee.

"I think we'll be okay," Lee said. "It doesn't look so bad."

Except Lee was always late for everything. They had missed several planes relying on his timing. If it was inevitable that part of life be complicated, Jack wanted it to be over something important, like a death in the family—not missing a plane. Some challenges were unavoidable, but missing planes wasn't one of them.

"Look at that—typical."

"What?" Lee asked.

Jack gestured over toward the logjam in the line to Lee. "The reason the line's jammed up is they only have four of those plastic trays to pass things through the radar scanning machine. So we're all standing in line waiting because they spent a billion on this airport terminal, but to keep costs down, they only bought four plastic trays."

They were the last passengers to board the big Airbus. Jack and Nu Yu sat together in two seats on the right and Lee and Kitty sat across the aisle from them in the middle. It was the first time he had traveled with Nu Yu. He didn't know her very well.

A half hour after takeoff, the flight attendants wheeled their breakfast carts up the aisle. Nu Yu listened to the menu announcement in Chinese. "They have beef with noodles or chicken with rice," she said to Jack.

"You go ahead; I'm not really that hungry."

She looked at him. "Maybe you'll get hungry later."

"No, I don't think so."

"I'm ordering the beef with noodles for both of us."

"All right."

The flight attendant set down the standard PRC airline meals in pink cardboard boxes: crudités, rolls and cake muffins, and hot food in aluminum foil trays. Nu Yu tore into her meal and finished it in no time.

She looked over at Jack.

"Here, take mine. I really don't want it," he said as he passed his beef noodles to her, and pulled his book out of his backpack.

Nu Yu smiled and didn't say anything as she opened the aluminum container of hot food and began eating again.

Once finished, she cleared the remains of breakfast off her tray. "I'm trying to learn about valuations," she said, taking out her notebook and shifting to face him. "You told us the other day that we should value a project we own on a pre-money basis, but on a post-money basis if we are seeking outside investors. I don't understand what this pre-money and post-money means."

Nu Yu was a little self-assured, but Jack was still impressed. She could have been content to be a corporate secretary and translator, the job he and Dr. Yu had hired her to do, but she was trying to learn. He put aside his book. "If it's our company, we must decide how much it's worth before we raise money—that's a pre-money valuation. An investor wants to know how valuable something will be after the investment—that's post-money."

"Okay, I understand," Nu Yu said. "But why doesn't the investor want to know the pre-money value, too?"

"They probably would; that's not a hard and fast rule," Jack said.

"Hard and fast?"

"A figure of speech."

"I like that one. It sounds like a Kung Fu action movie."

An hour later, the teaching lesson over, Jack looked over at Nu Yu studying the fashion advertisements in the airline's in-flight magazine. *It sounds like a Kung Fu action movie.* The only other time Jack had spoken to Nu Yu, when they had been sitting together at lunch with the others and it had somehow come up that earlier in his life he had been an art student, she had told him she had grown up wanting to be a kung fu action fighter. Thinking she was joking, he had started to laugh, then clammed up when he realized she was serious. Later, she had told him she sometimes wrote stories like the ones in Chinese action movies. Deriding movies like *Crouching Tiger, Hidden Dragon,* she told him they were made for Western audiences. He asked her what that meant, but she changed the subject.

He looked forward to showing her the Xiayang project, letting her see what he had achieved earlier in his life, then caught himself—who was he kidding? She wouldn't have the slightest interest in a hydro-electric project. He looked over at her again as she kept flipping through the pages of her magazine, acting like she didn't know he was staring at her. He was probably close to her father's age; she had been a schoolgirl when he developed Xiayang. He wondered what she had looked like then, wondered when she had become beautiful, and if she knew she was beautiful now.

Maybe she didn't think she was—part of her seemed self-assured, but she could be insecure, too. She was certainly self critical, especially about things he had never even thought about, like facial structure. She had spoken to him once in an offhanded way about people's appearances, evidencing a sharp awareness of facial structure, especially Asians', ticking off the differences between Chinese, Koreans, and Indonesians.

He looked at the right side of her face. He wondered if she was aware the left side of her face was more striking than the right. At least Jack thought so. Or perhaps she was overly conscious of the place below her right eye where a dark vein came close to the surface of her skin. Jack could see the dark color of the vein. When she laughed, the skin over the vein wrinkled. In his mind, it made her more interesting and less plastic, like what the gap between Lauren Hutton's teeth did for Lauren.

China was doing this to him, he thought to himself. Years earlier, he wouldn't have harbored any thoughts about Nu Yu, or even Lin. Lianhua? Definitely; but only her. Physically, none of them were his type. Blond hair and voluptuous curves didn't seem as important anymore. Jesus, what was happening to him?

Westerners would probably think Nu Yu was self-centered, he thought. He assumed she didn't think of herself that way, and would be dismayed to learn others might. She tried to be good; he could see that. But she was floating against one of China's dominant cultural tides, single child syndrome so ingrained people weren't even aware of the drawbacks of the phenomenon. He remembered conversations in America when eyebrows arched as mothers gossiped about the few single children in their universe, the catty consensus being that it led to selfish offspring oblivious to the feelings of others.

Jack wondered if Nu Yu had ever been in love with anyone; particularly someone older. Maybe she was capable of it, but probably hadn't experienced it. Things between them would never go any further, that was for sure. Even though he was her boss and she didn't know him well at all, she thought nothing of correcting what she saw as his Western foibles, telling him not to be too sarcastic or temperamental. Don't be too Western, she seemed to be saying; to her credit, it appeared she thought she was doing him a favor. He looked down at the hair on his forearm; she probably detested it. Probably thought he smelled, too.

Why on earth would a Beijing girl ever love a *laowai* man? Other than money, it was hard to find a reason.

The Airbus glided in over the foothills of northeastern Fujian and touched down at the Fuzhou airport. Nu Yu had organized a Prado Land Cruiser to drive them north. Lee rode shotgun, Kitty sat in back with Nu Yu, who slid into the middle of the back seat, telling Jack to sit behind the shotgun seat, where there was more room. As the car pulled out of the terminal and headed north, none of them said anything for a long time, just looking out the window and watching the countryside roll by.

Jack turned and caught Nu Yu looking at him. She averted her eyes, turned, and looked over his shoulder back out the window.

"There's the Minjiang," Jack said 30 minutes later, as they crossed over a ridge and dropped into the wide mouth of the Minjiang valley. The scene of his greatest business failure looked green and dewy. He wouldn't talk in the car about what had happened there years earlier. It would make him even older, and no one would care about it anyway.

"It's beautiful. It looks wide and clean," Nu Yu said.

Well, she liked the river; that was a plus. "Wait till we get upstream. It's even nicer. Too warm for trout, but very nice."

Nu Yu ignored his comment about the trout. Maybe she didn't know what to say when her boss started talking about fish, or maybe she just didn't know what a trout was. The Prado cruised up the gleaming new four-lane highway that ran alongside the river. The driver told Jack they would be at Banzhou in two hours. Five years earlier, the trip had taken a day.

Arriving at the Banzhou site in the early afternoon, they were escorted into the project office to meet Mr. Jin, the owner. After introductions, tea and fruit, Mr. Jin ambushed them. Although he had previously agreed with Lee to sell the project to Middle Kingdom for $63 million, Jack's target price range of $1.4 million per megawatt, Mr. Jin had changed his mind. He would only part with Banzhou for $90 million, a 40 percent increase.

Lee shook his head back and forth disgustedly as he listened to Mr. Jin's remarks.

When Mr. Jin had finished and Nu Yu had translated, Jack said to Lee, "What's the deal? I thought this guy was firm at $63 million."

"He was, until you showed up," Lee said, laughing but rueful.

"Sorry."

Jack and Lee laughed some more, and Mr. Jin, thinking he had them on the ropes, started laughing too.

Lee and Kitty had a side conversation with Mr. Jin, and then Jack brought them back to the topic at hand. "Nu Yu, please tell Mr. Jin we have already executed a memorandum of understanding with him at $63 million. We expect him to honor it. We are prepared to close in two weeks at which time we will give him a check. This is a good deal for him. We know he will very happy."

Nu Yu translated, Mr. Jin responded, and she turned back to Jack. "He says he doesn't have to sell to us. There is another big foreign buyer that spent $200 million last month in Zhejiang province to buy the Luosha projects. If we don't meet his offer, he'll sell to them."

Jack and Lee looked at each other and the two of them laughed again. Mr. Jin joined in once more, exposing several missing front teeth.

Jack turned to his side and spoke to Lee. Nu Yu would be polite, and Jack didn't want to be polite with Mr. Jin any more. "Tell him, Lee."

In Chinese, Lee set the record straight for Mr. Jin, who maintained his expression with some effort. Lee was the best Chinese guy Jack knew when it came to being confrontational and tough. Not theatrical, he was just matter of fact, but possessed the ability to handle conflict, something most Chinese found difficult. Lee finished and looked over at Jack and the others and nodded, starting to get up from the table.

Jack stood up and turned to Nu Yu. "Please tell Mr. Jin we're going upriver and we won't be coming back," he said, extending his hand to Mr. Jin, who also stood up with a surprised look on his face as Nu Yu, red-faced at the Westerner's abrupt behavior, informed Mr. Jin they were leaving. As the group filed out into the parking lot, he turned to Lee and said, "Let's go see Xiayang."

Five minutes after their Prado had pulled out of the Banzhou project parking lot, Lee's cell phone rang. It was Mr. Jin—he would take their deal, after all.

They pulled into Xiayang about four o'clock. Above the opposite bank of the river, the great green mountain lay sleeping, the sun starting to slide down its back shoulder for the evening. Jack looked out over the bund at the rapids downstream from the project. It was the dry season; the water ran clear and hard, like the good days he remembered. The fishermen were still there, on the banks of the stream and below the dam in the long narrow boats.

Upstream of the village, the Xiayang hydroelectric project, the 40-megawatt project Jack had built with Wuhan Turbine, sat low and squat in the middle of the Minjiang, churning out kilowatt hours, oblivious of what it symbolized to the man who made it possible standing on the bank.

He looked at Nu Yu. She wouldn't want to hear anything about that. He thought about when he had taken the silvery herring out of the rapids, and the big carp that had snapped his rod; she wouldn't want to hear anything about them, either. He had brought his rod case. But he could just imagine the consternation on Nu Yu's face if he told her he was going to throw a line into the Minjiang. Forget it.

As they pulled up to the project gate, Jack pointed to the golden Chinese letters on the powerhouse and asked Nu Yu, "What does that say?"

"Xiayang Hydroelectric Project."

"It should say New Land Power Corporation's Xiayang Hydroelectric Project."

"Well, your project is beautiful. It's the nicest one I've seen."

She didn't have to say that. "Thanks; that's very nice of you."

"No, I mean it. I can't believe you came here and built this so long ago."

"It wasn't *that* long ago."

She actually laughed. "I'm sorry; it's a long time ago to me. You must have been the only foreigner doing this in China then."

"Yeah." He stood gazing across the river, listening to it run, and thinking about everything that had happened. "You know, Nu Yu, if I could wish for something, I wouldn't want the project back. I'd take the years instead."

"Why? You should have no regrets."

"I don't, but I'd still want the years."

"Why?"

"Everyone your age in this country thinks I'm halfway to my grave."

She blushed, exhaled slowly, and looked away, clamming up until after they left.

The next day, they planned to depart Nanping at noon to catch a three o'clock plane from Fuzhou to Beijing. With the morning free, Jack and the others decided to climb one of the mountains across the Minjiang. They met in the lobby of the hotel fronting the southern side of the river and headed along the riverbank toward a footbridge a quarter of a mile upstream. Hundreds of people gathered in groups on the comfortable promenade bordering the river, some doing tai chi, others practicing martial arts, walking or sitting on benches.

They mounted the stairs of the footbridge and began crossing the Minjiang. They came down on the other side of the river to an impromptu market at the base of the mountain they planned to climb. "Four sticky rice," Lee ordered in Chinese to the peasant vendor. "And four soy milks and some vegetable dumplings."

Lee took the food and started handing it out. Nu Yu and Kitty, who had just eaten breakfast at the hotel 30 minutes earlier, wolfed theirs down. Jack's food was delicious, the way he always found peasant food in China. Even things that sounded bad to him, like soy milk, tasted surprisingly good.

Starting up the mountain, Jack walked ahead of the others, arriving at the top earlier and seating himself on a rock to take in the view. "You shouldn't sit down after strenuous exercise," Nu Yu said to him, panting as she struggled up the last steps. Jack looked to see if she was joking—he hadn't even broken a sweat—but she was serious. She had no sense he was in excellent shape, let alone an athlete good enough to audition for professional football scouts. To her, he was probably just like her father. Just bigger, hairier, and a *laowai*.

Chapter 42

You Learn Something New Every Day

When the car picked him up at the hotel on the way to the airport to return to New York, Jack was surprised to find Nu Yu riding shotgun; Tommy, his driver, usually drove Jack to the airport alone. Nu Yu said hello, but otherwise didn't speak. Sitting behind her as the car sped down the freeway to the airport, Jack reminded himself he had no idea what she thought of him. In the few times they had talked, Nu Yu's primary mission with Jack seemed to be cultural reform.

But maybe it was simpler than that—maybe she was just letting him know he wasn't Chinese, that not behaving the way Chinese men did was problematic. Being polite, opening doors, and saying "Ladies first," just confused things—most Chinese women were accustomed to following behind the men. And why crack jokes if they weren't funny?

Arriving at the airport, Tommy took the departure ramp, dropped them off at the entrance with Jack's luggage, and went to park the car. Nu Yu walked just ahead of him toward the baggage carts, and then turned to face him. "Jack, there's something I must ask you." She stood there looking at him uncomfortably, as if she had just gotten into an accident and was surveying the damage. "Can we be good friends?"

For a moment he just concentrated on the expression plastered on her face. Trying to take something away from her question, her eyes wouldn't let him. She glanced over toward the baggage carts, and then back at him.

He didn't know what to say. Had he been too obvious, too forward? Maybe his bad jokes had somehow given her the sense he was being too familiar with her.

She exhaled, turned and walked over to fetch a cart as Jack numbly followed behind her. Not allowing Jack to do any work, she took his bags, put them on the cart and pushed it up to the counter, handed Jack's passport to the ticket agent and filled out his departure card. The ticket agent checked Jack's bag and handed Nu Yu his boarding pass, luggage claim check, and a pass for the lounge.

They walked silently together toward the departure counter where customs personnel checked passports for the last time, the two of them wordlessly watching the maelstrom of travelers abandoning their baggage carts and kissing their loved ones goodbye.

Jack took his backpack off the cart and Nu Yu pushed the cart off to a corner, turned, and came back to Jack with a look of resolve on her face. Tommy walked up, saw something was up between them, pulled out his cell phone, and gave them their privacy.

They stood there awkwardly, the crowd swirling around them.

"I guess I said something wrong," Nu Yu said.

"No, no. It's all right. I thought maybe I did. I just don't know what your question means."

"You mean to be friends?"

"Yes. Look, I'm happy to be your friend. That's not it. I'm not sure why you're asking me. Did I do something wrong?"

She just looked at him with a puzzled expression on her face.

"What I mean is … oh boy, how do I ask this? Are you telling me you want to be something more?"

Her face flushed, and she appeared even more confused.

"Okay, okay, good, forget I said that," he said that, a stupid grin on his face.

"You're my boss. I need your permission."

"My permission? To be friends? In China, do people do that?"

"I don't want you to think I don't know my place. But I like to be able to talk to you. I can learn things from you. If that's all right with you."

"All right, now I understand. Of course we can be friends."

She smiled at him, a look of relief on her face.

"I just don't know, though, to be honest."

"Don't know what?" Nu Yu asked.

"How to do it. I don't think I've ever been good friends with a girl before."

Nu Yu examined him, trying to pull his meaning out of his eyes. "In China, women have men friends."

"Friends like me?"

She hesitated. "Well, no, not just like you."

"Look, you're from China; I'm from somewhere else. I'll have to work at it."

"You shouldn't have to work at it. It should just happen."

"I'm sure you're right."

"You must go now," Nu Yu said. "I'll see you when you return next month."

"Sure. See you."

She turned and started to walk away, then stopped, and came back. Standing in front of him, not looking into his eyes but over his shoulder, she held his shoulders, leaned up, and kissed him on the cheek.

"That's what friends do in the West, right?"

"Yes," he said, grinning at her. "At least, I do."

"All right, then," she said, mimicking his speech. She smiled, turned away, and disappeared into the crowd.

Jack remained where he stood, looking after her. He turned and looked over at Tommy; Tommy looked back at him. Without saying a word, they both shrugged their shoulders, smiled sheepishly at each other, shook hands, and Tommy ran to catch up with Nu Yu as Jack pushed into the line funneling through the customs counter out to the foreign world.

The scrum of Chinese in front of him jabbered at the blue uniformed custom agents attempting to review the clutch of passports thrust at them.

Holding his passport in his hand, Jack walked through the counter past the agents. They declined to stop him, and kept harassing the Chinese.

Chapter 43

The Place to Be

"**A**ttention passengers. We are experiencing some turbulence. Please return to your seats."

Turbulence. Couldn't the airlines have picked another word? Bumps? Anything but a long word with an *r*. The flight attendants tried hard, but few got it right. It didn't seem fair.

Dropping down out of the sky on his return trip to Beijing, Jack tried to remember a flight in China when he hadn't experienced turbulence, and couldn't. Neither could he recall the last time he had been on a plane there with an empty seat in economy, or one with anyone other than *laowai* traveling in first class.

Landing in Beijing and threading his way through the crowd past baggage claim, Jack was looking for Tommy when he spied Kitty and Coco. Standing behind the railing outside the baggage carousels, they were playing and laughing with each other, like two young Siamese cats. The girls in the Beijing office were all close friends; Jack often saw them leaving the building at lunch holding hands, their way of soaking up enough affection from a nearby source to make it through the workday.

He pushed through the crowd to them. "Are you guys here for me?" Jack asked.

"No, we just thought we'd hang around at the airport," Coco said, standing looking at him in her counterfeit UGG boots, a sarcastic grin on her face.

"Well, thanks. You could have just sent Tommy, you know."

"He's off today, so it's our job," Coco said.

"Well, they could have gotten someone else. You didn't have to, Coco; thank you. You too, Kitty," he said, instantly regretting his words as the smiles left their faces. Thanking them was too serious. He needed to lighten them up; his jokes wouldn't work, either. "Look, it's still early. Why don't we stop and have a drink at the Pavilion."

The girls looked at each other. "Okay," they said in unison.

Pushing through the airport's scrum of drop-offs and arrivals, they piled into Coco's Jeep Wagoneer, curled out of the parking garage through the tollbooths, and entered the flow of traffic on the highway heading downtown. A light rain was falling from the summer sky, but traffic was moving. Coco hit the gas and accelerated, gunning the Jeep down the left lane as if she was on an American interstate.

"You drive like a man," Jack said, sitting in the shotgun seat beside her.

"Hey, watch it," Coco responded, her forehead furrowing as she faked a frown while the corners of her mouth curled into a smile, her eyes never straying from the traffic in front of her.

"You know what I mean."

Coco swooped the Jeep around a laggard in the left lane going 30 miles an hour. "Sunday driver," she said, shrugging her shoulders.

"How long have you had your license?" Jack asked as Coco floored the Jeep up the right lane and veered back left to the passing lane.

"Two years," she said, gunning the Jeep down the straightaway at 60.

"Jesus."

"A long time, right?" Coco said, smiling at her reflection in the windshield.

"I'll tell you the answer when we get to the Pavilion," Jack said.

A few minutes later Coco swerved off an exit ramp, took the streets for a mile, and veered in to the Pavilion parking lot behind the Worker's Stadium.

"I always wanted to come here," Coco said, looking in one of the restaurant's windows as they walked along the sidewalk to the entrance.

"Yeah, me too," Kitty said.

"Well, why haven't you?" Jack asked.

"Too many *laowai*," Coco said.

"Yeah," Kitty agreed.

The Pavilion had a bar inside and tables outside on a lawn protected by a canopy of sycamores. A majority of the customers were *laowai*, most of them looking like people from the foreign diplomatic corps housed in the embassies nearby.

"You guys get a table over there," Jack said, pointing to a group of tables outside. "I'm going to use the restroom."

Returning outside a minute later, Jack walked up to the table for two the girls had selected. "Okay, am I supposed to sit on the grass?"

They both looked up, a red-faced look of surprise on Kitty's face, Coco oblivious, her head deep in the menu. "Sorry," Kitty said, embarrassed; they moved to the next table where there was more room.

"All right, what would you guys like to drink?" Jack asked them when they had taken their seats on teak chaises covered with stuffed white pillows, and he had taken a cigar out of his pocket, bit off one end, and lit the other.

The girls didn't respond; both of them were studying the plastic menu filled with colored photos of drinks.

"I don't think you want to order your drinks off a menu," Jack advised.

"*Laowai* don't, but we do," Kitty said.

"Suit yourself."

"Suit yourself," Kitty said, mouthing the phrase to herself for future use. She held the menu up for Jack to see. "What is this one?"

"A Pink Lady?"

"Yes. Is it strong?"

"No, it's a cream drink made with almond liqueur. It's sweet; you'll probably like it."

"I'll order that one, then," Kitty said. "Wait a minute; what's that green one she's having?" She asked, pointing over to where the waiter was bringing a drink to someone at the next table.

"It looks like a Grasshopper."

"I've changed my mind. I like green better than pink; I'll have one of those."

"All right. Coco, how about you?"

"I'm the designated driver; I'm having an iced latte."

"The designated driver. Where did you get that from? It's not an expression I've heard in China."

"Of course not—it's American," Coco said and she waved toward the waitress. "*Fuyan; fuyan.*"

"So you heard an American say that?"

"About 50 times."

"Really? Where?" Jack asked.

"On American television, silly," Coco said, looking over at Jack as if to say "Where've you been?"

Jack took a long drag from his cigar.

"Can I ask you something?" Coco asked him.

"Sure," he said, not at all sure.

"My boyfriend wants to get married next month. The 16th is a lucky date. May I take the day off?"

"Sure," Jack said, relieved. "I didn't even know you had a boyfriend. I hope this doesn't mean you're quitting."

"You kidding? We're just getting married. We can't even afford a wedding yet; that'll be next year. And we have to buy an apartment and furniture."

As Coco ticked through her shopping list for the upcoming nuptials, the waitress came over and asked them in English what they wanted. Jack ordered the drinks for the girls and a Mojito for himself. As he placed his order, Coco and Kitty craned their necks, scanning the crowd, and fastened on a Chinese guy at the table across the way from them. The girls whispered between themselves in English, either because they didn't want the Chinese guy to hear, wanted Jack to overhear them, or both.

"He looks ideal—tall and intelligent," Coco said.

"Yes, very good looking," Kitty said.

"We were all like that once," Jack said.

They looked at him like they didn't know who he was, and then went back to their conversation.

"Kind, too," Kitty added.

Jack took another pull from his cigar. "How can you tell all that looking at someone you've never met?"

"You just can," Coco said.

"Where's he from?" Jack asked.

"Beijing, I think," answered Coco, nodding her head as she stared at the guy. "Beijing, for sure. And I don't think he's 30. Perfect for you, Kitty."

"I'm not sure. Beijing men can't be trusted."

Finishing his drink, Jack knew better—intelligence and trustworthiness were desirable characteristics for Mr. Right, but not essential—the key was to be young and Chinese.

After they closed on four new Fujian projects, Jack asked Leilei, who seemed to have an advance line on every new hot spot in Beijing, to organize an office party to celebrate.

There was nothing like The Place back home. In the center of Beijing, The Place was an open air plaza set between two multistory buildings. About 40 feet above the floor of the plaza, a screen formed a ceiling stretching between the buildings and running a hundred yards off the street back to the rear of the complex. As Jack looked up, an aquarium scene undulated across the screen's surface, with pink, orange, and red fish floating like multicolored dirigibles across the night sky.

Their initial stop for the evening, CJW—"Cigars, Jazz, and Wine"—was on the right of the plaza in the rear. Dark and smoky inside, CJW's first level was a dance floor. Dinner patrons sat in tables along balconies upstairs, where a wine collection was arrayed in racks and refrigerated coolers from floor to ceiling along the entire rear wall.

The band for the evening was a group of African-Americans from New York City. Taking a break, the troupe stood talking at the bandstand.

Jack asked Kitty to order him a drink and went out on the floor to talk to the band.

"Where you guys from?"

"New York City," the trumpet player said. They seemed happy to see an American. Jack's being white wasn't problematic in Beijing; after all, they were all foreigners.

"So am I. What part?"

"Upper West Side."

"I lived at 100th and West End for years," Jack said.

One of them with a stickpin earring grinned, pointed his thumb at himself, and said, "Broadway and 135th."

"How about you?" Jack asked the female singer.

"I'm from Memphis, honey."

"I could tell," Jack said.

"What are you doing here, man?" the trumpet player asked Jack.

"Making money, same as you."

㊀   ㊀   ㊀

After dinner, Jack danced with all the girls in the office. None of the Chinese men danced.

The trumpet player was just launching the first heroic notes of Bunny Berrigan's *I Can't Get Started* as Nu Yu walked up to his table.

"Can you show me how to dance to this?" she asked Jack, tilting her head toward the band.

"Sure," he stammered, getting up from the table and following Nu Yu as she walked out onto the empty dance floor. He took her left hand in his, wrapped his right arm around her waist, and began to whirl her around the floor. It was the first time he had danced to slow music with a woman in China. He could feel Nu Yu's heart fluttering.

"I thought you were the shy and retiring type," Jack teased as he stepped and turned to the music with Nu Yu in his arms.

"Shy and retiring?" she asked, looking back at him, her eyes cool and dark.

"It means ..." he started to say, and then caught himself as she shook her head back and forth.

"I know what it means," she said.

"So why did you ask me to dance?" he asked, holding her closer and moving them across the floor.

"I wanted the experience," she said.

"Like eating Western food for the first time," Jack said.

Nu Yu displayed no reaction. He never knew whether his jokes were bad, or she hadn't understood, or she simply chose not to respond.

As the singer crooned the lyrics, Nu Yu said, "I recognize this," turning her head to better catch the melody. "It sounds very familiar."

"It's a song from the *Chinatown* soundtrack."

"You know the words."

"I should. It's the story of my life," he said, thinking of them all, of Lin, and Lianhua, and China.

"Without karaoke, China's economy would collapse." Explaining karaoke to Jack as they left The Place, Lee was only half joking.

The Regal was near the Worker's Stadium in a complex with a dozen other discotheques, bars, and restaurants. The club's entryway was manned by a phalanx of Chinese guys in tuxedoes and Amazon-like Chinese girls in tight, short black dresses who moved back and forth escorting groups into the Regal's cave-like entrance.

As Leilei led the way in a shimmery, fringed dress, the other girls from the Middle Kingdom office—Kitty, Xu Xu, Nu Yu, Coco, Marcy, a secretary in the engineering group, and Junzi Tong, a Beijing University student they had hired on a summer internship—filed in. Pete, Whitey, Dr. Yu, and Jack were right behind them. Walking down the dark corridor, he felt speakers pulsing behind the walls. As an Amazon geisha came out of a door to the right, he was barraged with a cacophony of noise, including a combination of produced sound, some Western and some Chinese, and unspeakably bad singing.

Their room was high-ceilinged and entirely lined in plush, black felt. A pit-like singing area surrounded on three sides a table covered with bottles of liquor and other drinks, and faced a floor-to-ceiling screen. The liquor collection was heavily weighted with branded, dark alcohol—Johnny Walker, Crown Royal, Courvoisier—that no one in America drank anymore, and beer. No vodka, gin, rum, or wine. At either side of the singing pit were computers programmed with Chinese and English songs.

The Amazon geishas took drink orders, offered menus, and helped program the karaoke computers. Leilei and Kitty appeared to be experienced karaoke hands, and asked people what songs they wanted to sing. Dr. Yu was already standing up and singing a song that appeared from the video to be an excerpt from a Chinese historical war movie. Jack was surprised at his booming singing voice, later learning this was the only song Dr. Yu performed; with his usual efficiency, he got his obligation out of the way early.

Everyone crowded around the computer screens, perusing the song selections. Most selected Chinese songs; the universe of English song titles was limited. Kitty scrolled though the English song titles, turning to Jack.

"Was Elvis Presley black or white?"

Favorite songs kept popping up, the group clamoring for their inclusion, often because they were under the impression it was an American favorite. Like *Sailing*. Someone told Jack it was a Rod Stewart song, but he had never heard of it.

There were two aspects of volunteering to sing a song. One issue was the lyrics and the melody—if Jack didn't know all the lyrics, could he read them off the screen fast enough not to lose the pace of the song?—and the other, unanticipated challenge was the video. Selecting *Bye Bye, Love* by the Everly Brothers had seemed like an easy decision to Jack—it was a great American anthem and he knew the lyrics by heart—but when the video came up, he recognized his mistake. Phil and Don Everly were on the screen singing and strumming steel guitars in a black and white, newsreel type film, probably made when the song was originally recorded in 1957, complete with static and white snow in the film background. Standing up on the stage singing the song, Jack's status as a dinosaur was confirmed.

By contrast, the Chinese numbers were usually the opposite—insipid lyrics and melodies, but filmed using slick videos featuring couples no more than 20 years old who always seemed to be walking down a lane with cherry blossoms floating down out of the sky.

Jack sat on the left side of the pit, smoking a cigar. He was surprised by the performances of the Beijing staff, but then caught himself—they probably did karaoke every weekend. Nu Yu sang one of his favorite Chinese songs, the theme song from the movie *Curse of the Golden Flower*. Coco insisted on doing all the hip hop numbers, and Kitty, the most dedicated entertainer, sang any song unclaimed by others, either in English or Chinese.

Even Marcy, who never spoke in the office, belted out a Chinese love song. When Marcy finished her number, Jack watched her return across the room to where she was sitting on a couch with Pete. Pete, who had lived alone for a long time, probably because he talked about engineering to anyone forced to listen, looked uncharacteristically content. He and Marcy were just sitting there, not saying anything and watching the performances. Every once in a while, someone else at their table would say something to Marcy in Chinese, and inevitably, Pete leaned his head, semi-permanently attached to Marcy's, requiring she translate every word, just like Pete had once tried to do with Kalin.

The Middle Kingdom group spent two hours going through 30 to 40 songs. Jack was just lighting up another cigar when he realized everyone was getting ready to leave. He stubbed out the cigar, took a last sip of his drink, and got in line to file out of their room. Pete and Marcy were right in front of him, slowly shuffling toward the door.

"Are you all right?" Marcy asked Pete as they stood behind the group funneling out the door. Pete didn't seem to be in much of a hurry.

"Sure."

"You're not tired?"

"Well, it's been a long day, young lady."

"Maybe you've had too much to drink."

"Not me."

"I didn't know you drank Courvoisier."

"I don't drink Courvoisier."

"But you were drinking it back there."

"It's all they had."

Marcy looked at Pete in the glare of the spotlight over the club's entrance as they exited the club. "I'm going to tell this taxi driver to take you home."

"Okay. How about you? Do you have money?"

"I'll get another one. Yes, of course I have money."

"Make sure you put in for it."

"No, that's not important," she said, waving her hand.

"Make sure you do, Marcy. One last thing," Pete said through the open window as he got into his taxi.

She looked at him without speaking. The taxi driver was gunning the gas.

"Did you sing that song for me?"

She just looked at him as the taxi driver pulled out of the club's driveway.

Looks like Pete was right, after all. The girls did like him, at least this Chinese one did, Jack thought standing by himself in the rain as he watched the taxi's red tail lights recede in the night.

Chapter 44

Bulls in the China Shop

"You've got to do something about him. Pete's out of control," Lee said, sticking his head in Jack's office.

"What's he done now?"

"This has nothing to do with me—I don't care one way or the other," Lee said. "But Ms. Cheng is really angry. Without telling anyone, Pete sent Marcy back to her hometown to get a passport. She just left; no one knew where she was. Four days later, she comes back. Ms. Cheng asked where she had been, and Marcy says, 'Pete sent me home to get a passport.' She had to go to the consulate in Shenyang and camp out in their offices. She was gone all that time and never even called in. So Ms. Cheng yelled at her, and, get this"—Lee bent over laughing—"Marcy said she didn't care what Ms. Cheng said; said she works for Pete now." Lee howled. "Can you believe it?"

"I wouldn't want to be that poor girl when Ms. Cheng gets done with her," Jack said.

"And the best part is Pete told Marcy to get a passport because he's trying to take her stateside."

"He told you that?"

"No, but you and I both know what he's up to."

Jack walked down the hall to Pete's office and nudged open the door.

"Pete, got a minute?"

"Sure, Jackie. Come on in and sit down."

"Let's take a walk outside if you don't mind," Jack said.

"What's up?" Pete asked as they walked out the front door of the office into the wide reception area off the lobby of the 25th floor of the Poly Centre, the office building where Middle Kingdom had relocated after closing the Merritt Partners deal earlier that year. The air smelled vaguely rank, like all Chinese office buildings. Jack had never been able to understand why they smelled that way, especially the Poly Centre—it was one of the nicest office buildings in Beijing.

"Pete, you just can't do this stuff," Jack said as they stood looking out over Beijing's western ridgeline.

"What stuff?"

"This game you're playing with Marcy. Look, we're trying to run a business here. Ms. Cheng is all pissed off because Marcy disappeared for four days on your say so. And what's this about her getting a passport to go stateside?"

"Jackie, I can explain."

"I doubt it."

"So Ms. Cheng turned me in." Pete shrugged and stared off at across the Beijing rooftops. "She never liked me."

"Ms. Cheng didn't do anything of the kind. I found this out through back channels. But now we have to fix things before the whole office blows up. We can't play favorites here."

"Look Jack, this experience has been a little trying for me. It's one thing to be part of a working group where you are welcome, and quite another to be shunned. Despite all the camaraderie I've tried to foster with the Chinese engineers here in Beijing, they've made it clear they would prefer I not be here. That little girl is the only one who makes me feel welcome."

"Pete, I know how lonely it is here. But whether the engineers like you isn't important for the job I need you to do. So don't let it be. And you've got to operate on China rules. Ms. Cheng's in charge of the girls."

"What about Marcy, Jack? Can I take her back to America?"

Jack shrugged. "That's up to Marcy, isn't it?"

"I think she wants to be with me."

"Look Pete, the key to getting by in China is to not allow things to affect you personally. If you get bothered when your Chinese colleagues drop hints they don't want *laowai* around, or you get attracted to the cute little Chinese girl and fantasize she really likes you—as opposed to the truth, which is she's no different from a dog following the person who feeds her—you've lost. Most Chinese people know our game—we're here to make a few bucks, and when we're done, we're going back where we came from. And that's fine with them."

"But what if the game changes? What if you end up caring about someone here?"

Jack listened to himself, looking into Pete's eyes. Who was he kidding? Neither of them believed what he was saying. He could see Pete looking at him; probably reading his mind. Maybe even detecting his feelings about Lianhua. "Look, I don't know about that."

"You're just saying you would handle it differently," Pete said.

But Jack couldn't say that, and Pete knew it. "What I'm saying isn't gospel, just a guide to everyday life here," Jack said, looking his friend in the eye. "Do I try to take my own advice? Sure; I try. Things are just different in China, that's all. Only the brave—or the foolish—should venture beyond casual friendship."

"And you don't see yourself ever being brave or foolish," Pete said, as if knowing Jack was going to try.

Chapter 45

Gum on Your Shoe

It was like having a bad dream. A month after traveling through the timeless hills of Fujian looking at hydroelectric sites, and a week after spending an evening with Amazon geishas, Jack was back in New York, sitting in court looking at Bill Dickle's hound dog face on the witness stand.

Jack forced himself not to listen. He could hear Elizabeth now. "No good deed goes unpunished." After the Xushi deal, it had been Jack's idea to give Dickle a written agreement—treat him like a human being—and she had just shook her head as he put it into the mail.

And now he had been whipsawed. Normally, when it came to undeserved compensation, Jack had always been the pushover; Elizabeth had been the tough one. "Pay them," Jack had always said. He wasn't hiding from anything, he told himself, just efficiently sidestepping a problem and moving on.

Until Dickle. It was the principle of the situation. Baoqing Bioengineering had paid Davis Brothers a retainer, and then the company had flat-out lied to him. Dickle had to know, but now Dickle had the nerve to petition the court for Boxwood's portion of the retainer fees. Send Dickle a check when he had defrauded them? No way. Jack lived up to his obligations, but fraud changed things. Dickle was a liar; Jack wasn't going to give him a penny.

When he got the arbitration papers, he had been surprised. Not because he thought Davis Brothers was on the holy side of the issue—according to the contract, Dickle was due his split of fees from the Baoqing deal—but because he couldn't understand how Dickle thought he was going to sit up in front of the judge and defend himself.

Until Tom Flemish, his litigation counsel, told him the Baoqing Bioengineering fraud wasn't an issue in the case.

"You've got to be kidding," Jack said.

"I wish I was," Tom Flemish said. "Unfortunately, you signed a contract with Dickle, and that's what the case is about. The fact that Dickle and the client conspired and lied about the state of the company's business is immaterial."

Jack just sat and stared at Flemish.

"You can just pay him and get this over with," Flemish said.

"To hell with that," Jack said.

"That's what I thought you'd say," Tom said, and then proceeded to outline his strategy for the case, which hinged on a lame theory alleging Dickle hadn't provided the services the retainer contract required of him.

"Tom, he didn't do anything, anyway. He was a finder. If the judge asks me if I relied on Dickle, I'm not going to lie. The guy was a crook; why can't we just say that?"

It was his turn to testify. Jack walked up to the witness stand trying to remember everything Tom told him. "Don't bring up Dickle's fraud or his poor character."

The clerk swore Jack in, and he looked over at the judge.

"Mr. Davis, did Mr. Dickle respect Chinese people?"

It was all downhill from there. Even though Jack had to pay Dickle his portion of the retainer plus legal fees and court costs, he wouldn't have done anything differently.

Walking back to the office, he glanced up at the robin's-egg-blue sky between the canyons of buildings running perpendicular to Park Avenue. It was a July afternoon in New York—early morning in

Beijing. The girls from the office would be asleep now; so would Lianhua. He tried to bring her face into focus, without success. Nine thousand miles away from the Middle Kingdom, walking past St. Patrick's Cathedral, the pigeons flapped their wings over his head as if announcing something.

Back in his office, he futzed to avoid thinking about anything bad, making a new pot of coffee, straightening the chairs around the boardroom table and sorting the mail. Flipping through the University of Chicago magazine just in, he scanned the table of contents. In a full page color montage on the inside cover was an eye-catching advertisement: the University's affiliate in Hangzhou was sponsoring a fall travel package to China spiced with the type of event the University's intellectuals loved: "Portraits of Tibetan Children; Glorious Paintings by Lianhua." The opening was at the West Lake Hyatt gallery on Saturday evening, a little over one month away.

Chapter 46

There and Back Again

It wasn't until his plane had lifted off from Beijing for Hangzhou that he started to feel really stupid. Flying somewhere to see an art show and hoping to talk to someone who probably wouldn't even remember him? He had lost his senses for sure.

No, he thought as he looked out the window at the last orange beams of sunlight slicing through the purple evening haze. It was simpler than that; he was pathetic. Being crazy was defensible; there was no excuse for what he was up to.

He only got as far as the taxi line at the Hangzhou airport before being reminded that whenever he traveled alone in China, bad things happened. He leaned into the windows of several taxis, trying to pronounce the name of the art gallery to their drivers with no success—the hacks just looked back at Jack derisively before finally experimentation paid results. "Hyatt, Hyatt hotel." Bingo. The driver nodded his head and grinned, flashing Jack a dentist's nightmare.

Jack shoehorned himself into the back seat of the tiny beat-up taxi, and the driver sped off for downtown Hangzhou. Scrunched in the taxi, the meter rattling in front of him, Jack breathed through his mouth to avoid the smell of garlic and the cigarette fumes, trying to remember Lianhua's face. His difficulty underscored the futility of what lay ahead— if he couldn't remember her, there was no way she was going to remember him.

The schizophrenic driver didn't help. Whenever smoking a cigarette, he went into automatic pilot, idling along with the other autos in the middle lane of the highway, but as soon as he flicked the spent butt out the window, the guy became crazed, jamming his gears and zipping past trucks in the breakdown lane, placing Jack's head three inches from being reduced to dust by the road's concrete barrier walls.

Exiting the highway, they cruised down the ramp and into the streets of the West Lake area of the old city. Jack started to feel better. Old Hangzhou could do that to people. He leaned back in his seat and watched the bicyclists weaving hypnotically in and out of traffic in front of the taxi. Stately sycamores lined the streets, their dry summer leaves soaking up the mist coming off the lake. Dark shapes of people floated along the boulevard ringing the water's edge. Boat noise echoed over the lake.

The taxi pulled up into the driveway of the Hyatt complex. Jack looked the place over—he hadn't been there since the Luosha deal closed six months earlier—and then glanced at his watch; he was late. The show would be over in less than an hour. He paid the driver and walked into the hotel lobby, checked in, gave his bag and some small bills to the bellman, and headed toward the art gallery off the north side of the lobby.

As he approached the gallery entrance, his misgivings returned. A pack of television cameramen and others holding klieg lights and reflecting screens swarmed around the doorway, focusing on people who appeared to stop and pose. He didn't want to go inside; it looked like a circus. Maybe he could see her from outside.

A *laowai* with curly white hair on the sides of his otherwise shiny head tried to catch Jack's eye. "You must be with the University," the man said. He was standing with a younger Chinese man wearing wraparound sunglasses and dressed in black with heavy hardware around his neck.

"No," Jack said. "Well, not now, anyway; I graduated some time ago."

"Are you on the university tour then?"

"No."

Jack craned his neck to peer through the gauntlet of people. The show was going to be over soon. He was going to have to push through.

"This is my friend Mr. Qing," the man with the shiny head and the fuzz continued, introducing the young Chinese man, who, watching the crowd, didn't turn his head.

"Hey, man."

"Nice to meet you, too," Jack said, looking around to see if there was any way to sneak into the gallery space through a side door.

"Are you going in?" the man asked. He was wearing a tweed jacket with suede patches on the elbows, the sort of jacket a lot of people at the University of Chicago wore.

A group of young Chinese women in stiletto heels, too much makeup, and lots of jewelry made their entrance; flashbulbs exploded.

"I guess I'm going to have to try," Jack said. "How about you guys?"

"That's why we came, but this looks formidable," the man said.

"Say, Mr. Qing," Jack said to the young Chinese man, who turned his shades toward Jack. "You've got the battle gear; come on, you go first."

Mr. Qing's shades kept pointing at Jack.

"You're the man," Jack told him, nodding his head at Mr. Qing for encouragement and motioning toward the entrance.

Mr. Qing looked at the swarm of media people, looked back at Jack, and then strode into the fray, semi-posing and flashing a smile, Jack and the bald man following behind him as a few misguided photographers wasted more flash bulbs.

Through the gauntlet, Jack tapped Mr. Qing on the shoulder. "Thanks very much for the escort. Just one question—do you ever take those shades off?"

Mr. Qing grinned and shook his head.

Inside, the crush of people was only slightly less intense. Jack stepped a few paces out of the entryway, stopped, and looked at the work hanging on the walls. The buzz of the room vanished. Lianhua's portraits commanded the space. They were striking, especially ones he hadn't seen before, of Tibetan children, their expressions as serene as the mist falling on the lake outside, but somehow hardened into an ethereal maturity by the rigors of life and death at four thousand meters.

He didn't have to search to find Lianhua. His idealized vision of China was standing right in front of him, as composed as her paintings, wearing a purple embroidered peasant smock and dark harem pants tucked into black riding boots, her long black hair piled on her head and fastened with a silver pin.

A crowd of well wishers stood in front of her, extending pen and paper for autographs. On one side, she was flanked by an entourage of young Chinese men, all dressed in black or denim, adorned with jewelry and American baseball hats worn backward on their heads. The local Hangzhou *savants,* no doubt.

Jack paid no attention to them. He was studying the guy with them, standing next to Lianhua. Tall for a Chinese man, he had a long aquiline nose, a ponytail of black hair trailing halfway down his back, and was dressed in a black Chinese peasant shirt and pajama pants. He looked Tibetan. Lianhua held his arm.

As Jack stood there taking in Lianhua and her retinue, he saw her look directly at him. He couldn't tell whether she recognized him or not, but she didn't move. It didn't matter. He wasn't going to make any more of a fool out of himself than he had already. She was with someone, so there was no reason for him to stay. It had been worth the shot; but most larks just don't work out, and tonight would be another one of those.

Taking one last minute to look at the paintings on the walls, he pushed back through the crowd clogging the entrance and walked outside into the cool black night. Crossing the boulevard separating the hotel from the banks of West Lake, he stopped to watch a group of old people silently whirl in unison through their tai chi ritual, following the movements of an instructor clad in red robes and wielding a sword in both hands.

Probably where he was headed one day soon he thought, standing on the wide, stone covered quay, the soft drizzle of the late Hangzhou summer matting his wavy hair, still brown but threatened with strands of silver.

He needed a drink. He walked back across the street into the lobby of the hotel and found a seat in the lounge.

He had thought the evening might go differently, but he was going to be drinking alone. Not that he minded, in general. Most of the time, he was all right with being alone—it was the only time he could think. Just not all the time. Not tonight. The waiter delivered a wine list. At least the hotel offered a decent selection, he remembered from his days there doing the Luosha deal. He ordered a glass of Australian pinot gris, asked the waiter for a match, and spent a moment lighting a Cohiba, thinking about the disappointment in the other room.

He looked up to see Lianhua walking purposefully across the lobby.

As Jack watched her, she strode to the front desk and spoke to the girl behind the counter. After a moment, the clerk motioned for Lianhua to join her at the concierge desk. Lianhua, the clerk, and the concierge put their heads together and spoke in low tones for a minute, and then the concierge shook his head back and forth. Lianhua stood and exhaled, a look of frustration on her face, as she absentmindedly surveyed the room.

Jack was looking right at her as her eyes stopped on him. She made a loud exclamation in Chinese, turned to the concierge and the girl, saying *xei xei* several times, and then walked across the lobby toward Jack. She wasn't smiling, but her expression, not as resolute as a minute before, was more tentative.

"I'm so sorry," she said from halfway across the lobby, shaking her head back and forth as she walked. "I tried to find you. They said they were not allowed to tell me if you were staying in their hotel."

At first, Jack didn't understand her, and looked behind him to see if she was speaking to someone else. "Are you talking to me?" Jack said to her, standing up as she got to where he had been sitting.

She was breathing hard. "Mr. Davis, yes?"

"Yes, that's right. You remembered my name."

"Oh, yes, Mr. Davis, of course I remember you. I'm very sorry. In the other room, it was very busy. I saw you, but I looked again and you were gone. I thought maybe it was dream, like when I met you."

"Well, that sounds like a nice explanation to me."

The two of them were just standing there, surrounded by people sitting in the lounge looking at the Chinese princess who had burst into their midst.

"Can you stay?" Jack asked. "Sit down, please. I should have already offered. Here, take my chair," he said as he turned to call the waiter. "*Fuyan,*" he said, pointing to his chair and signaling a request for another. "Would you care for a drink?"

"Yes, Mr. Davis. I'd like some tea," she said at first, still standing up. "No, no, no," she said, waving her hands in front of her face, closing her eyes and bowing her head slightly. She opened her eyes and looked up at him. "I'm sorry. My mind change. I would like a glass of wine."

"I'm having this. Would you like some?"

She looked down at his glass on the table. "I prefer red, I think. Maybe I will have two." She giggled.

Jack looked at her, realized she had meant it, the crow's feet around his eyes crinkling. "Two it is." When the waiter returned with a second chair, he ordered two glasses of pinot noir and another pinot gris for himself, and motioned for Lianhua to sit. "Please."

"Thank you, Mr. Davis."

"Call me Jack. In Hong Kong, you said it was all right to call you Lianhua, right?"

"Yes," Lianhua nodded.

She sat opposite him in her armchair. He looked carefully at her in front of him for the first time. Looking back at him, she reached up and pulled the silver pin out of the bun on the top of her head. Her black tresses tumbled down long and full behind her head, the scent of her hair floating over him. She reached and spread her hair behind her shoulders, framing her face and setting off the diagonal lines of her eyes and cheekbones.

The waiter brought the two glasses of pinot noir to Jack, who set them down in front of Lianhua. She took a sip, paused, and then took another, larger one. Jack watched her skin start to turn pink, then red. She had to know it, looking silently back at Jack, but kept drinking.

She was the most beautiful Chinese woman he had ever seen.

She kept looking at him and smiling, not saying anything.

"I can't believe how beautiful you are."

Now her face really flushed.

"When I drink wine my face turns pink."

"But that's part of it."

"My skin gets warm, too."

He reached up slowly and put his hands on her face. She let him, looked back at him and didn't avert her eyes, but didn't say anything.

"I'm sorry, say something if I'm offending you. I just had to touch your face." He held her face in his hands a moment longer, looked at her without saying anything, and then quit while he was ahead. "Do you like the wine?"

"It's very good; very light. I don't think I've had red wine like this before, at least not in China."

"Yes, most places in China don't serve pinot noir. At least you have enough to last for a while," Jack said, nodding at the two glasses, trying to keep a serious look on his face. "I don't recall ever seeing a Chinese woman order a glass of wine before, let alone two."

"I like wine. I take it when I travel for my shows. To relax. And I need it tonight," she said, smiling as she spoke in her precise, careful manner. She took another sip of wine.

"Why tonight?"

"My show. And seeing you."

He didn't say anything. If it weren't for the ponytail man in the other room, he would be exhilarated, but the picture of her arm in his was impossible to forget.

"First I see you in Hong Kong many years ago, then no more. I think maybe never," Lianhua said.

"Yes, I've only been back to Chairman Roo's office once since then," Jack said.

"Where have you been, then?"

"I am in China every month. Different parts of the country."

"All over China, then," Lianhua said.

"Well, I've been a few places here, but I'm no Mr. China."

"Mr. China? Who is that?"

"It's the name of a business book about China popular with foreigners."

"When did you come here first?"

"To China? Ten years ago."

"That's a long time ago for a foreigner to be in China. Do you like Chinese people?"

Jack smiled and hesitated. "I love them, laugh with them and sometimes at them at the same time. Know what I mean?"

"I don't think so, no. Tell me."

"Well, I like most Chinese people very much, but even the normal ones I like are different from my American friends—they take some getting used to."

"I don't want to be a normal Chinese person so you must tell me what you mean."

"I will."

"And there are some Chinese people you don't like, I'm sure."

"Well, I like most people. There are really no Chinese people I don't like, although I'm suing some Chinese guys. I've actually never done that before—I've never sued anyone, not even an American."

She didn't say anything. Maybe she didn't know what a lawsuit was.

"I'm sorry. I'm keeping you away from your art show. You probably should get back."

"Oh, no, is okay. Too many people; too busy."

"But they're here to see you."

"Is okay. I spoke with many people; the show is finished." She waved her hand.

"Was it a good show? Did you make money?"

"I'm sorry; make money?"

"Listen to me, trying to reduce everything to business. Did you sell any of your paintings?"

"Yes," Lianhua said, nodding.

"That's good. Are there any left? Maybe I can buy one. If I can afford the freight, that is; I don't know how much they cost."

"I'm sorry. The freight?"

"Oh, that's just an American idiom. The freight means the price; I'm saying I don't know if I can afford the price. We Americans use idioms for half our speech. I've got to remember not to use them so much."

"I love English idioms—I'm trying to learn them all."

"Stick with me then; I'll teach you more."

"Stick with you?"

"See?" Jack laughed.

So did Lianhua. "I would like you to have one of my paintings," she said.

"Why do you say that?"

"They're like my children. I want them to be with people I like."

"Do you paint them all on site in Tibet?"

"No, I go there every year and take many photos; then I paint at my studio. In 798, in Beijing. Have you been to Tibet?"

"No; they don't let many foreigners in now."

"But you must go. To know China, you must know Tibet."

Not only was the woman sitting across from him a wonderful artist and beautiful, but she actually seemed interested in him, in his view of her country and what he had to say—about art and English idioms, of all things—and she didn't seem to care if he had money or not. But maybe she was just good, as they all seemed to be, at hiding her true feelings.

"Does your boyfriend have a lot of your paintings?" Might as well get to the bottom of things.

"No understand," she said, shaking her head back and forth. "Boyfriend?"

"The man in the other room with the ponytail."

"Oh, no, sorry." Lianhua put her hands to her face and laughed, her black eyes sparkling. "He not my boyfriend. Jin my brother."

"Your brother?" Jack asked, as Lianhua nodded her head. "Well, that's a relief."

Lianhua looked at Jack for a minute without saying anything, and then took a sip of wine from her second glass of pinot noir. "Relief?"

"Never mind," Jack said, "I was just saying something I shouldn't have."

Lianhua looked at him and said, "Another idiom, I think," and frowned. "I think I should tell you; I have boyfriend," she said, her face more serious. "A small one."

"A small one? Am I allowed to ask what that means?" Jack said, laughing so as to resist caring. Her offering an explanation was a positive, at least.

"He lives in France. I only see him once a year," she said, remaining serious. Her expression didn't change as she asked, "You have a girlfriend, yes?"

Jack looked back at Lianhua and said, "The short answer is no, but it's a big subject—how much time do you have?"

"Oh, I guess I must go to bed soon."

"There I go again—I was just using a figure of speech."

"You mean like an idiom."

"Sort of."

"So you mean your girlfriends need explanation."

"Yes."

"I'd like to hear. Perhaps you can tell me some time."

"I hope so. Would you like another drink?"

"No, I'm going to bed."

"I'll go up with you."

They took the elevator. It stopped at her floor first. The door opened, Lianhua started to walk out, and he placed his foot where it would block the door, took her wrist, and guided her back around to face him. She looked at him, surprised and confused.

Jack pulled Lianhua toward him gently, went to kiss her, she moved her head sideways and he brushed his lips against her temple, then he held her more firmly and kissed her lightly on her cheek.

She blinked and recovered, gamely putting on a smile, the elevator door banging into the two of them.

"Have a good sleep," she said to him.

"You, too."

The elevator door closed and the car continued up to his floor. He was surprised—she hadn't expected him to kiss her and didn't know what to do. It was hard to believe, but he felt positive she hadn't been kissed goodnight very often. He knew people didn't kiss casually in China, but he didn't care—he was glad he had done it. He hadn't meant it to be casual with her.

The elevator came to his floor and he got off and walked down the hall to his room. He felt good about her. Not physically, although he was sure if he let his guard down that would follow close behind, but it didn't have to be that way. He had just wanted to feel good about a woman in China, and then there she was, the person he had dreamed about for three years, sitting across from him in the Hyatt Regency in Hangzhou.

As opposed to ending up with someone through convenience, let alone a sense of obligation or inevitability, he had pursued his vision of China, found her, and kissed her goodnight. That was enough, at least for now. He lay down on the bed in his clothes.

The rain fell across the lake all night long.

Chapter 47

Close but No Cigar

Seat 2K should have his name on it, Jack Davis thought as he settled into the first class seat on the window to begin his monthly flight from New York to Beijing. Jack always flew Air China Flight 982 from JFK to Beijing, and Monita Chen, his travel agent, always booked the same seat for him.

Flying economy to China was out of the question. The seats were too small and the rear cabin was always filled with flocks of Chinese tourists chattering and laughing in loud groups all night, along with the usual assortment of latter-day American hippies and National Geographic tour groups clad in Birkenstocks and tee shirts who didn't bathe or shave any part of their bodies based on some misguided theory this would effectively combat globalization as they jetted across the Pacific bearing their culture like malignant seeds invading on the wind.

Tommy was waiting for him in the street outside of customs, sitting in Middle Kingdom's Mercedes van. They greeted each other but didn't need to talk much—Jack liked that about Tommy.

He watched the highway begin to rush by as they emerged from the tollbooths and Tommy pushed the van over to the left into the passing lane. It was late August, the end of summer, and drizzly. Humidity hung over the city, pressing the smog and the soot of Beijing groundward. Big bright spotlights flared alongside the roadway as men worked the midnight shift, using hand tools, digging and pounding, planting and watering, exhibiting the same methodical determination as a colony of ants.

Pulling off the Second Ring Road at the Dongsishitiao Qiao subway station, Tommy drove around the corner down a tree-lined street and into the entrance of the Swissotel. The hotel faced out across the intersection of the Second Ring Road and Gongrentiyuchand Beilu, where one of Beijing's original nine gates had stood until 1960 when Chairman Mao demolished the city's walls. Across the street was the Poly Centre, Middle Kingdom's Beijing headquarters. On a clear day, Jack could see the serrated ridgeline of mountains beyond, west of the city, 30 miles away.

When in Beijing on the weekends, Jack preferred boutique hotels like the Bamboo Garden with its gardens and moon-gated walls, but he stayed in the Swissotel during the week. He liked the neighborhood. Right around the corner were embassy neighborhoods and quiet streets where he could take a walk and sit in a café, have some coffee, and read the newspapers before plunging into the day.

Also, Illya, the manager, always gave him an upgrade. As he said good night to Tommy and came through the big revolving door into the hotel, he saw Illya in the lobby.

"Well hello, Mr. Davis. Nice to see you on this beautiful evening."

"What's so beautiful about it, Illya? It's almost midnight and your bar is already closed."

"Please, Mr. Davis, for you the bar is always open. I have a Cohiba and a glass of Hennessey waiting for you," Illya said. "Please join me and tell me what's happening in America."

"I'll take you up on that; let me take my things up to my room first."

"My dear Mr. Davis, please, you must let us do our job. Jimmy, take Mr. Davis's luggage to his room while he joins us for a nightcap."

Jack reached out and gave the bellboy a 20-quoi note. No one tipped in China, except in five star hotels in the very big cities where there were a lot of foreigners. Otherwise, handing out tips wasn't regarded as generous, just stupid.

He had a cigar and two glasses of cognac with Illya, then went up to his rooms. They had given him a small suite facing west out the front of the hotel. The rooms were trimmed in teak and mahogany. Between the bedroom and the sitting room was a wet bar Illya had stocked with red and white wine, port, cognac, and Jack's favorite Cohiba cigars. A purple orchid sat in a vase on the desk.

Jack unpacked, got into bed, and slept fitfully. Waking at five o'clock in the morning, he rolled over and looked out at the gray mixture of fog and smog. In the coolness of the early morning, the heating vents on top of the building across the traffic circle spewed a thin mist of condensate up into the pewter sky, while the last of the night's renegade traffic, jerrybuilt tractors and mopeds that could no longer contend with modern Beijing's vehicle scrum, scurried back to wherever they came from before the rush hour began to rev up.

It was the one time in the day when Jack was open to the world, when he left himself unguarded, wasn't trying too hard or puzzling what could go wrong or just in the middle of something, when he asked himself what he was doing and why he was there. He rubbed his eyes and looked at the ceiling, then around at the room. Alone.

㊌   ㊌   ㊌

"What are we supposed to say to her?" Coco asked Jack.

Coco, Tommy, and Jack were in a taxi on their way to 798, Beijing's sprawling artist district out by the airport.

"What's that supposed to mean?" Jack responded, looking straight ahead to make sure the driver didn't get lost.

"We don't know anything about art or painting," Coco said. "She's going to realize we're just playing a game for you."

"Speak for yourself, Coco. I know about art," Tommy said. "I've been to 798 a bunch of times."

"Who you kidding? You went there to buy stuff for your apartment, just like me."

Tommy laughed. "Yeah, Coco, I'm really into decorating."

"First we have to find her," Jack said as the taxi dropped them off at the entrance to 798. He paid the driver, looked down the main walkway, and started walking in the sticky afternoon sun, peering into the buildings, Coco and Tommy keeping up alongside him. "Look, just to repeat, thanks for coming, guys," Jack said to them as they fanned out on the wide sidewalk. "I don't care what you say to her; I just don't want her to think I'm stalking her or something like that."

"Yeah, Jack, but if things work out, you'll be in conversation with a beautiful artist and I'll be stuck with Coco," Tommy said as Coco punched him on the arm.

Three blocks into 798, right on the main walkway, Coco pointed on the left-hand side at a low row of studios sitting side by side. "There's her studio," Coco said, pointing from where she stood under the scratchy shade of a dwarf sycamore to the single level storefront displaying Lianhua's paintings in the window.

Walking toward the entrance to the studio, Jack thought about the words he would say, as he had since they said goodbye in the elevator in Hangzhou a month earlier. And he still blew it.

"Hello," Jack said as he entered the studio and Lianhua looked up from where she sat painting at her easel. "I had to try to find you."

He thought she seemed pleased, but also embarrassed, as she blushed. "How are you?" she said, standing awkwardly.

"Better now," he said in a low tone. He knew he shouldn't do that, especially with Tommy and Coco there, but the look on her face totally disarmed him—he may as well have swallowed truth serum. "These are my friends Tommy and Coco," Jack said, as his co-conspirators edged into the entrance behind him. "We were just in the neighborhood," he said, laughing as the four of them looked at each other. He didn't know if anyone understood the American expression, but the others all laughed, too.

"I'm going to control myself and say hello Chinese style," Jack continued, and reached his hand out to shake Lianhua's.

But as if she had remembered the elevator and thought about him and had known what he had been thinking, she leaned over and offered him her cheek. When he kissed it, she let him kiss her again on the other side of her face, as Tommy and Coco stood embarrassed, looking up at the ceiling.

In the Tibetan restaurant Lianhua had suggested for dinner, deep chanting music vibrated in low tones, raising the hairs on the back of
his neck.

"I usually don't like music at dinner," Jack said to Lianhua, "but
I'd listen to this anywhere."

"They are monks," Lianhua said, but otherwise ate without speaking. A quiet, blue darkness crept across the city, climbing the peaks
west of Beijing. The Oriental sun showed the last of its orange embers
through a notch in the mountains, a cigar tip about to expire.

"The Yak meat is delicious, especially with this red wine. Here,
try some," Jack said to her, trying to put some Yak on her plate.

"No, I don't eat animals," Lianhua said, shaking her head back and
forth. "I am Buddhist."

"So no animals for you. How about fish?"

"Fish okay."

Jack leaned back in his chair. Lian bowed her head, concentrating
on her food. She rarely looked him in the eye, but he didn't think it
was because she didn't like him. More a Chinese woman thing.

"When I go back to the States tomorrow I'm going to talk to my
friend Virginio Ferrari," Jack said to Lianhua. "He's a sculptor from
Italy I used to work for in Chicago. He says the art world is moving
to Asia and he wants to come here before he dies."

"He won't die if he makes art," Lianhua said. "Artists keep living
as long as they are working. But is good idea. You must tell him to
come."

"Maybe I will, then," Jack said. "He'll need a place to work."

"We can speak to my brother," Lianhua said. "Jin knows all the
sculptors; the fabricators too. He can help."

"Okay," Jack said, feeling like he was at the top of a big ski run,
figuring out if it was too steep or that he should take it. He sat looking
at her, not saying anything.

"Are you all right?"

"I'm fine. Just not looking forward to withdrawal, I guess," Jack
said.

"Withdrawal. What is withdrawal?"

"It's what happens when you experience something really good, like a narcotic, that totally takes over your body and inhabits you, and then it is taken away. Your body reacts physically to the loss—that's withdrawal."

She stared at him. "We should go," she said.

At the curb out in front of the restaurant, she stood next to her car. He stepped next to her and said, "I'm going to kiss you goodbye." He kissed her on her left cheek next to her ear; she didn't pull away, but let him do it. He kissed her on her right cheek, holding her around her waist and pulling her body to him tightly and smelling her hair. She let him kiss her again, even seeming to hold him close for an instant.

He didn't know what to do next. "I'll miss you," Jack finally said.

"I miss you too."

Chapter 48

Penny Wise, Pound Foolish

"Listen to you—it must be the travel routine. You sound like you're going native," Whitey said to Jack. "What's happening with Mr. Xu and the lawsuit?"

"Not much," Jack said. "Finishing discovery this month."

Jack was back in New York, standing at the bar in the Harvard Club having a drink with Whitey. Their conversation was an idle one, falling back on an easy subject, Davis Brothers' Chinese investment banking clients, the penny wise and pound foolish ones, how with them it was always about dollars and cents, never principles. Around them, as the workday ended and evening descended, a collection of professors, business people, regulars, and strangers gathered in the splendid room with the maroon walls and photographs of JFK, FDR, and Teddy.

Listening to himself, he heard the bitter edge of his old Chinese anecdotes rubbing smooth. For starters, rehashing the same tired subjects just betrayed his lack of conversation skills. Anyway, Chinese investment banking clients were in the rearview mirror; he was moving

449

from the business of raising money for others to managing his own hydroelectric company. But the truth was, after everything Dr. Yu had done for him, the hard work by the girls in the Beijing office, and Lianhua—especially Lianhua—he was no longer comfortable joking about the shortcomings of the Chinese. Let someone else do it.

Chinaside more than stateside, he hadn't liked it at first, accepting the grind as the price of having a successful hydroelectric business. In the past, as the day had approached each month when he would have to strap himself in and return to the PRC, he had turned his thoughts to his upcoming tasks, and tried to block out the regret he felt over leaving his sons, and his second thoughts about the human misdemeanors piling up on the other side of the Pacific.

But lately he felt as if he was in the early stages of a chemical transformation. He had started to actually look forward to returning to China, of all things. *God almighty.* "You're right, Whitey. I am starting to feel different about the place," Jack said. "Probably something in the water," he said, grinning at his brother.

"Well, get me up to date," Whitey said. "I'm not over there as much as you."

Jack stood there drinking his Tom Collins as a good-looking *laowai* woman—definitely too much time in China, Jack thought to himself as the Mandarin word was the first to enter his mind—came into the bar on the arm of a short guy with fuzzy hair and glasses. The man was speaking very loudly to her about a real estate deal, but the woman wasn't listening, instead saying hello to Paul, the bartender. She was tall, taller than the fuzzy-headed guy, and wearing heels and a gray skirt, and kept looking over at Jack. The guy ordered a Zombie.

He looked back at her. It seemed like the old days; standing in a bar stateside, a good-looking woman looking at him. She wasn't kidding; one glance told him that. It would be easy, he thought, before he caught himself. So what? It was just nice to know; stateside, at least, he wasn't regarded as a dinosaur because he was close to forty. But what would be the point? Besides, Lianhua had permanently altered his view of what constituted a woman worth paying attention to.

He turned back to where his brother stood. He could retell the one about his client Mr. Loa at Yangling—the soybean king—and how he and his management team had come to New York and booked their hotel rooms two to a room even though Mr. Loa was worth $100 million. And how Mr. Loa snored and his roommate, the CFO, couldn't sleep and looked dreadful every morning, stammering through the presentations Loa made him stay up to memorize.

Or the one about Mr. Liu of the Brightway Corporation, the blowhard, how Jack told him the road show would begin Tuesday morning at nine o'clock and how Mr. Liu had arrived on the doorstep of the New York office in a disheveled state at eight o'clock, his clothes looking like he had camped in them and his hair sticking straight off the back of his head; and when Jack asked what had happened Liu told him instead of flying direct from Beijing to New York, he had gone from Beijing to Hong Kong to Narita to Anchorage to Vancouver to New York and in the process had been delayed 20 hours and lost his bags; and when Jack had asked why had he taken the long way, for God's sake, Mr. Liu said to save $200; and how Jack had had to take him around the corner to Brooks Brothers where Mr. Liu had to spend $2,000 for new clothes for the road show.

But he wasn't going to cover old ground with Whitey. Ever since New Land, they had been angry at China, and eager to pile on. But it would be more honest and truthful to tell Whitey how his feelings had changed, though maybe he wouldn't want to hear it.

"Well, business is good."

"You're not really answering my question."

Jack sighed. "It's still tough not to be cynical."

"Over there? Impossible, I would say."

"But I'm just not going to do that, Whitey."

"Why not?"

"What would it say about us? We'd be no better than mercenaries. We're in China working alongside our partners, clients, and employees, making money under the guise of mutual trust and respect—but telling jokes about them behind their backs? That's pure hypocrisy."

"So leave."

Jack laughed, but he was not amused. "Too late for that. China's starting to look like destiny—mine anyway. It's not a perfect situation. But that's how it is."

"But Jack, put the average businessman over there in the right situation, and he turns into a liar and a thief."

"Don't forget Ms. Cheng's old Chinese proverb: 'If the water is too clear, the fish will die.'"

"So we're supposed to let them steal as long as it's manageable?" Whitey asked. "That'll never work. Where do you draw the line?"

"We're in China, Whitey. It's their way. Just because it's not our way doesn't make theirs bad."

"But what happens when their way conflicts with ours?"

"Then we owe it to ourselves—and to them—to help them live in the clear water, or figure out how to live in dirty water ourselves, or both."

"Or we could just hire women," said Whitey.

"Well they're not all perfect—look what happened with Lin; Kalin, that is—but based on the performance of the girls in our office, I've given that idea some serious thought myself."

"And don't forget, Kalin was probably just a product of the Chinese system."

"What Chinese system?"

"You know, the system that burdens her with a retired mother and father and two sets of grandparents, while she's the only member of her extended family in her generation. How can young people in China today be anything but selfish, with all of their relatives focused down on them every day, the kid's job representing their only meal ticket and security blanket?"

"I think there was more going on with Kalin than that."

"Well, you know what it is, right?"

"Know what what is?"

"The reason Chinese women are so much better than the men."

"Well, I think the Chinese men are under more pressure."

"Nope."

"All right, what is it?"

"The cerebral cortex," Whitey said.

"The cerebral cortex?"

"I'm telling you. You know how in elementary school the girls are all smarter than the boys because the cerebral cortex part of their brain develops faster?"

"Yeah?"

"Well, in China it's a permanent situation."

"Get out of here."

"I'm not kidding." Whitey laughed and ordered another drink.

Jack sighed. "The truth is I don't want to be cynical. It's different now. You ever read *Tortilla Flats*?" he asked Whitey, referring to John Steinbeck's cultural notebook on the mistake prone but loveable Mexicans living above the cannery in Monterey, California.

The fuzzy-headed guy was continuing to harangue the good-looking woman about his real estate deal. Glazed over, she was stuck with him, for the night or longer, Jack couldn't tell. The guy was on the part about rent rolls and the cap rate, but she wasn't listening, standing there looking at Jack, practically leaning on him.

She just wouldn't be worth it.

"I thought we were talking about China," said Pete.

They *were* talking about China. To most people over there, he was probably just a *laowai* with money. He had once thought his investment banking clients liked him, but now realized they probably didn't. Their bowing and supplication was just a sham. They made him feel like a king, but that was only because they wanted him to feel that way. Comfortable and satisfied—and eminently capable of being taken advantage of.

But clients were always different, even stateside. He just really liked the people he worked with. Especially Dr. Yu. And Lee. And all the girls. The girls all tried so hard for him, doing things they didn't fully understand, things he told them they had to do because people in the West did things that way and expected it, and they accepted what he said and put their heads down and did it, trying hard to do it and harder still to please him.

But it was really Lianhua. Could he really be in love with a Chinese woman? It was as if he was inside someone else's skin.

"I changed my mind," said Jack, watching the *laowai* woman as she walked out of the bar a minute later.

Book Five

CHINA HAND

Chapter 49

Men and Women

Jack woke up in his room in Lime Rock in the early morning, knowing where he was by the smoky traces of old fires blown down the chimney by the wind, and opening his eyes to gaze at the pictures of his boys on the mantle. After doing his exercises, he padded downstairs in his stocking feet into the gun room, and pulled on his waders. Fetching his small stream rod, he walked in to the Salmon Kill across the road and caught a few unsuspecting trout before breakfast.

His office door creaked from lack of use when he opened it. The stack of telephone message slips that had always greeted him on the message desk had dwindled to an uninformative handful: his bank account overdraft had been automatically funded; the Harvard Club requested his donation for the Employee Retirement Fund; and opening day at the Hollenbeck Club for pheasant shooting was being moved up to the first Saturday of October, since the poults were hatching earlier due to global warming. He crumpled up the slips and tossed them in to the trash can in the corner, stepped over the pile of magazines and junk mail, made a few calls and left.

On the weekend, he drove his Suburban down the road to Watertown to pick up the boys at their boarding school. Putting his arms around them in front of their embarrassed friends, he handed out presents from China and some poems he had written for them on the plane, and piled everyone into the truck to take them to breakfast in town. After breakfast, they went home and played touch football on the front lawn for several hours until they tired and went to lunch in Salisbury. In the afternoon, they hiked on the Appalachian Trail above the farm, and then went to dinner and a movie that night.

Sitting at the charity pancake breakfast at the town fire hall Sunday morning, one of the twins said, "Daddy, why can't we do this every weekend?"

When Jack didn't reply, his oldest followed up. "Why do you have to keep working so hard, Dad?"

Sometimes he wondered, too. "I guess it's about something called a high-water mark. All men have a high-water mark—each of you will one day, too. Anyone know what that is?"

"No," the twins said at the same time the older boys relied, "Yes."

"Napoleon's was Waterloo, Lee's Gettysburg, but you guys knew that," he said, looking at his two older boys, who nodded, having heard him discuss the topic for most of their lives.

One of the twins asked, "What's your high-water mark, Daddy?"

"I'm happy to reply it appears to be too early to tell."

"Why does that make you happy?" his oldest asked him.

"Well, I used to think I passed my high-water mark a long time ago, when your mother was alive; when things were really good, before everything went downhill."

"So if you thought it was all the way back then, what have you been doing the last few years?"

"Trying to make sure it wasn't. And trying not to make the same mistake twice."

"What mistake?" his second oldest, the serious one, asked.

"Thinking things can't go wrong."

He dropped them off back at school on Sunday afternoon. Kissing them goodbye and telling them he loved them, he returned to

Beijing, where after two weeks he would come back and do it all over
again.

The prop plane bounced down onto the tarmac in Zhongdian, returning Jack and Whitey to the northwest corner of Yunnan to look at
more high-head hydroelectric projects for Middle Kingdom. It was late
at night when they arrived and collapsed into bed at the small inn where
they stayed when in town.

Jack awoke as the last stars faded into the whitish dawn of the
Tibetan sky. His window was glazed with a thin sheen of ice; opening
it, he looked over the valley fields brushed with silvery frost. He lay
down on the cotton throw rug covering the cobblestone floor of his
room, did his exercises, and then showered and shaved. His cell phone
couldn't pick up any reception, so he deferred his call stateside to the
boys until he got to a better place. Getting ready to leave his room to
meet Whitey for breakfast, he turned and saw himself in the mirror on
the wall beside the bathroom door.

With little gloss of youth left, the man looking back at him had
crinkles around his eyes and the beginning traces of spots on his hands.
His brown hair had a hint of silver and his expression was already filled
with the self-doubt of age. Next year, he would be 40.

Who was he kidding— high-water mark still ahead? Maybe, if
it just involved business. But business was only part of things; sure,
he wanted to be good at it, but it wasn't everything. It just consumed
a lot of time, making it easy to overlook the important things
in life.

He turned his head and pushed the specter in the mirror from his
consciousness, collected his wallet and his passport and closed the door,
retreating toward the dining room and a place in the light of day where
he could hide a while longer.

"Good morning," Whitey said as Jack walked over to his table and
sat down. Whitey was already in the middle of his meal. He ate large
breakfasts—hard-boiled eggs, toast, yogurt, fruit, and juice—and never
gained an ounce.

Jack put down his things on the seat opposite Whitey, ordered some coffee from the waitress, and went to the breakfast buffet to get some *congee* and toast. He liked breakfast in Yunnan, where the food was lighter but curiously Western, as if the European travelers on the ancient trade routes had influenced Tibetan kitchens. It was better if he ate something—his Chinese friends and staff became visibly nervous when he didn't, as if he was going to otherwise expire, and somehow become their responsibility. Or maybe it was just they were more comfortable when everyone was doing the same thing.

He returned to the table with his food and listened while Whitey described their week's mission. They would cross west through the mountains and drive down the Lancang and the Nujiang to Mangshi in the southern end of the province, Whitey said. Jack told him where they were on the subject of finances. Otherwise, they focused on their food.

"We've sure been doing this a long time," Jack said, as much to himself as to his brother.

Whitey didn't say anything. They had been together all of their lives, and didn't need to talk much to know what was on the other's mind. A response would be gratuitous, and besides, when he didn't say anything, Jack would fill the void.

"Do you ever wonder what for?" Jack said, lifting his head up and looking at his brother directly for the first time that morning.

"I haven't had a chance to, and I hadn't thought you did either, that is until the last few months."

Jack looked at Whitey and didn't say anything. He added some hard-boiled egg and bread crumbs to his *congee,* mixed the porridge in his bowl, and then ate it with a porcelain spoon. He asked the waitress for another cup of coffee, and turned back to Whitey. "Listen to me. How stupid can I be," he said, looking at Whitey. "I should be ashamed of myself. A year ago, I would have killed to be in the position we're in now. All we wanted was a chance to earn a decent living doing something we love, and now we've got it. That ought to be enough, right?"

"That's never enough, Jack. You know that."

Jack was about to say something more when he looked at Whitey's face, and saw a close likeness of the man he had seen in the mirror of his room earlier that morning. Talking to Whitey about what was on his mind, he would sound like a complete fool. He scolded himself silently, put his head back down over his food, and continued eating.

Finished with breakfast, they gathered their things, checked out of the inn and headed with their Chinese engineer to their Prado Land Cruiser. It was a big, breezy day. High clouds blew in on a south westerly wind from Tibet, the same wind that had blown out the haze the previous afternoon. Unimpeded, the sun shone brightly. When a cloud crossed in front of the sun's rays, the air grew icy, but after the cloud passed and the sky opened back up, it warmed up again as the heat bore down on the land. In a few minutes, the car rolled up the plain to the northwest corner of the Zhongdian valley, took a hard left through the notch in the mountains, and headed down to the Yangtze.

After navigating down the harrowing, winding road to the river, they drove south for another hour. Coming through a small river village, sitting in the back seat of their Prado, Jack and Whitey both looked out the window on the landward side at a man and woman walking down the road.

"Ever wonder why you see lots of *laowai* men with Chinese women, but not the other way around?" Jack asked Whitey out of the blue.

"No," Whitey said, "I don't. It's pretty obvious. The women are different here, that's for damned sure."

The Prado pushed south along the Yangtze, leaving the village and the couple behind.

"What makes you say that?" Jack finally asked.

"In America, they remind us every day their happiness is our responsibility," Whitey said. "Over here, there's still a concept—admittedly antiquated by Western standards—of women serving their husbands. Big difference, if you ask me."

"Definitely not something that would play stateside. But do you think they're really like that here?"

"That's what they say. When you add that to the general instincts of Chinese people to please foreigners, it probably makes for a very different experience."

"But it's probably not love."

"Who knows? If love is desire, admiration, and respect, my guess is once they're beyond 25 and have abandoned the idea of falling in love for more practical things, most Chinese women are happy with two out of three."

They drove another mile without speaking.

"You know, business is getting very good, and I think it's going to get even better," Jack said, "but now that I'm not consumed with fear over how I'm going to pay the bills at the end of the month, I'm looking around and realizing that other than my sons, my business, and my home, there's not much going on in my life."

"Sounds like a lot to me. What else is there?"

"A woman would be nice."

"Easy to say, but the truth is, you're only thinking about that now. For the last few years, it was the furthest thing from your mind," Whitey said.

The Yangtze churned through a dark gorge as the Prado came around the corner to a straightaway where the river and the land flattened out into a broad, sun-dappled piedmont.

"Do you have someone in mind?" Whitey asked.

Jack didn't answer.

"Chinese?" Whitey asked.

"It's probably not going to happen."

"Why do you say that?"

"Well, take the Chinese girls in the office. As far as they're concerned, we're already old men, and big and hairy too."

"I don't know; I'm not convinced age matters much here. I see a lot of Chinese girls with older *laowai* men."

"Yeah, but they're bought and paid for. There's no way they have any true feelings for the guys they're with."

"Don't be so certain, Jack. Chinese women are different. You can't tell what they're thinking, and don't forget their financial motivations. Chinese women are under pressure *laowai* women don't experience in their worst nightmares; they have their parents and even grandparents to think about, and no brothers or sisters to share the load. With all that in mind, where's a girl in China going to find a guy like you?"

"I've never believed in that; besides, I don't think money's going to change anyone's true feelings."

"Money does more than you think, Jack, especially in China."

"Yeah, but in reality, if I loved someone but she was just with me for the money, life would be horrible."

"Reality is disappointing, Jack. China is better."

Chapter 50

Catch and Release

"Could you help me find the Bookworm?" Jack asked Lianhua on the telephone one day after work when he had returned to Beijing.

"The Bookworm? What is this Bookworm?"

"It's a special bookstore in Beijing for English reading audiences. I read about it in the *Wall Street Journal*. It's near Sanlitun, but I can't find it by myself."

She came to his office after work and they flagged a taxi at the circle out in front of the Poly Centre bound for Sanlitun, Lianhua directing the driver as they drove eastward. Sitting next to her in the back seat, close enough to touch her, he looked at her from the side, following her profile from the top of her head down the left side of her face to her back.

He felt good when they were physically close. He liked looking at her as she sat at her easel painting in her studio in 798, especially in the summer when she took her shoes off and curled her toes around the corner of the table. She would look up as he looked at her, smile back at him and return to her work. He loved to watch her concentrating on her work. She became oblivious to people around her—or that was the impression she gave.

"Whose writing do you like?" Lianhua asked him as they edged past the Worker's Stadium in the heavy afternoon traffic.

"Do you mean fiction? Right now, I'm reading *Playing for Thrills* by Wang Shuo."

"No, I mean Western writing."

"Ernest Hemingway. Especially his Nick Adams stories."

"Why do you like the Nick Adams stories?"

"They're about fishing," Jack said.

"Fishing? You tell me about that once. I don't like fishing," she said, wrinkling her nose and making a face.

"No, no, it's not what you think," he said. "You're probably thinking of someone pulling a big smelly carp out of the Yangtze," he said to her as she nodded her head. "This fishing is clean and wonderful, and so are the fish."

"But I don't like killing fish or animals," Lianhua said.

"I don't kill them," he answered.

"What do you do with them, then?"

"Release them."

Then he told her about fly fishing, about walking down a path in a hemlock forest among the ferns with the sun streaming through the branches like light coming through the windows of a cathedral, wading in the river, the rapids gurgling a cantata in the background, and sleeping under a purple sky filled with stars.

She sat next to him in the taxi, listening. He could practically see her pulse at her temples. As fragile as an eggshell, and as impressionable as a young colt, her dark, warm eyes took in what he said and stored it all away.

"So you release them." She thought about that some. "So much work. If you're hungry, and you catch a really big one, you must keep it, I think."

"No, the big fish are the ones you release for sure."

"Why?"

"Because they are the beautiful ones, their skin lustrous and pure and healthy; they're the best ones," he said, looking at the smooth sheen of Lianhua's face and her full lips held together as he spoke.

"But you're hungry," she protested. "Maybe it's all right if you eat it," she said, looking at him.

"Sometimes I eat the small ones."

"So the better the fish, the more chance you release it."

"Yes, except the perfect fish—the fortune fish. That one you don't let get away."

"Aha," she smiled. She had caught him. "You eat that one."

"No, you mount it and put it on a wall."

"And worship it?"

"Yes."

"It seems shame to kill the best one," she said. "But she probably get caught anyway. Worshipped on a wall better than ending up in a pan, I think."

"What gave you the idea the fish was a female?"

A few minutes later, the taxi delivered them to an alley off Sanlitun. The Bookworm was in a building a few steps down the alley, on the second floor at the top of an outdoor staircase.

They browsed through the stacks in the library section first. "So what's your favorite English novel?" Jack asked Lianhua as he appraised the books on the shelves.

"That's easy," she said. "*The Gadfly*. I read it many times."

"*The Gadfly*?"

"You don't know?" she asked, surprised.

"I don't think so."

"You must."

The lady at the sales counter looked up. "I'm sorry; I couldn't help overhearing your conversation," she said. "*The Gadfly* is much better known in China than abroad. It's a Victorian-era novel about a man named Arthur Burton, written by Ethel Lillian Voynich. She was an Irish woman who married a Russian partisan; hence the book's popularity in Communist China a few decades ago."

Jack thanked the lady as Lianhua said, "Arthur Burton is my favorite foreigner. He was a revolutionary martyr. And even though he was hideously disfigured, the heroine loved him anyway. As I would."

"You mean you admire him; you like his fortitude, his spirit."

"Yes, all that. I like loyalty. And kindness, too."

"So you could love a man like that?"

"Yes, I like those things in people. So I could love a man like that. Yes."

"A foreigner. Not a Beijing guy."

"No, I wouldn't be interested in a Beijing guy. Beijing guys think they are too cool."

"How do they get that way?"

"I don't know. They just are."

"So no Beijing guys for you; just disfigured revolutionaries."

Chapter 51

China Hand

"On my trip to Yunnan I saw an elephant," Jack said to Chad Champion over the telephone from Beijing, briefing him on Middle Kingdom's activities. "Not a real one," he continued, "just a very good deal."

"A hydroelectric project?"

"No. A silicon metal smelter. Right downstream on the Binlangjiang from our hydro project in Mangshi is the largest silicon smelter in China. It's still under construction. The owner, Mr. Tao, has run out of money. If we wanted to target him, he's a sitting duck."

"So what's the deal?"

"We could acquire a 70 percent controlling interest for $17 million, which as near as I've been able to figure is about a two-year payback, assuming construction is completed on time. We don't have to put up all the money at once—we would make progress payments as construction is completed—but we'd have to fund the first payment by the end of next month."

"Have you squeezed the seller as far as you can?"

"As far as I can without creating a resentful partner. There's a Taiwanese polysilicon manufacturer waiting in the wings with another offer. Our offer is slightly less, but Mr. Tao's leaning our way because we would take the company public and he would get some upside. The Taiwanese deal is a total buyout."

"How much do you need for the first payment?"

"$1.5 million. As you know, I can put up a small piece but it wouldn't be much. And I'm really sorry about calling with a deal that needs to be funded on such short notice."

"Don't worry about it. That's what I want you to do when you see something good. Have Elizabeth put the papers together and get them over for me to review."

"Thanks, Chad."

"No; thank you. If you see anything else like this, let me know."

The Yunnan trip also resulted in several additional hydroelectric project acquisitions for Middle Kingdom, and the company was able to close an additional round of private equity. At $500 million of assets, the company's balance sheet was as large as Catapult Energy's had been. Word about Middle Kingdom was spreading fast in the capital markets, and investment bankers were calling.

In the spring of 1995, Jack gathered Middle Kingdom's senior management team in Beijing to hear pitches from investment banking firms interested in being a managing underwriter for the company's IPO. Bankers from a half dozen firms, having skimmed through Middle Kingdom's business plan, told management they were geniuses for conceiving it, and fawned over Jack and the others to an embarrassing point. After a brief internal discussion, followed by dozens of frantic follow up e-mails and phone calls from the bankers, the Middle Kingdom team selected Merritt Partners to lead the IPO, with Morgan Joseph also named a managing underwriter for supporting Middle Kingdom when no one else would.

After the interviews, Jack met Elizabeth, in from New York, in the Executive Lounge of the Swissotel for dinner. A waitress brought them menus as Elizabeth briefed Jack on what was going on stateside. "And

Duncan Leeds keeps calling. He says you promised him in Hong Kong he could get in on the ground floor of the Middle Kingdom deal?"

"Duncan Leeds," Jack said, shaking his head. "He's the last guy I would ever invite to do that. You know, I'm trying to think of any time Duncan ever asked me to participate in one of his good deals."

"You can't, because he hasn't. Face it, Jack, he just uses you. He gets his own deals all lined up, never has any room for you, and then, when he gets cold feet, he calls you up to vet the transaction so he has a second opinion. And for whatever reason, you continue to be nice to him."

"He's all right. And I've always liked his wife."

"He's a jackass. Stop wasting time with him; we'll all be better off."

"Let me tell you something, Duncan is no fool. If he thinks enough of Middle Kingdom to keep begging to be included, we must really be on to something. And Chad just confirmed it."

"Of course we are—you know that. What did Chad say?"

"I told him about the silicon deal in Mangshi and he said he was interested. He asked for you to pull the papers together and send a package over to him."

"You know how nervous this makes me. Just when Middle Kingdom is getting its sea legs, you've got to complicate things by going off on a different tangent with a brand new transaction. And I hate being the one to have to tell you."

"You know, it's all right for you to keep the brakes on," Jack said. "I want you to do that—you know my capacity better than I do. And you're a better judge of people."

"I just think you don't appreciate that I've got to rain on the parade in order to keep this place under control."

"Look, Elizabeth, I do, but we can't save our way to heaven."

"Meaning?"

"We're not done yet, is all. A lot of people have invested money *into* China. It's another level entirely to pull off a liquidity event like an IPO, when investors can take their money *out*. Very few have done that. When we get Middle Kingdom's IPO printed, people are going to throw money at us. If we were smart, we would think about organizing a place to put it."

"Meaning?"

"Instead of doing one-off transactions like Middle Kingdom, we should create a fund, and establish a brand and identity for ourselves."

"Well, for once, you would get some recognition of what you've accomplished here."

"We've all played a role. And don't forget, Chad's already the lead investor in Middle Kingdom. If we did this silicon deal, it would be simple to execute. It's the same players; we'd use the same lawyers and the same papers, too. We've just got to get our principal investment efforts in China a little more formalized, and we'll be able to do more of these deals."

"As usual, I'm the last to know," Elizabeth said. "It sounds like you've already got this all figured out."

"You're not the last to know—you're the first, as you always are."

She softened. "So what's the downside?"

"Well, this is going to sound stupid, but I don't want to be a cynic," Jack said.

"Why? Cynicism is healthy, if you ask me."

"Look, I don't want my relationship with this country to be one-sided, to just suck the place dry. I'm putting down real roots here. I just want them to find water."

"As long as the water isn't too dirty for us, or too clean for them," Elizabeth said, folding her napkin and getting ready to get up from the table.

"Remember, the people here are fighting their history. Mao took away all their basis of morality—thanks to him, for a couple of decades there was no religion; no school; in the Cultural Revolution, many didn't even have parents."

"Other than that, it's a great country. Look Jack, don't you get it? With all the money you're making, you've got no choice. You've got to be here. So what's the fund going to be called?"

"The China Hand Fund."

"Like a China hand at the turn of the century, an old expat coming to the PRC to help international parties look after their interests? Someone who knew the country enough to be cynical but loved the people anyway?"

"Exactly, as long as you forget the old part."

"Sounds good, but remember, if you're not careful, you'll suffer the same fate as them."

"What's that?"

"Dying confused about which country is your home."

Chapter 52

Chinese Handcuffs

Jack met with Chad and organized capital commitments to the fund from Victor Capital and Davis Brothers totaling $50 million for the upcoming calendar year, and Elizabeth filed the papers for the China Hand Fund in Delaware. The fund's initial investment was the silicon smelter.

The fun started the following month.

"I guess I'm going to have to postpone that investor tour we had planned for Mangshi," Jack said to Elizabeth, looking out the window of the Graybar building at the leaves dropping in the chilly autumn air. "Mr. Tao says he's got a start-up problem, and needs more money."

"Terrific. This deal's not even a month old," she said. "Has someone told Tao he's got to make his request in writing?"

"I told him. He's been on budget so far."

"Not anymore."

"Well, it's not like it's going to do us any good to say no. It's our business; he owns only 30 percent."

"Maybe 20 percent after this. I'll bet you anything there's bad news coming, and if so, we should cram him down."

"I'll let you know when I get there."

Taking the direct flight out of JFK the next day, he laid over at the Swissotel in Beijing, went to the office the next day, met Junzi Tong, and they caught the late morning plane to Kunming. The trip was Junzi's first travel assignment working for China Hand, and Jack had hesitated before taking her. He needed a translator, but the conversation with Mr. Tao might get animated, and he had no sense of her fortitude. A scholarship student who had just graduated from Beijing University, Junzi came from the small mountainside village of Han Wang in Yunnan near Middle Kingdom's Binglangjiang project, and spoke the local dialect. That is, when she talked—Junzi was very shy. She hadn't said two words to Jack since he had hired her at the beginning of the summer.

On the trip, Junzi didn't speak at all to him. Arriving in Kunming with two hours before they could catch the next leg to Mangshi, they stopped at a newsstand so she could buy a fashion magazine. Next to the newsstand, a flower shop stocked with the fall crop of Yunnan flowers—lilies, dahlias, and birds of paradise—spread their fragrance throughout the terminal. Finding a café, they sat down for lunch. Junzi ordered a chicken dish, vegetables, three types of dumplings, noodles, and two bottles of pear juice. They had eaten on the plane, but maybe she was hungry.

The waitress went off to the kitchen to place the order, and Junzi opened her magazine and started scanning the photographs. She kept flipping through the pages, oblivious of Jack's presence, or knowing but not caring.

The food arrived. Junzi put down her magazine and busied herself with lunch. Jack watched her eat; she concentrated on her food like a heron ready to spear a fish. Without Junzi saying a word, they finished lunch, she paid the bill and they headed toward the gate for Mangshi. Junzi lagged behind, browsing in the windows of the shops; their plane was scheduled to leave in less than five minutes. Jack looked over his shoulder at her; she made no attempt to catch up. On the airport sound system, Jack heard a few bars of Train's *Drops of Jupiter*—the words about the girl tracing her way through the constellations could have been written about the girl straggling behind him.

She wasn't really *with* him—they were just heading to the same place at the same time.

In the afternoon heat, their plane dropped through the towers of white clouds floating like castles over the Burma plain and bumped onto the tarmac alongside Mangshi's orange tile-roofed airport terminal. The tropical sunshine beat down, wilting the flight attendants waiting at the bottom of the stairway holding pink parasols for the passengers as they came off the plane.

Mangshi's terminal reminded Jack of the one in Key West. The taxi drivers looked the same, standing alongside the fence separating the parking lot from the baggage area like birds on a rail, in shorts and tee shirts, talking in small groups, hoping to get a fare from the arriving flight, but if not, hanging around until the next plane flew in, no big deal.

Their driver followed the other cars raising a cloud of dust that marked the route back to Mangshi, whizzing alongside farmland dotted with Dai women bent over row crops or knee deep in water. The women stood and straightened their backs, staring at the big metal machines rocketing through their world, and then bent over to spend the rest of their life doing what they had been doing before.

They pulled into the lobby of the Hotel Mangshi. It had been almost a year since Jack had last been there. Mr. Tao stood inside the front door waiting for them. After checking in and washing up, they walked around the corner to find dinner. Mr. Tao and Junzi led the way, speaking together in low Chinese tones; Jack brought up the rear. The sidewalk was lined with towering banyan trees, their roots and runners extending like muscled brown boa constrictors, pushing up the bricks of the sidewalks and inching under the road, rendering the thoroughfare dark and gloomy.

They arrived at an open air market and sat down at a peasant restaurant in wicker chairs around a table. A young waiter brought chopsticks, sunflower seeds and peanuts. Two Dai women appeared holding trays, one with beheaded chickens and the other with live fish flopping feebly in the candlelight. Junzi approved the offerings, and the women took them back to the kitchen.

Except for them, the restaurant was deserted. Junzi and Mr. Tao attacked the peanuts and sunflower seeds while continuing their conversation in Chinese, while Jack watched some boys playing pool in a lighted alcove across the way. He tried to interest himself in their game, but it was impossible. They were terrible.

The Dai women returned in a few minutes carrying trays of dishes of hot food, and set the dinner around the table: chicken, fish, mushrooms, tarot paste with spices, celery, and *bok choi*—enough for 20, Jack figured. The only concession to Junzi's foolishly excessive ordering was the entire meal wouldn't cost more than 10 dollars. As they ate, Junzi and Mr. Tao kept speaking in Chinese. When they were full, Junzi paid their bill and they walked back to the hotel.

No one had said a word to Jack in hours, When they got back to the hotel, Jack went into the lounge, ordered a Mai Tai, downed it in two gulps, took the elevator up to his room, and went to sleep.

It was nice to be loved.

㋌ ㋌ ㋌

They got to the silicon smelter before eight the next morning. Jack told Junzi not to announce their arrival—he wanted to look around himself, see what the place was like when no one knew the *laowai* investor was on the premises.

Inside the factory, Jack could see cranes transporting slabs of cooled silicon metal to a staging area where they were dropped and broken into large chunks on the concrete floor. An army of Dai women, their faces sooty but beautiful, bright eyes shining out from underneath hats and scarves, sat on the concrete floor wielding 20-pound hammers and pounded the chunks into gravel-sized stones.

"Just thank your lucky stars you don't have to do that for a living," Jack said to Junzi as they watched the women working.

She looked at him. "I'm a professional."

"That's not written somewhere in the heavens, Junzi. I'm just saying that we're lucky to be doing what we're doing instead of what they're doing, that's all."

"But they are Yunnan peasants."

Jack looked at her. He could ask her where she came from, but that might be too unkind.

Mr. Tao appeared, and Jack and Junzi followed him to his office. As soon as the tea was poured, Jack asked Junzi to have Mr. Tao describe the start-up problems with the furnace.

"The furnace problem doesn't matter," Junzi said to Jack.

"It doesn't matter?" Jack asked. She had such an innocent expression on her face—he must have misunderstood her.

"No," she answered.

"And why is that?" Jack asked, telling himself to be patient.

Junzi looked at Jack, and seemed to hesitate as she listened to herself continue. "Mr. Tao told me yesterday evening. He's happy to be able to tell you the news—he's arranged to sell the company to Mitsubishi for a big profit," she said, glancing at Jack and from his hardening expression beginning to realize she had strayed out of bounds.

"For how much?"

Junzi translated Jack's question to Mr. Tao; they spoke in Chinese for 10 minutes; she looked sideways at Jack several times. Mr. Tao kept talking to Junzi in Chinese, as if Jack wasn't in the room.

"Mr. Tao says the deal will be good for all investors, including you," Junzi said, trying to smile with little success.

"How much, goddamn it!" Jack said, raising his voice.

Junzi looked at Jack wide-eyed. Mr. Tao stopped talking.

"How much does this goddamn guy expect to get when he sells the goddamn company we've paid for with our goddamn money," Jack said. "Before I tell him how stupid he is, I'd like an answer. Please."

Junzi looked down at the table, and then lifted her head and said something to Mr. Tao. He responded, and Junzi turned back to Jack and said, "Forty million dollars," looking like she was about to cry and wincing as her answer escaped her lips.

Regretting his outburst, Jack toned it down. "Sorry, Junzi. It's not your fault. But that's not Mr. Tao's decision, and he knows it. Does he have any idea of the valuation proposed by the investors we've lined up?"

She said something to Tao again. He shook his head.

"About five times that—200 million dollars."

When she told him what Jack had said, Tao broke into a wide grin. His excitement remaining on his face, the creases on his forehead gone as his eyes widened and his ears seeming to flare off his head, Tao jumped up from his chair, held out his hands with both thumbs up, came over to where Jack sat and shook his hand. "Okay," he said. "Okay."

"Yeah. Okay, sure. You're not okay," Jack muttered. Speaking to Junzi, he said, "Come on, let's get out of here. I don't want to look at him anymore." Jack got up from the table and walked out of the room, Junzi running after him.

After a silent ride from the factory back through town, as they pulled up at the Hotel Mangshi and Jack opened his door to get out, Junzi ran around from her side. "Mr. Davis, I think I must speak to you."

"It's all right, Junzi. I'm sorry I lost my temper back there. That's not fair to you; it's your first assignment. I should have known better."

"My grandmother was a peasant."

Jack stood in the lobby entrance of the hotel, looking at the three Dai women cleaning the stone entryway to the hotel; two of them were barefoot.

"Our teachers told me not to tell anyone from outside my village that I came from a peasant family," Junzi said, looking like she was going to cry.

"I'm sorry," Jack said, putting his hand on her shoulder as she looked away. "Really. I shouldn't have said anything to you; it was none of my business. Listen, all of us come from common roots. Don't worry about it."

"That's not what I'm worried about, Mr. Davis."

"Look, you don't have to call me Mr. Davis; Jack's fine."

"It's what my professors told me about *laowai;* about you. They told me not to talk to you; they said that *laowai* were just here to make money and leave, and then the Chinese people would be left with the problems of operating the business and the country, that we shouldn't tolerate any interference."

Jack looked back at the three Dai women. Wearing hotel uniforms, they had changed spots, the two barefoot ones cleaning the glass revolving doors and the one with shoes polishing the brass handrails of the entryway.

"All right, Junzi, why are you telling me this?"

"I just can't do it, that's all. I wanted to talk to you about it at lunch yesterday, but I was trying to do what I was told. And what Mr. Tao was telling me last night was wrong."

"And why is it wrong, Junzi?" Jack asked, wanting somehow to comfort the poor girl.

"It's your money, that's all. Maybe Mr. Tao has to operate the business, and maybe he knows more than you about that, but it's your money."

"Well, Junzi, I think you've got a real future at this," Jack said, grinning as she wiped her eyes and looked at him, blinking. "Come on, let's get you some lunch; you must be starving—you haven't eaten in an hour."

㊍ ㊍ ㊍

A week later, Jack and Xu Xu flew out of Beijing on their way to Nanning to meet with Mr. Qi, a man who owned an ethanol plant near the coast at Fangchenggang.

Xu Xu was from Chengdu. Many Chinese accepted as common knowledge the notion that Chengdu was home to the country's most beautiful women, especially if they were from Chengdu themselves. With Xu Xu, Jack saw little room for argument; she was exquisite, possessing the classic doll-like facial structure prized by the Chinese, soft and flawless skin, and a wonderful figure. And having graduated from a university near Toronto, Canada, Xu Xu had a Western, compulsive sensibility about her job that Jack valued highly.

Arriving at the Nanning airport, Mr. Qi picked them up and they drove two hours southeast through the limestone hills of central Guangxi province to Fangchenggang. It promised to be a spartan evening. Since they were just staying one night and there was no hotel nearby, they would bunk in the employee dormitory on site.

The highway was straight and new, and theirs was the only car on the road. The road resembled an interstate highway, but better, its civil works fashioned from hand-hewn stone, the rockwork still whitish and clean, accented by plantings of bougainvillea and hibiscus.

Rolling through the middle of nowhere, Jack saw women in straw hats and bare feet sweeping dirt and debris off the edge of the road, as if the miles of concrete were a dirty patch of rug in their living room. A thunder storm squalled. Squadrons of gardeners, covered with dirt, retreated under the bridges to avoid the rain—perhaps they should have taken advantage of the free shower.

Along the side of the road, the large green and white directional signage looked similar to counterparts in the United States, except for the instructions: "Don't Drive Tiredly."

He looked over at Xu Xu next to him. Her eyes were closed; she had fallen asleep. A few minutes later, the driver pulled off the highway down an exit ramp and Xu Xu woke up. She groaned. "I feel so bad about where we're staying," she said to Jack as the driver drove them through a strip-like commercial area on the outskirts of Fangchenggang.

"Don't worry about it," Jack said.

"No, I mean it; you shouldn't have to stay there," she said.

They visited the factory in the afternoon and then discussed the deal with Mr. Qi over dinner. The good peasant food—mainly vegetables and tofu with heavy spices—was served in the company cafeteria on the first floor of the dormitory where the employees and their families lived. They ate quickly. Xu Xu finished early and got up to speak to a woman in the kitchen. After accepting two shots of *baiju* from Mr. Qi, Jack was ready to call it a night and head to the cot in the corner of his room.

Xu Xu and the woman from the kitchen approached Jack, Xu Xu holding some towels and the woman carrying a plastic bucket full of steaming hot water. "Sit back down for a minute," Xu Xu said to Jack. "She's going to give you a foot massage."

"Oh, no, she doesn't have to do that."

"It will help you sleep. Besides, it's part of our job."

"Xu Xu, it's not part of your job. It's okay."

"Sit down, take off your shoes and socks, and put your feet in the water," Xu Xu said to Jack as the woman placed the bucket of water on the floor in front of Jack.

The truth was, it sounded wonderful, so Jack did what he was told and put his feet into the bucket. The water was warm and soothing. Xu Xu laid out the towels alongside the bucket. The woman knelt down, put her hands in the water and began to rub Jack's feet, then lifted each one out of the water on to the towels and started massaging the toes on his right foot.

"Jesus, that feels good."

"I told you," Xu Xu said, a satisfied look on her face as she watched the woman continue her work. "It's part of our job."

After 30 minutes, the woman was done with the foot massage. She spoke in Chinese to Xu Xu. Xu Xu responded, gave her some RMB, and turned to Jack.

"She asks if you need any additional service."

"Additional service?"

Xu Xu just looked straight at Jack, her black eyes not changing their expression.

"Oh," Jack said, starting to laugh and then catching himself before he did anything insulting. "Please tell her the foot massage was plenty for today."

水　　水　　水

The plane carrying Jack and Lee and Tommy to Xinjiang had been locked in the clouds all the way from Beijing, two thousand miles east. Sitting in a window seat, Jack looked out as a blue hole opened up in the white cumulus, and saw the sun for the first time in three hours. A minute later, the plane shot into the clear, and the Tian Shan, a huge, snow-covered mountain range, emerged beneath them from out of nowhere, as if a craggy brown and white lizard had crawled under the plane.

They lost elevation rapidly as the snowfields topping the Tian Shan rose up to meet them.

Tommy sat in an aisle seat, craning his neck to look out Jack's window at the snow. When he saw Jack looking his way, he raised his thumbs up and said, "Good skiing country."

"I'll say. All we'd need is to take two days to hike up there."

Before hiring Tommy, Jack had reviewed his resume—an under-graduate degree in accounting—and had assumed he would be another bespectacled kid looking as if he had spent the first 20 years of his life in a mushroom tent memorizing equations, and would be insulted that he had to begin his training period doubling as Jack's driver. But Tommy showed up, ready for anything, and was a handsome devil to boot, tall and athletic, with a ready smile.

The plane coasted in over the mountain range, gliding over miles of glistening snowfields and green pine forests, not a dwelling or road in sight, until it landed in Yining, a city in the high Xinjiang desert 60 miles east of Kazakhstan. Once on the ground, Jack could see that most of the Han Chinese were army personnel, and most everyone else were minorities, dominated by the Uighurs, the Turkic group that had dominated the culture of the region for centuries.

Outside of Yining's city limits, the land didn't evoke China at all, appearing more like Central California before World War II. There were very few people to be seen, a welcome prospect, and the human settlements seemed simple and primitive. Vineyards and orchards stretched along the sunny, dusty highways, framed in the distance by snow-capped mountains and cobalt skies.

The Ili He, the Yining region's major river, drained southward alongside the highway from the Borohoro Shan into Kazakhstan. Before their departure, studying a map showing the waterway and its tributaries, Jack had told Tommy to throw a few of the fly rods he had brought over from stateside into a bag; if there was time, they would see if there was any decent fishing to be done.

Harry Guo, the owner of the silicon carbide investment opportunity they were considering, was waiting for them at the site. They toured the project, spent two hours in a question and answer session, and went to dinner. On the way to the restaurant, Mr. Guo and Lee were locked in conversation, and it was only while getting out of the car that Lee said, "By the way, Jack, Harry's telling me don't forget, we're in East Turkistan. We shouldn't expect a normal Chinese meal."

"Whatever that means," Jack said.

The restaurant's interior resembled the inside of a grand nomadic tent. Poles held up a canvas ceiling; they sat on pillows and rugs, and tapestries covered the walls. A harem of Uighur girls, wearing tights and gold lame jackets, their midriffs bare, served them. After appetizers, a score of dishes followed from the kitchen, capped by a large platter carrying the charred head of a lamb.

"That poor thing was probably outside in a pasture a couple of hours ago," Jack joked with Lee.

Harry Guo leaned over to Lee, and they spoke in Chinese. "A little longer; Mr. Guo says it takes six hours to roast a spring lamb," Lee said.

"Close enough," Jack grinned. "What's he up to now?"

Mr. Guo had stood up and, holding the lamb's ear in his left hand and a knife in his right, was sawing the ear off the head. Detaching it, he gestured for Tommy to come forward.

"He's telling Tommy that if he wants to grow into a leader like you, he must learn to listen by eating the ear of the lamb."

"There's one good reason not to be young," Jack said.

The sun was high in the sky the next morning as Jack, Lee, and Tommy walked along the bank of the Ili He, up above Mr. Guo's project, back in the Borohoro Shan east of town. A light wind rustled the bulrushes along the stream. Jack walked ahead of the others, trying to determine if there were bugs coming off the water; he couldn't see any.

"I think whatever they're taking is down below the surface," Jack said, pulling a few brown and green wooly buggers out of his fly wallet.

"Aren't the worms always down there?" Lee asked. He had not fished much before.

"Here, Tommy, tie one of these on," Jack said. "Give me your rod, Lee." Jack tied a wooly bugger on Lee's rod, then his. "All right; I'd try to trail these guys right down by the logs below those light rapids," he said, pointing down the stream. "I've put small weights on your line, so watch out for snags."

Before Jack even had his fly in the water, Tommy had hooked a fish down below the logs. A minute later, Lee had one as well. Jack went to examine the fish. They weren't trout, and they weren't bass. "Boys, I have no idea what these fish are, so my vote is we throw them back," he said.

"Hey, I'm just happy to have caught one," Lee said.

Jack tweezed the flies out of their jaws and put the two fish back into the water. He would walk upstream to throw his line in; the other fish in the pool around the logs would have figured out they were there, and all the commotion would spook the fish downstream as well.

An hour later, no one had caught anything else and it was time to head to the airport.

"You know, I could come back to a place like this," Jack said, sitting on a tree stump, smoking a cigar and gazing out over the valley of the Ili He looking west toward Kazakhstan.

"It's like Chinese handcuffs, know what I'm saying?" Lee said.

"You mean those woven tubes kids put over their fingers?" Jack asked.

"That's right. The more you pull away, the tighter they hold on to you."

㊌ ㊌ ㊌

"Michael Rudd from Broad Street Capital keeps calling," Elizabeth told Jack a day later when he called in to report on the three China Hand deals he had looked at.

"About what?"

"He says he wants to be an underwriter on the Middle Kingdom IPO," Elizabeth said.

"Broad Street Capital is a tiny firm; they can't help us."

"I know that. Look, he's your friend. Do me a favor. Take his phone call next time and tell him yourself. No one can get any work done with these investment bankers calling every day."

"I'll tell him."

"One more thing. This China Hand Fund activity is already gumming up the works. Next month, you're supposed to fly to Shuozhou to look at Mr. Wu's electrode company, and take the train overnight to Baoding the next morning to look at four more businesses Ms. Cheng has lined up. We don't have any interpreters. Do you know someone in Beijing you can hire for a few days?"

Chapter 53

Midnight Train to Baoding

Mr. Wu and his driver took Jack and Lianhua from his factory to Datung.

They drove slowly at first coming out of Shuozhou because there was snow on the roads. Then the snow tapered off and they drove fast for about two hours. It was late at night and there was no traffic on the highway. A grapefruit moon hung low in the sky, bathing the snow-covered mountain ridges with a yellow-silver sheen. In the valley that held the road, the chimney stacks of the coal-fired power plants reached up to the darkest part of the night sky, issuing plumes of heat that shrouded the landscape with incendiary ash. They were on the lee side of the Heng Shan mountains. There was no warming sea air there, and it was 25 degrees below zero.

Jack sat next to Lianhua in the rear seat of the Lexus and looked at her hands clasped in her lap. They were soft and white, the skin translucent and completely smooth; her nails were polished but clear. She wore no jewelry except a thin band on her ring finger and a wispy chain bracelet on her other hand. She used no makeup. She could have been drawn by a calligrapher's brush—all dark lines, her eyebrows thin and sharp, cheekbones high and wide, body long and thin.

She stared straight ahead, watching the roadway coming at them fast. He looked at her from where he sat. Her eyes were black and doe-like and he could see into the sides of them, but no further.

They made Datung around ten o'clock. The train station was in the center of town. It was framed with blue neon and sat in a huge square.

"I'm starving," Lianhua said. "We can go in there and get some noodles."

She pointed to an all-night restaurant on the edge of the square marked by a façade of red billboards and red lanterns. She started to walk back across the square to the restaurant, and Jack followed her. She wore a long black coat that was down to her ankles. It wrapped around her tightly and made her look taller. Her long black hair was tucked into her coat and a scarf wrapped around her neck. Her face was pure white in the moonlight, her cheeks flushed and pink from the cold and her eyes and eyelashes dark and shiny. They walked fast toward the restaurant, but Mr. Wu ran after them and motioned to the car, and wouldn't let Lianhua say no.

The driver kept their luggage at the station and Mr. Wu drove them across the square to the restaurant. He parked the car and they went inside together. There were big, thick, clear plastic drapes hanging over the doorway to keep out the cold. They lifted the plastic over their heads, and pushed away the drapes and people shoving in and out.

The waitress came over to take their order.

"What would you like?" Lianhua asked Jack.

Lianhua always ordered for them when they were together. Trying to do a good job as his temporary assistant, she managed the trip money and kept the expenses and bills, too.

"I don't know. What are you going to have?" Jack said. The menu was in Chinese; there were no pictures.

"I'm thinking of getting the chicken noodles," she said.

"I'll have that too," Jack said.

Jack listened while Lianhua and Mr. Wu went back and forth about the menu with the waitress. Jack wondered if anyone in China ever just ordered the first thing they saw on the menu.

"We'll have two noodles with chicken and some cabbages and pickled cucumbers," Lianhua said to the waitress in Mandarin. Mr. Wu was a vegetarian.

"No chicken noodle. Only beef noodle." The waitress was speaking to them in broken English, as if she had decided that even Lianhua and Mr. Wu didn't look like people from Datung.

"Only beef noodles," Lianhua to Jack.

"Beef noodles are fine," Jack said.

They ate quickly, then pushed their way back out of the restaurant, down the snowy steps to Mr. Wu's car, and drove back across the square to the train station.

A station officer with a megaphone directed people pushing their way into the station, blaring through his megaphone at the hordes shoving to get through the door. Everyone needed a ticket. It was almost eleven o'clock at night.

The officer looked at Jack and Lianhua and didn't ask them for anything. Foreigners usually didn't get stopped in China, and they wouldn't stop Lianhua or Mr. Wu and the driver either. The stairs of the station and the entryway were covered with what was once a carpet, but was now a mat with the color and consistency of snowy mud. It squished as they walked over it into the station. They had to have their luggage scanned in order to get inside.

The station was full of people. Some were standing in line; others were sitting in chairs or lying down and sleeping. They carried boxes and bags tied up with rope or string. Their clothes were dirty, their faces grimy and their hair spiky and unkempt. Most of them were chattering happily. They were going home for Spring Festival.

Mr. Wu and the driver carried their bags to the VIP waiting room. It was locked. No VIPs were expected for the midnight train. Mr. Wu went and found the station manager. He unlocked the VIP room, and Jack and Lianhua went inside. There were nice leather couches and it was warmer than in the station hall. Mr. Wu and the driver waited outside.

"You said you would show me some of your poems," Lianhua said when they were inside.

Jack took his computer out of his bag, plugged it in and turned it on.

"When you read poems, remember to read slowly," Jack said. "I know you know that, but poems are only good that way."

"Aren't you going to read them to me?" Lianhua asked.

"No, you can read them. Just read them slowly."

The computer came on and Jack opened it up to one of his poems; it was not his best one but he decided to start with it because it had special value to him. Lianhua read the poem slowly. She whispered the words to herself. She wouldn't read the poem too fast anyway because she was very precise with her translation and always wanted to grasp every word. She was very good that way.

She finished the first poem, and didn't say anything. Jack decided to select another poem. He thought the second one was better.

Lianhua read the second poem, mouthing the words slowly and carefully.

"I like this one."

Jack knew she would like the second poem. It was a better one. He had written it for one of his sons at the end of his high school football career. It was less sentimental, and the words worked better, and he knew she would appreciate that more. He realized he should have read the poems to her aloud because the best part of the poetry was the way it was read, but it was too late.

The station master came in with their tickets. The cold air gusted in behind him and turned the air in the VIP room to ice. Jack packed up his computer. Mr. Wu and the driver came in from the outside, took their bags and heavy down coats they would use on the trip, and walked quickly back out the door to the train. They took the VIP exit and got to the train before the other passengers.

Lianhua took the tickets from the station master and examined them. Jack and Lianhua were in Car 9, Compartment 1. Jack's ticket cost 179 yuan because he was in a bottom bunk, which was larger; Lianhua's ticket cost 173 yuan because she was in a top bunk. Jack wanted Lianhua to take a top bunk—the higher bunks were warmer than the bottom ones.

They climbed up the stairs to the cabin of the car and entered a hallway. The floor was wood and covered with a frayed carpet. There were wooden rails to hold on to and seats that folded down off the wall of the hallway outside of each compartment door. Radiators along the baseboard hissed quietly.

The conductor pointed in the direction of Compartment 1. Jack and Lianhua walked down the hallway toward their room with Mr. Wu and the driver following them and carrying their luggage. The doors to most of the compartments were open. The rooms were filled with people talking, smoking, peeling oranges, cracking nuts, and unpacking food and clothes from their parcels and bags. They all stared at Jack as he walked by; they stared at Lianhua, too.

At Compartment 1, Lianhua slid open the door. Nobody was inside. The room's furnishings were worn but serviceable. The compartment was about nine feet square, and held two bunkbeds, one on each side of the room; the bottom bunks a little above the floor, and the top bunks high up by the ceiling. With thick mattresses, the beds were clothed with white cotton pillows and comforters over muslin sheets. Above each berth, there were hooks, hangers for clothes and webbed netting to hold toilet articles, and night reading lights. In front of the lace curtain backdrop over the window between the beds was a night stand with a carafe of water and a small vase of flowers.

Mr. Wu and the driver carried their luggage in and hoisted it onto the racks over the door of the compartment. They hung up the coats and unpacked some oranges and water they had brought.

Jack and Lianhua shook hands with Mr. Wu and the driver. They said goodbye and left.

The conductor came by and Lianhua gave the conductor their tickets.

"Could you ask her how many stops between here and Baoding, please?" Jack asked Lianhua.

She spoke to the conductor. The conductor counted her fingers on both hands and said the names of the stops in Chinese.

"Nine," said Lianhua.

"Jesus," said Jack, "how are we going to get any sleep?"

Lianhua didn't say anything, but just looked at Jack the way she did when he said something that didn't deserve a response. She took off her shoes and started to climb up into her bunk. There was a metal bracket that folded down off the wall and a handle to grab on to. She started shinnying up the bunk. Jack took her foot and guided it to the step. He wanted to lift her up but she didn't need him to. She turned on her reading light and started arranging her bed and her clothes.

Jack stood by the side of her bed and looked at Lianhua. She didn't look at him, but kept arranging her things. "I'm going to kiss you goodnight," he said. He stretched out and brushed her cheek with his lips. She looked at him, smiled slightly, and looked back down at her things.

Jack stooped down and got ready for bed. He spread out his comforter, took down one of the coats Mr. Wu had hung up, balled it up and stuffed it under his pillow and took off his shoes. He turned off the ceiling light in the room, and lay down in his clothes. He crossed his legs, folded his arms around himself, and looked out the window where the moon was waiting to follow them when the train left the station, thinking about decades ago when he had taken the "Empire Builder," a Union Pacific dome liner, from Chicago to Seattle to see his grandparents, lying in bed with his mother looking at the shooting stars flying across the American West.

Lianhua was whispering on her mobile phone. He lay in his bed listening to the murmur of the words he couldn't understand, heard the station master's loud warning to get aboard, felt the train lurch, blinked as the phosphorescent lights of the station beamed into their window once they cleared the awning over the track and then gazed out at the big country as they pushed off for Baoding, eight hours away.

Jack asked Lianhua if she was all right and she didn't say anything. She hadn't heard him, he decided.

She was still speaking on her phone. She laughed once. "My brother Jin asks if I'm naked!" she cried.

Jack thought about that. It felt good to think about things like that, even though he wasn't going to do anything about it. He felt good just thinking about it, traveling with the elegant, beautiful Chinese painter on an old train in the middle of nowhere in China, the temperature about 25 below outside and them with an all-night train ride through the mountains in front of them.

He felt as good with her as he had felt with a woman in years. He hoped he could feel this way some more, but he didn't know if he could or if she would let him. He knew it was about something in her, but guessed it was really more about something in him now too, something that let what he felt about her be enough for now. He didn't think he needed anything more now.

Jack didn't want to confuse Lianhua, but he thought he might be. He liked her, liked being with her, and talking to her, but it was more than that. She was the first Chinese woman he had thought maybe he could be in love with. He just couldn't speak to her about it. That would really ruin things. Then they would have to be serious and deal with things, and for what? What good would come of it? He didn't want anything to change. Better to have it the way it was, but he hoped he was not confusing her. He thought he had to be, though. Or maybe she wasn't confused at all, but just putting up with him, thinking maybe he could arrange another art show for her in New York.

The train rocked and clacked and picked up speed. The cold air outside streamed in under Jack's bed. It was probably 20 degrees in the room underneath his bed, but Jack was comfortable. He liked sleeping in his clothes.

Lianhua was done with her phone. Soon Jack could hear her breathing above him, her breath soft and slow. Jack closed his eyes. He couldn't sleep but he tried and he didn't mind that he couldn't.

Around one o'clock in the morning, the train stopped at a station. As it started rolling again, the door to their compartment slid open and a peasant girl entered. The peasant girl was young, short, with bushy dark black hair and dark black eyes. She wore a white jacket with a black turtleneck sweater and jeans.

She never looked at Jack. She moved quickly and deftly in the room, like she had done it a lot. She hung her jacket on a hanger, and put her toiletries in the netting over the bottom bunk opposite Jack. Then she sat down on the bunk, took off her shoes, tucked them underneath the bed and fell asleep.

Jack lay there, thinking about Lianhua. He especially liked her, just liked thinking about her, looking at her, and talking to her. That's all he wanted to do with her—it was enough. He liked to kiss her, but kissing her to say hello or goodbye, or especially good night—that was enough. He didn't know if she liked him to kiss her, or not. Maybe she just tolerated it. It could be a Chinese thing; he didn't know.

At five o'clock the peasant girl got up with no prompting. Soon afterward, the conductor opened the door and told the peasant girl something in Chinese.

Jack turned over and looked at the peasant girl. She was sitting still on her bed, her bags packed beside her, looking out the window. Jack could see the moon shining on her face and her sad black eyes. Pretty in a rough kind of way, she kept looking through the window at a single spot on the horizon, her eyes not moving, looking out at her life until the train came to a halt, and then she was up and out of the room and gone.

Jack listened to see if Lianhua was all right. He could hear her breathing. He wished he could stand up and look at her face and feel her breath and smell her, but he didn't do that because he knew she wouldn't like it. He loved looking at her face, just staring at her face. Sometimes she saw him doing that, and asked him to stop.

When it was close to seven o'clock, the conductor opened the door and asked Jack in Chinese for the tickets again. Jack didn't understand why she was doing this, because it was the same conductor who took their tickets in Datung and Lianhua had already given the conductor the tickets when they got on the train, but Jack had learned in China they kept asking for things this way, checking up on everyone, the people in charge glad to have something to do, no matter how mindless.

Jack responded by pointing up to Lianhua's bunk. Lianhua's hand emerged from under the covers with the ticket stubs, the conductor checked the stubs and kept them, and Lianhua disappeared back underneath the comforter.

"How did you sleep?" Jack said after a few minutes.

Lianhua didn't answer.

"Could you take this water bottle?" she said five minutes later.

She was up. Her hand extended a water bottle down to Jack, who took it and put it on the night table.

Ten minutes later, Jack looked up and saw Lianhua's legs sliding over the top bunk as she tried to climb down. She had on gray socks and some type of dark gray leotard. He guided her foot to the metal step and then she started to come down.

"I'm going to the washroom," Lianhua said.

Jack lay back down on his bed and turned away to give her privacy. He didn't want to see her when she had just gotten up, and he didn't want her seeing him that way, either.

She came back in less than 10 minutes. Jack was surprised; Lianhua looked radiant. Her face was luminous, and her hair was neat and even. She was smiling.

"How did you sleep?" Jack asked again.

"Fine. Okay, I guess. How about you?"

"I didn't sleep much at all," Jack said. "Did you notice the girl who was in here for a few hours?"

"I think so. I remember someone coming in and then leaving afterward. It was a girl?"

"Yes," Jack said, "a peasant girl."

They packed up their luggage and coats. They left the rest of the oranges and the water in the compartment and lugged their bags down to the end of Car 9. They stood there as other people began to congregate in the alcove of the car, waiting for Baoding, the train gliding through the brown and gray outskirts of the city, the sky still dark royal blue to the west, but giving way to pink patches of dawn eastward.

The station loomed up, the train ground to a halt, the air brakes hissed, the people pushed forward, and Jack and Lianhua climbed down the steps of the car with the others and spilled into the Baoding terminal.

Jack looked at Lianhua one last time. He wished there was some way he could keep this vision of her forever, of her face in the cold at Datung and her smile in the morning when she first awoke and came down out of her bunk and he saw her. She looked at him, saw him taking her measure, and let him this time, not turning away, smiling back at him, her being coming out of her face at him, just looking forward to doing her job that day and doing it well.

They stepped out together and were swallowed up by the mass of people getting off the train and pushing through the gate and out of the station, into the acrid, incinerator-laced air of Baoding. Lianhua took Jack's computer case in stride and started looking for their driver.

Chapter 54

Chinese Checkers

"**W**hat a strange-looking place," Lianhua said. "Why did they make the buildings like this?"

Arriving at the textile company after lunch, the car bearing Jack and Lianhua turned off the highway into a set of garish black and gold-painted iron gates, the paint chipping badly and the gates beginning to rust, and proceeded a half mile down a long promenade with buildings on either side, their façades consisting of precast concrete columns, pilasters, fret work, friezes, and fenestration composing an unnatural architectural marriage of Versailles and an auto repair hanger. Behind the vulgar concrete skin were sewing mills in which hundreds of women sweated, turning out millions of garments sold back stateside.

"This is what happens when you mix a grandiose person's hubris, a trip to Europe, and a few quoi," Jack said.

"Hubris," Lianhua said to herself.

The factory was empty. Mr. Ho, Ms. Cheng's finder contact for the day, had told them the owner had given the workers the day off. Jack knew better—no self-respecting Chinese businessman ever gave a worker the day off unless it was a government-mandated holiday, and the workers wouldn't want the day off in any event; they'd want to work and get paid.

There was no activity because the company was floundering. Looking around, Jack figured the place would go belly up by year end. Most of the textile businesses in the wealthier eastern provinces had already gone west or farther south to Cambodia and Laos where the workers were still willing to work for slave wages, which the Chinese around Baoding— only 90 miles from Beijing—would no longer tolerate.

They pulled up to the building at the end of the driveway. The most florid structure, it served as the company's headquarters. In addition to a precast roccoco façade, the building was embellished with a circular courtyard and driveway, 30 stairs leading up to the main entrance, balconies, peaked dormers, and fauve slate roof tiles. The owner himself waited for them at the top of the stairs.

Jack, Lianhua, and Mr. Ho walked up the stairs and shook hands with the great man. He didn't look Jack in the eye, but turned and looked impatiently at his attendants and managers assembled behind him, as if he was late for an appointment and wanted to turn this tedious activity over to them.

"*Ni hao.*"

"*Ni hao, ni hao, ni hao.*"

After Mr. Ho spoke to Lianhua, she turned to Jack. "This is Mr. Liu, the owner and general manager. Mr. Ho would like you to know Mr. Liu is one of the most successful entrepreneurs in Baoding."

"Mr. Liu looks very overweight, resplendent in his suit and white socks, and more than a little desperate."

Lianhua looked at Jack with a puzzled expression and hesitated. She did not understand it when he became cynical or sarcastic. Jack felt bad for her, and angry with himself—wasting his emotions on this guy was childish.

"I'm sorry; it was supposed to be funny. It just didn't come out that way. Go ahead."

Maintaining her serious, somewhat removed expression, Lianhua continued to interpret. "Mr. Liu will show us around personally. He apologizes the factory is not operating today because of his gift to his workers."

"What would he do with the money?"

"What money?"

"Sorry, I don't mean to sound short with you. It's him. I just get like this when someone treats us like fools."

"Why do you think he believes we're fools?"

"I'm going to make you a prediction."

"What's a prediction?"

"Describing what will happen in the future."

"Okay."

Now she smiled. She liked games. It was very hot as they stood there at the entrance to the grand offices, Mr. Liu sweating and mopping his brow even though it was January and grabbing a bottle of water from his attendant, Mr. Ho looking at Jack and trying to figure out if there was going to be a deal or not, his cell phone ringing nonstop. It was about two o'clock in the afternoon, and the empty courtyard was stone silent. A fly lit on the tip of Mr. Liu's nose.

"He's going to tell us he needs the money for working capital."

"What does that mean?"

"Well, first of all, it means he doesn't need the money for permanent capital—he doesn't want to expand his mills. We want to put money into a business in which things are going well enough that the owners want to expand production. But that's not what Mr. Liu wants to do, because his existing mills are in decline since his labor costs are rising. So he is either marginally profitable or losing money. And because he has been spending money like a drunken sailor on these silly buildings, he probably has run up a big loan and needs some cash to stave off the bank. So he is looking for a fool to bail him out of his mistakes—or what he will call 'working capital.'"

"What do you mean, spend money like a drunken sailor?"

"I'll tell you later. Go ahead—ask him."

Lianhua spoke to Mr. Liu, and then turned to Jack, trying not to smile. "He says he needs a small investment for working capital."

"Let's get out of here."

At the end of the long day, they drove back to Beijing, sitting next to each other in the rear seat of Mr. Ho's Mercedes, Jack looking out the window at the fields and the trees as the red ball of the sun began dropping toward the horizon of the western sky, the workers bending up and down raking hay, raking up and down, up and down, up and down.

Jack looked back at Lianhua. She was sleeping. He liked taking trips with her, sitting next to her, looking at her eyes and her face and smelling her hair. He enjoyed talking with her. She spoke so well and she could talk with him about art and literature and museums and movies and was interested in everything he told her, and she told him about books of Chinese literature he should read because she wanted him to know about the real China. He answered her questions about business and about America, and he asked her questions about China and about men and women, and as long as the subject wasn't her or them she tolerated him and answered them. He tried to make her laugh, but he wasn't funny, and they both knew it, but sometimes she laughed anyway.

He looked again at her next to him. She was still asleep, her head against the seat rocking back and forth as the Mercedes navigated the bends and curves of the highway. Her lips closed, then opened slightly, and then closed again. He wanted to touch her, just lightly for a moment, before the trip was over and she went home and he went away. He wished he didn't have to leave.

She awoke as the driver veered sharply off the highway into a gas station. Rubbing her eyes, Lianhua stretched, looked at Jack, smiled, and then looked around her at the gas station.

"How are you?" Jack asked.

"I'm all right, just sleepy," she answered. "How are you?"

"Better now."

"You always say that."

The tank filled, the driver pulled the Mercedes out of the gas station and back onto the highway, Lianhua sitting close to Jack, watching the country roll by. When they slowed to enter a tollbooth and the driver turned to fish some bills out of his wallet sitting on the console, she pulled away from him. Jack looked over at her. "Mr. Ho's driver knows people in your office," she said. "I don't want any gossip."

As they sped away from the tollbooth, Jack looked over at Lianhua, who was looking away out the opposite window. "Do you believe in platonic love?" He figured she probably wouldn't know what it was;

maybe if he didn't offend her and was ambitious enough, he would take a chance and rephrase his question.

But it appeared she understood. Her eyes got very wide. She stared hard and straight ahead, exhaling with a low sound. She turned and looked at him, her face reddening slightly.

"Yes, I think I do."

"Well, okay. So do I."

"Okay." She went back to staring at the farmland along the highway.

Chapter 55

Chinese Fire Drill

"**W**hen's the last time you played?" Alan Lim, the managing director of investment banking at Merritt Partners, asked Jack. Alan took his golf seriously.

"Too long ago to be anything but a burden, Alan," Jack said. "You guys just go ahead without me."

"Come on, Jack. We need you to round out the foursome. Besides, it's China—golf is different here."

"Like everything else."

Saturday morning, Alan, Lee, Tommy, and Jack drove in Alan's Lexus an hour north of Beijing to the Pine Valley Golf Club. Nestled at the base of the rocky foothills rising up off the Beijing plain, China's imitation of the famous U.S. golf club resembled in name only the course Jack had played with Jimmy Laurel years earlier. But if opulence and grandiosity were the measuring sticks, the brazen club in Beijing was the clear winner over the stodgy men's retreat in the New Jersey pine barrens.

As Alan drove them up to the entrance to the club from the highway, 30-foot high bronze statues of Roman charioteers whipped their steeds atop stone gates. Driving through the entrance, they passed through guards in white uniforms trimmed with gold braid holding ridiculous salutes. An army of gardeners labored along the roadway planting spring pansies. Coming alongside a fairway, Jack could see the clubhouse floating over the landscape a mile away—there was no tree larger than a bush on the entire course. On a shale-covered ridge in the distance, the Great Wall ran eastward toward the sea.

Exuding the feel of reproduced furniture, the main clubhouse was a crude copy of a French chateau, its pillared portico sheltering a trio of attendants awaiting Alan's Lexus as it rolled up the graveled drive.

Assigned lockers, they changed into their golf clothes, and then headed for the pro shop, their golf cleats squishing along the hallway. At the pro shop, a contingent of young Chinese girls waited for them— caddies. Jack couldn't remember ever playing golf with a female caddy. The girls wore uniforms, tan pants, and red and yellow checkered blouses and plantation hats with long, exaggerated bills to shield the sun, the kind Jack had seen in the old pictures of Chinese women working on the pineapple plantations in Hawaii.

Heading for the first hole, Tommy drove their cart, Jack rode shotgun, and their caddies stood on a metal platform affixed to the rear of the cart.

"So, Tommy, how's life? Have you made a mistake and gotten married while I've been stateside?"

"No, no, not going to do that anytime soon, boss. Life's okay. Working hard on the appraisals for our latest hydroelectric acquisitions. We should have them finished soon."

"Ms. Cheng running you ragged?"

"Yeah. She went with us to the site last week—we had to work through the weekend."

"Does she have you guys sleeping two to a room?"

"Yeah, but it's okay. I don't mind."

Jack always played golf well when it didn't matter, and his first drive proved no exception. "Gushot," his caddy said, holding her hand along her visor to shield the morning sun, following Jack's ball as it rose through the wind toward the hole.

At the next hole, he heard it again. "Gushot."

"Tommy, what's she saying?" Jack asked. "Is she speaking to me in Chinese?"

"When?

"Just then."

"She's just saying 'Good shot,' I think."

"Okay. Hey Tommy, you know what's the best thing about golf in China?"

"Female caddies?" Tommy said.

"No one keeps score."

㧍   㧍   㧍

When they came off the course, Gushot gave Jack a card with her name and a number on it. Thinking she was letting him know he could call her, he turned to Alan. "Hey Alan, how do we tip the caddies?" There was no way he was going to call her, but at least he could give her some money.

"Don't worry about it Jack; we'll handle that," Alan said.

"Well, Gushot was terrific, so please do me a favor and take care of her."

"You may see her again before the end of the day."

At the door of the locker room, attendants were waiting with towels. As one cleaned and polished his golf shoes and put them in a new equipment bag, Jack got undressed and took a shower. Coming out of the shower in a robe, Alan was waiting for him.

"Foot massage or regular?"

"We get a massage?"

"This is China, Jack."

Jack put on a robe and followed Alan down the hallway from the locker room to the spa. Gushot, her caddy togs traded for a pajama-like outfit, stood waiting for them with a group of other girls.

"Gushot's a masseuse?" Jack said, turning to Alan.

"Part of her job. She gave you her card, right?"

"Yeah, she gave me some plastic card with her name on it; I thought she wanted me to call her."

Alan laughed out loud. "Well, that's between you two, but the idea is if you like the caddy, you can select her for your massage."

"A proper adaptation of China's 'additional service' concept."

"Something like that."

The spa room contained two massage tables arranged side by side. New Age music echoed through the stone-tiled space; *xiao* flutes trilled, and then a gong sounded and deep voices began to chant.

"So what kind of massage are we getting?" Jack asked Alan.

"The full treatment; I've got a few things I'd like to go over with you."

Gushot seated Jack and Alan, and she and the masseuse Alan had chosen lifted their feet into buckets of warm water, served them ginger tea, and began massaging their feet.

"It's about Middle Kingdom's valuation, Jack," Alan said, sipping his ginger tea. "As you know, when you're in Hong Kong next week, Angelina Chen, Merritt's senior analyst, will give us her final word on what Middle Kingdom is worth in order to launch the IPO."

Jack was listening to the music, trying to determine what type of instruments were playing. He sipped some ginger tea, then took some more, surprised something hot could taste so good after eighteen holes of golf. Gushot kneaded the ball of his left heel with her thumbs.

"Alan, we've beaten this topic to death. Asian hydroelectric companies are trading around 20 times EBITDA. So give us a fair discount—say 17 times—and we've got a billion-dollar company. We do a qualified IPO at $15 a share, and you and I have a deal."

Alan cleared his throat. "I'd do that tomorrow if I could, but I'm not the analyst—Angelina is. You realize, if the IPO valuation doesn't exceed $1 billion, the preferred shareholders get the whole company— you and the other common holders are wiped out."

"I'm painfully aware of that, as you might imagine."

"We just don't want you to worry, Jack. We'll take care of the senior management."

"What's that supposed to mean?"

"We've designed a very lucrative restricted stock program for you. Just because Merritt's preferred is going to cram down the common doesn't mean Jack Davis is going to lose out."

Gushot worked out the kinks in the toes of his left foot. "Look, Alan, how do you think I'm going to show my face to Chad Champion and the other common shareholders if Merritt crams down the common and word gets around I've received a huge stock option package from you guys?"

"Jack, Chad's a big boy."

"Alan, listen to me. No thanks."

"All I'm saying is, if there's a problem, you'll be taken care of."

"Well I've got a fail-safe solution," Jack said as Gushot began on his right foot.

"What's that?" Alan asked.

"Just tell Angelina to value us above $1 billion."

"Approve Angelina's valuation this evening, and we're on our way," Alan said to Jack, taking the telephone call in his hotel room at the Mandarin Oriental. "Merritt's Gulfstream is gassed up and waiting at Hong Kong International."

Jack hung up with Alan, ate a late lunch in the Café Causette, read the papers, and left the hotel on his way to Merritt's offices, walking through Statue Square past the HSBC lions. Waiting at the traffic light to cross Queens' Road Central, Jack watched as hoards of afternoon commuters—Chinese and foreigners, back office workers and bankers, natives and expats—rushed along in a river of humanity. In the midst of everything going on around them, shirtless workers in a construction ditch in the middle of the road raised their picks and pounded up and down on the dirt and rock, oblivious to the hubbub. The light changed, Jack crossed the road and took the escalator up to Merritt Partners' offices in Citi Centre.

On the fifteenth floor, a Merritt receptionist escorted him to the big, double mahogany door entrance to the firm's boardroom. Jack walked in, and the 30 people assembled in the room stood and began to applaud. Jack knew it was largely from a sense of relief. For the army of Middle Kingdom advisors—investment bankers, lawyers, auditors, and other specialists—it had been a long year slogging through due diligence reports, completing background checks, writing prospectuses, auditing statements, preparing SEC filings, and canvassing the market. They were ready to celebrate; close the deal, and bonuses were right around the corner.

Alan took the floor.

"All right, everyone. Attention, please. We've got some premarket-ing business, the SEC authorization call should come at eight, and then we'll hear Angelina's thoughts on valuation. Vahan, do you want to cover the premarketing issues?"

"Sure," Vahan said. Head of capital markets for Merritt, Vahan stood up and looked down the slope of his Cyrano de Bergerac–like nose at his notes. "After a month of circling the globe and meeting institutional investors on your behalf, Jack, Merritt has developed heavy interest in the Middle Kingdom IPO. The deal's in good shape, and with a little luck, might even be oversubscribed."

"What's your definition of a little luck?" Jack asked.

"Fidelity has placed a 30 percent order; we'd like to be able to fill it."

"I'm not surprised," Jack said. "This deal's right up their alley, I would think. What's the catch?"

Vahan hesitated, looked over at Alan, and plowed ahead. "Fido's usual raft of conditions: they want you to change your employment contract, invest $5 million more in the company, and they want the right to approve the CFO for the next three years."

"Forget it," Jack said. The mood in the room immediately threat-ened to lose much of its festive feel.

Vahan and Alan both sputtered in protest. "But Jack, it's Fidelity."

"I know it's Fidelity. But you guys know better than to knuckle under to them. They've been playing this game for years—with anyone who'll let them, that is. And you know the secret to dealing with them, too—just say no."

"But Jack, it's a 30 percent order."

"That's terrific for you, Vahan; your job's done. But the last thing I need is Fidelity owning a big piece of Middle Kingdom and Jamie Florence over there making my life miserable. No thanks."

"But Jack."

"No."

Crystal, Alan's associate, barged into the room. "The SEC just called. We're good to go."

The electricity in the crowd returned. Alan and Vahan huddled in a corner, sorting out the Fidelity conundrum. Behind a bloodless pallor and a pair of wire-rimmed glasses, Angelina Chen, Merritt's senior electric power research analyst for Asia, stepped to the podium.

"After careful consideration of the data provided me, Merritt Partners' research department recommends valuing Middle Kingdom at $600 million, financing the IPO at a range of $10 to $12 per share."

The air left the boardroom as if it had been sucked out by a huge noiseless vacuum cleaner. Jack shrugged his shoulders as he looked at Alan, stood up, and without a word headed for the door.

"Jack," Alan said, running alongside him and trying to keep him from leaving, "the markets are on a downhill slide anyway. Let's wait to see what the future holds; maybe things will improve."

As soon as Angelina started speaking, Jack had known the Merritt IPO wasn't happening. "I doubt she's going to change her thinking anytime soon," Jack said over his shoulder to Alan as he kept walking, breasting the double doors of the boardroom and stepping into the elevator. Arguing with analysts was as useless as trying to win disputes with auditors or policemen.

Jack emerged from the Citi Centre onto Garden Street, unsure of everything, from what time it was to the future of Middle Kingdom. As the breeze off the harbor flushed out the heavy air hanging over Central, he looked around, trying to get his bearings.

The workday's purposeful commuters had given way to young couples strolling along the tramways bound for the restaurants and clubs of the new IFC. The girls all looked the same: Victorian-looking booted high heels, thin rectangular black glasses, and bleached jeans. Compared to Lianhua, wannabes. And maybe that's all Middle Kingdom would be, too.

Chapter 56

A Walk on the Wild Side

Receiving Alan Lim's resignation by e-mail, Jack scanned the language: "We at Merritt Partners ... regret the conclusion of our analyst ... must abide by her independent decision ... advise Middle Kingdom to wait until market conditions improve...."

Market conditions. To hell with market conditions. It wasn't about market conditions; it was about Merritt's senior analyst valuing Middle Kingdom cheap so the firm's salesmen could blow the stock out. Meanwhile, Jack and his shareholders were expected to forfeit millions.

"Hey Elizabeth, did you get this Merritt e-mail?"

"Yes, I'm holding my nose," Elizabeth answered from down the hall.

"I'll forward it to the others. Let's have a conference call with the board an hour from now."

㊌　㊌　㊌

"What are we going to do?" Dennis Galileo started things off.

"Look, just because a Merritt Partners analyst says we're only worth $12 a share doesn't mean it's true," Jack said. "If we can get in front

507

of people and tell our story, I still believe enough of them will invest so that we can get a deal done at $15."

"So what are you saying we do?" Richard Abderman asked. "We can't go to the other bulge bracket firms. With Merritt folding, word's already all over the Street. We're damaged goods. We've got to persuade Merritt to change their minds."

"That's not going to happen," Jack said. "Our only chance is to take matters into our own hands."

"Impossible," Richard said. The rest of the board remained quiet, meaning they agreed with him.

"I did it once before," Jack said.

"When?" Richard asked.

"New Land Power," Jack said, superstitiously wondering if invoking his life's low point would jinx him. "Remember?"

Richard didn't speak right away; he remembered, all right. "Which firms would you use this time?"

"No-name firms," Jack said.

"For instance?" Richard asked.

"Morgan Joseph and Broad Street Capital, for starters," Jack said. "My guess is they can get a syndicate formed. Right, Dennis?"

"Watch who you're calling a no-name firm. And the truth is, I don't know," Dennis said. "We'll try our best, Jack, you know that. But I don't know. Why do you say Broad Street?"

"Michael Rudd has been all over me to play a role in our IPO," Jack said. "Now we'll see what he's made of."

❀ ❀ ❀

"Hey, buddy," Michael Rudd said when he picked up Jack's phone call. "What's going on?"

"We're not going to use Merritt Partners for the Middle Kingdom IPO," Jack said to him. "I thought you might want to get involved."

"Are you kidding? What do I have to do?"

"Nothing. Consider this phone call your formal invitation," Jack said.

"All right, but who's going to be the lead underwriter?" Rudd asked.

"What if I said you?"

When Dennis Galileo brought Michael Rudd to Beijing for the first time for Middle Kingdom's IPO due diligence sessions, Lee figured the best way to get him on board was a karaoke evening.

But this time they didn't select the Regal, nor were the girls from the office invited. Outside and inside, Le Club looked just like the Regal—the building was similarly sheathed in black-tinted glass, a group of Amazon geishas guarded the entrance, and after walking down an identical smoky corridor, the room they entered look just like the one they occupied at the Regal. The difference was the girls.

As soon as Jack and the others sat down, an Amazon geisha walked in leading a line of beautiful Asian girls across the singing pit as if they were participants in a police station lineup. The Amazon geisha spoke in Chinese to Lee, and Lee looked over at Jack.

"Jack, you go first."

"What are you talking about?"

"Just pick one, and then Dennis and Mike can do the same."

"No, no, I'm not going to do that," he muttered.

"Come on, Jack, you're going to embarrass these poor girls," said Dennis. "Just pick one; it's not like you have to marry her."

Dennis was right; Jack's reticence was getting the girls in the lineup nervous. They were dressed in yellow, but otherwise, there was no difference between them and the Amazon geishas. All tall and thin, with long black hair, they were beautiful, and made up like rock stars. The tallest one, standing in the middle of the pack, stared back at him.

"All right. In the interest of not ruining anyone's evening, I'll take the tall one in the middle," Jack said, laughing at Lee's gleeful expression.

Lee spoke to the Amazon geisha running the auction. He turned back to Jack. "Congratulations. Her name is Helen."

As Helen got her instructions from her handler, she stepped out of the line, came over to where Jack sat in the singing pit and sat down next to him.

"Hi, American guy," she said, holding out her hand. "I Helen. What your name?"

"I'm Jack," he said, shaking her hand. "How did you get the name Helen?"

"Someone tell me I look like Greek lady with same name," she said.

"Helen of Troy; Agamemnon's wife; Paris's lover. The woman that started the war of the ancient worlds," Jack said as he looked at her.

She smiled blankly. "You know Helen?"

"Yes. She looks just like you."

Helen seemed happy with this information, and as everyone else paired up, busied herself with her responsibilities. She asked Jack if he wanted something to eat, and when he said no, took off his shoes, got him a bourbon and soda, and a Cuban cigar. Then she asked him what songs he wanted to sing, and punched the selections into the English title computer.

Over the din in their room, as if blasted out of a foghorn, a voice blared in the next room, sounding like someone on a public address system: "The 8:30 express train to Tianjin is delayed due to technical difficulties. Please stand by for more announcements."

"What the hell was that?" Jack asked Lee.

Lee wore his conspiratorial smile. "What happens in China stays in China," he winked.

"Seriously," Jack said. "It sounded like there's a train station next door."

"That's the idea. The club gives the guys a cue, and they all dial up their wives and tell them they'll be late. A public service announcement, courtesy of Le Club." Laughing, Lee picked up the microphone and began singing *Sailing*.

Helen turned to Jack. "Me like you," she said, pointing first at herself with her thumb and then poking him in the chest with her forefinger. "But just friends. Okay?"

"Sure, Helen. Don't worry about it."

"Me worry. I like friends; no boyfriends."

"It's okay, Helen, I promise. We'll just have a good time tonight," Jack said, laughing as he watched Dennis and Mike Rudd sing Creedence Clearwater Revival's *Born on the Bayou*.

"I have secret." She had a big smile on her face.

"A secret? What's your secret?"

"This not my real job."

"No kidding. What's your real job?"

"I flight attendant. China Eastern." She raised her forefinger to her lips. "Secret. I lose job."

"Sure. You're just doing this on the side. How come?"

Helen looked at Jack with a quizzical expression on her face.

"Why two jobs?" Jack asked, holding up two fingers as the din of the room washed over them.

Her eyes opened wide and she smiled slowly as if he was asking her why the sky was blue. "Money," she said, rubbing her fingers together in front of him.

Jack sang a few songs, and had another bourbon and soda. The bourbon tasted good with the Cuban cigar. He watched his friends sing and laugh and thought about how the night felt good, like the old days. Except it wasn't the old days. The old days had ended in a crevice, but he had survived them and climbed out. He was in China now, business was good, and the future looked even better. He had a third drink. He liked Helen, the beautiful, full-figured Amazon geisha holding his arm as she sat next to him. She was nice. But that's all she would ever be.

He downed another drink.

When Dennis pleaded with Jack to sing *MacArthur Park,* he took the microphone and stood up shakily. He shouldn't have had so much bourbon. Helen held him up as he finished the last bars of the song.

The last thing Jack remembered was the tracks from Lou Reed's *A Walk on the Wild Side.* He loved the song, and tried to stand and join in the chorus, but his friends had other ideas.

He woke up at the Swissotel a few hours later. He was in his shorts, sprawled on an angle across the bed. Still in her yellow sheath dress with her shoes off, Helen was curled up on the upper corner of the bed. The nightstand light backlit her face. She looked worried. She reached over and rubbed the hair on his chest. "I like," she said.

"That's hard to believe."

"I like you."

"I like you too, Helen. But you're too nice to be here. How did you get in?"

She pinched her face in incomprehension and looked at Jack.

"Okay, let me put it this way. Me no kiss you, okay? Go to sleep."

She looked at him and as she comprehended what he was saying, a big soft smile came across her face.

"Me kiss you one time."

She kissed him, then went to the bathroom and returned with a warm wash cloth. She swabbed his forehead and behind his neck and ears. She rubbed down his back and arms. When she was done, she rolled Jack on his back, pulled his legs around parallel with the bed and covered him under the sheets. Putting on her shoes and coat, she came to the nightstand by his head and wrote something on the notepad.

"Telephone number. You call me?"

"Sure."

She leaned over him, the smell of her filling the air, kissed his cheek, and left.

Later that night, he awoke and fished Lianhua's telephone number out of his wallet. He would call and ask her about Lijiang. He should have done it a long time ago.

Chapter 57

One Rainy Night in Lijiang

The next day, he awoke late, called Lianhua and met her at the Starbucks around the corner from Tsinghua University where she taught painting.

"Look, this month has been complicated with the preparations for the IPO and everything else," Jack said to her when they found a seat, "and I'm heading stateside tomorrow. I won't be back for the better part of a month, and when I'm back, work will begin all over again. So I'm planning to take a few days off next time. I was thinking about going to Lijiang. I'd like to do some fishing, and if I feel too guilty about neglecting business I could go look at a few hydroelectric sites nearby. I'd like you to go with me. We could stay in a little inn somewhere. Two rooms, of course."

He took a deep breath.

Lianhua looked at him carefully, her flat black eyes soft like a kind animal's. She didn't speak for several moments. "Who else would come?"

What more could he have said? He had stated his case clearly. He wanted to take her away, to go on a trip with her, just the two of them. She probably didn't understand; probably thought he was merely discussing next month's business plans. He had taken a shot and failed; now when he explained the details, she would surely say no.

"No one. It would just be you and me."

She looked at him, and then looked away out the window at the lines of traffic idling at the red light on Tsinghua West. Then she looked back at him, her eyes steadying on his. "Okay." She nodded her head up and down slowly, then turned and looked out the window again.

㊌   ㊌   ㊌

Jack called the Leisure House, a small, provincial inn for Chinese tourists in Lijiang, and organized two rooms. The inn was owned by Tina Chen and her family, people Jack had met when he had first arrived in northern Yunnan to look at hydroelectric sites. There were no foreigners at the Leisure House; they didn't know about it since it wasn't in the English guidebooks, and didn't accept credit cards. Jack wouldn't stay in provincial inns in the eastern part of the Mainland but preferred them in China's western countryside, where the people were ethnic minorities and things were clean and the food was good.

He reserved a room with a loft bedroom off the courtyard for himself and a room for Lianhua on the floor above him with a window and a balcony so she could look out over the city. Tina would send her brother to pick them up at the airport, and he would double as Jack's fishing guide when he went fishing for *zunyu* in the hills above the city.

On his trip to China the following month, after finishing all his business two days early, he and Lianhua left Beijing on a Thursday morning, connected through Kunming, and touched down in Lijiang in the early evening. Tina's brother, instructing them to "Just call me Chen," was waiting for them in a tiny van.

As they chugged up the highway toward Lijiang an hour away, Jack looked out at the green hills of northern Yunnan. The mountains to the east were low and sloping, while the ridgeline to the west was sharp and pointed with jagged peaks. Up ahead the seven snow-covered crags of Jade Dragon Mountain poked through the fog. A thin layer of clouds hung low over the far end of the valley, shrouding Lijiang's Bethlehem-like rooftops and misting a quiet rain on its cobblestone streets.

The two passengers looked out the window as the van crossed the darkening plain, the squeaking noise of the windshield wipers the only break in the silence. He didn't care that it was spring and out of season in Lijiang, or that it was raining. It rained a lot in Lijiang. He liked how the rain washed down the city and kept it clean and filled its streams with clear, cold water.

Entering the back streets of town, Chen's van passed through the gates to the old part of the city and turned up a long narrow alleyway lit with red lanterns. The alleyway ran between high stone and terra cotta walls, and was punctured at irregular intervals with wooden gates and doorways above stone stairs set back from the thoroughfare.

The rain was picking up as they arrived at the gate to the Leisure House. Built as a quadrangle house centuries earlier, the inn's gate was marked by a wide set of wooden doors studded with brass clasps, gate cymbals, and hinges. Drum stones decorated the base of the gate's stone stairway.

Chen opened the door and showed them in. The wings of the house faced a central courtyard area. On the right and straight ahead were two-story buildings containing larger rooms on the ground floor and balcony rooms above, and to the left was a manger-like wing for the Chen family. In the cobblestoned courtyard, a small fountain dribbled water into a pond filled with lotus flowers, with tables, chairs, and umbrellas scattered around.

Two old men played Chinese instruments, the soft notes wafting across the courtyard. Two cats wrestled with each other on the edge of the pond, guests speaking in Chinese watching them as if they were paid entertainment. There were no *laowai*.

Tina greeted them at her reception desk, and spoke to Lianhua in Chinese while she prepared their paperwork. Finished with their arrangements a few minutes later, Tiny dispatched Chen to take their luggage to their rooms and led them to some patio chairs, poured them puer tea and said goodnight. Behind the sounds of the Chinese music, the fountain gurgled quietly and the rain beat a faint staccato on their umbrella. After she finished her tea, Lianhua excused herself to get ready for dinner.

㊣   ㊣   ㊣

Jack entered his room off the courtyard. It was very clean. A large vase of pink lilies sat on a table in the middle of the room, filling the air with fragrance. The first floor was a sitting room containing the table and two chairs and a futon that served as a sofa, with two floor-to-ceiling doors of wooden screen carvings and lace curtains facing the courtyard. A narrow, ladder-like wooden stairway in one corner of the room curled upstairs to a loft bedroom providing a large window that opened out over the courtyard.

Jack took off his jacket, lay down on the couch and looked up at the oiled wood of the ancient, roughhewn ceiling as he listened to the Lijiang rain drumming softly on the roof tiles.

He thought hard about what he needed to do. He couldn't crowd her—he wouldn't ask her the types of questions that would make her feel cornered. He shouldn't say anything about the two of them. And he couldn't ever let himself think maybe she cared for him, just a little, or fool himself into thinking he could hold her or kiss her, let alone anything else. He had to be really careful when he was feeling good, especially when he had several drinks, when he would look at her and realize how beautiful she was and want her so much.

He had no idea how he was going to do it, but he had to try.

㊣   ㊣   ㊣

Lianhua called to him across the courtyard. She was hungry and wanted to go to dinner.

They closed the gate behind them, turned left down the darkening lane and headed toward the center of Lijiang, following the streams and moving toward the lights and the noise of the central square. Jack looked up at the sky. It had stopped raining and the clouds had grown less ominous. He had worried the rain of the late afternoon would continue and wash away their evening. He wanted everything to be perfect but he knew he had to be careful; when he was anxious that way, small provocations would set him off and he would ruin things. He breathed deep and often, willing the evening to go its own way.

The lane led them to a set of tall stone steps intersecting a larger cobblestone thoroughfare lit by red lanterns and more people. Jack and Lianhua turned left and began looking for a restaurant. She had said she was hungry, but that didn't prevent her from detouring into several clothing shops along the way. Finally she pronounced herself famished and surprised him, saying she wanted Western food.

They came upon an Italian restaurant at the intersection of the lane with a stream running under an arched stone bridge. Inside, the dining room was clean and simple. A waitress seated them at a rustic table with wooden chairs. From where they sat, he could look out over the water as it ran under the bridge. Jack looked down where the streambed was illuminated by the light from the restaurant, and saw long, lime green grasses trailing in the clear water. Trout could live in a stream like that; he was certain of it. Lianhua ordered for both of them, selecting lamb chops for him, a vegetable omelet for her, together with a large dish of green vegetables, what she termed "staples"—noodles and potatoes—and a bottle of Italian red wine.

In the next hour, he had his longest conversation yet with Lianhua. He was sitting across from her, Western style, and could watch her as she spoke. He avoided speaking about personal things or about them, so when she did, it surprised him.

"I told my boyfriend about you," she said.

"You did? What did you say?"

"I told him I was coming here with you. He was unhappy. He said all rich *laowai* want Chinese girlfriends."

"But I got the impression he was a *laowai*, too. He's French, right?"

"Yes; French *laowai*."

"You told me he is a small boyfriend."

"Yes."

"Does that mean he's short?" Jack tried to laugh.

Lianhua shrugged. "I only see him once each year."

"Why is that?"

"I must paint every day, and he doesn't like my painting."

"How could someone not like your painting?"

Lianhua shrugged. "That's what he say. Maybe he doesn't like the rest of me."

"What's not to like," Jack said, smiling.

"He knows I want to have baby."

Oh, Jesus.

After dinner, they walked back to the Leisure House. Jack took Lianhua's hand and wrapped it under his left arm. She let him for a few minutes, and then, as if it took her some time to realize what was happening and thought about it, relented, taking her hand back. The walls along the alleyway seemed to grow taller and darker, the raindrops splashing beads of cold water on his face.

When they arrived back at the Leisure House, Lianhua said good night and went up to her room.

The rain stopped. Jack came out from his room and found a seat in the courtyard. Tina brought him some tea, and when he asked, said of course he could smoke a cigar. He lit a Robusto, sipped the tea, and looked up into the indigo evening. The Southern Cross dominated the heavens, diagonally across from the moon trying to emerge in the darker eastern end of the Tibetan sky.

Above him and directly under the moon, Lianhua stepped out onto her balcony and looked over the city. A moment later, when the light went off in her room, Jack looked up again. She was still standing on the balcony, staring out into the night.

Someone was walking on the cobblestones outside his room. He rolled over and looked out, not knowing what to expect, gamely hoping it was Lianhua. But it was just the two cats, playing with a gourd-like stone half as big as them.

It was early the next morning. The sky had cleared. Not yet light, Jack could still see the moon and the last of the evening's stars hanging above the city. The air was cold and damp. He turned on the nightstand light and read in bed.

An hour later, from her window up above his room, Lianhua called him to breakfast. He took a cold shower, shaved, and put on his tan gabardine pants and fishing shirt and his boots.

Lianhua was already in the dining area across the courtyard when he arrived. The inn's standard breakfast consisted of a porcelain mug of warm soymilk, toast with jam, plain *congee,* and hard-boiled eggs; there were also other things like pickled vegetables that Jack just looked at.

Chen came into the dining room and told Jack they needed to leave to get to the river by feeding time.

"Do you think the water will be all right?" Jack asked him.

Chen grinned, holding his right hand in a fist, thumb up. "Very good, Mr. Jack. You catch *zunyu* today."

They finished breakfast a minute later, put Jack's rod case and their things into Chen's van, and drove down the lane out of Lijiang up into the Tibetan foothills.

㊌ ㊌ ㊌

Slowed to a crawl above the hills where they left the trees behind and came up into the mountains, Chen's little van chugged through the switchbacks. They had to go high up to get above the silt in the streams from the farming and the mining and the runoff. When they reached the pass, a residue of winter snow lay in dirty, pockmarked piles along the road.

The van picked up speed, the strain of the climb over. The stream was clear coming out of the pass, but maybe they were too high. The water had to be clear—not too clear, so there was something for the fish to eat—and cold, but not too cold, or the *zunyu* would stay asleep.

Around the corner, Jack saw the small lake sitting at the base of the snow-capped mountain, reeds and bulrushes providing cover in one corner, the stream falling away down the canyon to the southwest, back the way they had come. He looked sideways at Chen. Chen kept driving, looking straight ahead and not saying anything, but a minute later pulled the van off to the left onto a flat pitch of ground next to the road, turned, and looked at Jack.

"This fortune fish place," he said, grinning. They got out, and Jack assembled his rod and got into his waders. Lianhua, silent the whole ride, walked back down the road with her camera.

Jack put on his polarized sunglasses and stalked the bank of the lake, first looking for hatch coming off the surface, and after seeing none, stared into the clear water among the reeds for shapes or movement.

He walked around the corner of the lake toward where it was jammed up against the vertical wall of the mountain, watching where the freshet from the glacier spilled down the rocks to fill the lake.

As the sun poked through the early morning haze for the first time, he saw whitish bugs rising up through the mist coming off the water. He put on a dry fly, a Royal Wulff, pushed some silicon into its feathers, flipped his line up and back over his right shoulder, and after one cast dropped the fly into the food lane formed where the freshet spilled into the lake. Nothing. The fly drifted back toward Jack, the line sinking under the water.

Jack's eyes followed the yellow line down into the greenish brown water, and fixed on the school. *Zunyu.* Lots of them; at least 30 trout, 10 feet down, their dark shapes crossing over his line, gliding through the depths of the lake. He looked over at the bank; Chen stood watching him, while Lianhua was down the road, taking pictures of the mountaintop.

Jack reeled in his line, cut off the dry fly with a clip strung from his vest, opened his fly box, and tied on a beaded mayfly streamer laced with some of Ritchie's hair. He looked back out at the lake, saw a light swirl on the surface betraying the school below, clocked the line back and forth and laid it in front of the oncoming path of the fish.

A trout hit immediately. Probably the lead fish; it would be a big one. As the fish realized the thing in its mouth wasn't food and shot toward the depths, Jack set the hook. The trout took 30 yards of line out toward the middle of the lake, came back around, then ran out again and returned once more, the line going slack as the fish made a run for the reeds.

Jack reeled fast, keeping his rod tip up and the line taut, hoping to slow the fish before it could reach the safety of the bulrushes, gently pulling on the line to drag the fish toward the shoreline without losing it. When he pulled hard, the fish broke the surface. It was huge; probably 30 inches long and over a dozen pounds.

The trout got to the edge of the reeds. Jack started wading into the lake. He had no choice—if the *zunyu* and the line got tangled up in there, the fish would stay hooked and ultimately die. The water was only a few degrees above freezing, and despite his thick rubber waders,

Jack felt the shock from the cold run up his spine. He kept pulling on his line, guiding the fish toward the edge of the reeds close to the shore, where he would have a chance to get to it and save it.

The bottom of the lake was slippery and ran steeply downhill. Jack kept wading toward the reeds as the water got deeper. The big fish was right on the edge of the reed cover, caught in a clump of bulrushes 10 feet away, and thrashing in a pointless effort to escape. Frigid water streamed over the top of Jack's waders, filling them and making his legs as heavy as lead, pulling him down, and threatening to take him under. If the bottom kept dropping off, he was in trouble. On the shore, he heard Chen call to Lianhua in Chinese, and her footsteps as she came running back up the road.

As he got to the fish, the water reached his chest. Feeling his heart pounding from the freezing glacier runoff, he reeled in the rest of his line, wrapped a loop of line around his neck and let his rod drag in the lake behind him so he could take the big *zunyu* in two hands.

Holding the slippery trout as tightly as he could, he pulled the line off the reeds, turned, and with the fish offered out in front of him, moved slowly toward shore, Chen standing on the bank, a worried expression on his face, Lianhua snapping pictures through the telephoto lens of her camera. When Jack got to the shore, he lifted the fish out of the water into the air in front of him, trying to look it in the eyes. It looked away—it was Chinese. He looked up at Lianhua. She avoided his gaze and looked at the fish, quivering in the reflection of the blue sky mirrored in the water.

"Are you all right?" she asked him.

"Sure, I'll be okay," he said to her, looking over at Chen who had a worried look on his face.

"Mr. Jack, you come out of water now," he said to Jack, sliding down the gravelly bank of the lake and offering his hand to Jack. "Very cold water."

"Just a minute," Jack said, putting the fish down in the grass along the shore. "Can you take my rod?" he said to Chen, pulling the line loped around his neck out of the lake and handing it to Chen. "I've got to revive this fish."

"You won't keep it?" Lianhua said, her eyes wide and hopeful.

"Well, I should, you know," Jack said, holding the big *zunyu* in both hands and moving it backward and forward in the water, forcing oxygen into its system. "This is the fortune fish," he said. "Remember what I told you?"

"You keep her and worship her," she said to him.

"Right," he said. He was almost done; the fish was starting to revive. He didn't notice his hands were blue and shaking. "You're not supposed to let the fortune fish get away, remember?"

"Yes," she said, bowing her head.

"But I'll let her go this time. For you. Take one last picture," he said, holding the fish and pulling the fly out of the its jaw with the pliers on his vest clip. Placing her down in the deeper water, he pointed the *zunyu* out to the lake, released it, and gave it a nudge. They watched it swim numbly away from the bank, recover, flip its tail, and disappear.

㊟ ㊟ ㊟

Chen drove back down the mountain to a small lodge where Jack bathed in warm water and changed into dry clothes. They ate lunch. Afterward, Jack threw his line into the stream behind the lodge and caught several good-sized trout on wooly buggers. He kept two trout and released the others. The sun stayed high in the sky until late afternoon. Then the clouds blew in again, it rained, and by the time they got back to Lijiang the weather had returned to its state early the previous evening.

Back at their inn, Jack gave the two *zunyu* to Chen, told him one was for his family, and asked him to clean and bone the other for dinner. Jack walked down the alleyway into town and bought a bottle of Australian white wine. Tina sautéed the fish with light oil and scallions, and served it to them with thin slices of Tibetan potatoes and green beans.

Jack and Lianhua went to bed early. The next morning, after a rare deep sleep, Jack woke early again, opened the window of his room to let in the breeze, and read for several hours until Lianhua announced she was up and hungry.

For their last evening in Lijiang, Jack ordered a horse cart to take them to town. The driver selected a route through a part of

Lijiang they hadn't visited before and dropped them off in a crowded, noisy place where costumed dancers, joined by tourists, held hands and bounced in circles to a band of musicians playing local music. Veering down a crowded lane, they stumbled into a night-club area: On their right, a group of Taiwanese singers in spangled pantsuits sang *Jumping Jack Flash* to an audience of *laowai* housewives, while ahead, a four-foot, 200-pound Chinese man danced hip hop on a stage.

They slumped down at a table in the first restaurant they saw, and ate dinner surrounded by Chinese tourists squawking on their cell phones. Finishing their meal, they left to find their little horse and cart waiting for them on the edge of the bedlam. At the inn a few minutes later, Lianhua announced she was going to her room.

"Stay out here for a few minutes, can't you?" Jack asked.

"I'm tired."

"I'm sorry about dinner."

"It was nothing. I don't care."

"I do. It's our last night together. Please?"

"All right, then. But only few minutes. It's late."

It had appeared there was no one in the courtyard except the two men playing their instruments and Tina's cats, but as Jack became accustomed to the darkness, he saw Tina and Chen sitting on the porch of their office, Chen smoking a cigarette, the tip glowing when he took a drag. The fountain gurgled. A spray of light rain drummed a pattern on the umbrella over their heads. Jack wasn't sure if Chen and Tina could hear them or how much English they understood, but he didn't really care.

"This is better. Thanks for staying with me."

What she said next cut a hole in the silence of the courtyard. "I'm sorry. I really am tired. But it not that. You understand; I'm not silly little Chinese girl who spoil you. You have too many of those, maybe."

He didn't know what to say, but he actually felt good. He hadn't thought she paid any attention to those things, let alone cared. "I don't care if any of the others spoil me. But if I get them to stop, would you start?"

As Lianhua jumped up and clomped up the stairs to her room, out of the corner of his eye he could see Chen doubled over laughing.

禾 禾 禾

Chen approached Jack as soon as he had finished breakfast.

"You should see the Dongba."

"There's a Dongba here?"

"Yes. Dongba is guide to the Naxi here; the leader of Naxi church."

"A church? Here?"

"Yes, yes. Not a church like yours. I don't know where name come from."

"Maybe the European explorers."

"Maybe. Dongba priest. Give wisdom. Foreigners, too. You see. They know women," Chen said, raising his eyebrows at Jack.

"All right. Thank you."

"Tina say you go see Dongba. Take Dongba *zunyu*," he said, handing Jack the trout he had given Tina yesterday, wrapped in brown paper.

"No, no. It's for your family."

"Please. Give to Dongba. Important. Please," Chen said, nodding his head up and down as he pushed the package back into Jack's hands.

They went to see the Dongba later that morning. As Chen drove Jack and Lianhua in his van through the streets, the city was shaking off the night. Women used thatch brooms and water from the streams to scrub the cobblestone sidewalks, as children in uniform shirts and backpacks trundled down the lanes toward school.

Chen dropped them off at the Dongba's seminary cottage, a wooden, shrine-like building set along the southern end of the Black Dragon Pool, Lijiang's main spring creek that percolated up out of a deep green hole at the foot of the mountainside.

Along the front of the cottage, supplicants already stood in line, waiting for an audience with the Dongba. The wooden boards and beams of the cottage were blackened with age, and smelled dry from a hundred summers. Hibiscus bushes planted along the walls sent tendrils climbing up the building's drainpipes and over a doorway leading into a sunny courtyard where three old men sat snoozing on a bench along the wall. Dongbas. Somewhere inside, deep voices chanted, the vibrations from the sound waves pulsing through Jack's body.

When it was their turn, Jack and Lianhua stepped inside and were escorted by a man acting as a docent and interpreter to a table in an alcove where a little man stood in a long yellowed robe that dragged along the floor. On the Dongba's head sat an octagon-shaped hat with flaps, giving him the appearance of an undersized Elizabethan jester. The table and walls of the room were covered with drawings reminiscent of Egyptian hieroglyphics.

With a quizzical expression covering his wizened, brown face, the Dongba looked first at Jack, then at Lianhua, then back at Jack. Ancient and wispy, he seemed like he might float away in a strong breeze, but the moment the Dongba spoke chant-like in a deep voice, Jack forgot the man's tiny size and apparent fragility.

"The Dongba asks where you come from," the docent said in excellent English.

"I am from America; Lianhua is from China."

The docent nodded at Jack and Lianhua as he spoke to the Dongba. Lianhua fidgeted, turned her head, and looked at Jack.

The Dongba concentrated on Lianhua for a moment, and spoke to the docent. "She is not your wife, the Dongba says," said the docent.

"No."

"But you have many questions about her. She has only one for you."

Jack looked at the Dongba and the docent, and then at Lianhua, who stared back at him.

"I guess I do. I don't know what things are proper for me to ask a Dongba," said Jack."

The Dongba said something in Chinese and the docent translated. "Are you too old for this woman?"

Jack and Lianhua looked at each other; Jack laughed. Jack turned and looked at the Dongba as he spoke. "It's not like that between us. At least not yet," he said, feeling Lianhua's eyes on his head.

"For your question," the docent said turning to Lianhua, "the Dongba asks what is your blood type?"

"O," she said.

"And you?" The docent asked Jack.

"A positive."

"So he has a good blood type for you," the docent said to Lianhua after conversing with the Dongba for a moment. "And your son won't be bald. Many *laowai* are bald but this man has a full head of hair."

"Who said anything about a son?" Jack asked, turning to Lianhua who stood silently, staring back at the Dongba.

Without any prompting, the Dongba stood up at the table and began chanting. Picking up a brush, he dipped the tip in a pot of black ink and began painting strokes on a parchment. Jack was focusing on the Dongba's face as he chanted when Lianhua made a sound, exhaling loudly. Jack looked over at her and then down on the table as she pointed to the drawing.

The parchment was covered with drawings of *zunyu*.

The Dongba finished the drawing and sat down. The docent spoke in Chinese to Lianhua, who took some money out of her bag and paid the Dongba. As the Dongba handed the drawing to Jack, Lianhua prodded him under the table. Remembering his instructions, he handed the Dongba the trout Tina and Chen had given him that morning.

The little man unwrapped the package, examined the fish, and said a few words in Chinese to the docent. "The Dongba asks if the *zunyu* was the best one," said the docent.

"No, it wasn't," Jack said. "The best one is still in the lake at the foot of the big mountain where I caught it." As the docent repeated Jack's words, the Dongba locked eyes with Jack for a moment. "Does the Dongba know where more of the *zunyu* live?" Jack asked the docent. "I don't know of many places with *zunyu* in China."

When the docent told the Dongba what Jack had asked, the Dongba laughed, exposing white teeth framed square with gold caps. "The *zunyu* are the Dongba's secret," the docent said, laughing softly.

The Dongba smiled at Jack for another moment, bowed his head, and then turned to Lianhua, speaking to her directly in Chinese. When he had finished speaking to her, Lianhua told Jack she would return and walked to another part of the museum, leaving Jack alone with the Dongba.

The Dongba watched her leave, and turned back to Jack. "Is she a virgin?" The docent asked on the Dongba's behalf.

Jack wanted to laugh, but managed to remain respectful. "I don't know. But it doesn't matter."

The docent and the Dongba spoke between themselves, and as the Dongba looked back at Jack, the docent asked, "Where does she live?"

"Beijing."

"Ah, a Beijing woman," the docent said, and conferred for a moment with the Dongba. "The Dongba says Beijing women marry for either love or money."

"She has money."

"Very difficult, then; you can't change her." The docent conferred again with the Dongba. "The Dongba says she is not your religion; she is Buddhist."

"That doesn't matter either."

The Dongba's small brown eyes locked on Jack, and spoke in a low tone to the docent. "She will want to have a baby," the docent told Jack.

Jack stared back at the little man in the robes, who kept looking at Jack. "You must choose," the Dongba said in Chinese, the docent translating.

"Choose what?" Jack asked, swallowing.

"Your life or hers."

Jack just stood there, looking at the Dongba and thinking about what he was hearing.

"The Dongba says it would help if you were closer to the *zunyu*," the docent said.

"Can he tell me where they are?" Jack asked the docent, who leaned over and whispered to the Dongba.

The Dongba stared back at Jack as he spoke in Chinese to the docent. "Take this drawing now; it will help you," the docent said. "The Dongba says if you can't find more *zunyu,* come back. Maybe he will show you then."

The Dongba began chanting again. The interview was over.

On the ride home, Lianhua said, "You surprise me."

"What do you mean?"

"I didn't know you want to speak to him about me."

"Sorry."

"Don't apologize. *Laowai* always apologize," she said as Chen drove them down the lane toward the inn. "What you want to know about me?" Lianhua asked.

"Only what you want to tell me."

"I tell you about the baby."

"Yes, you did."

Lianhua stared straight ahead as Chen's van bumped along the cobblestones of the narrow road.

Jack looked at her. "Is there anything else you want to know about me?"

She was quiet a minute more. Chen pulled up to a traffic light, pulled the gearshift into neutral, and lit a cigarette. He took a long drag; the end of his cigarette glowed bright orange and then dimmed. The light changed; Chen glanced back at Jack for a split second, blew a cloud of smoke skyward, and put the van in gear.

Lianhua said, "No, I don't need know more about you. I have enough."

"Me too."

As the van wobbled down the cobblestone street, Jack leaned over and kissed the side of her face; looking straight ahead, she let him. The van's tires thrummed over the stones in the lane as he held his head next to her, his lips bumping on her temple, his face buried in her hair.

He would give her whatever she wanted.

For some reason, Tim Drake's song *Which Will,* the one about which guy the girl would love, one he hadn't heard in 30 years, floated into his head as if he had heard it yesterday.

They left Lijiang late that afternoon.

Chapter 58

Tea and Oranges from China

"I've got to go back to New York tomorrow," he said to Lianhua a week later. Sitting with her in her studio at 798, the warm afternoon sun streaming through the windows, he watched her paint, mentally paging through his calendar and calculating his return date.

"So, I will see you soon, then," Lianhua said.

"Well, not that soon. I won't be back for almost a month this time."

"I think too long for you to be away from China," she said. "You like a fish that lives in a river and then goes to the sea; you must take care to return to fresh water."

"And you think China is my river?"

"Yes," she said, putting down her brush and looking at him, "I think so." She added some turpentine to the squish of dark blue on her palette and mixed it with a palette knife. "I say I see you soon because I will be in New York, too. For a show." She applied some of the paint to the dark water under the lotus flowers as he looked at her.

"You'll be in New York?"

"Yes. Ten days." She flattened the deep blue tone of the water where it got darker until the leaves seemed to float on the surface of the pond.

Jack smiled and scratched his head. "Were you going to tell me or just let me find out by walking past Gagosian's gallery again?"

"I tell you now."

He stood and looked at her as she smiled up at him. She turned back to her canvas and kept painting, floating over the scene behind her, her spirit submerging into the pond and blending into the colors of the deeper water.

"Well, I'll see you in New York, then."

"Yes," she said, her dark pupils open as she merged with her canvas, eyes crinkling for a moment in goodbye and then widened again as she reemerged into the depths of the picture.

水   水   水

"The powder room is through that door," Jack said to Lianhua, pointing to the hallway running off the Grill Room at the Harvard Club, as Dennis was talking to him at the same time. He turned to look back at Dennis across the table.

"The what?" Lianhua asked.

Jack looked back at her. "The pow ... oh, listen to me; you don't know the English they use in American suburbs, do you?"

Now she was totally confused. "The washroom," he said to her, using the commonly used Chinese term. "It's through that door. Come on, I'll show you. Be right back, Dennis."

Jack led Lianhua through the dining room, causing heads in the great hall to turn and gaze at the beautiful Chinese woman in the Oriental garb, and returned to the table a minute later.

"Hey Jack, tell me about her," Dennis said, waving at the waiter for some more iced tea.

"Nothing to tell," Jack said, looking at the expensive watch on the waiter's wrist as his salad was placed in front of him. "She's my attempt at cultural exchange, that's all," he continued with a straight face.

"Sure, Jack."

"No, really."

"Who do you think you're kidding? She's enchanting. I didn't see anyone halfway that attractive the whole time I was in China. How'd you meet her?"

"All right, Dennis. You've got me. One night in Beijing she took me down to her place near the river where I heard the boats go by and spent the night beside her, and I knew she was half crazy but that's why I wanted to be there, and then she fed me tea and oranges that came all the way from China. ..."

"Wait a minute. You were already in China."

Watching Dennis's face, rapt with attention, as he listened to the words borrowed from Leonard Cohen's *Suzanne,* Jack couldn't contain himself any longer and started laughing, stretching his hand across the table and patting his friend's shoulder.

"A stupid joke on my part, Dennis. Just words to a song. It's just a cultural exchange, I swear."

"Well, I'm going to suggest to my partners we institute the same program at Morgan Joseph. Maybe we'll start with some of those long-legged girls from the karaoke club."

Chapter 59

Knock on Wood

Jack was certain Mr. Xu didn't know how U.S. law worked or what a lawsuit was, since the legal system in China was only 15 years old and thinly applied. But the engagement agreement between Davis Brothers and Xushi Wire and Cable Corporation stipulated disputes would be settled in the United States District Court in Connecticut. And now that Xushi owned Copperwire, a U.S. entity, they had vulnerable assets in the United States as well.

Tom Flemish, Jack's attorney on the case, sent Mr. Xu several subpoenas. When they went unanswered, Flemish altered his deliveries from subpoenas to notices indicating Mr. Xu would be held in contempt and subject to fines and criminal prosecution. Meanwhile, Xushi and its attorneys kept dreaming up legal maneuvers to chew through Jack's money and motivation, and the case wound through months of depositions, interrogatories, filings, requests for papers, e-mails, and telephone logs.

Jack hadn't wavered, shelling out over half a million in legal fees. Finally, after over two years, Xushi could no longer elude the day of reckoning. A bench trial was scheduled to commence the following week in Connecticut federal court, the Honorable Peter C. Dodge presiding, who indicated he expected to clear the case off his docket before 1995 ended.

Chris Cao's e-mail arrived the following day. He and Mr. Xu planned to fly to New York to discuss a settlement. Would Jack be in the City?

Jack was in New York, but ambivalent. Davis Brothers' claims were for more than $10 million, and he was convinced they were legitimate. And he looked forward to the day when Chris Cao and Mr. Xu would be subject to the rigors of a U.S. court of law, forced to answer yes or no questions and not be able to lie. But he had already spent way too much on the case. The trial and inevitable appeals would cost another half million.

At noon, Jack peered around the dimly lit corners of the King Cole lounge in the St. Regis hotel on Fifth Avenue. He saw them in the back, in one of the last bar smoking sections anywhere in New York City.

Standing up to greet him, Mr. Xu looked more overfed than ever. Just managing to button his two buttoned seersucker sports jacket around his waist, Xu's diamond-encrusted belt buckle shone out from underneath as if it were electrified. He wore his usual alligator shoes.

Chris Cao was more understated, wearing a tweed jacket even though it was summer, and black, square-toed shoes like those worn by the day traders in the third-rate firms on Wall Street. He had actually been able to coax a moustache onto his upper lip, and had to be proud he had produced hair on his body somewhere other than the top of his head.

"J_Jack, how are you?" Chris said as he bounded up from his chair and shook Jack's hand with both of his, all he had to do to telegraph how the rest of the conversation was going to go.

Mr. Xu got up and while smiling, tried to demonstrate similar enthusiasm, shaking Jack's hand as well.

They all sat down. Jack ordered a green tea. The conversation went around in circles for a half hour, as it had to. Jack didn't mind. He had no urgent matters that day, and on the offhand chance a real settlement could be reached, would be relieved to stop paying his lawyers. And he didn't object to the company of either man. Chris Cao, well meaning if lacking backbone, was one of the more capable CFOs Jack had worked with in China, and Xu was interesting when he spoke about the wire business or his cars, if vapid otherwise.

Mr. Xu emptied half of his fancy gold package of cigarettes before Chris, detecting Xu's raise of eyebrows, steered the conversation toward the subject of the lawsuit.

"The truth is, Jack, we really like you. This lawsuit was such a mistake. All the two sides have done is pay the lawyers."

Jack kept his eyes on Chris as he spoke to show him respect, wondering as he listened if Chris had any idea how predictable his words sounded.

"You guys got a lot of bad advice," he said when Chris had finished his opener, "but worse yet, you acted on it. My firm did exactly what you asked us to do, and you still terminated us."

"Jack, the contract said we could."

"No, Chris," Jack said, shaking his head, "the contract didn't say that. Ben Jackass said you could. What you guys are missing is the law's sense of fairness. No matter what the words say, in America if someone hires me to do something and I successfully complete the task, I'm owed money. I did what I was hired to do, and Xushi Wire and Cable Corporation owes Davis Brothers over $10 million."

Chris looked sideways at Mr. Xu, turned his eyes to look somewhere over Jack's shoulder, and said, "We're prepared to settle today. Two million dollars in cash and we'll throw in another million in stock. That's a huge payday, Jack."

"Thanks for the offer, guys," Jack said as he took a last sip of his green tea and stood up from the table. "I'll think it over."

Chris scrambled to get up; so did Mr. Xu, hurrying to stub out his cigarette. Expecting to haggle Chinese style for hours, Jack's quick decision surprised them both. Maybe they would start to figure out how bad off they were.

Mr. Xu and Chris stood there numbly, smiling at Jack, not saying anything and not knowing what to do. Jack didn't like seeing people in their position, even them.

"You'll think it over, then?" Chris looked at Jack.

"Sure. Sure I will."

On the way out, Jack fished his cell phone out of his pocket, called Flemish, and told him to get ready for trial.

Chapter 60

Fortune Fish

"*Ni hao,*" Lianhua said when Jack answered his cell phone. He had been back in Beijing for two days.

"Hello, Lianhua. When did you get back from New York? Did that collector buy anything?"

"I tell you at dinner. Come to Pure Lotus; it's a Buddhist restaurant run by monks near my home."

The restaurant was decorated with antique Chinese furniture. Her hair in braids, Lianhua was already seated when he arrived, waiting for him in a tiny private room enclosed with carved wooden screens and filled by a bench seat on either side of a table adorned with a bouquet of lotus flowers.

"You like this place?" she asked.

"I love this little room," Jack said, ducking his head as he stepped through the doorway.

"It is an old piece," Lianhua said, "the bedroom chamber of a Chinese princess."

Jack raised his eyebrows as he eased into his seat. "I'm not going to tell you what I'm thinking."

"Is what you supposed to think."

Half paying attention as he picked up the menu, Jack did a double take. Usually she looked away, but not this time. "Well, they sure don't have anything like this in New York," he said slowly.

"No, but they have women there dye their hair blond and wear mink coats and diamond earrings. I think they all after you," she said. "I'm not one of those."

"You mean I can't persuade you to dye your hair blond?"

She held her hands over her face, laughed, and then looked up. "No blond fish."

Jack smiled. "I don't want a blond fish," he said. "You think you're a fish? Is that a Buddhist thing?"

"Not Buddhist thing. Dongba thing. You like a fish. When I'm away from China, I like a fish too. I need to get back to my water."

"What if it's too clear?"

"What you mean?"

"My friend Ms. Cheng says Chinese people can't live if the water's too clear," Jack said. "They need to enjoy a little black art in their life—maybe something slightly criminal, like a little squeeze off the top—or like a fish in water that's too clear, they're not happy."

"I think maybe Ms. Cheng right," Lianhua said across the table. "But not just stealing. You don't understand all Ms. Cheng say; maybe words mean something else, too."

"Meaning?"

"Some Chinese like be naughty."

"What kind of naughty?"

"Naughty." Lianhua opened to the menu and began flipping through the dishes. The waiter took her order a few minutes later; she asked him to bring Jack a wine list.

"Pinot noir again?" he asked Lianhua when the waiter returned.

"Yes," she said, looking up from the table at him from her deep black eyes. "Two glasses." She smiled.

They talked, and the waiter returned with a bottle of wine and poured it. Lianhua drank hers quickly, and poured some more into her empty glass.

"Another already?"

"Yes; tonight it is very important."

"This reminds me of the first evening we spent in Hangzhou," he said, as she nodded wordlessly. "Did I surprise you on the elevator?"

"Yes," she said, looking at him calmly. She almost never looked directly at him.

"But it was all right?"

"It was like dream."

The food came—vegetables in a lotus leaf bowl, a soup made with Tibetan potatoes, and a seafood stew. She insisted on serving him.

"Thank you," he said.

"Needn't thank me, my dear," she said.

While he ate, she drank several glasses of wine.

"I want you come to my house, see my paintings," Lianhua said to him.

"I would love that. When?"

"Tonight."

They parked her red Volkswagen in a vacant space along the hutong, locked it, and walked a few steps to her doorway. Along the dark alleyway, someone was walking a dog while a couple hurried by, the woman's arms wrapped around the man's waist.

"It is simple home," Lianhua said as they came to an entrance and she unlocked the red door. Inside, a narrow hallway was lined with shoes and boots. Lianhua took off her shoes and lined them up along the wall; Jack did the same. Putting on a pair of slippers, she handed a pair to him. "I bought these for you today—see if big enough."

He looked at her, but she had turned and was already walking down the hallway to another part of the house. He put on the slippers. They fit. He never wore slippers.

He walked past the screen where Lianhua had disappeared and came into a small living room. The entire space was lined floor to ceiling with paintings: portraits of Tibetan people, old crinkly men and women, children with looks of defiance and strength on their brows, and beautiful young girls standing in holiday finery. Along one wall in front of an empty chair, an easel held an unfinished landscape of a lotus pond.

Tibetan music began playing a moment later from a room in the back of the house. As Jack started down the hall toward the music, Lianhua reappeared, walking toward him holding a candle in a bowl shaped like a lotus flower. With her free hand, she signaled Jack to follow her as she turned through a doorway covered by a thin tapestry.

He found himself standing in her bedroom. She put the candle dish on a sideboard and turned toward him, putting her hands on his shoulders and looking up at him in the candlelight. "My dear," she murmured.

He put his arms around her and held her, feeling her ribs and smelling the fragrance of her hair. She lifted up her head and began kissing him, first on his mouth and then on his neck, and back to his mouth again, and then dragged him to her bed.

"You can make love to me now, my dear. No worry. Nothing happen today."

"If I said I loved you, would it spoil things?"

He stood at her door in the chilly Beijing night.

"Buddhist way is you only say things you mean."

He started to say something more to her, but she put a finger on his lips to shush him. "My dear," she said, kissing him one last time as she gently pushed him out the doorway. He looked at her face in the moonlight, turned, and walked down the hutong toward the main road and a taxi home. Looking up at the clear night sky, he tried to find the North Star, couldn't, and then reminded himself he was on the other side of the world.

Nine thousand miles across the Pacific. It was as if crossing the sea had changed him, short-circuiting his directional compass and making China his magnet, like a seagoing trout in a foreign river, pushing upstream through the brine-filled current and filling with resolve as he neared the cold, clear water of the highlands.

He stood a long time on the corner looking for a taxi, watching the cars maneuver on the boulevard like a school of fish. He didn't understand why he hadn't been able to find many trout in China. They all got where they did the same way—he was sure of that—but something had gone wrong in China. At least where he had looked so far. But he hadn't been everywhere. Particularly the high country; they could be hiding there.

He had to find them. If he could find them, and clear water, it would be all right to stay for her.

Chapter 61

It's Enough to Make a Man Religious

Around half past two on a May afternoon, the Poly Centre started to shake.

"Jackie. Earthquake," Pete said in a low tone as he stuck his head into Jack's office.

"Jesus." The antique porcelains in Jack's cabinet rattled against the glass panes. He stood up at his desk. "*Jesus*. You're right. We've got to get everybody downstairs."

Jack and Pete walked fast but at a controlled pace down the hall into the bullpen. Some of the girls were on the phone, others were standing at the window looking down to the ground, as if to get their bearings. Xu Xu was standing by her desk, a worried look on her face.

"Xu Xu, listen to me," Jack said. "Get everyone out of here. Take the stairs down to the ground. Don't let anyone use the elevators," he said as he and Pete went down the hall, opening office doors, and rousting the remaining inhabitants.

水 水 水

With hundreds of others from the Poly Centre, they waited down on the street for about an hour. When the aftershocks came, rattling the buildings around them some more, Jack sent everyone home. No one knew the tremors had rumbled all the way across China from Yunnan, more than a thousand miles away.

They heard from Mangshi later in the afternoon. Pete called him to say a huge earthquake had hit southern Yunnan. The epicenter was northwest of Mangshi, near Middle Kingdom's Binglangjiang hydro-electric project.

The following evening Ms. Cheng called Jack about Junzi's father. Live on national television, a broadcast reporter at the school in Han Wang, the Yunnan village at the epicenter of the quake, had inter-viewed four young girls who had been pulled out of the rubble 24 hours after their school building had collapsed. When the reporter asked them how they had managed to survive, the children said Mr. Tong, their teacher, had protected them with his body, saving their lives, but costing him his.

In the week that followed, the enormity of the Mangshi earthquake became apparent to the world, as Chinese and international television featured the disaster every waking hour. Images of the carnage saturated the media: piles of rubble, grim-faced soldiers and police; husbands, wives, sons, and daughters crying over lost loved ones; and citizens tearing at tomb-like piles with their bare hands. Jack saw Mr. Tong's face everywhere, usually followed by images of Junzi, a child forced by a media desperate for good news to grow up overnight, numbly repeat-ing the virtues of her dead father, now a national hero.

Lying next to Lianhua under a down comforter, he traced his finger along the dents at the base of her back, separating the trailing strands of her hair and exulting in the smoothness of her skin. The cool air of a Beijing spring morning streamed in the bedroom window.

In the other room, Lianhua's alarm clock, featuring a DVD of Buddhists from Nepal playing animal horns, clicked on.

"My dear," she said, rolling over sideways toward him as she spoke.

"Yes?"

"Nothing, my dear. I had dream. I needed to check you really here."

"I'm here."

"My dear, I worry."

"About what? The earthquake?"

"About you, my tiger. You don't leave me. If you leave me, I cut my hair."

"I won't leave you, my dear," he said. He hadn't thought he would ever say that to a woman again.

㐀 㐀 㐀

"I adopt four girls from earthquake," Lianhua told him at dinner a few days later.

"What do you mean? Permanently?" Jack asked.

"No, no, my dear. Just for now. Their Living Buddha same as me. Parents died. My brother and I will care of them for a short time. Then they meet new parents."

"Why not you?"

"No." She shook her head, looking down at her plate. "Maybe foreigners."

"Will you go to Yunnan to see them?"

"Yes, this week."

"Maybe you'll like them when you meet them. I'll bet you could keep them if you wanted to."

She looked at him once, and then looked back down at the table. She wasn't going to talk more about it.

"Well, it's very nice of you and Jin," Jack said.

"Maybe you come to Yunnan, too?"

"I guess I should, right?"

"Yes. Many Europeans are going. You speak to your Italian friend Virginio. Maybe you make sculpture for monument."

㐀 㐀 㐀

"Virginio, I hope you can do it. The whole world needs to help," Jack said over the telephone to Virginio from the Binglangjiang project later that week.

"I remember the earthquakes in Italy," Virginio said. "Such a disaster, my God. I still have pictures in my mind."

"Sketch out some of the pictures, then. We can use them to make a sculpture. Dr. Yu knows many of the leaders here. The school where Junzi's father died wants to put up a memorial to honor the teachers who died there—there were fourteen of them."

"My God, such a disaster," Virginio said again. "My work in Verona is tired. To come to China would be fantastic."

Jack and Virginio spoke for a half hour longer, and Jack made arrangements to send Virginio tickets to Beijing the following week. Next, Jack spoke to Dr. Yu and Elizabeth. They organized a group to pay for the memorial, contributed cash, and got on the phones for more.

"Where are you right now, Richard?" Jack said when he got Richard Abderman on the telephone.

"Where else would I be on a Thursday morning at seven thirty? I'm sitting in my kitchen. Where the hell are you?"

"No, Richard, you're sitting in your kitchen on Park Avenue in New York City."

"That's right, what about it?"

"Richard, listen to me. I'm at Binglangjiang in Yunnan, where a month ago it rained concrete from the sky. They've got 80,000 confirmed dead and another 20,000 rotting under piles of rubble. We need you to send some money; everyone from Middle Kingdom is sending something."

"All right, all right. Why didn't you say so, already. Sure I'll send money. Just tell me where."

㊖   ㊖   ㊖

Jack and Lianhua rode with Junzi and Virginio in army jeeps with the government officials taking them down through the streets of the village to the school where Junzi's father had died. Along the sides of the roads, collapsed buildings lay in heaps, the smell of the thousands of dead still trapped inside wafting up in the humid Yunnan air.

Their caravan pulled up alongside a clock tower, its hands stopped at half past two, the time the quake struck.

"Why are some buildings still standing?" Jack asked Junzi.

"They will leave some of them to be part of a museum," she said. "That's my street, right over there," she said, pointing to a corner across the way. "I used to go for lunch to a store on that corner every weekend."

Jack didn't ask her to point out where the school had been.

Jack couldn't read Chinese, but the posters on every corner advertising for missing children didn't require any understanding of the language. Every time Lianhua saw one, she started to cry. Jack wouldn't let her buy the newspapers.

To pry Lianhua out of the devastation for the day, Jack took her with him when he visited the Binglangjiang hydroelectric site. A hundred miles west of Mangshi through the tea gardens and forested mountaintops of southwestern Yunnan, Binglangjiang had taken a blow from the quake—the employee dormitory had collapsed, but luckily everyone was at work or at school—but was still producing power.

Mr. Huashui, the owner of a local construction firm, stood waiting for them outside the Binglangjiang dormitory, looking like every other contractor Jack had ever done business with: beer gut covering his belt, shirt tail hanging out, and shifty eyes only willing to find Jack's for split seconds. Together with his son, a young man with a squirrel-like face whose hair cut gave him the look of a sea urchin, they discussed with Jack the repairs the building would require as Lianhua interpreted.

After finishing their conversation about the project work, Mr. Huashui and his son turned to go when Lianhua detained them, explaining in Chinese they needed a contractor to fabricate and install a sculpture in Han Wang in memory of Mr. Tong and the other teachers who had died at the school. Could they help?

Jack watched Mr. Huashui and his son as they listened impassively to Lianhua. No chance; Jack would have bet money on it. Mr. Huashui farted. Lianhua finished with her plea, Mr. Huashui looked at his son, they shrugged their shoulders and responded with a few words.

She turned to Jack, expressionless, and hesitated for a moment. "Don't act surprise; if you do, maybe he change mind."

"What do you mean, change his mind? What's he going to do?"

"He will build it. You tell him what to do."

Jack tried to remain stone-faced. "You're kidding. This guy volunteered to fabricate and install the whole thing?"

"Yes."

"How much does he want?"

"Nothing," Lianhua said. "He had relatives who died in Han Wang. Everybody did."

Chapter 62

A Chinaman's Chance

The stock market remained stalled through the first half of 1995, and then started picking up for no good reason, as if someone was pumping up the Street with hot air.

"Don't fight the tape," Jack said when Lee questioned the substance of the rally. "I think it's now or never."

They were gathered in DLA Piper's conference room in front of the speakerphone, with the other members of the Middle Kingdom board and Michael Rudd of Broad Street and Dennis and Mary Lou from Morgan Joseph on the line. "All right, let's get started," Jack said. "Mike, Mary Lou, who else can you add to the syndicate?"

"Well, it's just Broad Street and Morgan Joseph at this point," Michael said over the telephone. "But I'm confident we'll be able to line up a European firm to cover the funds over there and a clean tech specialist as well. Any contacts you have would be greatly appreciated."

"I'll put a list together. How much do you think we can raise?" Jack asked.

"You tell me," Mike replied.

㊌ ㊌ ㊌

From the table, Jack could watch Lianhua cooking in the kitchen. When he stayed with her, she always made him the same breakfast: a banana pancake with a fried egg on top, pear soup, and tea.

Down the hallway on Lianhua's DVD recorder, the Nepalese monks blew their horns. Looking outside through the window, Jack could see the red ball of the sun struggling to break free of the Beijing smog, washing a pinkish hue along the hutong. The heat from the factory chimney across the street billowed white smoke into the sky.

"My dear."

"Yes?" Lianhua answered.

"After we dedicate the sculpture next week, I must leave to do the Middle Kingdom IPO," he said.

"Oh, my dear," she said, cleaning her hands with a dishtowel and walking out of her kitchen to look at him. "How long?"

"A long time."

"How long, my dear?"

"Four weeks, I think," he said, although he really didn't know. It might be longer.

"Oh, my dear. You will get sick."

"No, no. Don't worry about me. I'll be fine."

The monks on the stereo stopped chanting. The fried eggs popped in the skillet. Lianhua stood in front of him, still cleaning her hands with the dishtowel.

"My dear, we will miss the day again."

There it was. "Well, it's not just one day, is it? There's more than one day," he said.

"No," she said. "Only one day for sure."

"We won't miss it the next time, my dear. I promise."

"It's all right. You have your family."

"No, I told you. That's all right."

"Leave me some of your clothes," she said to him.

"I think all my clothes here are clean; you washed them yesterday."

"I want to sleep with them so I smell your body." The eggs popped again in the skillet. Lianhua went back in to the kitchen.

Chapter 63

Be Careful What You Wish for

The Boeing 737 descended through the Yunnan haze. At 5,000 feet, the sky over Kunming opened up. Patches of sun dappled the clouds, telling Jack the weather for the sculpture dedication ceremony would be tolerable. He looked across the airplane cabin at his four sons. They had all been in China before, but only Fake China; this was their first trip to Yunnan.

To Yunnan to honor the dead. The "Glorious Dead." He remembered looking up at the words on the stone war memorial in Statue Square in Hong Kong, standing in the grass next to the blunt obelisk as the cars rolled politely, silently, along Harcourt Road. It was an excellent monument, the language noble as it recalled men from a bygone era.

But the words surely seemed false today. He looked at his sons sleeping in their seats. Dying wasn't glorious. Especially not for children.

They gathered in Han Wang on the hot and steamy June afternoon in the park behind the new school the government had built to replace the one that had collapsed with Junzi's father and the others inside. The elements of the sculpture stood under a group of young trees in the center of the park, covered with construction tarpaulins. Ropes attached to the tarps led skyward to Mr. Huashui's hoist that would, at Jack's signal, unveil the work.

A month earlier when Jack and Virginio had started working on the sculpture, it consisted of a single piece, a 20-foot wide oval of stainless steel with four spirits of brass gaining freedom above it. Later, the piece had evolved into an environment nestled in the park grass, with stainless cubes crashing in random piles around the oval center-piece, several of them upright so observers could sit and contemplate what had happened.

A large crowd had already assembled around tables covered with refreshments when Jack and the boys arrived. Junzi and her mother stood off to one side, talking with Nu Yu and Kitty and the rest of the Beijing staff; Jack and Dr. Yu had sprung for the cost of flying everyone out for the event since they had all worked long hours on the project.

Elizabeth, Whitey, Pete, and Bobby McDermott had flown in from stateside. So had everyone from New York who had contributed to the memorial—his brother Greg and his friend from Harvard, Sam Sheppard; Chad Champion from Victor Capital; Henry Morgan, Frank Joseph, Dennis and Mary Lou and John Pickens from Morgan Joseph; Mike Rudd from Broad Street; Jack's board member, Richard Abderman; his lawyers, Jonathan Katz, Gene Batty, and Frank Pine from DLA Piper, Darren Offset from Gusov Ofsink; Tom Flemish from Olshan, Grundman; Raymond Nu and Winnie and Maggie, his audi-tors from Ernst and Young; and Jack Morris, the financial printer Jack had used for every deal over the last 10 years—all standing under the trees in the shade, sweating in their suits.

From China, Sam Lu and David Ng from Merritt Private Equity were there, as were many of Jack's Chinese clients who had contributed to the memorial. Even Mr. Xu and Chris Cao from Xushi Wire and Cable Corporation, still locked in legal combat with Jack, showed up, Xu the only Chinese guy in a suit.

Thanks to Dr. Yu, the governor of Yunnan was there, as well as the mayor of Mangshi, the surviving government leaders of Han Wang, officers from the military's evacuation force, and a large group of friends and relatives of those from the school who had perished.

Used to monopolizing the spotlight, the government officials were overshadowed by the religious attendees. In a patterned white robe, the Dongba sat with the docent on folding chairs. Standing with Lianhua and her brother Jin were a group of Buddhist monks in red, yellow, and white robes, a few playing drums or tambourines and bells while one spoke to a Catholic priest representing the Italian consulate.

Jack brought the Dongba a glass of cold lemonade, and the ceremony got started. As an official from the school stood up to the microphone at the speaker's dais and raised his hands, people stopped talking and the monks stopped playing. The governor said a few short words and the mayor spoke, followed by a general from the army. People were getting hot and tired as Jack stepped up to the dais, introduced Virginio, thanked everyone for attending, and asked the docent if the Dongba could offer a prayer.

The docent whispered in the Dongba's ear, and the Dongba stood, eyed the centerpiece of the sculpture, walked toward it with his arms raised holding a wand and began to chant. The monks encouraged everyone to gather around the sculpture, and Jack motioned to Mr. Huashui at the hoist to unveil it. As the tarpaulins lifted and disclosed the stainless steel and bronze forms, and the gloom and dust of the Han Wang quake reflected off the metal and dissipated into the Yunnan sky, Chinese and foreigners reached instinctively for each other's hands and circled around the memorial, silently staring at the work, not knowing what to do next.

He wouldn't have done it himself, let alone picked *Sailing* as the anthem, but afterward Jack was glad someone had started singing; he was fairly certain it had been Dr. Yu. Jack heard a few flat, wobbly notes, some people started humming, and then everyone began to sing. The monks picked up the rhythm, booming their drums and shaking their tambourines. Jack didn't know the words, but most of the Chinese and a few of the foreigners did, and even people who didn't know the words managed to sing the refrain, locking hands and arms, swaying back and forth.

"God, I need a drink," Dennis said as the bus pulled up to the entrance to Kunming's Green Lake Hotel, enabling the stateside foreigners to escape the afternoon's humidity in the air-conditioned lobby lounge. "Tsingdao, please," he said to the first waitress he saw.

"Do you think I can smoke this in here?" Richard asked Jack, holding up a Macanudo as long as a baseball bat.

"This is China, Richard."

"Does that mean yes or no?"

"Of course you can. They're not politically correct here," Jack said. "Not yet, anyway."

"Speaking of not being politically correct," said Mary Lou to Jack, "if I didn't see it with my own eyes, there's no way I would believe you made that sculpture."

"I didn't make it," Jack said. "Virginio made it; I just ground some of the welds. Who told you that?"

"Virginio did," Mary Lou said.

"My dear, please tell them I didn't make the sculpture," Jack said as Lianhua walked into the lounge.

Lianhua smiled at Jack, but didn't say anything at first. "You make," she said when the silence became too painful, and then seemed shocked when Mary Lou, Dennis, and Richard hooted at Jack.

"Excuse me, guys, let me talk to Lianhua a minute here. Hey Dennis, order me a Tsingdao the next time you get one."

Jack took Lianhua to a corner of the lounge. "That was nice today, didn't you think?"

Lianhua looked down at first, then lifted her eyes to look at Jack's face. "My dear."

"What?"

"I think I know you, but maybe I don't," she said to him, looking down at the ground.

"You know me, Lianhua."

"My dear, I see you today. You have full life," Lianhua said. "You don't need me."

He had known she was thinking it, watching her as she looked at him during the ceremony. "No, my dear," he said.

"Yes. You already have your sons, your friends. I just make problem for you."

"No, no. Don't say those things."

"I take you away from them. Those people think I'm bad."

"They don't, Lianhua. They like you."

"Maybe you too nice for your own good, Jack Davis."

㊌ ㊌ ㊌

"I'm thinking I could come here, Lianhua," Jack said to her at her home in the hutong when they had returned from Yunnan to Beijing. "There's nothing left for me stateside."

She lifted her head and looked at him. "Your sons, Jack."

"I know. I've been thinking a lot about that. I'll bring them with me."

She looked at him apprehensively, and slowly shook her head back and forth. "They must be happy."

"They will be. In the long run, they'll thank me."

She looked past him in silence.

"My business is all Chinaside today," he offered.

"You can travel here for your business," she said, avoiding eye contact with him. "What about your friends?" she asked after a minute of silence.

"My friends? Really, my only day-to-day friends these days are here—the people in my office in Beijing," he said.

"They not your only friends. What about your old friends?"

"My old friends? My college roommates? My business school friends; people from the old days, from Catapult Energy and New Land? They're wrapped up in the layers of their own families, their own routines, their own lives, Lianhua. There's no room for me."

"Those people in Yunnan? They came all the way from America for you."

They did; he knew that.

"They would miss you. And you'd miss them. I know you."

That much was true. Maybe he didn't spend much time with them, but they represented a life to him. And maybe that was it. Stateside wasn't any one thing—just a life.

He wouldn't miss any one sport that much, but all of them together—that was different: baseball from April to October, then the World Series; football from Labor Day until the bowl games over the holidays and the Super Bowl in late winter; college basketball after Christmas, following Georgetown and hoping for the Final Four; and then in between, the Masters; the Indianapolis 500; the All-Star Game; the U.S. Open tennis tournament.

He had no doubt he could get by without them, but it was pointless to think about replacements. He wasn't going to get interested in Ping Pong.

He looked at Lianhua. She was watching him. "What?"

And what about the newspapers? Chinaside, the *New York Times, USA Today,* and the *Wall Street Journal* were watered down, day-late affairs; reading them felt like eating cardboard.

And the holidays that had given life a familiar, comfortable pattern: President's Day, Memorial Day, July Fourth, Labor Day, Halloween, Thanksgiving, Christmas, and New Year's. He would have to just make do, but replacing them with Dragon Boat Racing Day, or celebrating Chairman Mao's ascension October 1, didn't seem like things he could get excited about.

He wouldn't sell the farm. They'd visit from time to time. There weren't any upland birds in China, that was for sure, but just as long as he could find someplace good to fish, he'd survive.

He looked up at her. She was still staring at him.

"What?" he said again.

She had the same look on her face as the time he had tried to teach her how to fish.

She had stood in the middle of the stream, casting her line, looking good to him. He had been happy. She told him later she really didn't want to catch one. She was doing it for him, she said, but she didn't really want to catch one. He had tied on a barbless hook, so there was no way she could snag the trout accidentally—either she would have to catch the trout, or the fish really wanted the fly, or both. And she had hooked one, and when she lifted her hands in surprise, she set the hook. And then it was right there in the shallows, tugging on her line. He had been excited, looking over at her, grinning stupidly before he saw the pained expression on her face.

Jack had taken her rod, reeled the trout in, and taken it off the hook, holding it as it quivered in his hands. Looking up at her, he almost dropped the fish when he saw the look of horror on Lianhua's face. He released the trout back into the stream, watching it with Lianhua as it shot a baleful eye up toward its captors before flipping its tail and turning downriver.

"It's a life, Jack. The same as yours," she had said to him that day in her house on the hutong, looking at him before she turned away and drifted downstream in the current.

Book Six

THE LONG WALK HOME

Chapter 64

Trial and Error

"**A**ll rise," the bailiff intoned as Judge Dodge entered the courtroom from his chambers.

The United States Federal Court, District of Connecticut, was ready to resume its Wednesday afternoon session. The high-ceilinged courtroom overpowered the small group of people assembled within. Besides the judge and his staff, two lawyers representing Xushi Wire and Cable Corporation sat at the defendant's table on the left, Tom Flemish and his assistant counsel sat at the plaintiff's table on the right, and Jack, Mr. Xu, Chris Cao, and some minor witnesses sat in the benches behind the participants' railing.

"All right," Judge Dodge began. "So Mr. Cao, is it your testimony that after Mr. Davis and his firm had done everything you asked them to do, that is, successfully raised the money for your company's IPO, you believed you could simply terminate their contract and deprive them of the future compensation to which they were entitled?" asked Judge Dodge.

"Y_y_yes, Your Honor."

"Mr. Cao, let me suspend for the moment my curiosity as to your reading of the contract. The question I have for you is a simple one: What kind of person does something like that?"

As Jack sat in the courtroom watching the carnage, his antipathy for his Xushi opponents evaporated. He felt badly for them. Undergoing a brutal, embarrassing experience, they were marooned stateside in a land of true justice, far from China's Mafia-like system of conflict resolution. Together with their foppish lawyer, they were being exposed for what they were—a collection of dissembling liars saying whatever they thought was necessary to accomplish their ends. Saying, in sworn testimony, to a United States federal judge, statements like: "Your honor, those written words don't mean what they say." Jesus. It was pathetic.

Carl Richards, Esquire, Xushi Wire and Cable Corporation's defense counsel, performed criminally on his client's behalf, evidencing nothing in the way of legal skills or even basic intelligence. His appearance didn't help. Long sideburns dribbled down from his unevenly shaved head, intersecting a pair of bug-eyed glasses propped at a lurching tilt across his face. Shod with a pair of tan pointy shoes affixed with metal gizmos, his midsection bisected by a fat azure tie extending only halfway down his pot belly, his clothing seemed more appropriate for a barker selling used cars.

Richards's courtroom demeanor was cartoonish. With herky-jerky motions, he abandoned his podium at unpredictable intervals to hop around the room, adding the phrase "Is that correct?" as punctuation to the end of every statement, whether directed at defendants or plaintiffs.

Xu and Cao seemed like they too had cooperated with a costume designer from a grade B movie. Jack almost didn't recognize Chris Cao. He had parted his hair in the middle of his head and flattened it across his scalp, appearing Mandarin-like as he spouted long-winded, wishful answers to the judge. Mr. Xu was sartorially splendid in a Tommy Hilfiger suit for which he probably wasted $500, accented with a pair of whitish gray socks, all the better to show off his neon-like crocodile shoes.

For most of the day, the judge grilled Chris Cao. Jack cringed; it was difficult to watch. At three o'clock, Judge Dodge asked both counsel to approach the bench. Even though Jack was sitting 30 feet away, the courtroom was quiet; he could hear the judge's words clearly.

"Mr. Richards, I must advise you that your case is not going well. You may wish to consider using the court's arbitration services. Otherwise, at the rate things are proceeding, I don't believe your client is going to appreciate my decision."

"Oh, no sir, we're fully confident we can persuade you of our case," Richards said.

Judge Dodge stared at him. "So that's your conclusion? You intend to continue?"

"That's what my clients have instructed me to do, Your Honor," Richards said.

Jack looked at Richards's face. Although sincere, he was oblivious.

"All right," Judge Dodge shrugged.

Two days later, the court awarded Davis Brothers $7 million in damages.

㊌   ㊌   ㊌

The next week on a bright sunny day, Jack walked north on Park Avenue to say a prayer of thanks at St. Bartholomew's, taking in the red geraniums in their flower boxes along the medians. He passed the building where Catapult Energy had had its offices, stopped to check whose name currently adorned the building, and continued walking north past the Waldorf.

It was a normal Park Avenue interlude: in a six-block space, he ran into several people he knew. But otherwise, the day felt otherworldly. His acquaintances were all *laowai*. After all the time Jack had spent in China recently, seeing business acquaintances on Park Avenue in New York City was like encountering people from another life.

And so it had been.

Chapter 65

Third Time's the Charm

When it had been their deal, Merritt Partners had estimated the IPO road show would last a week. They would see more than a hundred institutions, but most of them would be in groups, for lunches or dinners. A piece of cake, Alan Lim had said.

The good news was Jack had contacts at those same institutions, but the bad news was that if he wanted them to listen, he would have to go to them individually. Working with the Broad Street and Morgan Joseph syndicate members, they lined up over a hundred one-on-one meetings. The road show would take over a month, each day beginning with a morning call at half past seven and ending with a dinner meeting. They would be lucky to have a handful of group meetings.

"Do you think there's other guys who have ended up doing this?" Jack said to Elizabeth as they sat in his New York office waiting for the car to take him to the airport to begin the Asian leg of the road show.

"You mean put together their own IPO with a bunch of no-name underwriters and sell their deal themselves?" Elizabeth said. "No, not a chance. No one else is that crazy."

"Come on, what choice do we have?"

"What choice do we have? I'll tell you what choice we have. We could do what everyone else would do—give up, sell the company, take some profits, and call it a day."

"Yeah, but I'm not doing that."

"I know, but you asked," she said as Will Francis came in and announced the car was downstairs. "You sure you don't want any of us to go with you?"

"I'm sure. Just keep the company running. I'll be back in six weeks with the money."

Two hours later, Jack was on a plane bound for Singapore.

㊌ ㊌ ㊌

The final, stateside leg of Middle Kingdom's IPO road show began at an analyst breakfast in Boston on a June morning. Jack had survived pitching investors in Asia—Singapore, Hong Kong, and Shanghai—as well as in Europe—Paris, Geneva, Zurich, Frankfurt, Milan, and Lugano—and the United Kingdom—London and Edinburgh.

Standing in front of the crowd at Boston's Harvard Club, he felt it. Not quite a dizziness, it was as if the oxygen in the room had been replaced by a fuzzy yellow gas, enabling him to see the past decade of confusing years.

He looked out at the group of analysts, and recognized the same blasé, smugly cynical expressions he had seen during his first presentation for Catapult Energy 10 years earlier. He had always worked hard for them, but they remained removed, as if he was on one side of a glass barrier and they were on the other. That he should make tons of money for them was expected, and didn't merit as much as a thank-you, while failure meant that all along, their initial suspicions had been correct—he was a liar.

As the crowd ticked through the same questions he had been asked during all three of his IPOs—how many megawatts does the company own? What's your gross margin? Is this your full-time job?—he stood patiently, doing the same thing he had done the day before, and would do the next, and the next, until this IPO too was hopefully concluded.

Some things had indeed changed. For this iteration, he had a new adversary—the Chinese analysts. Possessing no attention span whatsoever, and less manners, they luxuriated in stateside's buy-side rules of etiquette: insulting the supplicants was allowed, just part of the fun. And beyond that, Jack was fair game for a special reason—if they hadn't thought of the business themselves, no *laowai* could go to their backyard and build a billion-dollar company. There had to be something wrong.

Jack had just fended off one Chinese analyst's statement averring that it was common knowledge that all hydroelectric projects in China had the same erosion problems as Three Gorges when a slim New England woman in the back of the room rose, her name tag identifying her as Moira Sullivan of Bay State Financial, waving her pencil in the air.

"So why should I think you'll be any better off in China than all those other foreign companies over there who were cheated and mislead?"

"Only one reason, ma'am. In China, it's all about dollars and cents. Not politics; not local cultural issues. Just dollars and cents. Crass, but refreshing, right?"

"And the dollars and sense verdict on Middle Kingdom, Mr. Davis?"

"Hydroelectricity in China is unique, Ms. Sullivan. It costs the customer less than the alternatives—simple as that."

"Is this your last road show, Mr. Davis?"

"As long as I get the money."

㊌   ㊌   ㊌

Sitting in his office in New York City when it was all over, the $100 million from the IPO in the bank, he put his cigar down and turned to Elizabeth. "You know, I don't feel any different."

"You're not—just 10 years older."

"You know what I mean."

"I know exactly what you mean. But don't forget, you're the one who always said 'Money just makes life more convenient.'"

"Well, that should be true now, I guess."

"Maybe, maybe not."

"What do you mean?"

She just looked at Jack and didn't say anything.

"Come on, I really don't know," he said to her.

"Haven't had time to think about it, right?"

Chapter 66

Two Out of Three Ain't Bad

"**Y**ou're early, Mr. Davis. Mr. Galileo's table is right around the corner. We'll call upstairs and let him know you've arrived."

"No, you don't have to do that. I'll just sit and wait, thanks."

He and Dennis had agreed to meet Richard Abderman at the Sea Grill, the place where the three of them had first spoken about investing in a Chinese hydroelectric company three years earlier. Jack never arrived early, but he wanted to sit in the quiet elegance of the Sea Grill, watch the skaters, and not think about anything—or maybe think about everything.

The maitre d' escorted Jack to Dennis's favorite table, tucked in the corner, providing privacy and an unobstructed view of the rink outside. He ordered a glass of Sancerre from the wine steward, and looked around as the restaurant's wait staff, dressed in the Sea Grill's royal blue blouses, finished their final tasks before the noon lunch crush.

Outside through the picture window, the day was big and blustery. According to the calendar, summer had been a fact of life for over a month, but a pod of gray clouds from Canada whisked northwesterly across the sky, blowing a cold shower of big wet raindrops across Manhattan for five minutes before running out to sea.

The skating rink was jammed. Tourists stumbled around the perimeter, while moderately talented high school girls from the suburbs dodged them. The rink's self-appointed stars stayed in the center, executing clumsy versions of camels and spins and doing their best to disdainfully ignore the mass of centrifugal travelers.

The Sancerre was good and cold. Jack hadn't had any breakfast and the alcohol went into his system quickly. He sat in the corner, content to watch the pieces of the day assemble around him.

Two elderly ladies were shown to their seats at the table next to him. Without speaking to each other, they opened their menus and began reviewing the options. One asked, "What are you having?" and before the other could respond, followed up with, "I'm going to be good."

Don't be good, he thought to himself. Look at yourself. What are you waiting for? It could be over tomorrow. You've been good all your life. You don't have to do it anymore.

Dennis walked in before the wine fooled Jack into trying to give the ladies some advice. "Jack. Great to be with you today." He shook Jack's hand and they braced each other's shoulders.

"It's a great day, Dennis, and a lot of it has to do with you."

"Don't be silly. You did most of it. Ritchie's on his way. Before we discuss life after the IPO, I hear congratulations are in order regarding your court case."

"You know, Dennis, that trial was difficult."

"Trials always are."

"No, I don't mean it that way. I'll tell you, I used to wish I could take advantage of a court-like venue with some of my Chinese investment banking clients. And last week, I got my opportunity. But in the end, it felt horrible. Despite everything, those guys were my friends before things deteriorated. I still like them. They didn't mean me any harm. They just got bad advice. I wish I could have helped them."

"Help them? They cheated you. 'Help them,' Jack? You're too nice."

"No, they're okay guys; they really are."

"Well, you're the one who always is telling me the Chinese love us and they hate us."

"Unfortunately, it's true. Anyway, the judgment's one thing, but the best thing to happen to me recently is Middle Kingdom's IPO."

"Who are you kidding? The best thing to happen to you is Lianhua."

"Very funny."

"I'm not trying to be funny. Before Richard gets here, what's the latest?"

"What do you mean, what's the latest?"

"What do you think I mean? I want to know what's happening between you and that gorgeous Chinese woman."

Jack shook his head back and forth. "Nothing. Nothing is happening between us."

Dennis looked at Jack and realized he was being serious. "Well, I'm truly sorry to hear that. In Yunnan, it looked like you were really fond of each other."

Jack looked up at his friend, and wondered what purpose would be served by more discussion of the subject. "We were, Dennis, extremely. The truth is, she's not only beautiful, but maybe the most considerate person in the world."

"Now we're getting somewhere."

"No, it's not what you think."

"Why do you say that?"

"What would you say if I told you that she left me because she knew the life she wanted for herself wasn't right for me?"

"She did that?" Dennis looked serious as he stared down at the table, and then looked up and eyed Jack. "If someone like that really exists, you should go back to China, find her, and never let her out of your sight."

Chapter 67

Easy Come, Easy Go

The sky was midnight blue when he arrived in Lijiang on the last flight from Kunming. Chen picked him up in the little van. At the Leisure House, Tina gave him the same room he had the last time he had stayed there, when Lianhua was in the room above him with the balcony and called him for breakfast every morning, when his hopes were sitting right in front of him and he felt like he could reach out and touch them.

Early the next day, Jack dressed, took breakfast at the inn, and walked through the deserted lanes of Lijiang to the Dongba seminary by the Black Dragon Pool. It had rained during the night. The July evening had turned unseasonably cold, and the edges of the streams showed traces of ice.

At the entrance to the seminary, the attendant was asleep behind the window of the ticket booth. Jack left some RMB on the sill of the booth and walked down the main path around the Black Dragon Pool. In the chilly air, ripe red hibiscus flowers were dropping from their vines, and fat white magnolia blossoms oozed fragrance down waxy leaves.

At the entryway of the seminary, the docent stood watching as Jack approached.

"Good morning," Jack said, relieved to see the solution to his language problem. "The Dongba said I could come back, remember?"

The docent nodded wordlessly, and escorted him into the Dongba's study. Dressed in his robes and hat, the Dongba was painting characters on a scroll when they arrived. He turned and looked at Jack, put his brushes down and motioned to the seating area next to a small fountain.

They sat down together. The docent served them tea. The Dongba looked closely at Jack, and leaned over and said something matter-of-factly to the docent. "The Dongba says your princess is gone," the docent said.

"Has she come here?"

The docent paused to look at the Dongba and then turned back to face Jack. "No."

"I thought she might have," Jack sighed.

The Dongba said something to the docent. "She is not in Beijing, the Dongba says."

"I don't know where she is. Sometimes I dream about her," Jack said, wanting the Dongba's help but not knowing how to ask for it.

The Dongba said something more to the docent. "She wanted things you don't want, the Dongba says."

"It was okay," Jack said. "I wanted them for her."

The docent put his head next to the Dongba and whispered. The Dongba lifted his eyes up to gaze at Jack and spoke sharply. "That has never been good for you, the Dongba says," said the docent. "He says when you want those things for yourself, you may find her again."

Jack looked out the window as two black crows flew by. The three men sat in the quiet, dry warmth of the room. A thin aroma of incense filled the air as the fountain gurgled in the corner.

The Dongba stood up, as if the interview was ending.

Jack stood up. "What about the *zunyu?*"

"You haven't found them?" The docent asked.

"I haven't really looked. Sometimes I dream about them, too," Jack said.

The docent spoke to the Dongba, who walked around his table, rolled out a piece of parchment, picked up his brush, and began a deep, poetry-like tonal chant. As the Dongba kept chanting, the docent said to Jack, "The Dongba says some dreams are life, and some lives are dreams. You must live them to know the difference."

Jack kept looking at the Dongba as the tiny man chanted about his life. Then the chanting stopped, and the Dongba spoke to the docent.

"The Dongba asks where you will you go when you leave here."

"I'd like to find the *zunyu*."

The docent whispered to the Dongba, who looked at Jack and muttered a phrase to the docent.

"Is that all you seek?" the docent asked on behalf of the Dongba.

Jack shrugged, a sheepish half-smile on his face.

"He will show you," the docent said to Jack.

Jack nodded, and watched as the little man painted a stick figure of a man surrounded by mountains on the parchment, and then drew *zunyu* swirling in the air.

The Dongba finished the drawing with a flourish, straightened up and held it up in front of Jack, pointing to the right side of the parchment and talking.

The docent said, "The Dongba says the *zunyu* are up high, above the trees near the sun. When you're up there, you will find your fortune fish in front of the evening star."

When Jack left the Dongba's studio, the night's gray rain clouds had departed, replaced by high white puffs floating lazily across blue sky. There was no wind as he walked along the edge of the Black Pool. The water was dark and glassy. A lone trout rose and sent a single ripple shoreward. It was too cold for flies to hatch. Jack could see a school of *zunyu* cruising below the surface, trolling for food as the spring creek spewed silver bubbles up around them.

Turning down the main street of the old city toward the inn, he watched the shopkeepers open the gates of their stores, yawning as they began a new day. Women cooked on charcoal fires in front of their houses, their children playing on the cold cobblestones.

When Jack opened the wooden gate of the Leisure House, Chen and Tina were sitting at their table in the office to the right of the entrance, Chen drinking tea and Tina doing paperwork. They looked up at Jack, glanced at each other, and stood up.

Jack looked back at them as he stepped into the courtyard. The fountain bubbled as if someone was whispering his name. The cats played with the leaves growing out of the edge of the lotus pond.

As Chen organized a chair for Jack under one of the umbrellas, Tina disappeared into the kitchen and reappeared a moment later with a tea service, placing it on the table next to Jack and pouring him tea. She and Chen set to putting up the umbrellas around the patio, speaking to each other in Chinese as if Jack were not there, the guttural, sing-song sounds of their voices lapping over Jack like the fountain bubbling into the pond.

There was only one thing to do now. He would go up there, and try to find the right place. His home was thousands of miles away, but there had to be someplace like it between here and there, a place where he could fish and live in front of the evening star.

Chapter 68

High-Water Mark

The car came to a stop at the end of the dirt road coming southwest out of Xidang, the village where Jack and Chen had stayed the night before. Jack got out of the passenger side, stretched and checked his watch. He could hear the heat of the morning rushing skyward through the dark pines.

Chen put the van in park on the steep hill, and set the emergency brake. He got out, went around back and opened the trunk. He paused before handing Jack his rucksack and fly rod case.

"You sure you do this, Mr. Jack?"

"Thanks, Chen," Jack said, patting Chen on the shoulder as he started to take his equipment out of the trunk himself.

"I don't know, Mr. Jack. You think this good idea?"

"Yeah, sure it is, Chen. Sure it is."

"Those mountains very, very high, Mr. Jack. I don't know where fish are up there. Maybe no *zunyu*. Come back with me. Please. You come back with me now. We'll go fishing on my mountain, like last time. We catch very, very good fish."

"No, no, Chen," Jack smiled. "Out there, up there, that's where the *zunyu* are," he said, pointing up the path that began just beyond the clearing at the end of the road, the trees on either side framing the snow-capped peaks of the Kawa Karpo range as they glistened in the morning sun. "The Dongba told me." Traces of overnight snow dusted the shaded side of the trail. Wind bent the tops of the trees.

"I don't think so, Mr. Davis. I don't know where the *zunyu* are up there. You come back with me."

Jack hoisted his rucksack up over his shoulders and picked up his rod case. He looked at Chen one last time, smiled as he reached out and shook his hand, and then turned and started up the path toward the glacial peaks in the distance.

Chen stood watching after Jack long after he was out of sight.

The sun peeked through the black trees. The air felt brisk and cool. Jack could smell snow and the clean sky and the pines as he walked up the trail. At 15,000 feet above sea level, his heart beat rapidly. He walked a hundred paces, stopped, then walked another hundred paces, and stopped again.

Skirting a group of boulders and cutting up a skinny part of the trail, he came in to a clearing. A panorama of the valley lay below him. Xidang was several thousand feet down east in the distance. Wood smoke from cooking fires spiraled up from the village's stone roofs, merging into a gray column until the wind at the higher elevations dissipated it into the atmosphere.

Standing on top of the planet, Jack looked out across the curve of the earth toward where he was born.

He drew in a deep breath, felt the rarefied altitude, and thought about home, his mother and father waving to him from the driveway in front of their house, his sons, the flowers in the fields at the farm, all stretched out before him as he gazed up in the eastern sky over the remains of his life, the husk of the evening star waiting for him.

It was going to be a long walk home.

Chapter 69

The Long Walk Home

He had food in his rucksack but didn't stop to eat. He liked feeling hungry when he hiked, and he wanted to get above the tree line before noon. Close to freezing when he had started out, he felt good now, the clear dry air beating down from the cobalt sky. As the heat rose, the wind swirled loose snow up off the peaks toward the crescent-shaped remainder of the moon, white and charred after doing its evening work.

The path was old and lightly traveled, but serviceable, free of brush, and soggy only in sections. Tiny rivulets of snowmelt webbed the wall of the mountain like veins on an old woman's face. Up ahead another thousand feet above him, Jack could see snow drifts where the tree line ended.

At a steep section of the mountain, the path curled up around an outcropping of cliffs and rock and then dropped back down into the forest where it crossed another trail. The new trail was well traveled and the grass around the junction was beaten down and muddied.

Just beyond the junction, a stream crossed the path on its way down to carve the valley below. Clear water came rushing down from the mountain to Jack's right, flowed across the path, and went out of sight into the ferns and the forest down to the left. White and magenta flox dotted the sides of the streambed.

Jack slid the rucksack off his back and put it and his fly rod case on the dry ground along the bank of the stream. He knelt down and cupped his hands in the fast-moving part of the water, first drinking deeply, then washing his face and pouring the icy water over his head and neck. Jack loved drinking out of mountain streams, and was happy to be dirty and wet. He planned to walk all day and then sleep in his clothes.

Hearing the noise of a waterfall downstream through the trees, he stepped over the stream and through the ferns and hemlocks to look where the freshet cascaded out over a cliff.

The woman stood at the edge of the pool formed by the falls, dressed in the red blouse and headdress of a native, her body erect as she looked up into the sky. He couldn't see her face. Beyond her, Jack followed her gaze and saw Venus, the first and last point of light burning in the eastern heavens.

Still gazing at the sky, she put the palms of her hands together, raising them together over her head and then spreading her arms out perpendicular to her body. She turned and faced down into the pool. It was clear, its bottom lined with boulders and stones in the shallow end and mossy rocks giving way to tree limbs and stumps in the deep end where the waterfall entered, right below Jack.

Jack looked away from the woman toward the bottom of the pool. He could see *zunyu*, lots of them, swimming slowly in a loose school and gliding in and out of the shadows, the sun reflecting up off the lighter-colored rocks and making the bottom seem closer to the surface than it was. The trout stayed below the surface of the pool, gliding down to where it was cool and working off their morning meal, staying out of the sun and the warmer surface water, the school bending and swaying listlessly like the branches of the pines being gently pushed by the breeze, the fish sometimes in tight formation, then falling out, then moving back together again.

Jack looked back at her. She was naked now, her clothes on a rock, her headdress off and her long black hair trailing down her back, standing hip deep in the shallow end of the pool, looking down at the *zunyu*. Standing very still, she watched them carefully, a light wind coming through the trees and blowing her hair softly over her shoulders.

She slowly slid into the pool toward the fish, her head above the water, swimming a purposeful breaststroke that pushed low swells over the surface back toward the deep end of the pool.

Jack stood right above her. He looked at the *zunyu*. When she had entered the water, the fish had temporarily retreated, but now were regrouped and lay over the bottom in a circular school, floating and waiting.

She moved below the surface and began swimming underwater toward the *zunyu,* stroking slowly with her arms, her legs scissoring back and forth, her hair streaming out behind her.

The school of *zunyu* parted, and as she swam down to them they turned and headed off on either side of her toward the deep end of the pool, her legs changing to an up-and-down paddling stroke as the fish escorted her into the depths.

The sun shone on her back and the school, the scales of the *zunyu* sending sparkling glimmers of reflected sunlight up to the surface. The pool turned greener and darker at the deep end, the emerald shallows giving way to dark hemlock-hued depths, the swimmer and the *zunyu* pushing down into the void, going down deep to the coolness. Jack watched them, then lost sight of them in the deep green depths, thought he saw her legs softly paddling as the light came through the trees and shined momentarily on the deep part of the pool, then lost her again as the sun went back behind the branches.

Jack Davis knelt down to focus on the surface of the pool, leaning back on his haunches, getting comfortable, his eyes not leaving the water where he had last seen the swimmer. He would wait for her. He had all day.

About the Author

John D. Kuhns is a financier and industrialist who has been doing business in China for over 25 years. *China Fortunes* is his first novel.

In 1984, as the founder and Chief Executive Officer of Catalyst Energy Corporation, Mr. Kuhns was the first American to acquire commercial hydroelectric generating equipment from China, powering the company to its successful IPO and listing on the New York Stock Exchange. According to *Inc.* magazine, Catalyst Energy was the fastest-growing public company in the United States from 1982 to 1987, becoming a $1 billion enterprise.

Having closed IPOs for five companies, including some of the world's leading alternative energy businesses, Mr. Kuhns's most recent transaction was the January 2010 IPO for China Hydroelectric Corporation, China's largest owner of small hydroelectric projects, for which he currently serves as Chairman and Chief Executive Officer.

Kuhns Brothers, Mr. Kuhns's investment bank, raises financing for Chinese companies, and his private equity organization, the China Hand Fund, makes investments in Chinese companies.

Mr. Kuhns graduated from Georgetown University, where he was also captain of the varsity football team and member of the university's Athletic Hall of Fame; received a Masters of Fine Arts from the University of Chicago, where he was also an undergraduate teaching assistant in sculpture and drawing as well as the art and culture critic for the *Maroon*, the university newspaper; and received a Master of Business Administration from the Harvard Business School.

Mr. Kuhns has offices in Beijing and New York, and lives stateside with his family in Connecticut, where he fly fishes religiously.